THE CONSERVATIVES

ALSO BY PATRICK ALLITT

Catholic Intellectuals and Conservative Politics in America: 1950–1985

Catholic Converts: British and American Intellectuals Turn to Rome

Major Problems in American Religious History (editor)

Religion in America Since 1945: A History

I'm the Teacher, You're the Student: A Semester in the University Classroom

PATRICK ALLITT

The Conservatives

IDEAS AND PERSONALITIES THROUGHOUT AMERICAN HISTORY

YALE UNIVERSITY PRESS NEW HAVEN & LONDON

Published with assistance from the foundation established in memory of Philip Hamilton McMillan of the Class of 1894, Yale College.

Set in Scala type by Binghamton Valley Composition.
Printed in the United States of America.

Library of Congress Cataloging-in-Publication Data

Allitt, Patrick.
The conservatives : ideas and personalities throughout American history / Patrick Allitt.
p. cm.
Includes index.
ISBN 978-0-300-11894-0 (hardcover : alk. paper) 1. Conservatism—United States—History. 2. United States—Politics and government. I. Title.
JC573.2.U6A425 2009 2008042559
320.520973—dc22

A catalogue record for this book is available from the British Library.

This paper meets the requirements of ANSI/NISO Z39.48-1992 (Permanence of Paper).
It contains 30 percent postconsumer waste (PCW) and is certified by the Forest Stewardship Council (FSC).

10 9 8 7 6 5 4 3 2 1

For Deborah and Malcolm

CONTENTS

PREFACE

I WROTE my doctoral dissertation during the Reagan years on an aspect of American conservative history. Not many historians were studying conservatism then, even though it was becoming central to American political life. Since 1990 many excellent books have appeared, detailing and explaining elements of conservative history, philosophy, and politics. However, only one author, Robert Muccigrosso, has attempted to tell the whole story of American conservatism from the Revolution to the present, and his account is severely compressed. When Yale University Press invited me three years ago to write a much bigger history of American conservative ideas, I accepted gladly, in the belief that such a book would be interesting to research and would fill a gap in the historical literature.

As it turned out, there was a lot more to say than I had space for, and I have been forced to touch only lightly, or pass over in silence, many deserving subjects and personalities. I hope, nevertheless, that this book will be of use to students and general readers interested in the long history of American conservatism. The skeleton of the whole story is here, along with an explanation of its main themes. I introduce a large cast of characters, some of whom espoused ideas that are abhorrent by current standards. Whatever they believed, I have tried to give them at least a provisional hearing, presenting their ideas in context to show why, in their time, they were plausible and—to some readers—attractive. I extend the same courtesy to their critics.

I have tried not to read contemporary issues into the past and to keep my own opinions as far in the background as possible, in the hope that the book will be of use to readers from all points on the political compass. I am not arguing on behalf of conservatism or against it; neither do I assert that one of the many strands of American conservatism is somehow more genuine than others. My intention is to keep the rhetorical temperature low and to take each group—at least provisionally—on its own terms.

I am grateful to my editors at Yale University Press, Lara Heimert and Chris Rogers; to my agent, Jeri Thoma; and to my colleagues at Emory University, especially David Abraham, Joseph Crespino, Brooks Holifield, Frank Lechner, Jeffrey Lesser, and Daniel Spillman. Thanks also to my favorite readers elsewhere: Jim Fisher, Ernie Freeberg, Darryl Hart, Christine Rosen, Howard Seftel and the two very helpful anonymous peer reviewers for Yale University Press, one of whom, Leo Ribuffo, threw off the veil of secrecy. The dedication is to my much beloved sister and brother.

Introduction

FROM THE LATE 1970S to the early twenty-first century, American conservatism was constantly in the news. Conservative intellectuals challenged nearly all the liberal verities of the 1950s and 1960s. Powerful conservative think tanks served up a steady stream of policy proposals, and politicians from both major parties took notice. New media outlets like CNN and Fox began to approach the news from an openly conservative vantage point, and by the 1990s some politicians were disavowing liberalism because even use of the "l word" appeared to cost them popular support.

At the grassroots level such organizations as the Moral Majority and the Christian Coalition brought out the vote for conservative candidates. In domestic policy, support for the traditional family and for religion in public life, along with opposition to gay rights, abortion, welfare, and affirmative action, all won sympathetic conservative attention. Government began to dismantle decades-long welfare and busing programs. A succession of appointments under presidents Reagan and the two Bushes changed the character of the Supreme Court. In foreign policy, conservatives theorized the exhaustion of the Soviet Union, then celebrated the end of the Cold War, before looking ahead to new geopolitical challenges.

As the media charted this era of conservative dominance, however, it also noticed divisions within the conservative movement. Some conservatives wanted a vast defense establishment able to nullify all threats, to take on opponents anywhere in the world, and to spread the gospel of democratic capitalism worldwide. Others, especially after the Cold War, wanted a retreat to the historic American policy of isolation, leaving the rest of the world to its own affairs. At home, some conservatives favored a drastic reduction of the federal government, while others saw new opportunities for government intervention. Occasional well-publicized splits in conservative groups and among conservative politicians bespoke philosophical as well as pragmatic differences.

Where did American conservatism come from, what are its intellectual sources, and why is it internally divided? This book is dedicated to answering those questions, not just with regard to recent decades but throughout the history of the republic. Conservatism was not always a high-pressure "inside the Beltway" affair, and at times it almost vanished from American public life, becoming merely the preserve of scattered intellectual groups. There is, however, a strong, complex, and continuing American conservative tradition. Understanding it helps us understand the nation's history as a whole.

It is important to emphasize at the outset that before the 1950s there was no such thing as a conservative *movement* in the United States. Writing about conservatism throughout American history therefore creates organizational and semantic problems. Before the twentieth century, it was unusual for Americans to refer to themselves politically as *conservatives,* though many used the term as an adjective (as in "I take a conservative view of this issue"). I make the case that certain people throughout American history can be understood as conservatives, but with the important caution that this was not a noun most of them used about themselves.

For more than a century one of the major political parties in Britain has called itself Conservative. In the United States, by contrast, neither of the two parties has monopolized the political expression of conservatism. Here I argue that conservatism is, first of all, an *attitude* to social and political change that looks for support to the ideas, beliefs, and habits of the past and puts more faith in the lessons of history than in the abstractions of political philosophy. The attitude long predated the movement. Conservatives were skeptical and anti-utopian. They doubted the possibility of human, social, or political perfection. Their attitude toward politics was comparable to the religious idea of original sin: people are unable to act entirely rationally or selflessly, human plans will go awry, well-meant actions will have unintended bad consequences. Planned societies are therefore impossible, and the attempt to create them will probably lead to chaos or tyranny. Similarly, they thought that human imperfection made war a permanent part of the human condition so that hopes for a world free of conflict were delusional. They thought of progress as possible, but not inevitable, and worried that ostensibly progressive changes were really sources of degeneration and decay. When they advocated reforms, they appealed to tradition, national heritage, or the wisdom of earlier generations, sometimes claiming that their apparent innovations were really a way of restoring the conditions of a better time in the past.

Writers about American conservatism have often observed that the word itself has meant different things at different times and that there is no consistency in conservatives' beliefs about what should be conserved. This truth need not be surprising; conservatives have generally taken an antitheoretical approach to their world. American conservatism, moreover, has often been *reactive,* responding to perceived political and intellectual challenges. As the challenges and threats changed, so did the nature of the conservative response. Beliefs that once seemed radical later came to seem conservative. Arguments for the free market, for example, seemed radical in the era of the American Revolution, but arguments for the free market since 1917, when Soviet communism proposed a fully planned and centrally directed economy, have had a strongly conservative flavor.

Certain ideas and themes recur throughout the book. One is a suspicion of democracy and equality. In the early republic, democracy seemed threatening to many property owners and members of the educated elite. The Constitution had created a republic, but it did not mention democracy; to the privileged of that era, the spread of democracy could feel unsettling. They denied that all men are equal, except perhaps in the eyes of God, and they believed that mass participation in politics, far from enhancing liberty and justice, would be more likely to degrade the republic and replace virtuous leaders with demagogues. By the late nineteenth century, to argue openly against democracy was becoming difficult, but conservatives kept up a steady drumbeat of criticism against egalitarianism.

Along with doubts about democracy and equality, American conservatives generally shared the view that civilization is fragile and easily disrupted. Every generation must learn anew the importance of restraint, manners, deference, and good citizenship; the survival of the republic presupposes the virtue of its citizens. For more than two centuries, influential conservative writers have emphasized these qualities and argued for a highly educated elite as guardians of civilization.

Throughout conservative history, further, it is possible to trace recurrent fears about social dissolution. At times such fears became acute and led conservatives to call for drastic remedies. In the late 1850s, for example, many otherwise sober Northern conservatives became convinced that the republic was threatened by a vast slaveholders' conspiracy. At the same time Southern conservatives feared that the Republican Party planned to eliminate the slave system on which their society was built. The two groups, both acting on what might be thought of as conservative fears, brought about disunion and war. In the 1960s, similarly, conservative opponents of radical activism declared themselves the guardians of law and order and argued for a heavy-handed government policy that, in calmer times, they would have deplored.

On many other issues conservatism has meant different things at different times. The conservative attitude to the proper role of government, for example, has varied according to circumstances. Alexander Hamilton, as first secretary of the treasury, wanted to strengthen federal authority to supervise the nation's finances and to nurture economic growth. In the 1790s Federalists like Hamilton and John Adams dreaded the possible spread of the French Revolution to America. This unease led them to seek a closer diplomatic relationship with France's principal enemy, Britain. During the New Deal of the 1930s, by contrast, conservatives were men who *feared* big government, especially if it meant federal intervention in the running of the economy; in addition they favored isolation from European conflicts. The very thing Hamilton had tried to ensure, with a conservative end in view, was the thing a later conservative generation tried to forestall. American history provides numerous occasions when the most identifiably conservative Americans favored a strong and active national government and others when *opposition* to a strong national government seemed essential. Similarly, there have been eras when conservatism was almost synonymous with a posture of isolationism, and others when it went hand in hand with bold intervention abroad.

It is not unusual to find figures who can be thought of as conservatives on both sides of great conflicts. The pre–Civil War rivals Daniel Webster and John C. Calhoun, for example, each had the conservation of a cherished old thing in view (the Union for Webster and the tradition of limited government plus Southern slavery for Calhoun). The Civil War itself can easily be seen as the conflict of two conservatisms, with Webster's and Calhoun's principles and rivalry represented by the two sections and ratcheted up to a deadlier pitch. But if it began as the encounter of two incompatible conservatisms, pressure of events and the imperative to win led both sides to take dramatic and transformative steps—such as Emancipation, conscription, and the suspension of habeas corpus—that were anything but conservative in practice.

Conservatism throughout American history has often entailed the defense of privilege by the holders of privilege and has always been vulnerable to the accusation that it is really just the self-interested special pleading of men who have a lot to lose. At its worst it has indeed been little more than rich men's defense of their material advantages; conservatism's characteristic vices have been pessimism and complacency. When it is only special pleading, conservative writing is neither convincing nor interesting. When, on the other hand, it comes as part of a broader understanding of the world, embodying hidden or neglected insights about the human condition, conservatism becomes engaging. We so rarely hear arguments in favor of human inequality, for example, that we are in danger of forgetting that, for most of world history, inequality has been regarded as almost too obvious to require any justification. Likewise with democracy; the arguments against it are rarely voiced in public American settings today, so that it becomes easy to think of democracy as a natural or default situation rather than as an extremely unusual historical achievement. Yet conservative arguments against equality and against democracy were persuasive and influential to intelligent readers in many eras of American history, as were arguments in favor of slavery. We do not have to believe them, but if we are fully to understand the American past we should remember that serious people took them seriously.

CHAPTER ONE

The Federalists

IN THE HISTORY OF THE EARLY REPUBLIC, the term Federalist had two meanings. Both are important in the history of American conservative thought. First, Federalists were the politicians and thinkers of the 1780s who wrote the Constitution and argued in favor of using it in place of the Articles of Confederation. Their experiences since 1777 had convinced them that the Articles were too weak to hold the new nation together and that a stronger instrument of government was necessary. Their antagonists, the anti-Federalists, argued that the Constitution would rob citizens of their new liberties and would subordinate the states to an overmighty central government, that it was, in effect, counterrevolutionary.

Federalist refers, second, to the politicians of the 1790s and 1800s who rallied around George Washington, John Adams, and Alexander Hamilton in what some historians have described as the First Party System. Although they did not constitute a political party in the modern sense and had a principled objection to the creation of political factions, in practice they shared views and collaborated on a wide variety of issues. At home they wanted a strong federal government guiding national economic policy. In foreign policy they favored Britain in the wars of the French Revolution. They feared French revolutionary radicalism and accused their rivals, the Jeffersonian Republicans, of being Jacobins (a reference to the instigators of France's Reign of Terror). Believers in social hierarchy, class deference, and restraint, they did not think the American republic should become a democracy. It is, accordingly, appropriate to think of them as conservatives, even though it is a word they rarely used to describe themselves.

CONSERVATIVE INNOVATORS

The Constitution was written by fifty-five men, meeting in secret, whose experience in the early 1780s convinced them that the republic was in danger. They wanted to preserve the nation for which they had fought against Britain and which, after Shays's Rebellion, seemed to be bankrupt, unmanageable, and about to break up. Their work was simultaneously revolutionary, in that it created a written blueprint by which the nation would live, and conservative, in that it drew from the wisdom of the ages and aimed to embody the political lessons taught by the experience of generations.

The document we now know as the Federalist papers was the new nation's first conservative classic. Its eighty-five essays were written at high speed and published in newspapers sometimes at the rate of four per week, by supporters of the Constitution seeking to persuade their fellow citizens that this new frame of government was necessary and good, that it would make the central government effective yet preserve their liberty. The essays, fifty-one of them written by Alexander Hamilton (1755–1804), twenty-nine by James Madison (1751–1836), and five by John Jay (1745–1829), were all published under the pen name "Publius" (a reference to Publius Valerius, who had banished the last king of Rome and founded the Roman republic). Most newspapers featured anti-Constitution or anti-Federalist essays on the same or adjacent pages, so that readers could follow arguments for and against each new element of the proposed Constitution.[1]

Hamilton and Madison differed on many issues, but in 1787 they agreed on the need for the Constitution and agreed to make Publius as consistent as possible. Both believed that the Constitution addressed hard realities better than the ineffective Articles of Confederation and was well attuned to human imperfection. As one of Hamilton's biographers says: "The two shared a grim vision of the human condition, even if Hamilton's had the blacker tinge. They both wanted to erect barriers against irrational popular impulses and tyrannical minorities and majorities. To this end they thought that public opinion should be distilled by skeptical, sober-minded representatives."[2]

The Constitution, they wrote, justifies an increase in the power of the central or federal government, which is essential if the nation is to hold together at all and not become a cluster of lesser federations. Because men are swayed by self-interest, because they are passionate, ambitious, and greedy, the Constitution places limits on how much power they can exercise, and for how long. Ordinary citizens contribute by electing representatives, but their choices are complemented by indirect elections (state legislatures, not ordinary voters, chose U.S. senators), and all are subject to an impartial, unelected judiciary. Under the Constitution the nation would, they said, be strong enough to face down all internal and external threats.[3]

A few of the essays have been acclaimed for their particular insight and for adapting old political ideas to new American conditions. The Federalist, No. 10, for example, argued that the vast geographic extent of the United States was a strength, not a weakness. It contradicted the conventional view that republics could prosper—and endure—only if they were small. Why might size be an advantage? The larger the republic, the more likely that it could assemble outstanding men as its legislators. "As each representative will be chosen by a greater number of citizens in the large than in the small republic, it will be more difficult for unworthy candidates to practice with success the vicious arts by which elections are too often carried." Further, the geographic and economic diversity of a large nation would inhibit the formation of any one overmighty faction. Different areas would have different material interests, which could compete without upsetting the whole system.[4]

Publius was careful to reassure readers that the reach of the federal government was limited to issues of collective concern that could not be taken care of locally. Individual states would conduct their own affairs and need not fear obtrusive federal officials; the Constitution was *not* creating a single, all-powerful national government. In the Federalist, No. 45, he wrote that "the powers reserved to the several States will extend to all the objects which, in the ordinary course of affairs, concern the lives, liberties, and properties of the people, and the internal order, improvement and prosperity of the state."[5]

Members of the revolutionary generation saw themselves as having overthrown a tyrant, King George III, and some were afraid that the Constitution might create a new form of tyranny. Publius explained in the Federalist, No. 51, that this hazard would be prevented through the separation of powers. Each section of the proposed government had a particular function. The self-respect of the people in that section would lead them to preserve it, protect its dignity, and prevent encroachments from the other sections. In this way human nature, despite all its weaknesses, would preserve separation of powers and prevent tyranny. In a classic passage that any conservative can read with pleasure Publius wrote: "Ambition must be made to counteract ambition. . . . It may be a reflection on human nature that such devices should be necessary to control the abuses of government. But what is government itself but the greatest of all reflections on human nature? If men were angels, no government would be necessary. If angels were to govern men, neither external nor internal controls on government would be necessary. In framing a government which is to be administered by men over men, the great difficulty lies in this: you must first enable the government to control the governed; and in the next place oblige it to control itself." In a nod to the principle of popular sovereignty the passage concludes: "A dependence on the people is no doubt the primary control on the government; but experience has taught mankind the necessity of auxiliary precautions."[6]

All eighty-five of the papers are written in a stylish eighteenth-century prose that requires a twenty-first-century reader's full attention. They never deviate into pious hopes and make no claim for the transformation of humanity, but exhibit, rather, a clear-eyed view of human realities and political experience, showing how thoroughly Madison and Hamilton had studied the fate of earlier republics and the characteristics of their decline.

The unanimous choice of George Washington (1732–99), the most famous and widely honored man in America, as first president, added greatly to the Constitution's legitimacy and its prospect of survival. At first Federalist had meant simply a supporter of the Constitution, by contrast with the anti-Federalists who opposed it. Once the document was in operation, however, two tendencies developed in the political life of the 1790s. We remember these groups as Federalist and Republican, though they were not political parties in the modern sense, in that they lacked the management and machinery to enforce party discipline on their members.[7]

The Federalists of the 1780s and 1790s did not describe themselves as conservatives, but they certainly hoped, with the help of the Constitution, to conserve a traditional social order that, as they saw it, was threatened by disorder from below and radicalism from abroad. Afraid that the chaos of the French Revolution, which reached its height in the Terror of 1793, might spread to America, they tried to preserve the old social hierarchy and to act as much like British gentlemen in the new republic, as the colonial elite had done a few decades earlier. Even their view of the American Revolution was conservative. Far from seeing it as a bold adventure in liberty, sweeping away the old British order of things to create a new and rational alternative, they saw it as an attempt to *restore* the traditionally balanced British constitution, which a grasping monarchy had corrupted in the course of the eighteenth century. They were, in their own eyes, "restorationists" rather than revolutionaries. One among them, Harrison Gray Otis (1765–1848) of Massachusetts, expressed this point exactly when he wrote: "Those [people] mistake altogether the nature of the political controversy between the American Colonies and the British Ministry, who suggest that our fathers were actuated by a *radical* spirit. They acted on the defensive, and contended only for *constitutional* rights and privileges."[8]

Their ideas about a balanced political system came from the old Whig tradition, which had grown out of English political controversies of the seventeenth and early eighteenth centuries. A generation of intellectual historians in the past three decades has shown the influence and power of these ideas for nearly all the American revolutionary leaders. "Country" Whigs, opponents of the king's court circle, idealized the classical republican tradition, derived from such Roman authors as Cicero and Tacitus, descending through Machiavelli and the Florentine humanists of the Renaissance, and taking more recent form in the work of the British writers James Harrington, Algernon Sidney, John Trenchard and Thomas Gordon. The ideal political system, according to this view, draws its legitimacy ultimately from the people but in practice balances monarchy, aristocracy, and democracy, preventing any of the three from dominating the others and creating a condition of ordered liberty. The citizens must be civic-minded but not ambitious, dedicated to the nation without looking on politics as an arena for self-advancement.[9]

The Revolution had, of course, brought monarchy to an end in the United States, and the new nation was determined to have no titled aristocracy. The historian Gordon Wood has shown that a new variant of classical republicanism developed under these circumstances, adapting the presidency to the role formerly held by the monarch, and the Senate to the role formerly held by the aristocracy. But president, Senate, and House were all, in the terms of the tradition, parts of the democratic element. Whether these substitutions would work remained uncertain. Fisher Ames (1758–1808), perhaps the most outspoken of the Federalists, doubted it. "The power of the people, if uncontroverted, is licentious and mobbish," he wrote. "It is a government by force without discipline. It is led by demagogues who are soon supplanted by bolder and abler rivals, and soon the whole power is in the hands of . . . the boldest and most violent." A virtuous aristocracy, "natural" if not hereditary, must restrain the common people.[10]

No one worried more about the lack of monarchs and aristocrats than John Adams (1735–1826), one of the seminal figures in the history of American conservatism. He thought President Washington should be exalted by being referred to as "His Majesty," rather than the humble "Mr. President," and argued that presidential vetoes should not be reversible even by a two-thirds majority in Congress. Adams feared the influence of the *philosophes,* a group of eighteenth-century French intellectuals who attempted to understand politics from first principles rather than on the basis of long historical experience. In his view these writers, including Denis Diderot (1713–84), Jean-Jacques Rousseau (1712–78), and the Marquis de Condorcet (1743–94), were unrealistic about the dark human passions and too willing to think the best of humanity, despite historical experience to the contrary. "Not one of them takes human nature as its foundation." Adams argued for a political system consonant with human realities, restraining men's passions and limiting their power. "The best republics will be virtuous and have been so, but we may hazard a conjecture that the virtues have been the effect of the well ordered constitution, rather than the cause." Adams, like Ames, was skeptical of the idea of human equality. In 1811 he remarked, "Equality is one of those equivocal words which the philosophy of the 18th century has made fraudulent. . . . In the last twenty-five years it has cheated millions out of their lives and tens of millions out of their property."[11]

Adams's three-volume *Defence of Constitutions* (1787) was as long-winded as the *Federalist* essays were concise. It argued against the idea—favored by Tom Paine and other revolutionary-era radicals—of a one-house (unicameral) legislature on the grounds that it was too democratic, too vulnerable to the transient passions of uneducated voters. Adams felt particularly proud of having written this attack on democracy before the French Revolution, with "its face of Blood and Horror, of Murder and Massacre, of Ambition and Avarice," and even suggested that it had inspired Edmund Burke's classic indictment, *Reflections on the Revolution in France* (1790). The *Discourses on Davila* (1790), Adams's translation of a seventeenth-century French book on civil war, interlarded with his own commentaries, was chiefly an analysis of human motivation in politics. Adams believed that no motive is more central in life than the desire to be noticed, admired, and emulated. Men's different ways of going about it and their different qualities make inequality inevitable. This insatiable craving could, of course, become dangerous; government must guide and sometimes inhibit it.[12]

The Federalists were landed gentlemen of wealth and high social standing who shared Adams's view that social hierarchy was natural. Skeptical of popular democracy, they believed that only the elite, only those privileged by property, education, and leisure, were in a position to participate in politics. It seemed clear to them that a poor man entering politics would use his position to enrich himself, whereas a rich man, needing no more wealth, would dedicate himself to the public good. Republican citizens, and especially leaders, must be *virtuous,* immune to the temptations of corruption and of perverting the government to serve private ends. Adams disliked elections, saying that "experiments of this kind have been so often tried, and so universally found productive of horrors, that there is great reason to dread them." He and his generation knew from personal experience that election day could often become unruly or violent, as voting took place in public and as rival candidates treated voters to whiskey and showered abuse on one another.[13]

The voters' job, as Federalist politicians and writers understood it, was to choose representatives from among the community's superior men, who would then govern on behalf of the community as a whole with virtuous selflessness, trusting to their consciences to act uprightly. William Richardson Davie (1756–1820), a North Carolina Federalist, told electors in 1803: "I never have and I never will surrender my principles to the opinions of any man, or description of men, either in or out of power; and . . . I wish no man to vote for me, who is not willing to leave me free to pursue the good of my country according to the best of my judgment, without respect either to party men or party views." He and his fellow Federalists would *not* represent their constituents' particular interests because to do so would encourage factionalism at the expense of the general good.[14]

Like later conservative generations, however, the Federalists learned that they had to adapt to new conditions if they were to have any effective political role. America *was* becoming more democratic, however they might deplore the trend, and to survive in politics they had to woo the voters. The historian David Fischer has demonstrated a generational divide between old Federalists, who could never make the switch to popular campaigning, and young Federalists, who realized after 1800 that they must create local, statewide, and national party organizations or else face political extinction.[15]

FEDERALISM AND THE POLITICS OF THE 1790S

As the 1790s opened, the very survival of the republic was in doubt. The American people, after all, had overthrown first the British government and then their own (as conceived under the Articles of Confederation) in the previous fourteen years. Maybe their new government under the Constitution would soon suffer the same fate. The Federalists understood that republics are rarely more vulnerable than in their earliest years, before their practices have had time to become traditions, and before their rituals have become time-honored through repetition. How could the Constitution's supporters expect more durability for their new system?

One way was by surrounding the president with the same veneration previously given to kings. The First Congress spent a lot of time discussing titles and etiquette, because of the Federalists' recognition that the national leader had a symbolic as well as a practical role to fulfill. Some liked the idea of making Washington president for life, or of creating a hereditary presidency. Federalists also created elaborate rituals for the celebration of Washington's birthday and July Fourth as they endeavored to create traditions for the republic. Stately processions on these occasions were designed to emphasize that republican America was quite different from the France of surging crowds and unruly mobs.[16]

The Federalists' trump card from the beginning was Washington himself. His unanimous election to the presidency in 1789 and again in 1792 gave the Constitution a prestige it would otherwise have lacked and prompted many dubious Americans to give the new system of government the benefit of the doubt, and the chance to prove itself. Washington modeled himself on the Roman hero Cincinnatus, whose fame sprang equally from his effective leadership in times of emergency and his willingness to *renounce* power after saving the republic. At the end of the Revolutionary War Washington had ostentatiously declined a permanent political role under the Articles of Confederation, and at the end of his two presidential terms, in 1797, he again surrendered the power that was his for the asking to return as a private citizen to his Mount Vernon farm.[17]

A second way to make the Constitution durable was to ensure that it did not suffer from the same defects as the Articles of Confederation. The work of Hamilton as first secretary of the treasury was, in this respect, as important as the presidency of Washington. Historians have long argued about whether Hamilton, a bold political innovator, can be thought of as a conservative, but evidence in favor of the idea is persuasive. He sought political stability under the Constitution, a strong union, and financial security for the federal government. In later periods of American history, when conservatives have favored a strong federal government, Hamilton has been their hero (though it is equally true that later conservatives who have favored states' rights or a weak federal government have cast him as their villain).[18]

Hamilton understood, first, that if the federal government was to endure, it must create its own version of the Bank of England, an institution of rocklike financial probity that could be trusted throughout the world. It must, moreover, win the support of America's wealthiest men. The way to ensure their support was to give them a direct financial interest in the survival of the republic, along with the confidence that it would always meet its financial obligations. He therefore argued strenuously and successfully that the new government under the Constitution should found a national bank and should take responsibility for paying off fully all debts incurred by the old government. It should assume the outstanding debts of the states as well, indicating its leadership in national finance. Even though this policy of accepting responsibility for old national and state debts created a heavy burden for the new federal government, he argued, it would strengthen the republic by giving leading citizens a material as well as a patriotic motive to support it.[19]

Along with the assumption of old debts and the creation of a national bank, Hamilton argued for a policy of government-subsidized industrial development. He believed the federal government should actively promote and support economic activities that would enrich and strengthen the nation as a whole. Recognizing that Britain's power was based on its growing industries, he planned to guide America down the same road. Such was the burden of his *Report on Manufactures* (1791). He was even willing to support industrial espionage if it could bring British technology to America. Hamilton, recognizing that America needed to catch up with Britain industrially, favored government subsidies and tariffs on imports to keep out the goods of rival nations.[20]

Tariffs alone were not sufficient to raise the money Hamilton needed to pay the annual interest on the national debt in addition to meeting the government's other costs. He therefore proposed to Congress an excise tax. His attempt to impose it on the farmers of western Pennsylvania set off one of the first crises of the new regime, a rebellion whose leaders declared that the excise was an attack on their livelihood. They refused to pay. President Washington, acting under Hamilton's guidance, recognized that he should assert the federal government's power in a dramatic way to prevent anarchic scenes like those of Shays's Rebellion a decade earlier. He therefore led an army of thirteen thousand men across the Appalachians to suppress this "Whiskey Rebellion." This was an immense and disproportionate force in reaction to a local uprising, but one whose sheer existence bespoke the federal government's power and determination.[21]

What else would help ensure social order and promote virtue? First was religion. The First Amendment to the Constitution declared that Congress should pass no laws relating to an established religion, but it said nothing about the states, several of which retained established churches for several decades after the Revolution—Connecticut until

1818 and Massachusetts until 1833. These two states followed the European erastian tradition, according to which the church was a branch of the state and subsidized by the state, unifying it and embodying its religious and moral will. Jefferson's alternative approach, expressed in the religious liberty statute he had written for Virginia in 1785, created the model that was emulated everywhere after 1833. Religious disestablishment seemed anarchic to its Federalist critics, who were willing to extend tolerance to members of other denominations but who could not imagine a society functioning successfully without a religious establishment.[22]

Most white Americans were literate in 1800, so Federalists and Republicans alike published propaganda against the other, much of it scurrilous and dishonest. A few Federalist writers, however, were serious literary figures. One was William Cobbett (1763–1835), an English visitor. Between 1794 and 1800 he lived in Philadelphia and wrote strident pro-Federalist pamphlets, then ran his own newspaper, *Porcupine's Gazette*. Historians of the American press have shown that he was the single most widely read publicist of the 1790s. Thinking of himself as a young radical and having expected to love America as a haven of virtue and liberty, he was bitterly disillusioned on arrival to find the common people "a cheating, sly, roguish gang," and he came to believe that the spread of democracy had also spread irreligion, disrespect for one's betters, the breakdown of the family, and a dangerous tendency to romanticize the French Revolution. In America, wrote Cobbett, he had "seen piety give place to contempt of religion, plain dealing exchanged for shuffling and fraud, universal confidence for universal suspicion and distrust . . . a country once the seat of peace and good neighborhood, torn to pieces by faction, plunged by intriguing demagogues into never-ceasing hatred and strife . . . a people, once too fond of what they called liberty to bear the sway of a British King, humbly bend their necks to the yoke, nay to the very foot, of a set of groveling despots." The groveling despots in question were politicians in the Jeffersonian Republican cause.[23]

For Cobbett and for any American of conservative disposition, the French Revolution, as it progressed, provided a vivid series of illustrations about how well-meaning plans could go horribly awry and how a deficiency in virtue, restraint, and balance could unleash destructive furies. No issue was more divisive in the 1790s than the appropriate American reaction, and the related question of how America should position itself with respect to Britain, France's principal foe. At the outset, in 1789, many Americans sympathized with the French Revolution, seeing its early stages as comparable to the early events of their own national drama fourteen years before. Jefferson, who was in France as American minister in 1789 and 1790, never forgot the exhilarating mood of hope and renewal the country was experiencing. By 1793, however, the execution of King Louis XVI, the mass guillotining of the aristocracy, and evidence of the Paris mob's terrible destructiveness had led Federalists to turn in horror against the whole thing and to denounce any Americans who still expressed pro-French sympathies. Hamilton detested the French Revolution. One of his admirers, Harrison Gray Otis, wrote that Hamilton's "penetrating eye discerned, and his prophetic voice foretold, the tendency and consequence of the first revolutionary movements." He early recognized, Otis added, that "the people of France, like every nation which surrenders its reason to the mercy of demagogues, would be driven by the storms of anarchy upon the shores of despotism."[24]

The rise of Napoleon to absolute power out of the turmoil of the Revolution, when interpreted through classical republican theory, confirmed the old idea that revolution in the name of the people could lead first to demagoguery, and then to tyranny. One by one the frail republics of Europe fell to Napoleon under a combination of threat and force: Holland and Genoa in 1797, Switzerland and Venice in 1798. These tragedies further alarmed the Federalists, underlining their anxiety for the durability of republics—especially those unwilling or unable to fight for their lives. In 1799, Fisher Ames wrote, "When we look at Europe and contemplate its political state, we seem to be treading on the crater of a half-extinguished volcano. Here, scarcely cool from their fusion, are the cinders of one republic, and there still smokes the brand of another. . . . Can we think there is a decree for the immortality of our republic, when every gazette from Europe is blackened with the epitaphs of nations once independent, now no more. Lately they had life and being; now they lie like mangled birds to digest in the French tiger's maw." Some Federalists even feared in 1798 that if Britain was defeated, France would attack America. Otis wrote his wife that year: "Should Great Britain be compelled to yield, it is my opinion that our liberties and independence would fall sacrifice. She is the only barrier to the dreadful deluge, and when that is broken down, it will be time for us to prepare to be good and dutiful subjects to the French."[25]

Federalists' anxiety over Napoleon's power, along with the French government's insult to American diplomats in Paris (the "XYZ affair"), prompted them to push through Congress the Alien and Sedition Acts (1797–98). This series of laws permitted the arbitrary deportation of aliens and made criticism of the administration in speech or writing an offense. Related laws sought to impede immigration and to extend the period between immigrants' arrival and their chance to take out citizenship from five years to fourteen. All the people prosecuted under the acts were Jeffersonian Republicans. Otis spoke for most Federalists when he justified these measures as a way of forestalling the migration of revolutionaries, particularly from France and Ireland, "who, after unfurling the standard of rebellion in their own countries, may come hither to revolutionize ours." National emergencies justified drastic actions.[26]

THE REVOLUTION OF 1800 AND THE MARSHALL COURT

Thomas Jefferson became president in the election of 1800. Unlike the Federalists he favored an agrarian republic. Dedicated, like them, to the classical republican tradition, he emphasized different elements in it. He saw the countryside as the home of virtue and cities as dens of vice. He believed that America, with its vast interior, could remain a farmers' republic for centuries, staving off the moral decay that had come to overcrowded urban Europe. There should be no established churches, he believed, property should be widely distributed, old hierarchies ought to be dismantled, and the wisdom of the ordinary voter was to be trusted. Central government policy should not favor the material interests of the strong. In opposition during the 1790s, Jefferson had opposed Hamilton's broad construction of the Constitution, deplored speculation, the central bank, and Hamilton's commercial policies (because he thought they would hasten an age of luxury and depravity) and had spoken out against the Alien and Sedition Acts. He saw his election as a return to the spirit of 1776.[27]

Federalists were horrified—perhaps taken in by their own propaganda. Some of them seemed to believe that America's own Reign of Terror was about to begin. Just before the 1800 election Timothy Dwight, the staunchly Federalist president of Yale University, asked: "Can serious and reflecting men look about them and doubt that, if Jefferson is elected and the Jacobins get into authority, those morals which protect our lives from the knife of the assassin, which guard the chastity of our wives and daughters from seduction and violence, defend our property from plunder and devastation and shield our religion from contempt and profanation, will not be trampled upon?" Several older Federalists retired from public life in disgust, after discovering that their wealth, status, and social position were no longer sufficient to ensure their political preeminence. Theodore Sedgwick, a landowner and the dominant political figure of Berkshire County, Massachusetts, for example, wrote: "The aristocracy of virtue is destroyed; personal influence is at an end."[28]

Despite such alarms the 1800 election was a vital moment in the history of American conservatism, because it established the principle that the losing party in an election admits defeat and moves peacefully into opposition. The Jeffersonians were quick to grasp this point, one commenting: "The changes of administration, which in every government and in every age have most generally been epochs of confusion, villainy and bloodshed, in this our happy country take place without any species of distraction or disorder." The history of electoral politics around the world is full of examples of losers refusing to honor the verdict of an election and of seizing power to exclude the winners. It is full, also, of winners arresting the losers or abolishing the electoral machinery once it has brought them to power. In 1800 in America, mercifully, the Federalists did not rebel and the Jeffersonians did not repress or outlaw them. Peaceful transitions have now undergirded American political stability for more than two centuries. We are so familiar with the idea that the losers of elections concede to the winners (confident that they will have another chance in later elections) that we can easily lose sight of what an achievement that is—the bedrock of a successful republic.[29]

Jefferson has been a venerated American symbol (at all points of the political spectrum) for so long that it is difficult to appreciate the ferocity with which Federalists denounced and dreaded him. First, he seemed to Federalists too willing to experiment politically and to take a rationalistic approach to politics rather than trust to experience and the wisdom of former ages. Noah Webster (1758–1843) had Jefferson in mind when he declared: "Never . . . let us exchange our civil and religious institutions for the wild theories of crazy projectors; or the sober, industrious moral habits of our country, for experiments in atheism and lawless democracy. *Experience* is a safe pilot; but experiment is a dangerous ocean, full of rocks and shoals." Second, Jefferson was a convinced deist but a Christian skeptic. And third, he was a slaveholder, whereas Federalism was becoming a regional party in the antislavery North. Federalist propagandists made the most of allegations about Jefferson's sexual affair with "dusky Sally," the slave Sally Hemmings. They juxtaposed his and other Virginians' rhetoric of liberty with the underlying reality that they had the tyrannical power of life and death over their slaves. [30]

Although the Federalists would never again hold the presidency, they did not disappear after 1800. They remained as a vocal minority in Congress, intellectually powerful as writers, preachers, and polemicists, and politically dominant for two more decades in New England. Fisher Ames's rhetoric became more colorful than ever; he wrote in a letter of 1806 that "our disease is democracy. . . . It is not the skin that festers—our very bones are carious, and their marrow blackens with gangrene. . . . Our republicanism must die, and I am sorry for it." Younger leaders like William Plumer (1759–1860) recognized that they would have to borrow some of the Republicans' electoral techniques and to start talking about the voters in a less censorious way. To one unbending Federalist, reluctant to enter the roughhouse of electoral politics, Plumer wrote: "Abjure . . . that uprightness which cannot accommodate itself to events—which cannot flatter the people—that stiff, ungracious patriotism, which professes to save the people from their worst enemies, themselves." He understood that in the democratic air of the new century few Americans were now willing to be told that they were inferior, and few thought of men richer than themselves as their betters. Cultivating public opinion had become essential to electoral survival.[31]

Jefferson's controversial acts, meanwhile, periodically reinvigorated the Federalists in opposition. One was the Louisiana Purchase. They feared that to make the already vast nation even bigger (as this act certainly did, doubling its territorial extent) was to increase the likelihood of its failure. As Americans fanned out far beyond the Appalachians, were they going to preserve the virtues of good republicans? Fisher Ames's 1805 gloomy anticipation of what would happen in the purchase lands was characteristic: "Safe in their solitudes, alike from the annoyances of enemies and government . . . it is infinitely more probable that they [Western settlers] will sink into barbarism than rise to the dignity of national sentiments and character."[32]

The Louisiana Purchase also affected many Federalists' ideas about the role of the national government. In the early 1790s, under Hamilton's leadership, they had favored a loose construction of the Constitution, arguing that a national bank and energetic federal aid to economic development were among its implied powers and that a strong central government was necessary. Jefferson and his "interest" had deplored that approach. In 1804, however, the roles were reversed. Jefferson interpreted his presidential powers under the Constitution broadly to justify the purchase, prompting the opposition Federalists to denounce it as an act of usurpation. As many subsequent events were to show, a loose construction of the Constitution could sometimes serve conservative ends and sometimes those of their rivals.[33]

Dismayed by the Louisiana Purchase and defeats in the elections of 1804 and 1808, the Federalists were further disheartened by Jefferson's embargo, imposed on American Atlantic commerce in 1807, and then by Madison's declaration of war against Britain in 1812. Federalists, having been pro-British ever since the early 1790s, grieved at anti-British antagonism, not least because it was ruinous to their material interests. Some believed that the Union was now being run by Virginians in the interest of their state and of the South. The rule by which three-fifths of slaves were included in the population count for matters of electoral apportionment gave the South artificial political strength, while the acquisition of Louisiana augured a vast increase for the slavery-dominated Republican Party. In states where the Federalists retained local ascendancy, they refused to permit state militiamen to serve in the national army, while New England's financiers, many of the wealthiest men in the country, refused to aid President Madison in funding the war.[34]

In 1814 a group of New England Federalists summoned the Hartford Convention to discuss the possibility of a northern secession from the Union. Only Massachusetts, Connecticut, and Rhode Island were officially represented, though New Hampshire and Vermont also sent observers. Such a meeting during war, tiptoeing to the brink of treason, was not the kind of thing the Federalists themselves would have tolerated from their rivals; they had passed the Alien and Sedition Acts under much less provocation in 1798. It was, however, an act of weakness, not strength, and the Federalists' weakness became fully apparent when the war ended, vindicating the republic's ability to survive. Federalists lost yet again in the elections of 1816, and their party began to break up.[35]

It was doomed by the spread of direct popular democracy and the growing belief in the equality of all (white) men. Certain powerful figures from the Federalist camp, nevertheless, lived far into the nineteenth century and, under different auspices, carried Federalism's conservative impulse with them. John Quincy Adams (1767–1848), for example, went on to play an important role in antebellum politics. An exceptionally gifted, scholarly, hard-working, and earnest young man, he had been groomed by his father, John Adams, for greatness. They were an exacting couple; a 1794 letter from father to son had warned: "You come into life with advantages which will disgrace you if your success is mediocre. . . . If you do not rise to the head not only of your profession but of your country, it will be owing to your laziness, slovenliness, and obstinacy." Son reciprocated with a letter of his own after father's election defeat in 1800. While "the common and vulgar herd of statesmen and warriors" had pursued their own self-interest, "it will be a great and glorious preeminence for you to have exhibited an example of the contrary, a statesman who made the sacrifice of his own interest and influence to the real and unquestionable benefit of his country."[36]

John Quincy made a judicious switch into the opposition party in 1809, when it seemed to him that the New England Federalists were putting regional above national concerns—he dismayed them by supporting the embargo. He certainly tried hard to live up to his father's expectations, serving as an American ambassador in Europe for four presidents, as secretary of state, and eventually—as specified in the letter—as president (1825–29). Like most of the older Federalists, he was skeptical about democracy and said he would "sooner turn scavenger and earn my living by cleaning away the filth of the streets than plunge into this bottomless filth of faction." This younger Adams, who kept an extremely detailed diary for fifty years, scrutinized his own motives closely—he had an active puritanical conscience and hated the idea that he was ever motivated by personal ambition. His lofty self-conception was consonant with the tradition of republican virtue he had learned at home, though he was perhaps not quite so selfless and averse to success as he imagined.[37]

Old Federalists were uneasily aware that they had contributed to bringing into existence the new world they detested. They might claim to love the old world of order, deference, and hierarchy, but many of them were skilled practitioners of entrepreneurial capitalism. The historian Steven Watts notes that "by upholding an ethic of commercial growth, entrepreneurial achievement and individual independence, this conservative cadre unwittingly helped to undermine the deferential, virtuous, and stable policy they rhetorically upheld with such emotion." He adds that their angry denunciation of the Republicans "came from an emotion born of culpability as well as horror." They knew that the new world was, in large part, their own creation.[38]

One remarkable element of the Federalist legacy is its contribution to the abolition of slavery north of the Mason-Dixon Line. It was an issue over which the Federalists were divided. The historian Larry Tise has shown that some Federalist clergy, North and South, voiced support for slavery. For the first thirty years of the republic's history, however, another group of northern Federalists opposed it. They never missed an opportunity to rebuke their Republican (and largely Southern) opponents for building their fortunes on African-American enslavement and argued that the virtuous republic would be better without human bondage than with it. It was difficult, they added, for Virginia slaveholders to be good republican citizens because their absolute power over their slaves' lives, and their tendency to pursue lives of ease and luxury, made them even more vulnerable to corruption and vice than one would find in the general human condition. (William Lloyd Garrison, the abolitionist radical of the next generation, began life as an apprentice printer at a Federalist newspaper, the *Newburyport Herald,* where he was introduced to the politics of antislavery.)[39]

Probably the most lasting and conservative achievement of the Federalists—one from which we still benefit today—was their role in creating a strong independent judiciary. Just before leaving office in the spring of 1801 President Adams appointed his secretary of state, the forty-five-year-old John Marshall, a Southern Federalist of strongly conservative convictions, as chief justice of the Supreme Court. Marshall was to remain in that position for the rest of his life, until 1835, and to define once and for all the Court's right to review the constitutionality of congressional legislation. Polls of American lawyers now rate Marshall as the best chief justice in the history of the Court. At the time of his appointment, however, he looked like a Trojan horse to Jeffersonian Republicans, a dedicated Federalist thrust into the heart of the new Republican administration.[40]

His decisions never betrayed party interest in the crude sense, though they certainly embodied Marshall's (and the Federalists') general idea of the direction in which America as a growing society ought to move, strengthening federal power, encouraging economic growth, and upholding the sanctity of contracts. He was a broad constructionist, remarking in one decision: "Let the end be legitimate, let it be within the scope of the Constitution, and all means which are appropriate, which are plainly adapted to that end, which are not prohibited but consist with the letter and spirit of the Constitution, are constitutional." He also worked hard among his brethren to get unanimity in judging cases, and established the principle of declaring the decision of the court as a whole, in place of the older method of letting each judge in a case speak for himself, with the result that decisions seemed more authoritative.[41]

Marshall inherited what was, at the time, the least significant branch of the federal government, a branch whose future was uncertain. He transformed it into an equal partner with the executive and legislature and created for it the stabilizing role it has played throughout almost the whole of subsequent American history. Among the earliest and most important cases decided under his guidance was *Marbury v. Madison* (1803), a case full of political pitfalls, around which he navigated skillfully. It established the principle that the Supreme Court was authorized to review congressional legislation and to decide whether or not it conformed to the Constitution. Establishing the principle of judicial review, which governments of all parties have accepted ever since, he placed a decisive brake on popular democracy. Judicial review, in effect, means judicial *supremacy*, giving immense authority to a highly educated elite, an elite, moreover, that is not elected and that could never gain power in the rough and tumble of electoral politics. In other ways, too, Marshall established the Supreme Court as a central conservative institution, and one that tended to enhance the power of the federal government. Three cases from 1819 were particularly important. In the first, *Sturges v. Crowninshield,* he ruled that Congress was entitled to pass uniform bankruptcy laws and that state laws contradicting them were unconstitutional. In the second, the *Dartmouth College* case, he enhanced the principle of the sanctity of contracts by overruling the New Hampshire state legislature's attempt to alter the terms of the college's original charter. In the third, *McCulloch v. Maryland* he overruled the state of Maryland's attempt to impose a tax on the national bank. All three of these cases promoted federal supremacy, as did *Ogden v. Gibbons* (1824), which confirmed the right of the federal government to supervise interstate commerce and to overrule state-granted monopolies if they got in the way.[42]

Beginning his tenure at the end of the Adams administration, Marshall was joined on the bench by a long succession of Republican appointees, nominated by presidents Jefferson, Madison, and Monroe. His learning, persuasive power, and authority combined, nevertheless, to leave him the dominant figure throughout his thirty-four years of leadership, converting to his views a succession of colleagues who might well have been antagonists. Even though he was one of seven justices on the bench (only later did the number, which is not specified in the Constitution, rise to nine), he wrote nearly half of all the court's decisions in those years. No colleague was more important than Joseph Story (1779–1845), appointed to the Supreme Court by President Madison in 1811. Ostensibly a Republican, Story soon came to share Marshall's views on nearly all important matters. More scholarly than Marshall (he doubled as a Harvard law professor), he also added intellectual gravity and weight of precedent to the cases they decided together.[43]

By the time of his death, in 1835, Marshall was afraid that the good society he hoped for, ruled by "the wise, the rich, and the good" was in danger from the spread of democracy and the ascendancy of Andrew Jackson. In fact, however, the supremacy of the Supreme Court was beyond dispute. As the legal historian Robert McCloskey notes, his death was almost as important as his life in ensuring this result: "Within a surprisingly short time the justices of the Supreme Court, regardless of who appointed them, were paying almost unanimous lip service to his memory; those who had chided him so willingly while he was alive now cited him, like scripture, in their own behalf and flinched at the charge that he would have disagreed with them." His successor, Roger Taney, was neither willing nor able to dismantle the great structure Marshall had built. We are by now so familiar with the rule of law, and with the

Supreme Court's central authority, that we can easily forget that it, like political stability, is not something that can be taken for granted.[44]

The Federalists' legacy includes much that later generations of conservatives could applaud: the rule of law under the Constitution, the preservation of a republic based on the principle of mixed government, peaceful changes of government through election, and judicial supremacy. They also tried to assure a stable financial basis for the federal government, national credibility in diplomacy, and protection to the wealth of the privileged elite. Hamilton and Adams, the two most brilliant Federalists, and most of their supporters, were unashamed of their elitism, regarding the existence of a virtuous natural aristocracy as vital to the republic's health; they took seriously the idea that inequality is both natural and desirable.

There is a less creditable side to the Federalists, which it also bequeathed to American conservatism. They chronically underestimated the ability of men in the social classes beneath them. From the 1780s right into the 1820s they complained incessantly about the anarchic tendencies of the lower orders and warned that democracy leads to disaster. America was democratizing rapidly throughout the era but showed no signs of revolutionary chaos, even if lower class men's respect for their "betters" was weakening. Gloomy and unadventurous, the Federalists saw the Louisiana Purchase and the rapid westward spread of the republic not as opportunities but as auguries of doom. And despite plentiful evidence to the contrary, they confused Jefferson and his party with wicked, French-style revolutionaries. From this distance the political continuities between the 1790s and 1800s are more striking than the discontinuities.

CHAPTER TWO

Southern Conservatism

THE SOUTH OF THE EARLY REPUBLIC was dominated by Jeffersonian Republicans, the Federalists' great rival, though many of them also were profoundly conservative. Their conservatism was different from that of Hamilton, Adams, Ames, Otis, and Marshall, however, just as Southern conservatism has been distinct from its Northern counterpart throughout much of American history. At times the two have appeared to be almost polar opposites. While the Federalists struggled to establish a strong central executive and a national economic policy, believing them necessary to national survival and prosperity, their antagonists in the South opposed both. In their view a strong central government, created at the expense of states' rights, would be the death of republicanism.[1]

Southern conservatism in the early republic reflected, in part, the region's economic interests. The area had few cities, and its principal activity was farming, namely, growing staples for export. In the colonial era it had specialized in tobacco, indigo, and rice. Eli Whitney's invention of the cotton gin in 1793 suddenly made it possible and profitable to market short-staple cotton; cotton became the South's basic export for the next seventy years and fueled an almost continuous boom, as plantation agriculture and slavery spread rapidly westward.[2]

To some extent conservatism correlates with economics and geography within the region. Southerners living on the exhausted tobacco lands of Virginia and tidewater South Carolina were more likely than participants in the western cotton boom to fear that they were presiding over a civilization in decline. As Bertram Wyatt Brown, the historian of Southern honor, remarks, "Virginia's economic and political decline from the mid-eighteenth century to the third decade of the following one was especially demoralizing for the 'old elite.' . . . But that prospect of declension—the fall of empires, peoples, and clans—had been the destiny of mankind for ages past. . . . Typically the moral lesson cast the southern mind backward, not forward to better times ahead." These were men who idealized classical heroes and cultivated the stoic virtues. The historian Drew Faust argues that many of the most gifted Southern writers of the antebellum era "found a special emotional resonance in the image of themselves as Jeremiahs—as prophets without honor speaking truth to an unheeding world."[3]

To be sure, not every slave owner, nor every Virginian, should be thought of as conservative. Thomas Jefferson, for example, was the owner of large estates and 180 slaves (about whom he suffered periodic bouts of bad conscience); nevertheless he had a philosophically and politically adventurous outlook, pioneered the abolition of state churches, and doubted much of the teaching of conventional Christianity. He might not have been the Jacobin his Federalist foes alleged, but neither can he easily be thought of as a conservative. Other slave owners too thought of themselves as forward-looking, entrepreneurial, adventurous, and commercially up-to-date, approving rather than lamenting the spread of democracy across the white South. The Old South became, if anything, more conservative with the passage of time. Intellectual innovators in the area fell silent, migrated north, or accepted their conservative neighbors' ideas, especially after 1830.[4]

RANDOLPH AND TAYLOR

The first assertion of southern conservatism after the defeat of the anti-Federalists did involve Jefferson—the Virginia and Kentucky Resolutions. Throughout most of the colonial period the tobacco colonies had enjoyed a policy of benign neglect by Britain, and they had risen up in arms when Britain began a policy of more rigorous administration. Similarly, in response to the Alien and Sedition Acts in 1798, which threatened federal intervention in local affairs, Jefferson (for Kentucky) and Madison (for Virginia), both acting anonymously, drafted these protests against centralized power. They stated that the Constitution was a compact among sovereign states and that states were justified in deciding whether Congress had exceeded its constitutional authority. States could, they said, "interpose" themselves against illicit federal legislation. Kentucky followed up with a second resolution the next year, adding that the state was entitled to "nullify" unconstitutional federal laws.[5]

Among the supporters of these resolutions were two old-fashioned and outspoken Virginians, John Taylor and John Randolph, the most articulate early representatives of Southern conservatism. A lineage of conservatism involving states' rights and small government can be traced from their speeches and writings through much of the next two centuries. Taylor (1753–1824), the elder of the two, was a Revolutionary War veteran, lawyer, planter, and slave owner. He represented Caroline County in Congress.[6]

Randolph (1773–1833) was the son of a wealthy planter, attended college and law school in the North, and, because he was too young, just missed the controversy over the Constitution, even though he entered politics in his early twenties. His eccentricities have always delighted biographers. As a young man he suffered a debilitating illness that made him impotent and affected his vocal cords. An observer from Massachusetts described Randolph addressing Congress at the height of his powers:

> His head is small and until you approach him near enough to observe the premature and unhealthy wrinkles that have furrowed his face, you would say that it was boyish, but as your eye turns toward his extremities everything seems to be unnaturally stretched and protracted. To his short and meager body are attached long legs which, instead of diminishing, grow larger as they approach the floor until they end in a pair of feet broad and large, giving his whole person the appearance of a sort of pyramid. . . . His long straight hair is parted on the top and a portion hangs down on each side, while the rest is carelessly tied up behind and flows down his back. His voice is shrill and effeminate and occasionally broken by low tones [of the kind] you hear from dwarves and deformed people.

He dressed in pre-Revolutionary fashions and traveled in an old English coach pulled by six thoroughbred horses. Touchy on points of honor, Randolph, in his fifties, fought a duel against Henry Clay—the only casualty, luckily, was his cloak, which suffered one hole. An early admirer of Jefferson, he turned against him for deviating from the austere republican tradition. An early admirer of Andrew Jackson, he turned against him, too, when he became, as Randolph saw it, a demagogue.[7]

Taylor and Randolph shared a broad pattern of beliefs. Strongly influenced by the English country Whig tradition, they eulogized farmers and the countryside while condemning the vices of city life. Taylor was usually down-to-earth—indeed monotonous—as a writer, but he had a mystical reverence for the countryside and for agriculture as the foundation of a virtuous society. His book *Arator* (1818) declared that in farming "the practice of almost every moral virtue is amply remunerated in this world, whilst it is also the best surety for attaining the blessings of the next." Manufacturing capitalism, characteristic of the rising cities and central to Hamilton's plans, he regarded as avaricious, grasping, and destructive of liberty. He wrote two influential pamphlets against Hamilton's measures in the 1790s. Randolph, similarly, loved farming and hunting, detested city life, and thought of the farmer's way of life, especially that of the pre-Revolutionary Virginian, as ennobling.[8]

They feared not only city life but also the federal government. If permitted to grow, it would pose the same threat as had the royal court in England; it would manipulate and bribe citizens, buying off their independence and silencing their criticism with jobs and sinecures. In the same way, a national bank would create a financial elite, enjoying government favor while luring ordinary citizens into debt and dependency. The notion of federal subsidies to advance nation-building projects like roads, canals, and a national bank, during the second and third decades of the century, dismayed them both, because such measures would weaken the independence of the sovereign states.[9]

Taylor's and Randolph's fear of big government was closely related to a fear of standing armies. They favored active state militias, whose effect would be to disperse rather than concentrate coercive power. The nation ought not to undertake foreign ventures, ought not to be expansive, and ought to leave its citizens to themselves as far as possible. Randolph declared that his principles were "love of peace, hatred of offensive war, jealousy of the State governments toward the General Government; a dread of standing armies; a loathing of public debt, taxes and excises; tenderness for the liberty of the citizen; jealousy, Argus-eyed jealousy, of the patronage of the president." He broke with many of his fellow Southerners by opposing the War of 1812. As he saw it, the war would benefit speculators, not ordinary citizens, would strengthen the federal government at the expense of the states, and worst of all would offer aid and comfort to Napoleon, whom he looked on as the greatest enemy of human freedom in the entire world.[10]

In the crisis conditions of the 1790s and early 1800s the nation was radically politicized. But in the view of Taylor and Randolph, less government is usually better. "The principles of free government in this country . . . have more to fear from armies of legislators, and armies of Judges, than from any other or from all other causes," said Randolph. He deplored active government and said the best legislature was one that passed no laws and whose members slept. Growing numbers of citizens had begun to assert their right to participate in political life, but Taylor and Randolph, just as they feared a strong central government, feared the participation of their poor and propertyless white neighbors. Randolph particularly feared "king numbers," the idea that a simple majority of voters should be able to make their views prevail. In his view, property holders alone should be entitled to vote, lest nonproperty holders come into power, seize the property of the haves, and constitute themselves the new propertied class.[11]

Not surprisingly, Taylor and Randolph did not believe in human equality. Randolph, in an 1826 speech, said that he rejected the principles asserted in the Declaration of Independence. "That all men are born free and equal—I can never assent to, for the best of all reasons, because it is not true." He added, "If there is an animal on earth to which it [equality at birth] does not apply—that is not born free—it is man; he is born in a state of the most abject want and a state of perfect helplessness and ignorance." Randolph's most famous declaration was: "I am an aristocrat. I love liberty, I hate equality." He believed that equality of condition was *un*natural and could be achieved only by tyrannical political action.[12]

Finally, Taylor and Randolph never enthused over the geographical expansion of the nation, never adopted the mood of what was later called

Manifest Destiny. Randolph, although he had voted for the Louisiana Purchase, later regretted it. He came to deplore the restlessness, pragmatism, and expansionism of the young nation, seeing these qualities not as signs of youth and health but as fatal to republican virtue. He voted against the admission into the Union of each new state in turn. In 1822 he wrote that "no government extending from the Atlantic to the Pacific can be fit to govern me or those whom I represent," because it could not embody "the common feeling and the common interest with the governed which is indispensable to its existence."[13]

The question of slavery underlay all other sectional disputes, becoming acute in 1820, when Missouri petitioned for incorporation into the Union. The North, with its larger population, was correspondingly stronger in the House of Representatives. North and South were, however, balanced in the Senate, because each state had two senators, no matter how large or small its population, and because the number of slave and free states was equal. The Missouri Compromise, worked out by political peacemakers, therefore specified that Missouri, entering the Union as a slave state, would be balanced by Maine, entering as a free state. The compromise also specified that henceforth new states could permit slavery only south of the Mason-Dixon Line (latitude at 36°30').[14]

Taylor and Randolph saw the Missouri Compromise not as a judicious act of political peacemaking but as further evidence of federal aggrandizement. After all, states were sovereign and ought not to be subject to dictation. If the federal government was permitted to decide questions relating to the makeup of states, such as whether or not they might permit slavery, they would soon be intervening against laws inside the older states too. Taylor wrote in *Construction Construed and Constitutions Vindicated* (1820) that the compromise had transformed the role of the federal government, which would now be the referee of controversies between the free-labor and slave-labor sections of the Union. Each section would think the worst of the other, and the long-term outcome would be civil war.[15]

JOHN CALHOUN

John Calhoun of South Carolina (1782–1850), a practical politician but also a skillful political theorist, succeeded Taylor and Randolph as Southern sectional leader in the 1820s. He carried on their advocacy of the country tradition, touting republican virtue against the hazards of an overmighty federal government. At the same time he began adapting the slave south to the expanding market economy. Says one historian: "Calhoun fashioned an accommodation between ancient republican ideals and the realities of modern commercial capitalism."[16]

Calhoun emerged as a regional leader during the tariff controversy of the late 1820s. Southern plantation owners, the richest and most politically influential men of their section, favored low tariffs. They—Calhoun among them—prospered by exporting raw cotton, mainly to England, and importing British manufactured goods and wanted few or no barriers to impede this trade. Northern manufacturers, by contrast, struggling to nurture industries in competition with more established British rivals, favored high tariffs, which would make British imports more expensive than their own goods. Each section feared that the other's tariff policy would damage its interests, and when the North gained the upper hand in Congress and introduced high tariffs (the "Tariff of Abominations") in 1828, some enraged Carolinians advocated secession.[17]

In the "South Carolina Exposition and Protest" (November 1828), Calhoun, writing anonymously, developed the themes of the Kentucky and Virginia Resolutions to argue the need for limited government and for safeguards against the tyranny of the majority. Individual states, already sovereign before the creation of the Constitution, he wrote, had certain reserved powers. If the federal government exceeded the powers delegated to it in the Constitution, the states were entitled to assert their rights by exempting themselves from that legislation. The Founding Fathers, he added, had recognized that different parts of the nation had different interests and that they should be free to pursue them. "The Constitution has formed the states into a community only to the extent that they have common interests, leaving them distinct and independent communities as to all other interests." In the Fort Hill Address of 1831 Calhoun elaborated: Avoiding use of the word *nullification,* he argued that a state was justified in interposing itself between its citizens and a federal government that had exceeded its constitutional authority and that the practice already had a long history. One Calhoun biographer notes that "every sentence that Calhoun wrote . . . was intended to show that there was nothing to fear in the Carolina doctrine; it was profoundly conservative."[18]

Calhoun also introduced the idea of "concurrent majorities," by which he meant the accumulation of evidence that all parts of a society, and all interests in it (rather than a mere numerical majority of voters), consented to measures of vital significance. One such measure would be a combination of strong majorities inside and outside of Congress, of the kind used to ratify constitutional amendments. The obvious objection to this theory was that in a complex society so many interests were involved, and so many possible veto powers, that the requirement of concurrent majorities would prevent any legislation from being passed; the checks and balances would paralyze the system. Besides, as later historians have pointed out, his apparent solicitude for minorities actually extended only to *propertied* minorities that were powerful in their own right. He certainly did not feel squeamish about the minority rights of anti-nullificationists inside South Carolina.[19]

In November 1832 a South Carolina state convention set aside that year's high tariff legislation, ordered citizens of the state not to pay the tariff on goods they bought, and threatened to secede from the Union if the federal government attempted coercion. It also called for volunteers to fight for South Carolina in the event of conflict, and at once raised twenty-five thousand men. From our vantage point these actions look like a rehearsal for the secession and civil war that would come in the 1860s. In Calhoun's view, however, such steps were salutary ways to *prevent* civil war, by demonstrating the state's resolve to resist federal tyranny. Military threats by Jackson and passage of a "Force Bill" by Congress led the nullifiers to back down, but their pride was saved by introduction of a lower-rate compromise tariff, a deal arranged by Henry Clay of Kentucky.[20]

No other state joined South Carolina in endorsing nullification. However, John Randolph, now close to death from tuberculosis and heavily dependent on opium and alcohol to get him through each day, persuaded his fellow Virginians to sign a series of resolutions declaring that Virginia, too, was a sovereign state, retaining the right to secede "whenever she shall find the benefits of union exceeded by its evils." The outcome of the crisis was ambiguous enough that nullifiers were able to claim their method had succeeded, since peace and the Union had been preserved, and tariff rates reduced.[21]

In later years Calhoun offered his mature thoughts on the principles involved in this and subsequent crises in his *Disquisition on Government* (written between 1843 and 1849 and published posthumously) and his *Discourse on the Constitution and Government of the United States* (still in draft at the time of his death, in 1850). The *Disquisition* went back to the first principles of political philosophy. It began by denying that men are born free and equal—implicitly rejecting the philosophy of the Declaration of Independence and all contract theories of government that involve an imagined state of nature. Indeed, he wrote, men are not born at all; babies are born into particular societies and eventually *become* men, but they become the men of these particular societies, rather than deciding, *as* men, that they will opt to join it.[22]

The government under which men live has to balance citizens' liberties against the needs of the whole society, while citizens have to be vigilant, lest the government become too powerful over them. Such liberty as citizens possess comes only through the existence and smooth conduct of government (not from nature), and is enjoyed to different degrees at different levels of civilization. Liberty, under these circumstances, is much more important than equality. Men may be equal before the law but they are unequal in every other way because of their different abilities and the different ways in which they work. Society benefits from these inequalities; they are essential to progress.[23]

The *Discourse* put Calhoun's general principles to work in an examination of the American political system. He repeated his earlier claim that the states had never surrendered their sovereignty when they created the federal government. They had, however, created it by use of the concurrent majority (ratification by a large majority of the states) and had built into it the checks and balances and procedural safeguards that prevented the tyranny of the majority. The concurrent majority promoted political comity by encouraging all parties to consider the needs of others in order that mutually beneficial legislation be passed. "By giving to each interest or portion the power of self-protection, all strife and struggle between them for ascendancy is prevented. . . . And hence there will be diffused throughout the whole community kind feelings between its different portions." All praise to the Founders. Unfortunately they had failed to specify that states could veto or nullify federal actions and had given the federal government too much power over finances. Trends initiated by Hamilton had come to an odious climax in 1833, when Congress, at Jackson's behest, had passed the Force Act, threatening military retaliation against a nullifying state. The future of the Union depended, said Calhoun, on a reduction of federal and presidential power.[24]

SLAVERY

The Nullification Crisis, a danger in its own right to the durability of the Union, was all the more threatening because of the question of slavery just below its surface. After 1830, white Southerners found themselves forced to defend the institution of slavery in the face of three rising challenges. First, they endured slave uprisings: Denmark Vesey's in 1822 and Nat Turner's in 1831, which coincided with the Nullification Crisis. Second, in 1833 Britain abolished slavery in its colonies, the sugar islands of the Caribbean. The British example challenged America to keep pace. Third, American antislavery advocates, taking heart from the British example, intensified their own campaign. Moderate and procedural at first, the antislavery impulse was transformed by the rise of a new militancy in the 1830s. "Immediatist" abolitionists like William Lloyd Garrison and Frederick Douglass came to dominate the movement.[25]

White Southerners, uncomfortably aware of Northern antagonism, refined a theoretical justification of slavery that had often been made earlier but that now needed greater intellectual weight and rhetorical vigor. Between the 1830s and the 1850s they began, in a variety of ways, to argue that slavery was not just a necessary evil but an actual good, beneficial alike to masters, slaves, and the society as a whole. Calhoun declared in a Senate debate in 1837 that slavery was "instead of an evil, a good, a positive good." In an 1848 debate he added that the rising antislavery agitation was based on "the false and dangerous assumption that all men are born free and equal" and on the fallacy that blacks were "as fully entitled to both liberty and equality as whites." This assumption did more "to retard the cause of liberty and civilization, and is doing more at present, than all other causes combined."[26]

Conservative historians in the twentieth century sometimes hesitated to dwell on their predecessors' argument for slavery, lest it appear to contaminate the conservative position on other issues. Russell Kirk passed over it in almost complete silence in his great classic *The Conservative Mind* (1953). There can be no question, however, that standing up for slavery was a thoroughly conservative thing to do. Nearly every society in the history of the world had had slavery in one form or another, as these apologists pointed out; far from being something strange and aberrant, it was absolutely normal. One among them, William Harper of Charleston, argued that civilization itself would never have begun or flourished had it not been for slavery. "Without it there can be no accumulation of property, no providence for the future, no taste for comforts or elegancies, which are the characteristics and essentials of civilization. . . . Since the existence of man upon the earth, with no exception whatever, either of ancient or modern times, every society which has attained civilization has advanced to it through this process."[27]

Taking the long view, Harper was surely right. Slavery had seemed normal and unremarkable almost always, almost everywhere, not least in the classical world with which Americans in the young republic so often compared themselves. The remarkable thing about Western Europe and North America is not that they too used forms of unfree labor but that, eventually, they abolished it. The work in recent decades of a group of superb Southern historians, Eugene Genovese, Drew Faust, Michael O'Brien, James Oakes, and others, has enabled us to recognize this point more clearly than previously. They have also reminded us that the slave owners were not shamefaced men doing what they knew was wrong but, rather, proud and honorable men doing what they genuinely believed was right, and that in matters of logic, history, tradition, and scripture they often got the best of the argument.[28]

Conservatives usually think of themselves as the guardians of civilization. Articulate slave owners felt confident that their peculiar institution was a civilizing force. Calhoun himself, for example, spent his entire life surrounded by slaves and slavery. He witnessed firsthand how their work enriched his family and how ownership of slaves gave him high social prestige. As one of his biographers remarks, "If slavery in the 1830s meant barbarism to Boston abolitionists like William Lloyd Garrison and Wendell Phillips, it implied civility to Carolinians of Calhoun's generation." The plantation owners viewed their system, with its mix of commercial enterprise and paternalistic slavery, as the high water mark of civilized life and ordered freedom.[29]

Calhoun's generation argued that slavery was good not just for the slave owner but for the slaves themselves. In a speech of 1839 Calhoun himself declared: "We now believe it has been a great blessing to both of the races—the European and African, which, by a mysterious Providence, have been brought together in the Southern section of this Union. The one has greatly improved, and the other has not deteriorated; while, in a political point of view, it has been the great stay of the Union and our free institutions, and one of the main sources of the unbounded prosperity of the whole." Racial differences were so great, these owners believed, that African Americans would be unable to live as free laborers side by side with whites. Calhoun argued that the contrast between slaves and free blacks in the North already demonstrated this point convincingly. In a letter to British ambassador Richard Packenham on the theme, he selected a few statistics from the census of 1840 to argue that insanity, blindness, and vice were far more common among free blacks than among slaves. The black population still in slavery, on the other hand, "enjoys a degree of health which may well compare with that of any laboring population in any country in Christendom" and a "high elevation in morals, intelligence, and civilization." In other words, slavery was protective of the slaves, offering them a better way of life than they might hope to enjoy if forced to fend for themselves. Besides, slaves were part of the family. Henry Watson, an Alabama plantation owner, wrote of slaves that "we feed them, clothe them, nurse them when sick and in all things provide for them. How can we do this and not love them? They too feel an affection for their master, his wife and children, and they are proud of his and their successes. There seems to be a charm in the name of 'master'—they look upon and to their master with the same feeling that a child looks to his father."[30]

Was the slave owners' belief in racial difference mere prejudice? They claimed that the new science of ethnology supported their ideas, but, much more important, so did the Bible. Southern clergy scrutinized their Bibles for arguments in support of slavery and racial distinction. Twenty-first century readers may be dismayed to see how easy that job proved to be, but it is hardly surprising. The Bible, Old and New Testaments alike, was written in a world where slavery was ubiquitous and where, so far as we can tell, the possibility of its abolition had never arisen. According to some interpreters, Ham, Noah's son, who shamed his father by seeing him drunk and naked, was widely believed to be the ancestor of all black-skinned people. Thornton Stringfellow (1788–1869), a Baptist preacher and one of the theological defenders of slavery, noted that God himself, cursing Ham, renamed him Canaan and said: "Cursed be Canaan . . . a servant of servants shall he be to his brethren." Later, when God chose Abraham to be the patriarch of His chosen people, He blessed him with an immense house of servants; Stringfellow demonstrated with lengthy exegesis from other passages that the word *servant* in Genesis meant the same as *slave* in modern English. Later still the Children of Israel, enslaved by the Egyptian pharaoh, objected to being slaves, but once they had escaped and occupied the Promised Land, they in turn enslaved other peoples, again with God's blessing. Moving to the New Testament Stringfellow was able to show that Jesus never objected to slavery. St. Paul in his Epistle to Philemon even sends a runaway slave back to his master with the message not to set him free but to treat him kindly, and to remember that they are brothers in Christ. Surely if God objected to slavery, Stringfellow argued, He would have said so.[31]

At the same time, of course, abolitionists were using their Bibles to denounce slavery, claiming that it violated the spirit of the Gospel. Southern divines usually got the better of the argument when it came to citing chapter and verse; they regarded appeals to the spirit of Christianity as too subjective, tending toward unorthodoxy. James Henry Thornwell (1822–62), a Presbyterian theologian, was critical of the abolitionists' theology and of the theory of social and racial equality that lay behind it. "The parties in this conflict are not merely Abolitionists and Slaveholders," he wrote; "they are Atheists, Socialists, Communists, Red republicans, and Jacobins on the one side, and the friends of order and regulated freedom on the other. In one word, the world is the battleground. Christianity and Atheism are the combatants, and the progress of humanity is the stake."[32]

Arguments from the Bible, however, are often designed to challenge uneasy consciences rather than to support complacency. As Genovese has shown, they were aimed not just at abolitionist outsiders but also at backsliders nearer home. Preachers like Thornwell and Stringfellow "peppered their communicants with calls for higher Christian standards and with slashing attacks on the un-Christian personal and social behavior of all too many slaveholders." Sermons on slavery regularly criticized slave owners for not living up to standards clearly established in the Bible itself. If they were negligent, cruel, or capricious, masters stood under divine judgment. When crises came about, including the ultimate crisis of defeat in the Civil War, many Southern preachers believed their section had suffered a divine chastisement for not living up to God's commandments.[33]

Proslavery writers were able to invoke the authority not just of the Bible but also of the classics—much venerated in that time and place. George Frederick Holmes (1820–97), a British immigrant who became an outspoken proslavery writer, noted that the Spartans had held slaves in their era of greatness. Plato, Aristotle, Thucydides, and all the most famous Greeks had lived with slavery too, without advocating its abolition, while the Romans, also proslavery, had conquered the known world. Edmund Ruffin (1794–1865), a Virginian agricultural scientist and proslavery writer, made the same point: "Slavery has existed from as early time as historical records furnish any information of the social and political condition of mankind." Such durability for the institution seemed to them further proof that the all-powerful God who rules the world cannot reasonably be thought to have everlastingly opposed it.[34]

As the radical abolitionist movement grew, proslavery conservatives moved over to the offensive in arguing for the superiority of their system. They compared working conditions on their plantations with conditions in British industrial cities and the new industrial cities of the American North. Here in the South, they said, we slave owners take care of our charges from cradle to grave. We bring them up as children when they are too young to work, nurse them in sickness, and provide them with care, shelter, and support in the last years of their lives when they are too old to work. In Britain and in the North, by contrast, employees are paid only by the hour for the factory work they have done. Factory owners do not attend to the welfare of their employees' children, do not pay pensions in old age, and do not compensate the many workers who are injured or maimed on the job. Of the two, our slavery system is kinder, gentler, and more humane.[35]

Insisting that their system was morally superior and that sooner or later the North would have to come around to something like it, they linked a broad array of religious and economic issues. In a bravura passage Eugene Genovese imagines a summary of the Southern conservatives' argument as they might have made it in addressing their Northern brethren:

> You northern conservatives share our revulsion against growing infidelity and secularism, against the rapid extension of the heresies of liberal theology, against the social and political abominations of egalitarianism and popular democracy, against the mounting assault on the family and upon the very principle of authority. You share our alarm at the growing popularity of the perverse doctrines of Enlightenment radicalism and the French Revolution—the doctrines of Voltaire, Rousseau, Paine. You share our fears for the fate of Western civilization. Yet you fail to identify the root of this massive theological, ecclesiastical, social and political offensive against Christianity and the social order: the system of free labor that breeds egotism and extols personal license at the expense of all God-ordained authority.

Only a widespread recognition that some form of unfree labor was necessary could reconcile the nineteenth-century's marvels of material progress with the ancient need for order, restraint, and virtue.[36]

By the 1830s, it was already easy to fear that as concentrations of industrial workers in cities got bigger, class conflict would get worse. Similarly, it seemed reasonable to suppose (as Karl Marx was then supposing in Europe) that as industrialization intensified, class antagonism would grow more acute until it burst out in proletarian revolution. Slavery, said its conservative defenders, avoids this problem by linking masters and slaves together in extended families rather than creating a stark antagonism between capital and labor. Slavery, in other words, acknowledges the reality of class stratification while reducing the likelihood of conflict.[37]

Probably the best-known defender of slavery is the autodidact George Fitzhugh (1806–81), whose books *Sociology for the South* (1854) and *Cannibals All!* (1857) took the argument to its extremes. Fitzhugh predicted that slavery would prove to be the ideal labor system for the future, not just for African Americans but for most *whites* too. Convinced of the absolute inequality of human beings, it seemed clear to him that most people need to be protected rather than liberated. The great fallacy plaguing America was the idea of equality, for which in large part he blamed Jefferson. He thought of the American Revolution as "an exceedingly natural and conservative affair; it was only the false and unnecessary theories invoked to justify it that were radical, agrarian, and anarchical." Those unnecessary ideas came from John Locke, "a presumptuous charlatan." Fitzhugh condemned not just Locke but the entire philosophical legacy of the eighteenth century. "The human mind became extremely presumptuous . . . and undertook to form governments on exact philosophical principles, just as men make clocks, watches, or mills. They confounded the moral with the physical world, and this was not strange, because they had begun to doubt whether there was any other than a physical world." Fitzhugh rejected all contract theories of government (Hobbes, Locke, Rousseau) in favor of the theories of Sir Robert Filmer (1588–1653), a seventeenth-century English monarchist and author of *Patriarcha*. Government is not based on individual consent, said Fitzhugh, following Filmer. It is, rather, an extension of the principle embodied in the family, bringing together people of different ages, sexes, abilities, and needs, for the sake of their mutual support and protection.[38]

Whatever the merits of the various proslavery arguments, Southern intellectuals knew that unfree labor was under attack throughout much of the world. Britain had abolished slavery throughout its empire by legislation of 1833. Did liberation bring wealth and contentment to those it had freed? Conservative defenders of slavery found plenty of reasons to say no. When John Randolph visited Ireland with his slave John, he was amazed at the degraded poverty he found there among the peasants. "I was utterly shocked at the condition of the poor peasantry between Limerick and Dublin. Why, sir, John never felt so proud of being a Virginia slave. He looked with horror upon the mud hovels and miserable food of the white slaves. I had no fear of *his* running away." In the same vein the abolition of serfdom in parts of Eastern Europe was, in the slaveholders' view, no cause for rejoicing. Thomas Dew (1802–46), president of the College of William and Mary, wrote that the freed serfs of Poland longed for renewed servitude and the protection it brought. "The traveler will now look in vain, throughout our slaveholding country, for such misery as is here [in Poland] depicted. . . . But liberate our slaves and in a very few years we shall have all these horrors and reproaches added unto us." Similarly, he claimed, the emancipation of slaves in the British West Indies had been disastrous to their welfare.[39]

Would slavery be able to retain its intellectual plausibility in an increasingly hostile world? Only if new generations of Southerners grew up believing in it. Education therefore became an important arena for proslavery intellectuals. Curricula varied, but nearly all Southern college presidents shared the belief that they must "counteract the growing transatlantic revulsion against slavery as a moral as well as social evil." Objections to slavery, frequently heard on such campuses as Jefferson's University of Virginia during the early years of the republic, became far less common after 1830. College presidents, usually teaching the capstone course on moral philosophy to seniors, wove a defense of slavery into their exposition; they "espoused a broadly conservative worldview that stressed the necessity for social stratification, the authority of the male head of household, and the basic tenets of Christian orthodoxy." This educational venture was largely successful. Young elite Southerners of the 1840s and 1850s appear to have believed just as much as their grandfathers—perhaps more so—in the legitimacy of the slave system, a belief many of them would eventually put to the ultimate test on the battlefield.[40]

Southern conservatives often spoke of themselves as Cavaliers and tried to place their society in seamless continuity with classical and European models, as though it were the logical organic outgrowth of civilization. But in reality they were locked into an industrializing world as producers of raw materials for textile factories, dependent on such capitalist innovations as railroads, steamships, banking, and credit facilities. Sometimes, despite their claim to be family patriarchs, they had to sell slaves to meet financial obligations or buy them to expand their labor force, in either case jeopardizing rather than strengthening the family integrity they claimed to honor. Sometimes, despite their assertion that the slaves enjoyed plantation life and lived well, the slaves rebelled or ran away. In other words, daily life reminded them that they could not always live up to their own ideals. Genovese writes that the work of conservative Southerners before the Civil War "constituted a massive attempt to 'create' the missing tradition by relating the plantation community to the organic communities of premodern Europe. They struggled to create a culture that would stand as a worthy heir to the best in the Western Christian tradition and prove a bulwark against the disintegrating tendencies of the modern world." Like so many others in American conservative history, they were vulnerable to contradictory pressures, economic and political, which in the long run doomed their system to destruction.[41]

The historian James Oakes adds that the most articulate patriarchal conservatives were, in any event, always a minority among slave owners.

These were the privileged elite who lived in long-established communities around the Chesapeake Bay, Charleston, Savannah, and New Orleans, or on the richest Mississippi land around Natchez. For them, stability, family integrity across the color line, and rejection of egalitarian politics were serious commitments. By contrast, he suggests, the majority of slave owners were always opportunistic businessmen, perpetually in motion westward, scrambling for advantage and regarding slaves and lands simply as useful assets in a volatile market. "Where most slaveholders believed in upward mobility and physical movement in pursuit of their goal of material advancement, paternalists preferred stasis and were appalled by the prevailing urge to move." Their point of view he catches beautifully in the remark of a slave owner who condemned "this miserable, selfish, avaricious and dastardly spirit of emigration," which "destroys all local attachments and all love of country." By contrast "every virtuous and patriotic citizen should feel himself bound to the soil which gave him birth, which has been the home of his father, and which contains the bones of his ancestors." Oakes cautions that we can get a misleading sense of the stability and conservatism of American slavery by regarding the literature of this minority as representative of the whole.[42]

Although the defense of slavery underlay their political and social thought, elite Southerners did worry about other issues, especially the rising tide of democracy that—like the slave controversy—intensified in the 1830s. For example, James Henry Hammond (1807–64), an ambitious South Carolina politician on the make, deplored the spread of universal suffrage, which had given poor whites "a power which they are totally incompetent to exercise—if not absolutely unworthy of it." He felt demeaned by the mass electioneering that was now required to win or hold a seat in state and national government, telling a friend, "I may be fastidious but I . . . thought there was no particle of honor conferred by an office obtained by coaxing and begging and intriguing." Such men fought an unsuccessful rearguard at state constitutional conventions, trying to preserve the requirement of property qualifications for office. Nathaniel Beverley Tucker (1784–1851), a law professor at the College of William and Mary, was revolted by the decision of Virginia's 1850 constitutional convention to widen the franchise. In his view it had created a tyranny, "insolent and base." In a letter to a close friend he asked, "What are our democracies, but mobs?"[43]

In this respect, if in few others, Southern antebellum conservatives shared a common point of view with the Federalist conservatives of the early republic. Both groups participated in an expanding market economy, but both felt uneasy at its political implications. Differing on the question of central government power, they agreed on the principle of human inequality. If poor and propertyless groups gained political power, they believed, demagogues would rule, jeopardizing the stability of a society that ought to be guided by privileged and virtuous elites. These shared conservative concerns would not be sufficient, however, to unite them in the rising sectional crisis of the 1850s.

CHAPTER THREE

Northern Antebellum Conservatism and the Whigs

HISTORIANS HAVE LONG REGARDED THE DEFEAT of John Quincy Adams in the election of 1828 and the turbulent inauguration of President Andrew Jackson the following spring as symbolic moments in the development of American democracy. Men and women of all classes paraded to Congress with Jackson, listened to his inaugural address (given outdoors for the first time), and then, by the thousands, attended a White House reception, trampling flowers, drinking heartily, and making a boisterous assertion of their equality. Conservatives deplored the spectacle; one lady described it as "a rabble, a mob, of boys, negroes, women, children, scrambling, fighting, romping," while Supreme Court Justice Joseph Story recognized in the event the "reign of KING MOB." Jackson exploited the possibilities of his office to the full. He defied the Supreme Court over the fate of the Five Civilized Tribes and compelled their banishment beyond the Mississippi. He threatened to use military force against South Carolina in the Nullification Crisis. Above all he declared war on the Second National Bank in 1832, just prior to his successful reelection campaign. Often contemptuous of Congress, he seemed to some old Federalists and conservative Southerners to be the tyrant long foretold in classical republican theory.[1]

In opposition to Jackson and his heirs arose the Whig Party, which competed with the Democrats through the 1830s and 1840s for national preeminence before falling victim to sectional tensions in the 1850s. Many of its most articulate writers and practical politicians, including Daniel Webster and Henry Clay, gave voice to a moderate conservatism. They sought to blend social stability with continued opportunities for economic modernization and specialization; they looked on society as an organism that linked past, present, and future generations. They feared the triumph of mass democracy (of the sort glimpsed in Jackson's inauguration), and they feared the moral absolutism represented by the rising abolitionist movement, which repudiated their own cherished principles of moderation and conciliation.

THE BANK WAR

Alexander Hamilton had supervised the creation of the First Bank in 1791 as part of his plan to make the federal government strong and the nation financially sound. Its abolition in 1811 had led to currency instability, prompting President Madison to organize the Second Bank in 1816. Its purpose was to manage the national currency, hold government revenues, support the treasury, and restrain the lending practices of reckless provincial banks. Like the Supreme Court it was supposed to be nonpartisan and immune from political pressures. The bank had been poorly led at first; then in 1823 President Monroe entrusted it to Nicholas Biddle, a man described by an English visitor as "the most perfect specimen of an American gentleman." Biddle (1786–1844), a prosperous and classically educated Philadelphian (he received a B.A. from Princeton at age fifteen), had already flourished as a diplomat, writer, and state legislator. In the 1820s he supervised the paying down of the national debt, established a currency that was recognized at par throughout the United States and abroad, and made loans to underwrite national improvement schemes. Looked at from an economic point of view the Bank of the United States seemed to be doing an excellent job under his guidance.[2]

Biddle's conduct of the bank's business, though effective, was, however, secretive. "The bank made its decisions behind closed doors," notes the historian Sean Wilentz, "and these decisions were made by a man who declared himself beholden to no elected official in the land. Biddle, with his haughty bearing and his presumption that democracy was demagogy, personified the Jacksonians' charges that the bank threatened popular sovereignty." Biddle's political friends convinced him that, despite

President Jackson's objections, he could be sure of getting the bank rechartered and that he ought to do it before the election of 1832 rather than wait until the original charter expired in 1836. He followed their advice, and, as expected, the bank won comfortable majorities in both houses of Congress. Jackson vetoed it, however, in a language that invoked the specter of class warfare, claiming that the bank's "aristocrats" were aligned against the "humble members of society—the farmers, mechanics, and laborers."[3]

Biddle was enraged by the veto message, which sounded to him like an echo of the French Revolution. "It has all the fury of a chained panther biting at the bars of his cage. It really is a manifesto of anarchy—such as Marat or Robespierre might have issued to the mob." Jackson won reelection handsomely, using the bank in his campaign speeches and literature as a symbol of the aristocracy he was pledged to destroy. In the ensuing years he removed the federal government's funds from the bank, transferring them to "pet" banks in the various states, and twice firing secretaries of the treasury who refused to cooperate with the policy. The Bank War marked a defeat for conservative economic principles, a defeat made all the more symbolically vivid by the clash of its two leading personalities. Within a few years a new political party, the Whigs, had come together in opposition to nearly everything Jackson stood for.[4]

WHIGS AND DEMOCRATS

The Democrats, honoring the memory of Jefferson, thought of America as essentially an agrarian republic. The yeoman farmer was the ideal citizen: he owned his own land, was independent, and was able to participate in political life on the basis of his natural virtues and common sense. Every citizen, farmer or not, had an equal right to vote. Politics should be the preserve of everyman, with representatives directly answerable to the voters. Higher learning among representatives and office holders was unnecessary and might be sinister. Even judges should be elected by the people rather than chosen from among the ranks of trained lawyers. Western expansion would ensure the continuing availability of free land for new generations of farmers far into the future. Democrats feared concentrations of power and concentrations of wealth, both of which were to be found in cities. They therefore favored small, weak government and had little interest in nurturing American industries. Centralized banks were, in their view, particularly dangerous; politicians and bankers were too liable to corrupt one another, creating a faction of power and wealth that would be the enemy of the ordinary working people. Better, they believed, to have fewer credit facilities and to be confined to the use of hard money; that would restrain avaricious commercialism and forestall the creation of permanent antagonistic social classes.[5]

The Whigs countered this vision at every point. They thought the nation should have a mixed and diversified economy, blending agriculture with commerce and industry. The vote should be a privilege, not a right, should be confined to property holders, and should be used to elect superior men of virtue and learning, who would then deliberate and vote according to their discretion rather than being tied to the voters' immediate interests. Higher learning among representatives and office holders was vital because politics is complicated and delicate. Judges should be rigorously trained in the arcana of law and should be exempt from electoral pressures. Cities, though potentially "luxurious" and "vicious," could also be centers of civilization, where wealth-generating industries could be sited, bringing prosperity to all. Sophisticated central banking was desirable, while controlled access to credit facilitated further expansion. In other words, the Whigs favored nearly all the characteristics of modern capitalist development: division of labor, specialization, banking and credit, and government policies dedicated to economic growth, all in the context of moral restraint, the rule of law, and respect for tradition. There might be differences of income and wealth, but social classes would ideally enjoy a natural harmony of interests. William Brownlow (1805–77), an ardent Tennessee Whig, was horrified by the Jacksonians' manipulation of class antagonisms as an attempt "to array the ignorant against the intelligent, the poor against the rich, the wicked against the pious, the vulgar against the decent, the worthless against the worthy, and thieves against honest men."[6]

The Whigs showed by the name they chose that they honored the tradition of the eighteenth-century British opposition and the ideals of America's Revolutionary generation. The English Whigs were heirs to the Glorious Revolution of 1688 and guardians of parliamentary privilege against royal tyranny. The American Whigs saw themselves in a comparable role, facing down the tyranny of the overmighty "King"

Andrew Jackson. In principle, they, like the Federalists before them, were suspicious of parties or "factions." In practice they soon learned how to work like a party, mobilizing voters to win elections, and succeeded in getting their candidates to the White House in the elections of 1840 (Benjamin Harrison) and 1848 (Zachary Taylor). Edmund Burke was one of their favorite writers: they shared his horror of the French Revolution, they admired his rhetorical blending of logic and sentiment in defense of tradition, and they shared his aversion to rationalist schemes for sweeping away the old and rebuilding society according to blueprints. Sixteen editions of Burke's complete works were published in America before the Civil War, seven of them in the 1830s alone.[7]

Like Burke, they admired self-restraint, balance, prudence, and respect for the law and tradition. They feared that the young nation was too violent, too prone to accept extralegal means of solving problems (lynching, dueling, plundering Indians). No wonder they were dismayed by Jackson. His populist swagger and high-handedness led some Whig writers to compare him to Julius Caesar, Oliver Cromwell, and Napoleon, famous tyrants from earlier eras who had manipulated popular passions to make themselves all-powerful. He seemed to personify the old Federalist claim that mass democracy gives rise to demagogues. The spread of democracy, however, had changed the permissible language of politics, and Whigs had to be careful to avoid giving the impression that they opposed universal suffrage. The Whig writer Calvin Colton (1789–1856), for example, deplored the effects of universal suffrage in his book *A Voice from America to England* (1839), addressed to a British audience, but gave the impression of favoring it in the Whig pamphlets he wrote for home consumption in the campaigns of 1840 and 1844.[8]

Colton, who lived for a time in England, was in many ways a representative Whig intellectual, one of the first actually to describe himself as a conservative. He deplored the rigidity of the English class system by comparison with America's ability to reward talent and hard work. On the other hand he admired British sensitivity to custom and tradition. "It is a real, substantial English virtue that keeps things steady, so that you may know what to depend upon, and it operates generally for the public good. Immemorable usage, in any country, if it concerns everybody, and relates to practical, everyday interests, is generally right, and may be presumed so." As Colton's biographer says, this could easily be a passage from Burke.[9]

Back in America in 1835, Colton believed that Jacksonian democracy was wrecking American politics. "American government as first set up [by the Founders]", he wrote, "was properly republican, with salutary checks on the popular will," but now it was "assailed . . . by a power called democracy," which threatened order and even civilization itself. He feared the effects of public opinion. "The great struggle in America . . . on which the fate of the Republic is suspended . . . is between the Constitution and Democracy. The Constitution is the bulwark of the nation's safety, but the dynasty of [public] opinion is constantly assailing it, and whether the Constitution will yet give way altogether and totter, and fall to the ground, remains to be proved." Colton's political ideal was "a representative republic governed by men of virtue, wisdom, learning, and property who, though ultimately responsible to the electorate, would be aloof from the turbulence and passions that infected the mass of citizens."[10]

Colton was also dismayed by the "devil" of radical reform that seemed to be sweeping the country. The excitement of evangelical revivals in the Second Great Awakening upset him. He decided to become an Episcopalian, to join a church that emphasized liturgy and ritual restraint rather than spontaneity, sudden conversion, and spiritual drama. He disliked perfectionist crusades on behalf of prohibition, sabbatarianism, and vegetarianism. Above all, although moderately opposed to slavery, he hated abolitionists. Their fanaticism, as he saw it, had transformed Southern slave owners from men who admitted the evil of the system into active defenders of it as a positive good. He also suspected that abolitionists were plotting slave insurrections and foresaw that abolition, if brought about suddenly or prematurely, would shatter the entire basis of the Southern economy, harming everyone, blacks and whites alike.[11]

Rufus Choate (1799–1859), another New Englander, expressed similar Whig ideas. A gifted courtroom orator and Whig congressman, much in demand on occasions of public celebration and commemoration, he admired Burke and despised Locke and Rousseau, rejecting their notion that society and the state are based on voluntary contracts between individuals. Choate thought of the American Revolutionary generation as a group of Burkean Englishmen who had resisted the innovations of George III and his ministers on behalf of tradition. Were they not the heirs of the Puritans, who had kept aloft the banner of human liberty in the dark days of King Charles I? The American Revolution, in other words, sat squarely in this long and time-honored tradition of preserving English liberties against the threat of tyranny. Choate, who was a fine classicist and amateur historian, linked these British antecedents to an even longer republican tradition, stretching from ancient Greece and Rome, through the Renaissance cities of Italy and Switzerland and Calvin's Geneva, to the America of his own day. He, like Colton, was no friend to slavery, but he deplored the radical abolitionists, regarding them as fanatics lacking respect for the Union.[12]

In a speech to Harvard Law School in 1845 Choate argued that lawyers were active agents in the conservation of the state because, in their daily work and in their invocation of precedent, they reminded citizens of the continuity of the generations that bind past, present, and future together in an organic national unity. "May it not one day be written, for the praise of the American bar, that it helped to keep the true idea of the State alive and germinant in the American mind; that it helped to keep alive the sacred sentiments of obedience and reverence and justice, of the supremacy of the calm and grand reason of the law over the fitful will of the individual and the crowd; that it helped to withstand the pernicious sophism that the successive generations, as they come to life, are but as so many successive flights of summer flies, without relations to the past or duties to the future, and taught instead that all—all the dead, the living, the unborn—were one moral person . . . that the engagements of one age may bind the conscience of another." Best of all, the law upheld liberty while enforcing order, reverence, and subordination. It would encourage Americans to think of the nation not as some temporary contractual arrangement but as something venerable and eternal.[13]

The Whigs' most influential economist was Henry Carey (1793–1879), a friend of Nicholas Biddle, who was also the first American economist to become well known and respected overseas. He approached economics pragmatically, taking the America around him, rather than abstractions about "economic man," as his starting point. As a result he was less pessimistic than the British economists Thomas Malthus and David

Ricardo. He believed that the right combination of entrepreneurship, government subsidy, and tariffs could turn America into an industrial power, making it economically strong and independent of British imports. To him, that meant diversification and specialization, making the most use of citizens' varied talents. "Highest . . . among the tests of civilization," he wrote, is a society's ability to find for all citizens "demand for their whole physical and mental powers." Denying Malthus's idea that wages always tend to sink to the subsistence point, he believed that tariffs, along with government support of infrastructure and education, would enable American manufacturers to pay well. As a result, citizens would become more prosperous and civilized than ever before. "The more perfect is [a person's] development the greater is his desire for knowledge, the greater his love for literature and art, the greater his desire to see for himself the movements of the world, and to learn from those who are capable of affording him instruction."[14]

The Whigs' political standard-bearers through the 1830s and 1840s were Henry Clay (1777–1852) and Daniel Webster (1782–1852). Along with Calhoun they were the most influential politicians of the period from 1820 to 1852 and the most prominent men *not* to become president. Clay, like Carey, favored federal aid to projects that promoted national development. His "American System" (as distinguished from the "British system" of laissez-faire and free trade) involved protective tariffs, federal highways, and subsidies to canals, river improvement, and railroads, a communications infrastructure to make America independent and strong. He dedicated himself to strengthening the Union, politically and economically, declaring in 1844 that "if anyone desires to know the leading and paramount object of my public life, the preservation of this Union will furnish him the key."[15]

Acutely aware, as a border-state leader (Clay came from Kentucky), of the need to reconcile the conflicting interests of the North and the South, he prized compromise and conciliation as among the highest political goods and was a skillful parliamentarian, good at trading favors and building coalitions. In consequence, like many moderate conservatives before and since, he was angrily denounced by more ardent spirits from both sections. Abolitionists condemned him for being a slave owner, for favoring only gradual abolition, and for promoting the compromises of 1820 (the

Missouri Compromise), 1832 (to end the Nullification Crisis), and 1850 (over the admission of California to the Union as a nonslave state). Southern fire-eaters, conversely, condemned him as a traitor to his section for opposing them and for conciliating Northerners who were antislavery. But if he had detractors, he also enjoyed the admiration and emulation of men who shared his goal of preserving the Union through compromise. Abraham Lincoln (1809–65) was one who grew up in Clay's shadow and declared later that he was "an old-line Henry Clay Whig."[16]

Daniel Webster, the Whigs' New England leader, was Clay's nearest rival for preeminence—the two of them sparred for the presidency through the 1830s and 1840s. Webster had been born and raised in New Hampshire, studied at Dartmouth, and worked as a lawyer and rising Federalist politician between 1800 and the 1820s. He made his national reputation through appearances before John Marshall's Supreme Court, in a series of cases that strengthened the power of the federal judiciary. In fact he appeared before the court 170 times, a record never since equaled. He too supported an active national policy to promote internal improvements and economic growth, under the aegis of a strong central government.[17]

A magnificent public orator in an age when public speaking was highly prized, Webster glorified the American past and the idea of the Union in rich and memorable phrases, helping to create around the Revolutionary generation, whose survivors were dying out by the 1820s and 1830s, an aura of mystical reverence. He was capable of provoking a high sense of excitement. An admiring friend wrote, after hearing one speech: "I was never so excited by public speaking before in my life. Three or four times I thought my temples would burst with the gush of blood. . . . When I came out I was almost afraid to come near him. It seemed to me as if he was like the mount that might not be touched, and that burned with fire." Webster also knew how to make audiences weep. The hardheaded Justice Story admitted of his speech before the Supreme Court in the *Dartmouth College* case: "Webster's whole air and manner . . . gave to his oratory an almost superhuman influence. . . . The whole audience had been wrought up to the highest excitement; many were dissolved in tears; many betrayed the most agitating mental struggles; many were sinking under exhausting efforts to conceal their own emotions." Others described him as "sublime" and regarded him as an almost superhuman figure deserving not just respect but veneration.[18]

In Webster's "Second Reply to Hayne" of 1829, one of his most famous political speeches, he spoke for six hours over the course of two days to an enraptured U.S. Senate that was crowded to overflowing with admirers. Denying the Southern claim, recently advanced by Calhoun, that the individual states were sovereign bodies superior to the Union, Webster made a logical and emotional case on behalf of the supremacy of the Union, ending with a peroration that foresaw the possibility of civil war. It became famous in its own right—much memorized by later generations of schoolchildren:

> When my eyes shall be turned to behold for the last time the sun in heaven, may I not see him shining on the broken and dishonored fragments of a once glorious Union; on states dissevered, discordant, belligerent; on a land rent with civil feuds, or drenched, it may be, in fraternal blood! Let their last feeble and lingering glance behold the gorgeous ensign of the republic, now known and honored throughout the earth, still full high advanced, its arms and trophies streaming in their original luster, not a stripe erased or polluted, nor a single star obscured, bearing for its motto . . . everywhere, spread all over in characters of living light, blazing on all its ample folds, as they float over the sea and over the land, and in every wind under the whole heavens, that . . . sentiment dear to every true American heart—Liberty and Union, now and forever, one and inseparable.

By the 1830s, as one of Webster's biographers notes, "his name had become symbolically attached to the concepts of Constitution, Union, and the stability and virtue of the age of Washington." Further, "in 1860 it was essentially Webster's vision of the Union which Lincoln articulated and the North responded to with such massive enthusiasm."[19]

EUROPEAN INSIGHTS INTO AMERICAN DEMOCRACY

Webster and Clay, like Calhoun in the South, were working politicians, practical men who sometimes paused to reflect on the theoretical implications of their work but who never forgot the actual situation to which they must react. At the same time two foreign visitors, one temporary and one permanent, were reflecting more broadly on the American political situation in its wider historic context. The first was Alexis de Tocqueville (1805–59), a twenty-six-year-old French visitor who spent nine months in America in 1831 and 1832, principally to study prisons. On his return to France he wrote a report on American prison policy but also, of far more lasting significance, the two astonishingly perceptive volumes of *Democracy in America* (1835 and 1840), perhaps the most influential and widely cited book about America in the nation's history. It was a pioneering work of sociology and has become a conservative classic.[20]

America represented to Tocqueville a premonition of the future. He treated democracy as an immense impersonal force moving through history, far too strong for anyone to stop. Therefore it must be understood, harnessed, and directed. In France, however, "democracy has been abandoned to its wild instincts, and it has grown up like those children who have no parental guidance, who receive their education in the public streets, and who are acquainted only with the vices and wretchedness of society." Tocqueville hoped his book about the world's most democratic nation would draw the appropriate lessons for France's democratic future while also pointing out the necessary warnings. Almost incidentally it gave Americans, as they began to read it in translation, food for thought about their own situation. Tocqueville is unequalled in his power to remain relevant on the strengths and weaknesses of democracy and on the relationship between liberty and equality.[21]

He found much to admire in America. Land was plentiful and ordinary citizens could, through hard work, prosper as farmers on their own land. They were thriving, educated, ambitious and enterprising. They stood up for themselves, had a high sense of dignity, never had to grovel to aristocrats, and were free to worship as they preferred. They even ruled themselves. Their nation also enjoyed extraordinary political stability—a point sure to be of interest to anyone coming from France after half a century of chronic instability. Tocqueville, some of whose ancestors had been guillotined in the Terror of 1793, argued that this stability came not just from the good qualities of the Constitution but also from the fact that citizens had created hundreds of voluntary and civic organizations at every level of society, which collectively had a profoundly stabilizing effect.[22]

On the other hand, Tocqueville found faults with America. First, it was a land in which money had become all-important and which tempted everyone to become a grasping capitalist. There was no refined upper class, and hardly anyone was devoted to intellectual distinction; they were too busy in their professions, so "a middling standard is fixed . . . for human knowledge." This mediocrity in turn led to excessive conformity. The pressure of public opinion could be tyrannical, stifling to individuality. All Americans, he found, were vain, hated to be censured in any way, and had an intense craving for praise. "Their vanity is not only greedy, but restless and jealous; it will grant nothing, while it demands everything, but is ready to beg and to quarrel at the same time."[23]

Second, the spread of democracy had discouraged the pursuit of statesmanship. Men hoping to play a role in public life could no longer present themselves to the electorate with the claim that their social position or their virtues entitled them to rule. Campaigning required them to disguise rather than advertise their superiority. As a result, politics attracted manipulative, unscrupulous, and greedy men who sometimes saw it as an avenue for self-advancement rather than for the exercise of republican virtue. Politics had become sordid and mediocre. In fact, every election marked a crisis. The president "no longer governs for the interest of the state, but for that of his re-election; he does homage to the majority and instead of checking its passions, as his duty commands, he frequently courts its worst caprices." Andrew Jackson was a case in point. In a little masterpiece of denigration Tocqueville described Jackson as the "slave of the majority," as one who was "perpetually flattering [their] passions" and acting in a way that undermined respect for the office of the president itself. "In his hands the Federal government is strong but it will pass enfeebled into the hands of his successor."[24]

Third, said Tocqueville, the idea of equality was widespread and dangerous. Today we find it easy to assume that liberty and equality go together; Tocqueville thought they were polar opposites, and what he saw in America led him to fear that equality might destroy liberty. "There is . . . a manly and lawful passion for equality that incites men to wish all to be powerful and honored. This passion tends to elevate the humble to the rank of the great; but there exists also in the human heart a depraved taste for equality, which impels the weak to attempt to lower the powerful to their own level and reduces men to prefer equality in slavery to inequality with freedom. Not that those nations whose social condition is democratic naturally despise liberty; on the contrary, they have an instinctive love of it. But liberty is not the chief and constant object of their desires; equality is their idol. . . . Nothing can satisfy them without equality, and they would rather perish than lose it." Egalitarianism, as he saw it, nurtured envy. The hazard was that an envious democratic people would strengthen government at the expense of liberty, using its coercive powers to enforce equality.[25]

Less renowned today but influential in the America of his time was Francis Lieber (1798–1872), a friend of Tocqueville who helped him while he was in America and who later translated his prison book into English. Prussian by birth, Lieber had as a teenager been a soldier in the army that finally destroyed Napoleon at Waterloo in 1815. Wounded in the battle, he later became a radical student who was in and out of Prussian prisons for his outspoken advocacy of liberalism (he too developed a lifelong interest in penology). Emigrating to America in 1827 and settling in Boston, he was delighted to find in this republic many liberties of the kind young Germans at home could only dream of, including freedom of speech and of the press and the right to participate in selecting a government. He became a citizen in 1832 and won a permanent academic post as professor of history and political economy at South Carolina College in 1836. He was an adventurous teacher, "one of the most distinguished American college professors of his time."[26]

Lieber was also a thoughtful writer on political theory. His biographer argues that "no one since the Federalists had developed a systematic political philosophy to meet the needs of the groups that were rapidly achieving control of the nation" and that Lieber filled the gap. The Whigs "continued to pay lip service to the natural-rights philosophy of the eighteenth century, ill-fitting though it was, since they had not yet evolved a new scholarly rationale to take its place." Lieber developed a political ideology relevant to the conditions of a rapidly growing industrial society, an ideology that "when it crystallized in the gilded age . . . bore unmistakable signs of his handiwork." He aimed to be highly empirical, basing his conclusions on solid facts rather than deduction from first principles. The United States, as Lieber saw it, thrived not because it was the embodiment of Enlightenment ideals but because it was an actual historical reality. Like Rufus Choate he used the metaphor of society as an organism. Its people shared not just a system of constitutional government but a pattern of affections and loyalties that stretched back over two centuries; they were racially, religiously, and linguistically united, and they enjoyed a wide consensus on the basic issues of life.[27]

Lieber's distinctive political ideas can be found in his *Manual of Political Ethics* (1838), *Essays on Property and Labor* (1840), and *On Civil Liberty and Self-Government* (1853). In thinking about politics it was necessary, he said, to give consideration to three distinct things: society, the state, and the government. Individuals participate in all three. They are from birth members of society and its basic unit, the family, which nurtures them. Society precedes the state and stretches across the generations, introducing each new individual into its world. The state is the collection of generalized rules that a society makes to promote order and justice. The government is the branch of the state that takes particular and positive steps in response to new problems and challenges. Citizens' rights are accompanied by obligations, and citizens achieve liberty by living up to these obligations. The society's institutions therefore should not be thought of as inhibiting or restricting liberty. Without them there would be no liberty at all—strong government and liberty, in other words, are inseparable.[28]

Property is as fundamental and natural as the family. Like marriage and the family, property predates the state. Lieber scorned the early socialists, who thought of property as theft. To him, on the contrary, property makes men fully human. The right to property, he wrote, was the right "to call the product of his own exertions his own, to accumulate as he chooses; to exchange it for what he desires, and to dispose of it for the benefit of his individual family. . . . Man yearns to see his individuality represented and reflected in the effects of his exertions—in property." Government ought, accordingly, to protect and promote property. Lieber was sympathetic to Whig schemes for government promotion of internal improvements but concerned to protect individuals from excessive government intrusion. "Act on individualism alone . . . and you would reduce society to a mere crowd of egotistical units, far below . . . the ant hill; act on socialism alone and you would reduce society to loathsome despotism, in which individuals would be distinguished by mere number." Like Tocqueville, he feared democratic absolutism and worried that the recent democratization of America would result in the tyranny of democratic majorities.[29]

Lieber, although he lived and worked in South Carolina for twenty years, was no admirer of slavery and did not enjoy living in the midst of it. On the other hand he was no admirer of abolitionism either, recognizing the destructive potential of a movement so highly charged with moral absolutism. He fell out with his former friend and protégé Charles Sumner over the issue when Sumner became an abolitionist, because he could foresee that it might lead to secession. America would then end up fragmented into many petty states, like Germany. To Daniel Webster, whose conciliatory views were more to his taste, he wrote that he felt more deeply on the subject than many Americans "because I am a native German who knows by heart the commentary which his country has furnished and is furnishing for the text of querulous, angry, self-seeking, unpatriotic confederacies." In 1856, as intersectional tension increased, Lieber finally quit South Carolina and was able to find work instead at Columbia University in New York City, to him a far more congenial post.[30]

We know that the Jacksonian era would end with secession and civil war. Americans living through the decades before 1860 were probably more struck by the fact that America achieved a peaceful transition through every electoral cycle while European life was punctuated by frequent revolutionary upheavals: in 1815, with the final defeat of Napoleon; in 1830, with the July Revolution in France; and in 1848, with revolutionary outbreaks in France, Germany, Rome, and much of Eastern Europe. This was the paradox with which Tocqueville and Lieber struggled—that an America whose democracy ought to make it *un*stable was actually much better at transitions of government than aristocratic Europe.[31]

Charles Eliot Norton (1827–1908), a young Bostonian, was skeptical about the revolutions of 1848. His book *Considerations on Some Recent Social Theories* (1853), published when he was only twenty-six and based partly on firsthand observations during a long European tour, cautioned American readers against the fallacies of the era's revolutionaries—Kossuth in Hungary, Mazzini in Italy, Louis Blanc in France, and others. Their assertion of peoples' right to liberty and republican government, he said, was an abstraction that took no account of actual conditions in Hungary, Italy, and France or of these countries' historical legacies. Their success would be mischievous, not liberating, because in much of

Europe the masses needed to be led by "the few who have been blessed with the opportunities, and the rare genius, fitting them to lead." Calhoun, likewise, predicted early failure for the French Revolution of 1848, arguing that the French had none of the qualities necessary for self-government and that the revolution would eventually place "absolute power in the hand of one man," a prophecy that came true three years later with Louis Napoleon's coup of 1851.[32]

These skeptical conservatives were a minority, however. When Louis Kossuth, leader of a Hungarian uprising against the Habsburg monarchy, visited America in 1851–52 and urged America to participate in his people's war against Austria, vast crowds greeted him enthusiastically, throwing torchlight parades and turning out in thousands to hear his speeches. His flowing moustache and loose-sleeved overcoat even influenced American fashions for a season. When Congress arranged a ceremonial dinner in his honor, however, some Southern conservatives accepted invitations from Georgia's Whig senator Alexander Stephens to an anti-Kossuth dinner—Southerners didn't want the U.S. government encouraging rebellions of any kind! Secretary of State Daniel Webster, also skeptical about Kossuth's ambitions, attended the pro-Kossuth dinner and toasted "Hungarian Independence" but was careful to give the exile no practical help.[33]

GUARDIANS OF CIVILIZATION

The generation born during or just after the Revolution took pride in America's political independence from Britain and had to decide whether to create a new culture to go along with its new politics or whether to model their cultural life on that of the Old World. Americans of conservative temperament believed they should preserve the best of the Old World and perfect it in the New. Many of them admired the European elite's antiquity, manners, and classical learning. How elegant that life seemed by comparison with America's rough-and-ready democracy. These conservative-minded Americans strove to model their educational, civic, and cultural life on the best of their European discoveries. They thought of themselves as gentlemen and deplored the coarsening of manners in Jacksonian America, even as they championed America's expansion, economic vitality, and lack of hereditary castes. Like so many others in American history, they were paradoxical conservatives.

The sense that America was deficient in what came to be called high culture is clear in the writing of George Ticknor (1791–1871). Graduating from Dartmouth, he spent two strenuous years studying at Goettingen in Germany, just after the Napoleonic Wars. Goettingen was then one of the world's leading universities, with a library superior to any in the United States. In a letter to his father he described the contrast between Goettingen and the American colleges he knew: "What a mortifying distance there is between a European and an American scholar. We do not yet know what a Greek scholar is; we do not even know the process by which a man is to be made one." According to an early biographer, "He was the first to acquire in the universities of Germany the scientific method of humane learning; the first to open to American readers the books of the great cosmopolitan poets and prose-writers—Dante, Montaigne, Cervantes, and Molière; the first to prove to the countrymen of these that a stranger from the wild lands over the sea might be a gentleman and a scholar, the peer of their ripest and best." Ticknor returned to Boston to take up an appointment as Harvard's first professor of Romance languages, in 1819. In subsequent visits to Europe he befriended many of its leading figures, including Lord Byron, Charles Lyell, Madame de Staël, King John of Saxony, and Talleyrand. His history of Spanish literature (1849) became the standard work not only in the English-speaking world but even in Spain, none of whose authors had yet written any comparable work. Ticknor championed the American republic to his European friends but urged his fellow citizens to build the educational and cultural institutions, in which America was then sadly deficient, on European models.[34]

From the 1820s to the 1860s Ticknor became, in effect, the guardian and promoter of high culture in Boston. He tried to transform Harvard from a provincial academy into a real college of humane learning. He proposed replacing the traditional grind of memorization and recitation with courses of lectures in each of the modern languages, in sequences of graded difficulty. Overcoming obstructive colleagues he succeeded at least in his own field and was able to introduce French, Spanish, Italian, German, and Portuguese to a generation of students who previously had had access only to Greek, Latin, and Hebrew.[35]

Ticknor was a prominent Bostonian as well and played the crucial role in founding the Boston Public Library (1854). Born and raised in a

Federalist family, he regarded himself as a gentleman and a member of the social and intellectual elite. In his view, however, this position imposed on him duties of civic leadership; he was far ahead of his time in seeking to ensure that the library's books would circulate freely and that poorer citizens would have access.[36]

Among his friends and contemporaries was Edward Everett, another figure in the establishment of an American high-culture tradition and another paradoxical conservative. Everett (1794–1865) was an intellectual child prodigy, a star student at Harvard, ordained and called to the pulpit of Boston's prestigious Brattle Street Church at the age of nineteen, and within the year appointed professor of Greek in an endowed chair at Harvard. Like Ticknor he studied at Goettingen, becoming the first American to earn a German Ph.D. (in philology) and among the first to encounter the historical-critical method in the study of ancient texts. Back at Harvard the young Ralph Waldo Emerson was one of his first, and most admiring, students.[37]

Everett's early career as a scholar of ancient Greece coincided with the era of Greek Revival style in America. Where Washington's generation had favored such Roman models as Cincinnatus, Everett's favored the Athens of Pericles, a democratic state but also one renowned for feats of arms. In the 1820s modern Greece was fighting its war of independence from the Ottoman Empire (the conflict in which the poet Byron volunteered and died) and seemed to offer an inspiring parallel to the young American republic. Everett tried to emphasize this ancient lineage. He often invoked Pericles and Homer in the orations for which he became nationally famous. In a Phi Beta Kappa address of 1824 he declared that Americans, in building their empire, must learn to model themselves after the virtuous ancients. They should also remember the ultimate ruin of Greece and Rome as a warning against neglecting the cultivation of virtue and honor.[38]

From Harvard, Everett went into politics. He was a friend of Daniel Webster and, like him, a Massachusetts Whig, an outstanding orator, and a person deeply committed to the cause of preserving the Union. He was, however, ill suited to the rough-and-tumble of Jacksonian political life and ended up resigning seats in both the House of Representatives and the Senate. One biographer notes that "he lacked . . . both taste and talent for the contentiousness, vulgarity, and violence endemic to the rapid democratization of American politics." He sat out the "bombast and buffoonery" of the Whigs' "Log Cabin and Hard Cider" campaign of 1840, spending the year in Paris instead. He then served as U.S. ambassador to Britain, where "he seemed peculiarly at home among the aristocrats."[39]

Everett's fame came principally as an orator, but he aided Ticknor in establishing the Boston Public Library and, as governor of Massachusetts, supported Horace Mann's foundation of a statewide public school system. On his return from his British ambassadorship he became president of his alma mater, Harvard, a position he hated. After having hobnobbed with Queen Victoria and the British upper classes, he now had to devote his time to disciplining a rabble of drunken students who nicknamed him "Old Granny" and loved to play practical jokes, such as nailing shut his gate, covering the chapel with graffiti, starting bonfires in Harvard Yard, and setting off firecrackers indoors. "Sobriety, dedication, decorum, and respect for the great humanistic tradition of the past as well as for its custodians were at the heart of his idea of the university," so the reality was a dismaying affront.[40]

Everett is remembered today, if he is remembered at all, as the man who gave the big two-and-a-half-hour speech at Gettsyburg in 1863, one that was instantly overshadowed by Abraham Lincoln's brief masterpiece, *the* Gettysburg Address. In the 1850s, however, Everett was still a nationally known public figure, speaking and fund-raising on behalf of preserving George Washington's Mount Vernon home as a national shrine and urging conciliation with the South. In a typical speech of the 1850s, he reminded a group Harvard alumni that "the conservative element is as important in our nature and in all our relations as the progressive element. . . . I doubt [any notion of] progress which denies that the ages before us have anything worth preserving." The historian Irving Bartlett sees him as a figure who "clung to an old-fashioned kind of republicanism" and "an important voice for an intelligent conservatism in the American context, a believer in the ability of people in the mass to improve themselves in ways rational, gradual, and connected to the virtue of past generations."[41]

While Everett and Ticknor were struggling to establish American branches of European high culture in Boston, Samuel Morse (1791–1872) was playing a similar role in New York. We remember him as the inventor of Morse code and the telegraph, but the first half of his life was devoted to painting and fine art. In 1826 Morse founded the National Academy of Design, to be run by artists themselves, on the model of Vasari's academy in Renaissance Florence. He had grand ambitions for it: "I shall not feel satisfied with a local institution; it must be the great institution of the United States, around which all true artists will rally. . . . Artists must have no local prejudices in favor of particularities. New York is the capital of our country and here artists should have their rallying point." The historian Thomas Bender notes that Morse was not only asserting the independence of artists from the old business elite but also "protecting the artistic enterprise from the emerging egalitarianism in intellectual and political life that was already as he spoke being identified as Jacksonian democracy." American artists must develop a living tradition of their own, but one that was tasteful, educated, and discriminating, in contact with the great European tradition to which it owed so much.[42]

In sum, it is possible to discern two distinct but closely related forms of conservatism in the American North before the Civil War. One was the political conservatism of the Whigs. Defenders of tradition, restraint, hierarchy, and moderation, they also supported the development of a modern mixed economy, in which there could be space for entrepreneurs and manufacturers as well as independent yeoman farmers. Advocates of specialization and social inequality, they wanted government by an educated elite, an approach to politics that emphasized compromise and conciliation, and a learned judiciary shielded from transient popular passions. They understood society as an organism that persisted through time, linking past, present, and future generations, rather than as a collection of individuals who had contracted with one another for the particular functions of government. Religious, though only moderately and sociably religious, they felt nearly as much reverence for the Founders and for the Union as for God.

The other element of antebellum Northern conservatism, voiced by cultural elitists and often shared by the Whig political writers, was the idea that true civilization was the culmination of centuries of tradition in the Old World and that America could become fully civilized only by emulating what was best in British and European high culture. America would reach maturity when it could contribute fully to this venerable civilization and protect its delicate structure. Despite its virtues, America had not yet, in the view of these cultural elitists, begun to rival old Europe educationally and artistically. Incidentally, this sense of cultural inferiority was to be durable among American conservatives and could still be found, a century or more later, among Anglophiles and devotees of *Masterpiece Theater.*

CHAPTER FOUR

Conservatism and the Civil War

THINK OF THE CIVIL WAR as a conflict between two types of conservatism. Conservative Southern slaveholders, aggravated for thirty years by abolitionists and then horrified by John Brown's raid on Harper's Ferry and the election of Abraham Lincoln, came to believe that only by separating themselves from the Union could they preserve their society and their way of life. Calhoun's works had convinced them that they were justified in doing so, and when they formed the Confederate States of America (CSA) they looked backward not forward, solemnly invoking the authority of the Founding Fathers. Lincoln, meanwhile, tutored by Webster and Clay, resolved at all costs to preserve the Union. He claimed the same Founders' heritage as his antagonists, insisted he was defending the common patrimony, and was careful at first to advance no radical program of political change.

The need to win the war, however, gradually forced leaders on both sides to adopt extreme measures, such as drafting men into their armed forces, suspending habeas corpus, imposing martial law, and radically rethinking the position of slaves, though they undertook these innovations reluctantly. Lincoln certainly never planned to be the Great Emancipator. This chapter explores the clash of rival conservatisms, showing how the sectional conflict intensified in the 1850s, eventuating in war and transformation. It also shows how, at war's end, much of the defeated white

South undertook a self-conscious program of conservative, backward-looking restoration in an attempt to re-create an idealized version of its former self.

NORTHERN CONSERVATIVES IN THE 1850S

The deaths of Calhoun, Clay, and Webster between 1850 and 1852 marked the passing of the generation that had dominated Jacksonian politics. The sectional conciliation that Webster and Clay had tried so hard to preserve broke down in a series of escalating crises during the 1850s: first, bitter controversy over the Fugitive Slave Law; then the Kansas-Nebraska Act and frontier warfare between pro- and antislavery factions in Kansas; next the Supreme Court's proslavery decision in the *Dred Scott* case (1857); and finally John Brown's attack on the federal arsenal at Harper's Ferry and his attempt to stimulate a slave rebellion in 1859.

This succession of dramatic events energized Northern intellectuals, many of whom realized the likelihood of secession and war. A group of conservative-minded writers, including Charles Eliot Norton, Frederick Law Olmsted, Francis Parkman, Henry Bellows, Francis Lieber, Orestes Brownson, and Horace Bushnell, became increasingly intolerant of the South, less because they were indignant about slavery than because they feared that the tyrannical "slave power" aristocrats were conspiring to spread their system westward at the expense of free labor, and were willing to destroy the Union to do it. The Union, as they saw it, was an organic unity, a living thing with common origins, shared virtues, and shared memories that could not lawfully be torn apart by an arrogant sectional faction.

Norton, already a critic of revolutionary trends in Europe (see Chap. 3), described the leading secessionists as "men of hasty temper, of arrogant and tyrannical disposition, of narrow minds." Frederick Law Olmsted agreed with him. Olmsted (1822–1903), whom we remember today chiefly as the architect of New York's Central Park, traveled widely through the South in the 1850s and wrote about it extensively. His influential articles and books had more to say about the inefficiency and slovenliness of the slave plantations he visited, and the system's tendency to turn the slave owners into petty tyrants, than about the suffering of the slaves themselves. The owners, he wrote, had "a devilish, undisguised and recognized contempt for all humbler classes." Slavery was harmful to America, in his view, because it was an uneconomic, inefficient, brutalizing, and backward-looking social system that robbed the slaves of all incentive and the owners of all tendencies toward conciliation.[1]

But if these Northern conservatives disliked the slaveholders' power, they equally disliked abolitionists. They regarded men like William Lloyd Garrison and Wendell Phillips, who wanted an immediate end to slavery, as no better than anarchists. Lieber described the immediate abolitionists as Jacobins whose uncompromising aim blinded them to a complex reality and threatened damage to society as a whole. Such single-mindedness, he wrote, "has never gained the ultimate victory though often a battle, and has never sown, planted, gathered, blessed, but always destroyed, embittered, ruined and cursed." The historian Francis Parkman (18923–93) wrote Norton in 1850, in support of that year's great Compromise, that preserving the Union was a much more important objective than either protecting or abolishing slavery. "I would see every slave knocked on the head before I would see the Union go to pieces, and would include in the sacrifice as many abolitionists as could be conveniently brought together."[2]

These Northern conservatives were intellectually at odds not only with the South and with abolitionists but also with transcendentalism. Ralph Waldo Emerson, best known of the Transcendentalists, was a radical, anti-institutional individualist who believed in the soul's direct link with God, without the need of mediating institutions like the church. His friend Henry David Thoreau argued the supremacy of the individual over what he took to be the drudging hypocrisy of society. The conservative patricians, by contrast, spoke up for society and its institutions as the things that make our lives possible, within which we and our families live and without which we are lost and powerless. Henry Bellows (1814–82), one of New York's most influential Unitarian ministers, shrank from assertive individualism. "Would that I could develop here, at a time so forgetful of the dependence of society on organization, the *doctrine of institutions,*" wrote Bellows in 1859, "the only instruments except literature and the blood, by which the riches of ages, the experience and wisdom of humanity, are handed down."[3]

Transcendentalism preached one form of individualism; the Second Great Awakening preached another. Charismatic preachers such as

Charles Grandison Finney had galvanized urban Protestants in the foregoing decades with a message of individual conversion and salvation. Horace Bushnell disapproved. Bushnell (1802–76) is best known today as a pioneering liberal theologian, but in his social and political views he was a conservative figure and a critic of revivalism. He had earlier deplored the abolition of established state churches, and he saw revivalism as a further threat to the stability of Christian communities. Christianity should grow through nurture in Christian families, he wrote, not through the individual conquest of stray souls, manipulated into a temporary euphoria by revivalists. Revivalism concentrated on the inner man but neglected "those duties of society, of good neighborhood, and good citizenship, in which human life is spent—the kind of graceful feelings, honesty, mercy, generosity—everything that is necessary to outward dignity and beauty."[4]

In the crisis conditions of the 1850s, respect for law and institutions led these conservatives not to resist but to obey the Fugitive Slave Law. Norton, for example, believed that there was an "absolute necessity" of "cultivating the spirit of obedience" to properly constituted laws, even those with which citizens disagreed. However wrong the law might be, he reasoned, citizens in a republic must not substitute the "right of private judgment" for the letter of the law; instead they must exercise their political rights by campaigning lawfully for revised legislation. As his biographer notes, "in an age of utopias Norton was an anti-utopian political thinker." Orestes Brownson (1803–76) took the same view. "No civil government can exist, none is conceivable even, where every individual is free to disobey its orders when they do not happen to square with his private convictions of what is the law of God." Government, Brownson added, is ordained by God; resistance is presumptively rebellion against Him.[5]

Many of these conservatives were patrician Whigs, members of the same urban elite as George Ticknor, Rufus Choate, and Edward Everett, and, in most cases, sons and grandsons of the old Federalist elite. They saw themselves as guardians of a jeopardized society, threatened by civic disorder from below, by the spread of luxury and vice at the top, and by the slave power of the South. The historian George Fredrickson writes that "they saw in secession a threat to conservative interests and to the stability and order of society."[6]

NORTHERN INTELLECTUALS AND THE WAR

A forlorn remnant of the Whigs, the Constitutional Union Party, ran John Bell for president in 1860; Edward Everett was his running mate. Everett had watched the unfolding events of the 1850s with dismay. As his biographer notes, "Like others Everett read Burke's *Reflections on the Revolution in France* and became a dedicated admirer of Burke. He distrusted the role of the passions, the role of the mob in social upheavals [and] the sudden prominence of generalities that were half-myths." His inclination had been to drop out of politics altogether after the Kansas-Nebraska Act, and he was dismayed by the rise of the sectional Republican Party, because he foresaw that its success would lead to disunion . "The South and the North are equally wrong headed," he told a friend, adding that "the ultra-ism of the North [is] more dangerous inasmuch as it is founded on truth and justice." His speeches on behalf of moderation and conciliation could not prevent the election of Lincoln. After that, and once the Southern states began to secede, he took the view that the Union should let them go, because "to hold . . . states in the Union by force is a preposterous idea."[7]

Among Northern conservatives Everett's was the minority view, however. More of them shared Lincoln's belief that the seceding states were still part of the Union but were now in rebellion. Critics of radical individualism, many of them looked on the outbreak of war as an opportunity to chasten it and to consolidate society by reviving the old martial virtues. Francis Lieber wrote to a friend: "When nations go on recklessly as we do, dancing, drinking, laughing, defying right, morality, justice [engaging in] money making and murdering, God in his mercy has sometimes condescended to smite them hard, in order to bring them to their senses and make them recover themselves." Henry Bellows felt the same way. He regarded the war as an opportunity to rediscover certain hard realities about life: the need for toughness, self-denial, and the virtuous dedication of oneself to the nation rather than to private gain. He expected war to revive the stern old Puritan virtues.[8]

Francis Parkman also agreed, especially on the matter of reviving martial virtue. A patrician conservative, skeptical of democracy, equally scornful of vulgar nouveau riche businessmen, industrial workers, slave owners, and Irish immigrants, Parkman was also an invalid. He had suffered from near blindness, piercing headaches, and heart palpitations ever since his adventures on the Great Plains with the Sioux Indians, which were the basis for his wonderful book *The Oregon Trail* (1849). Unable for reasons of health to serve in the army, he wrote regular letters to the press about the war, urging his fellow citizens to subdue the rebellion. They should welcome the higher calling of war over the degradation of business, because "a too exclusive pursuit of material success has notoriously cramped and vitiated our growth" and "a scum of reckless politicians has choked all the avenues of power." But now the war, "like a keen fresh breeze," has "stirred our clogged and humid atmosphere," and the nation would profit from it, emerging like another Rome, "clarified and pure in a renewed and strengthened life."[9]

In Parkman's view, popular government did not mean government by the common people. It should mean, rather, rule by a highly educated and self-aware elite that made no secret of its own superiority. He was unimpressed at first by Abraham Lincoln (America's "feeble and ungainly mouthpiece"), seeing him as the kind of nonentity thrown up by popular democracy. Whereas the three million Americans at the time of the Revolution had brought forth Washington, Franklin, Jefferson, Adams, and Hamilton, he wrote in another letter, the twenty million of his own day had brought forth no comparable heroic leaders. "The people have demanded equality, not superiority, and they have had it; men of the people, that is to say, men in no way raised above the ordinary level of humanity." The people, if they were to be saved, must "learn to recognize the reality of superior minds and to feel that they have need of them."[10]

An elite of exceptional men in politics should be drawn from the same class of men as its military leaders. Parkman criticized the Union Army's officer corps during the war, arguing that the officers were too similar to the men they led. They ought to be a class above, living by a strenuous code of honor, commanding unquestioning obedience, and regarding dishonor or cowardice as infinitely worse than death. The South, he was forced to admit, had the advantage in this respect over the North. "Through all the illusions and falsehoods with which that fierce and selfish aristocracy has encompassed itself, runs a vein of sound political truth." The South, being more hierarchical and aristocratic, was more adaptable to war.[11]

George Templeton Strong, like Bellows and Parkman, welcomed the onset of war. Strong (1820–75) was a great diarist whose day-by-day account of life in the 1850s and 1860s enriches our understanding of New York City's growth and of what a wealthy Whig citizen loved, hated, hoped for, and feared. He had been dismayed, in the years before the war, by endemic political corruption and by what he thought of as the brutal ignorance of Irish immigrants as they become more numerous and visible in New York. He hoped, when the war began, that "democracy and equality and various other phantasms will be dispersed." He also detested the enemy, describing Southern planters as "a race of lazy, ignorant, coarse, sensual, swaggering, sordid, beggarly barbarians, bullying white men and breeding little niggers for sale." Such intense dislike became common among Northern conservatives during the war, who felt they were fighting a war against barbarians, and to save civilized standards.[12]

Bellows and Strong became key figures in the Sanitary Commission, a quasi-official organization designed to support the government and the Union Army by bringing efficiency to what, at the start of the war, was a muddled and overburdened logistical system. Humanitarians like Walt Whitman, Louisa May Alcott, and Dorothea Dix hastened to the war hospitals in Washington to volunteer their unpaid services, believing strongly in the importance of empathizing with the war's victims. The commission's members, by contrast, took a hardheaded view of their role, accepted salaries, practiced efficient bookkeeping, preserved a strict chain of command and bureaucratic procedures, and prided themselves on their own version of military rigor.[13]

Not only should the war be prosecuted rationally and efficiently, they said; citizens should fight it in a mental state of absolute loyalty, forsaking all political quibbles for the duration. Nauseated by the political bickering and self-seeking they witnessed in Washington, commission members began to argue in favor of complete submission to the will of the government. Whatever the human frailties of its officers, said Bellows, the government is a quasi-divine entity, duly constituted and recognized by God. Bellows came close in 1863 to reviving the old "divine right of kings" argument on behalf of Lincoln. "To rally round the President—without question or dispute—is the first and most sacred duty of loyal citizens, when he announces not that the Constitution merely, but that the National life and existence are in peril." Public opinion, by contrast, was almost certain to be a misleading guide to policy: he referred to it as the "poisonous malaria sent up from the marshes of public prejudice."[14]

Strong leadership and uncritical support for it were equally essential. When President Lincoln suspended habeas corpus (the right to be charged and tried after arrest, or else to be released), the patrician conservatives did not balk but agreed that it was a necessary war measure, even though one of them, Leiber, had earlier written, in *On Civil Liberty and Self Government,* that suspension could be undertaken only by Congress. One of Lieber's friends, the octogenarian Horace Binney, wrote a series of pamphlets justifying the constitutionality, during wartime, of Lincoln's action. Binney (1780–1875) had grown up with the nation and in many ways embodied Northern conservatism. He was the son of a Revolutionary War veteran; an old Federalist lawyer and friend of John Marshall; later a Whig congressman who had led the unsuccessful fight against Andrew Jackson in the Bank War; and now a Republican. He looked at the rise of democracy as synonymous with the decline in virtue and, once the war had begun, was horrified to see fluctuations of public opinion impeding its conduct. "Is it possible that at such a time as this the same unruly popular will which has caused our decline in virtue for thirty years is to rule us in this war, to take the strength of our military leader, so that he cannot have his way, where his own judgment is so clear, but must yield to the ignorant, willful, perverse and often corrupt voice of the press, the politicians, the office-seekers, the office holders?"[15]

The war did not go well at first. Conservative writers realized that it might take years to subdue the South, but they did not flinch at the extent of Union casualties, even when they witnessed the carnage firsthand. Bellows argued that the nation needed a great and violent purge, such as the war was now providing. Early defeats like Bull Run, in 1861, which increased the probability of a long and costly war, might even be providential. Bushnell sounded the same note in a sermon entitled "Reverses Needed." Until now, he declared, America's foundations had never been clear. Was America an organic community, blessed by God Himself, or was it all a matter of "theories of compacts, consentings, reserved rights, sovereignty of the people and the like?" A long war would annihilate the second alternative, sweeping away Jefferson's "glittering generalities" once and for all and leaving behind the society based on "historic and morally binding authority, freedom sanctified by law and law by God himself." Norton made the same point in an *Atlantic* article entitled "The Advantages of Defeat." Premature victory might enable Northern leaders to persist in the "feebleness of character" that decades of peace and prosperity had bred in them.[16]

ABRAHAM LINCOLN

Lincoln deserves a place in the American conservative pantheon for one big reason: he led the nation to victory in a civil war that could have destroyed it, succeeding in this most basic of all conservative tasks. Conservatives of later generations, especially in the South, have often challenged Lincoln's conservative credentials, however, because in their view he ignored the states' sovereign right to secede, then invaded their homeland, while centralizing the federal government and transforming the constitutional balance out of all recognition. Lincoln is, to be sure, a complex figure. Entering the war with the limited intention of saving the Union, he found himself forced to take bolder steps if he was to succeed.[17]

Lincoln (1809–65) grew up in Kentucky, Indiana, and Illinois, as his family moved from the slave South to the free-labor Midwest. An ardent believer in self-help, a nonsmoker and nondrinker, he early lost his Christian faith, retaining no more than a deist's belief in providence, though he developed an exceptional facility with biblical quotations and analogies. Bookish, averse to physical labor, ambitious for fame and greatness, he became a successful lawyer and local politician in Springfield, Illinois, and a passionate advocate of the rule of law. "Let reverence for the laws be breathed by every American mother to the lisping babe that prattles on her lap—let it be taught in schools, in seminaries and in colleges; let it be written in primers, spelling books, and in almanacs; let it be preached from the pulpit, proclaimed in legislative halls, and enforced in courts of justice. And, in short, let it become the political religion of the nation; and let the old and young, the rich and the poor, the grave and the gay, of all sexes and tongues, colors and conditions, sacrifice unceasingly upon its altars." Joining the Whig Party in a Democrat-dominated area, he supported Henry Clay's American System and tried to promote industry, canals, steamships, river widening, and railroad schemes in his adopted state.[18]

He aimed to avert the spread of slavery into the West, to prevent the migration of free blacks, and to ensure that the region's population remain all white. He opposed slavery but was not an abolitionist and would have been content to see it continue in the states where it was already established. He did not believe in racial equality or racial integration. On the contrary, he shared with Clay the belief that the two races could not live together on equal terms and that free blacks ought to be deported to Liberia, Panama, or some other place outside the United States. His secretary of the navy summarized that Lincoln, "believing the Africans were mentally an inferior race, believed that any attempt to make them and the whites one people would tend to the degradation of the whites without materially elevating the blacks, but that separation would promote the happiness of each."[19]

After the breakup of the Whig Party, Lincoln joined the sectional (all-Northern) Republicans. His 1858 debates with the Illinois Democrat Stephen Douglas, widely reprinted throughout the states, revealed his astuteness as a politician and orator and made him nationally famous. The point of difference between the two great debaters was Douglas's belief in popular sovereignty—that the people of a new western state should be free to choose whether or not to adopt slavery—and Lincoln's rejection of it. The political philosopher Harry Jaffa notes that Lincoln "insisted that the case for popular government depended upon a standard of right and wrong independent of mere opinion and one which was not justified merely by the counting of heads." Moral rectitude, in his view, always trumped gross numbers, demonstrating that Lincoln had not been seduced into the "degradation of the democratic dogma."[20]

He was attractive to the Republicans as a presidential candidate in 1860 because he could reconcile conflicting groups in this new coalition: abolitionists from the northeast with free-soil westerners, former elitist Whigs with more populist westerners and antislavery ex-Democrats. He gained the Republican nomination in 1860 and the presidency in that November's election. Denying the Southern states' right to secede, he applied the lesson he had learned from Webster and Clay: that the Union was a single organism, one and individisble.[21]

Lincoln's early conduct of the war bore witness to his conservative inclinations. When two impetuous generals declared slaves in liberated areas of the South to be freed, he countermanded them on the grounds that suppressing a rebellion did not entitle the Union to attack Southerners' private property. To keep the nonseceding slave states of Maryland, Delaware, Kentucky, and Missouri from joining the Confederacy, he emphasized repeatedly that the war was *not* an attack on slavery, and he vetoed Congress's Second Confiscation Act of July 1862, which would have freed all slaves in rebel areas. Almost to the bitter end he favored gradual emancipation, possibly stretching on to the year 1900, with compensation for the slaves' owners. His "ten percent" plan for the readmission of rebellious states when fighting ended suggested a magnanimous eagerness to reintegrate the Union as quickly and painlessly as possible (whereas congressional Republican radicals wanted a far more stringent test for readmission). Above all he did not try to suppress elections, even when it seemed likely in 1864 that he would lose.[22]

The Gettysburg Address and the Second Inaugural are his two most famous speeches; together they nicely embody the paradoxical character of his American conservatism. The first, delivered at the dedication of Gettysburg Cemetery in November 1863, four months after the battle, followed a much longer address—two and a half hours—from Edward Everett, outlining the events of the war up to that point and a detailed account of the battle itself. Lincoln's two-minute masterpiece argued that the soldiers who died there had given their lives on behalf of the proposition that "all men are created equal," which had been stated in the Declaration of Independence more than eighty years earlier. They had fought also for the principle of government "of the people, by the people, for the people." These are democratic principles, said Lincoln, but they are also part of a sanctified national tradition that must be protected and preserved. They have been threatened or trampled down throughout the rest of the world, and are still under threat from the Confederacy, but are alive thanks to the Union's brave soldiers. In other words, the seeming novelty of the American republic is itself now a time-honored system deserving of reverence and worth fighting for. The biblical overtones of "four score and seven years ago" and "our fathers" hinted at a far more ancient lineage. The outcome of the war would affect not just the American future but the future of the entire world in its striving for liberty and self-government. This was a war to conserve the republic and vindicate equality.[23]

In the Second Inaugural, sixteen months later, and shortly before Appomattox, Lincoln repeated his determination to win the war, after which he would restore the Union as quickly and painlessly as possible, "with malice toward none, with charity for all." For a man who had left conventional Christianity behind, it was a speech drenched in biblical language, some of it of the harsh, Old Testament variety rather than that of Jesus the Savior. Unlike many preachers of the war years, Lincoln took a position of theological modesty, insisting that the North was *not* acting on behalf of God as a righteous avenger and that the war was *not* a crusade. Both sides might claim God's blessing, but "The Almighty has His own purposes." It would be better, he said, to recognize that both sides have sinned and both must pay the price that God exacts, even if it annihilates all the wealth created by slavery and sheds as much blood as had slavery itself. We all stand under God's judgment and are not free to appropriate the divine will to our own earthly ends. As the historian Allen Guelzo points out, this was an artful way of contradicting congressional Republicans to his left, who wanted a more draconian reconstruction: "It was an appeal against the Radicals . . . to an authority not even the Radicals were brazen enough to defy." And as Jaffa points out, it was a further reminder from Lincoln that democracy does not simply mean the will of a majority of the people, especially not when they have affronted God Himself.[24]

If Lincoln's actions and words through much of the war demonstrated humility and restraint, it is equally true that in other respects he took radical steps to achieve his conservative end, steps that prompted critics, at the time and since, to accuse him of tyranny. He assumed Congress's war-making powers when Congress was out of session, telling a close aide, "As Commander in Chief of the Army and Navy, in time of war, I suppose I have a right to take any measure which may best subdue the enemy." He suspended habeas corpus, refused to back down in the face of a rebuke from the chief justice of the Supreme Court, and periodically imposed martial law. He conscripted men forcibly into the Union Army when the flow of volunteers dried up. Above all, once convinced it was necessary for military reasons, he issued the Emancipation Proclamation (January 1, 1863), freeing all slaves in the rebellious states.[25]

Although the proclamation led to his gaining the nickname "Great Emancipator," he saw it chiefly as a war measure, made necessary by the Northern armies' slow progress—it did not liberate slaves in the border states that had stayed loyal to the Union. Nevertheless, the fact that the Union then won the war, facilitating the actual liberation of the slaves (a point confirmed in the Thirteenth Amendment) made this step one of the most dramatic in all of American history. The proclamation also specified that freed slaves could serve in the Union Army, and this too was significant. As the historian Mark Neely points out, "This momentous decision guaranteed a multiracial future for the United States. Eager radicals and grumbling conservatives alike realized that the President could not ask a man to fight for his country and then tell him it was not his country after all."[26]

NORTHERN DEMOCRATS

Northern Democrats faced an awkward situation during the Civil War. So many members of their party had joined the Confederacy that they were vulnerable to accusations of disloyalty. Their reaction to the events of those years demonstrates a different kind of conservatism, one that rejected the necessity of the war itself and condemned the radical measures Lincoln eventually found necessary to bring it to a victorious end. Northern Democrats regarded Lincoln not as the savior of the nation but as a tyrant and usurper, destroying citizens' rights, imprisoning those who spoke out against him, and upsetting the balanced Constitution by concentrating more power in the federal government than the Founders had intended.

In the 1850s many Northern Democratic newspapers had defended slavery, regarding it either as a tolerable evil or, in a few cases, as a positive good. John Van Evrie (1814–96), for example, the editor of the widely circulated New York *Day-Book,* believed in the absolute inferiority of African Americans, saw them as destined by nature for servitude, and regarded with horror the possibility of their becoming equal participants in a free-labor society. America was a republic of whites, he said, and when citizens realized that Lincoln's party stood for racial amalgamation, these politicians would be "knocked in the head as remorselessly as so many mad dogs by the betrayed, outraged and indignant freemen of the North."[27]

James Gordon Bennett (1795–1872), editor of the *New York Herald,* agreed, reciting many of the proslavery Southerners' favorite arguments. A Scotsman by birth, Bennett had lived for a time in Charleston before moving to New York. As his biographer writes about his editorial views: "If the abolitionists saw in the black man a white liberal struggling to get out, the *Herald* saw only a bloodthirsty savage whose primal passions must be restrained by the discipline of slavery." Throughout the 1850s Bennett's *Herald* opposed abolitionism, considered white Southerners' anxieties justified, and saw itself as the embodiment of conservative common sense, as opposed to the utopian crankiness of its chief rival, Horace Greeley's *Tribune*.[28]

After the election of Lincoln, some Northern Democrats regarded the secession of the slave states as justified. Bennett argued in December 1860 that Lincoln's party—elected but not yet in office—ought now to conciliate South Carolina or be ready to let it secede peacefully. "The people of the North will never give their consent to the raising of a standing army which, if successful in subjugating the southern states, would very soon be turned against their own liberties." Even when Bennett switched to supporting the war, he continued to hope that it would simply restore the Union, while preserving slavery.[29]

When conciliation failed and the war began, northern Democrats regarded Lincoln's war measures, especially the declaration of martial law and the suspension of habeas corpus, as the actions of a tyrant; they saw him as the destroyer of American liberty. He ordered the large-scale arrest of Southern sympathizers in the border states at the start of the war and created an espionage service that could arrest and detain people without trial and without notification of the charges against them. He subjected draft resisters to martial rather than civil trials, an order under which 13,500 citizens were arrested and imprisoned. He periodically suppressed antagonistic newspapers, including Van Evrie's *Day-Book,* imposed martial law in recaptured Southern states, and, most dramatically, declared all slaves in the rebellious states free. All these actions, justifiable in the eyes of patrician conservatives like Bellows and Bushnell, seemed like acts of usurpation to Northern Democrats, even those who supported the war.[30]

Clement Vallandigham (1820–71), an Ohio "Copperhead," was among Lincoln's most outspoken opponents. An old Jacksonian Democrat, he was a tenacious believer in strict construction of the Constitution. Never carried away by war fever, Vallandigham hoped that secession might be ended by a peaceful compromise. He indicted Lincoln for exceeding his constitutional authority, for imposing martial law, and for scheming to end slavery.[31]

Vallandigham's critical speeches of 1863 led to a dramatic midnight arrest by armed soldiers at his Dayton home. He was tried by a military tribunal, against whose constitutionality he also protested. In a letter to his constituents from prison he wrote: "I am here in a military bastille for no other offence than my political opinions, and the defense of them and of the rights of the people and of your constitutional liberties. . . . I am a Democrat; for Constitution, for law, for Union, for liberty; this is my only crime. For no disobedience to the Constitution, for no violation of law, for no words, sign or gesture of sympathy with men of the South . . . I am here today in bonds." Lincoln hoped that banishing Vallandigham to the Confederacy would create the impression that he was a traitor, but the Confederates themselves, recognizing that he was completely out of place among them, helped him escape to Canada. Other Northern Democrats cited his case as evidence of Lincoln's tyranny, among them George Pendleton, also from Ohio. "I have seen a citizen torn from his home at the dead hour of the night, his house broken into, his family terrified, and himself carried to a military prison, sentenced by a drumhead trial, and sent to a punishment unknown to our law."[32]

Many other conservative-minded Northern intellectuals denied, like Vallandigham, that the war should be fought to the bitter end. The novelist Nathaniel Hawthorne (1804–64), for example, another Democrat, steadfastly refused to be swept up in war fever. Much of the fiction for which he is best remembered is set in seventeenth-century New England, and nearly all of it explores the human condition in religious terms, emphasizing the power of evil, humankind's weakness in the face of temptation, and the near universality of folly and wickedness. Apparently upright figures turn out to be instruments of the devil, hypocrisy stalks the land, and even the most virtuous are prey to ruinous temptation. In many stories Hawthorne skillfully creates a mood of historical nostalgia, then lays bare the ugly realities beneath the façade. His fiction is among the most psychologically astute of the nineteenth century, always with a skeptical and pessimistic edge. Russell Kirk remarked that "Hawthorne dwells almost wholly upon sin, its reality, nature, and consequences; the contemplation of sin is his obsession, his vocation, almost his life. Here he becomes a major preceptor of conservatism."[33]

When most of the Deep South seceded in early 1861 Hawthorne believed the Union should permit it to leave, writing to an English friend: "As to the South, I never loved it. We do not belong together; the Union is unnatural, a scheme of man, not an ordinance of God, and as long as it continues no American of either section will ever feel a genuine thrill of patriotism, such as you Englishmen feel at every breath you draw."[34]

In July 1862, when the war was going badly for the North and much of the Northern press was drenched in patriotic rhetoric, Hawthorne, writing as "A Peaceable Man," struck a discordant note in the *Atlantic Monthly*. Though never proslavery, Hawthorne found he could sympathize with the mass of Southerners in their decision to secede. "It is a strange thing in human life, that the greatest errors both of men and women often spring from their sweetest and most generous qualities; and so, undoubtedly, thousands of warm-hearted, sympathetic and impulsive persons have joined the rebels, not from any real zeal for the cause but because, between two conflicting loyalties, they chose that which necessarily lay nearest the heart. . . . In the vast extent of our country—too vast by far to be taken into one small human heart—we inevitably limit to our own State, or at farthest, to our own section, that sentiment of physical love for the soil which renders an Englishman, for example, so intensely sensitive to the dignity and well-being of his little island." Hatred of the enemy was, accordingly, disgraceful and hypocritical.[35]

Hawthorne knew that the war would not bring about the millennium many Northern observers anticipated. War is destruction pure and simple, he wrote, and if it had any benign consequences, they would be incidental. "No human effort, on a grand scale, has ever yet resulted according to the purpose of its projectors. The advantages are always incidental. Man's accidents are God's purposes. We miss the good we sought and do the good we little cared for." Observing the ugly raw earthworks of a new fortification near Washington, for example, he at once thought not of their defensive effectiveness but of how their remains, decades later, would affect onlookers. They would "remain as historic monuments, grass-grown and picturesque memorials of an epoch of terror and suffering; they will serve to make our country dearer and more interesting to us and afford fit soil for poetry to root itself in." Such reveries, now delightful, would not have been at all appealing at the time to authoritarian conservatives like Parkman, Strong, and Bellows, who wanted unquestioning loyalty and maximum zeal for the cause.[36]

ORESTES BROWNSON

Writers about American politics, almost from the beginning, assumed that theirs was a Christian country, and by Christian they meant Protestant. The Catholic population, a tiny minority at the time of the Revolution, began to grow with emigrations from Ireland and Germany in the 1820s, 1830s, and 1840s. The first Catholic to make a significant contribution to American political writing, however, was the convert Orestes Brownson (1803–1876). His bishop told him after his 1844 conversion to accept all the conventional teachings of the Catholic Church on social and political themes and to take them on faith, but he found them inadequate or misleading. He was soon reading voraciously in the tradition of Catholic spiritual and political writers, reinterpreting them for his own time and place. The most articulate Catholic in America (potentially rivaled only by his friend and fellow convert Isaac Hecker), he prompted his old Protestant friends to look at Catholicism in a new light and urged his fellow Catholics to understand themselves and America itself in a new way.[37]

The American Republic (1865), which he published just after the Civil War, was the first book of basic political theory to be written by an American Catholic. Profoundly conservative, it argues that America comes closer than any other political system to fulfilling the Catholic ideal. It also argues that America brought to perfection a continuous political tradition begun in ancient Greece and Rome and nurtured through the long generations of Christian civilization. Brownson emphasized the essential rightness of the Union cause in the war and the essential fallacy of the Confederacy, but added that, ironically, most people on each side had not really understood the nature of the system for which they fought. "Catholics are better fitted by their religion to comprehend the real character of the American constitution than any other class of American, the moment they study it in light of their own theology."[38]

First, said Brownson, government is a positive good and not, as some Americans seemed to believe, a necessary evil. It is appointed by

God Himself (there is government even in Heaven). Church and state are separate but are derived from the same divine source. Government therefore has, and should have, the ability to exact the obedience of its citizens and to make a divinely sanctioned claim over them. Refuting a long tradition of political philosophy (Hobbes, Locke, and Rousseau), he added that governments of all kinds are *not* formed by compacts among peoples who until then have been living in the state of nature. Using the same metaphor as Francis Lieber, he wrote that society "is an organism, and individuals live in its life as well as it in theirs. There is a real living solidarity, which makes individuals members of the social body, and members of one-another. There is no society without individuals and there are no individuals without society." Men live socially and politically and have done so since the Creation.[39]

Second, Brownson argued that every nation has what he called a "providential constitution," a kind of living social reality, and that its government or written constitution will succeed only if it conforms to this underlying reality. The genius of the American Founders was that they recognized this truth and, after the failure of the Articles of Confederation, wrote the Constitution in conformity to it. Denying the Confederate theory that each state was sovereign, Brownson asserted that the United States was one entity. It has a central government and dispersed state governments, among which power is properly distributed, all working together harmoniously. In fact, the United States has finally solved the ancient problem of distributing powers so that the central government is not too strong and not too feeble, something neither the ancients nor the moderns in Europe were able to achieve. The written Constitution provides the mechanism but is able to do so only because it follows closely the unwritten providential constitution.[40]

Third, America, though its people increasingly think of it as a democracy, is essentially a republic, being democratic only in a very particular and limited way. Brownson cautioned against two errors in thinking about democracy. The first fallacy, common in the antebellum South, was the idea of "personal democracy" of the sort Randolph and Taylor had favored. Its supporters failed to appreciate the necessity of government over and above the individual and the demands it could rightly make on them. The second fallacy, common in the antebellum North, was the sentimental or humanitarian democracy of the abolitionists, which overemphasized the role of the state and would lead, if pushed to its logical conclusion, to socialism, an all-powerful state, and the political annihilation of human variation. Its advocates tended to forget that humans belong not only to the state but also to God and to the natural world, which are properly represented through the institutions of the church and property.[41]

As he surveyed the theoretical and practical politics of the last few decades, Brownson noted that Daniel Webster and Abraham Lincoln had been right about the primacy of the Union but that, ironically, they had been right for the wrong reason. Neither had grasped that the Constitution, and the Union it represented, were legitimate because they corresponded with the underlying unwritten providential constitution. Brownson added that Americans of all sorts, throughout the Jacksonian era, had mistakenly given a hero's welcome to liberal rebels from other nations, such as Kossuth and Mazzini. They had been too willing to heed Jefferson's rash and fallacious claim that every generation needs its own rebellion. No wonder the Confederates had felt entitled to secede. Compact theories of government, indeed, provide justification for such rebellions, whereas the Catholic theory restrains them. Jefferson Davis, like Kossuth and Mazzini, had rebelled against a duly (and divinely) constituted government; such leaders were an affront to political stability everywhere.[42]

Brownson angered his bishop by regarding the separation of church and state as an ideal situation. Most Catholics then accepted the shelter the First Amendment gave them but looked forward to the day when they could unite church and state, so long as the church in question was their own. Brownson, by contrast, pointed out that the American system used the minimum of coercion and permitted every person to follow his or her conscience. The tradition of two separate but divinely appointed "societies," church and state, had a venerable Catholic past, and the tradition was now, ironically, honored better in the American system than in those European nations where the church was yoked to the state. Protestant churches were as free as Catholic ones, it was true, but in the long run that did not matter. "In the United States false religions are legally as free as the true religion; but all false religions, being one-sided, sophistical, and uncatholic, are opposed by the principles of the state which tend, by their silent but effective workings, to eliminate them." Protestantism would perish eventually from its own follies; in the meantime the state need not persecute it.[43]

Protestant Christianity proved more durable than Brownson had expected, and Protestant voices remained far more influential than Catholic ones in American political debates for another hundred years. Not until after the Second World War would a later generation of Catholic writers play a significant role in the history of American conservatism.

THE SOUTH AND THE CIVIL WAR

The entire picture of what was happening in the late 1850s and early 1860s and what it meant looked completely different from south of the Mason-Dixon Line. Secessionists were conservatives in the sense that they wanted to conserve their distinctive society. They broke from the Union after the election of Lincoln in the belief that only by seceding could they preserve it. The Republicans did not threaten to end slavery, but they did pledge to prevent its spread further west. As a result, the political representation of the slave states would become an ever smaller minority in Congress and the Senate; free-labor interests would always outvote it. The rise of radical abolitionism since the 1830s and more recent troubles, such as the guerrilla fighting in "Bleeding Kansas" and John Brown's raid on Harper's Ferry, convinced many members of the Southern elite that Lincoln's party, despite its rhetoric, was in fact looking for a way to end slavery once and for all. Followers of Calhoun during the Nullification Crisis and the 1850 Compromise debate, they believed secession to be lawful because the sovereign states had predated the Constitution and surrendered only certain enumerated powers to the central government.[44]

Secession was, in another sense, the antithesis of conservatism, because it meant leaving behind a tried-and-true way of life and politics as usual, and because it was almost certain to provoke major unforeseen consequences. It was riskiest for the South Carolinians, who took the step first. They could not be sure that other states would follow their lead. They did not know whether Lincoln would permit them to secede peacefully or regard them as rebels. They did not know whether they would be able to create an effective new proslavery nation of their own, would be able to cooperate effectively with one another, or would gain diplomatic recognition abroad. Neither did the leaders know whether they could prevent political discontent from the Southern lower classes from jeopardizing their privileged position.[45]

The Fire Eaters, secession enthusiasts like Robert Barnwell Rhett of South Carolina, Edmund Ruffin of Virginia, and William Yancey of Alabama, led the way, but after Lincoln's election, members of the Southern planter elite like Jefferson Davis quickly asserted their control. The political life of every Southern state was dominated by a handful of wealthy slave-owning families. In South Carolina they called themselves the Chivalry and were accustomed to rule. Never an aristocracy in the British sense, since there were no hereditary titles and no House of Lords, they were nevertheless functionally similar to the aristocracy in that they were a rich, interrelated ruling class not easily joined by outsiders and were accustomed to having their own way politically. Haughty, proud, touchy on points of honor, and quick to duel, they also exhibited many of the characteristics of an aristocracy. The decision to secede was, for them, a combination of self-interest—they believed their power to be jeopardized by the Republican victory—and idealism, based on the principles worked out by proslavery writers and preachers in the foregoing decades.[46]

Not all members of the Southern elite favored secession, however. Some continued to believe that, regrettable though the Republican victory was, the South ought to remain in the Union. Alexander Stephens of Georgia (1812–83), for example, an old Southern Whig, "talked states rights but was clearly reluctant to abandon the Union, not only because he had a long and sentimental attachment to it, but because disruption would bring in its train unforeseen and, most likely, dangerous changes." To a Northern friend he wrote in 1860, "Revolutions are much easier started than controlled, and the men who begin them, even for the best purposes, and objects, seldom end them." Similarly, the South Carolinian Benjamin Perry (1805–86) had opposed nullification in the 1830s and favored the Compromise of 1850, both moments when the possibility of secession had arisen. In 1861 he wrote that his state's secessionists were "exulting over the destruction of the best and wisest form of government ever vouched by God to man. Fools and wicked fools, they know not what they do and may God forgive them." Once their home states seceded, however, these Southern Unionists had to decide where their primary loyalty lay. Most followed their states, even when they had misgivings, Stephens and Perry among them. They became active politicians and soldiers in the Confederacy.[47]

The Confederate Founding Fathers were aware that they were, at least in one sense, revolutionaries, but this was a role they tried to play down. They aimed to preserve the principle of states' rights, making the CSA a loose confederation according to the tradition of the Kentucky and Virginia Resolutions, and they modeled their constitution as nearly as possible on that of 1787 as a way of emphasizing continuities with the past. The historian Emory Thomas notes that "the nation framed and formed at Montgomery was the political expression of the Old South status quo. The practical moderate leadership which asserted itself in the 'morning after' aftermath of secession sought no new worlds; they and most of their fellow Southerners were well satisfied with the world that was." They had, he adds, "employed radical means to achieve conservative ends." In his inaugural address as president of the CSA, Jefferson Davis (1808–89) underlined the point by surrounding himself with traditional American symbols; he delivered it at the foot of a statue of George Washington on Washington's Birthday, February 22, 1862. He used the speech to affirm the right of secession and to deny that it was revolutionary.[48]

Davis and his fellow founders also claimed a divine sanction, arguing that the Confederacy, like Old Testament Israel, represented God's chosen people, endowed with a sacred duty to protect itself against Northern aggression. How wonderfully apt to their purposes was the verse from Jeremiah: "Then the Lord said unto me, out of the North an evil shall break forth upon the inhabitants of the land, and they shall fight against thee, but they shall not prevail against thee; for I am with thee." In at least some of the Southern states, meanwhile, secession conventions sought to roll back democratic reforms of recent decades, trying to place more power in the hands of the planter elite while restricting the political influence of poor whites. Like the Northern patricians, elite Southerners feared social and political turbulence from below—they looked on radical democracy as an instrument of either the Yankees or the devil. Ironically, however, they were more dependent than ever before on the good-will of the people they were striving to disfranchise, since poor whites would make up the bulk of the CSA army.[49]

Were Southerners, as some of them claimed, sufficiently distinct from all other Americans as to have a separate national identity? European theorists of nationalism of the early nineteenth century, including Herder and Fichte in Germany and Michelet in France, had argued that nationalism was based on distinct racial characteristics or distinct languages. Articles in *DeBow's Review*, the *Southern Monthly*, and the *Southern Literary Messenger* from 1861 and 1862 followed this lead by claiming that the people of the Northern states were "Saxons" and those of the Southern states "Normans," with essentially different racial characteristics. Others suggested that the North represented the Puritans or Roundheads of the English Civil War era, and the South the royalist Cavaliers. Even Southerners unconvinced by these analogies from English history believed they had a right to self-determination. They cited the era's many nationalist movements, but as the historian Drew Faust notes, they "were careful to dissociate the South from genuinely radical movements; it was the conservative European nationalism of the post-1848 period with which the Confederacy could identify most enthusiastically." She quotes an article from the *Daily Richmond Enquirer* that praised Polish resistance against Russia. "It is not the poverty, and plebeian or proletaire interest rising up against superior classes; rather it is the aristocratic and high-bred national pride of Poland revolting against the coarse brute power of Russian imperialism. . . . At bottom the cause of Poland is the same cause for which the Confederates are now fighting."[50]

Whatever the plausibility of such claims, the reality of having to fight for its existence almost from the moment of its birth prevented the Confederacy from retaining the distinctive features of the Old South. First, to create an effective army through conscription, whose soldiers could march wherever necessary under a unified command, it had to abridge the very same states' rights that had helped motivate secession in the first place. Second, it had to divert agricultural energies into growing more food and less cotton. Third, it had to industrialize as quickly as possible in light of the mechanized character of modern warfare and to intervene in the market to promote economic efficiency. Fourth, the exigencies of war led to the transformation of traditional social roles, relationships, and gender roles; as men went off to fight, women had to take on more roles than ever before. And fifth, before long the Confederacy, like the Union, had to suspend habeas corpus and other citizens' civil rights.[51]

Above all, the whole question of African Americans' situation and loyalties became acute. Slaves, as well as women, cared for many farms whose owners were away fighting with the armies. The more slaves learned about the issues involved in the war, the more likely they were to challenge the role they were being asked to play. They abandoned plantations in large numbers when the opportunity arose, and more than one hundred thousand enlisted in the Union Army. Confederate songs, poems, and paintings, far from reflecting this reality, depicted slaves as loyal to the system and as choosing to stay with their masters when given the option. But as Faust points out, "These treatments . . . implicitly recognized that the conflict brought slaves the chance to exercise choices about their destiny. . . . Confederates unwittingly imparted a legitimacy to the voices of their theoretically powerless black slaves, suggesting that their consent was somehow important." As Confederate difficulties intensified after 1863, the Confederate Congress began to debate the possibility of enlisting blacks as soldiers, even though the implication was that they would have to be freed as a quid pro quo. By the time of the surrender in 1865, the pressures of war had changed the Confederate states almost beyond recognition.[52]

Confederate defeat is attributable in part to the persistence of conservative habits and ideas among secessionists. One historian of the Confederacy writes that "the centralizing efforts of the Davis administration offended prominent state rightists, who began a continuing attack on the policies, even legitimacy, of their own government." Influential newspapers such as the Charleston *Mercury* and the Richmond *Whig* denounced Davis as a tyrant for his conscription policy and his suspension of habeas corpus. Georgia governor Joseph Brown tried to maintain personal control over Georgia's troops, in line with the principle of states' rights, rather than yield them to the military imperatives of the South as a whole. The Confederate vice-president, Alexander Stephens, himself a Georgian, feuded with Davis right in the heart of the CSA administration. Meanwhile, class antagonism between rich and poor whites, always a source of tension in the Old South, increased rapidly, as the poor felt they were shouldering an undue share of the burden. Disillusioned by social inequities, revolted by the opportunism, extortion, and profiteering of merchants and planters, and by their government's declining ability to support them, poor whites began to give up on the Confederacy.

The underindustrialized South was short of everything by 1863. It even lacked supplies of printer's type and paper—most Southern journals and newspapers had to close down as old equipment wore out, making it harder than ever to propagate the concept of Confederate nationalism.[53]

LOST CAUSE CONSERVATISM

The experience of defeat obliged Southern conservatives after the war to confront an unpleasant series of new realities. First, their attempt to preserve a slavery-based system had failed. Whatever its merits, that way of life had now come to an irrevocable end. Some among them speculated that God had decided to chastise His chosen people in the South because they had not lived up to biblical standards in caring for their slaves. Second, their theory of the distribution of powers, favoring states' rights over the federal authority, had been defeated, along with the claim that state sovereignty preceded that of the federal government. Now they were occupied by Union troops and forced to accept the Thirteenth, Fourteenth, and Fifteenth Amendments, which had abolished slavery and appeared to threaten white supremacy. The Freedmen's Bureau and black Republican appointees in government began to turn the tradition of Southern racial hierarchy on its head.[54]

Confronting these realities, of course, did not necessarily mean accepting them, let alone welcoming them. At once, and for years afterward, Southern writers wrote retrospective justifications of their cause, along with claims that Lincoln and the Republicans had violated American traditions that they themselves had struggled to conserve. Alexander Stephens's *Constitutional View of the Late War Between the States* (1867–70) was the heaviest of these justifications, written in the form of a fifteen-hundred-page debate between himself and three imagined Yankee interlocutors in the manner of a Platonic dialogue. With remorseless logic and exhausting, repetitive detail, Stephens's *Constitutional View* explains every issue in American history, from the ratification of the Constitution to the end of the Civil War, confirming the prior sovereignty of the individual states and the legitimacy of their decision to secede. The Yankees are thwarted at every turn of this vast conversation, and eventually admit as much.[55]

Commemorations of the Old South and the Confederacy quickly took on a tone of nostalgia and elegy. They romanticized the supposed harmony and beauty of the prewar society and mingled remembrance of the dead with remembrance of the cause for which they had fought. During the war itself the South had been riven by divisions and recriminations, but afterward these could be forgotten or minimized in favor of the myth of the Lost Cause. Central to Lost Cause mythology was the idea that a virtuous, godly people had justifiably seceded, had been attacked by the despotic Yankees, and had fought selflessly, shoulder to shoulder, against a numerically overwhelming foe. Edward Pollard (1832–72), one of the first Southern writers to use the phrase "Lost Cause," in an 1866 book of the same name, argued that the central issues all along had been states' rights, the preservation of white supremacy, and the superiority of Southern civilization. Admitting defeat on the battlefield Pollard wrote: "A war of ideas is what the South wants [now] and insists upon perpetrating. . . . All that is left of the South is the war of ideas. . . . In such a war there are noble victories to be won. . . . The war did not decide negro equality; it did not decide negro suffrage; it did not decide States Rights." In a second book two years later he asserted that white supremacy, rather than slavery, had been the principal issue all along.[56]

Pollard and many other defiant ex-Confederates, including John Esten Cooke, William Gilmore Simms, Albert Taylor Bledsoe, and Robert Lewis Dabney, helped embroider the myth. It quickly took on religious overtones too, so that ex-Confederates could affirm that they had been involved in a godly work. Their earthly mission had failed, but then, so had that of Jesus—the shattering of the South, in this telling, was comparable to Christ's Crucifixion. Stonewall Jackson and Robert E. Lee became, in memory, Christ-like figures, and annual gatherings of Confederate veterans, or meetings to unveil new statues of Confederate heroes, took place in an atmosphere of prayer and hushed veneration. Lost Cause ideology, conservative and backward-looking, exercised a coercive pressure on white Southerners, making it difficult for them to advocate collaboration with Reconstruction governments. When Robert E. Lee's wartime second-in-command, General James Longstreet, criticized his former commander and went to work for the new government, his former colleague Jubal Early branded him a traitor.[57]

Guardians of the Confederate flame regarded radical Reconstruction in the late 1860s and early 1870s as almost blasphemous. Reconstruction dismayed ex-Confederates by giving former slaves the vote, encouraging their participation in state politics, and appointing them to a wide range of state and federal jobs, under the supervision of an occupying Union Army. It was cruel, said ex-Confederates, to thrust African Americans out into the world in the mad belief that they could play a role in running it. Some of them regarded the abolition of slavery itself as an act of unkindness to people who needed paternalistic protection.[58]

Advocacy of the Lost Cause blended easily with the creation of the Ku Klux Klan. Founded in 1866 by Confederate veterans in Tennessee, the Klan summoned up the image of the old Scottish clans, familiar to many Southerners through the historical romances of Walter Scott. The post–Civil War struggle of the ex-Confederates took as its model the post-1745 struggle for Scottish independence after the failure of Bonnie Prince Charlie's attempt to regain the throne for the Stuart dynasty. Conservative white Southerners could understand the Klan as an instrument to uphold their region's honor and traditions—to them the burning cross was a symbol not of racial terrorism but of romantic Christian militancy on behalf of an endangered civilization.[59]

After ejecting the remaining Northern troops through the political compromise of 1877, Southern Lost Cause conservatives began to rebuild a South to their own liking. Calling themselves the "Redeemers" (another implicit comparison of themselves with Jesus), they instituted segregation laws and tried to restore traditional principles of social deference and hierarchy. Evocation of the old ways served to legitimate these actions. As one historian has noted, "Nothing is so striking about the New South as its resemblance to the Old South. If the Confederacy was a classic revolutionary experience for Southerners, then the New South was the 'Thermidor,' the conservative reaction." Another adds that Reconstruction had done more to solidify Southern opinion than the experience of the war itself. "The defeat of the Confederacy and the long intersectional conflict over Reconstruction solidified a distinct and separate image for the South. . . . Though the New South movement insisted that rational lessons should be drawn from defeat, promoters of the Lost Cause ultimately used emotions of loss, hurt, and pride to impose a myth of wartime unity."[60]

By 1871 the myth of the Lost Cause was spreading from the South to the nation as a whole. *Scribner's Monthly,* from 1870 to 1881, and then

The Century, under the editorship of a Union Army veteran, Richard Watson Gilder (1844–1909), featured dozens of stories about the South and the Civil War and promoted a talented group of postwar Southern writers, including George Washington Cable and Joel Chandler Harris, the creator of Uncle Remus. The collective impression given by these articles and stories conformed closely to the outline of the Lost Cause myth—that Southerners had fought honorably in a just cause, that they were resourceful, that their women were beautiful and self-sacrificing, and that they came from a land that prized tradition and ancient things, one in which race relations were benign, hierarchical, and peaceful.[61]

Henry Grady (1850–89), editor of the *Atlanta Constitution* in the 1870s and 1880s, showed how it was possible to adapt to new realities without foregoing the consolations of the Lost Cause ideal. Grady was slightly too young to have fought in the war. The most influential advocate of the New South in the 1870s and 1880s as a writer and orator, he used Lost Cause themes to make the case for blending the best elements of old Southern tradition with advocacy for the region's economic development. Central to many of his speeches was the tale of his brave father, Colonel William Grady, dying under enemy fire at the Battle of Petersburg, attended in his last moments by a faithful family slave. The anecdote captured in a highly personal way the pathos and emotional power of the Lost Cause.[62]

In influential speeches to Northern audiences in 1886 and 1889, however, Grady went on to say that the sweeping away of slavery was a providential step that had freed the South of a great burden, and about which the South ought not to be resentful. Now the region could modernize, industrialize, and develop its potential in ways that the old slave-plantation system would have inhibited. North and South could work together on behalf of a harmonious and prosperous future, but only so long as the North, while investing in Southern industries, permitted Southerners to deal with the racial issue in their own way. Any recurrence of Northern Reconstruction-style intervention would simply reopen old wounds and falsely impede the cause of white supremacy.[63]

Lost Cause conservatism was durable partly because it created ground on which a sectional reconciliation between North and South could take place. The historian Alan Nolan notes that "the reunion was exclusively a white man's phenomenon and the price of the reunion was the sacrifice of the African Americans." Margaret Mitchell drew heavily on Lost Cause mythology in writing *Gone with the Wind (1936)*, rich with chivalrous whites, contented slaves, and wicked Yankees, giving the myth a new lease on life far into the twentieth century. As we shall see in a later chapter, Lost Cause ideas influenced Southern contributors to the agrarian movement of the 1930s and to the Paleoconservatism of the 1980s and 1990s. They have not entirely disappeared even today, as controversies over how the National Park Service should treat ex-Confederate shrines bear witness.[64]

The Civil War came about not because powerful men wanted to change the world they knew but because they wanted not to. By 1861 conservative Southerners saw secession as the indispensable step to conserving their world, and they tried to minimize the revolutionary character of their conduct. Eager to retain control of their section, they fought against the Northern invaders and against the popular ferment of the South's poor whites in the hope of maintaining the familiar old world of plantation slavery. When they failed on the battlefield, they tried to compensate for defeat by creating a backward-looking, unequal, hierarchical society while comparing their experience to Christ's suffering and death.

Lincoln, conversely, reacted to secession by asserting the indivisibility of the Union and doing everything he could to sacralize it by an artful invocation of the Founders and the Declaration of Independence. As preserver of the nation at a time of crisis when it might well have splintered, he can certainly be thought of as a conservative, yet he was clearly conservative in a different way from his Whig and Federalist predecessors. Unlike them, he regarded democracy not as a vulgar threat to the virtuous republic but as a time-honored characteristic of American life. He honored the fallen men of Gettysburg for vindicating what was by then a *tradition* of American democracy, and he linked their sacrifice to the defense of equality. We might think of this approach as a kind of progressive conservatism, over against the defensive conservatism of earlier elites.

American conservatism has always had a paradoxical element, entailing the defense of a revolutionary achievement. But as I suggested in the Introduction, it is probably better to look at American conservatism in its changing contexts and to see it as reactive and attitudinal than to regard it as a commitment to certain unchanging principles. In this chapter we have encountered Lincoln making the conservative case for democracy and equality. In the following chapters we shall see other Americans making the conservative case for entrepreneurial capitalist individualism, even though capitalism has done more than anything else to transform the world in the last two centuries.

CHAPTER FIVE

Conservatism After the Civil War

INDUSTRIALIZATION AND NEW TECHNOLOGIES revolutionized the United States after the Civil War. Railroads linked previously remote areas, reducing cross-country travel times from months to days, and making possible for the first time the settlement and farming of the Great Plains. Large-scale production and refinement of oil provided a cheap illuminant and, later, fuel for automobiles. The mass production of high-quality iron and steel opened up new possibilities for high-rise buildings, strong light bridges, and a more durable urban infrastructure. Entrepreneurs and financiers grew rich in directing these changes; a few, such as John D. Rockefeller, Cornelius Vanderbilt, J. P. Morgan, and Andrew Carnegie, became household names for their astonishing (and sometimes unscrupulous) effectiveness.

Agrarian and urban critics began to challenge the dominance of the business elite in an array of reform movements that culminated in the populism of the 1890s and the progressivism of the early twentieth century. Business leaders and their intellectual allies responded by justifying their conduct, asserting its congruence with American values and with the laws of nature. Among the most powerful of these allies were the political economist William Graham Sumner, the steel-maker-turned-philanthropist Andrew Carnegie, and Supreme Court Justice Stephen Field. It is useful to think of them as conservatives, but conservatives of a kind even more paradoxical than Lincoln. What they wanted to conserve was an economic and political system dedicated to material progress and social transformation, in which the holders of private property enjoyed a high degree of protection from state intervention. They denigrated tradition, marginalized religion, and showed more sympathy for low-born but self-made entrepreneurs than for established elites.

American traditionalists in those same years were conservatives of a very different type. They were, in fact, just such unashamed elitists and advocates of high culture as Sumner and Carnegie scorned. They feared plutocracy (government by the rich), demagogues, and social revolution from below. Some, the mugwumps, dabbled in reform. Disdain for the entire political system, meanwhile, all but paralyzed others, notably Henry and Brooks Adams, the intellectually brilliant great grandsons of the nation's second president. As powerful and imaginative writers, the Adams brothers have won a permanent place in American conservative and literary history, though they were politically insignificant and exercised little influence over their contemporaries.

The years between the Civil War and the First World War also gave rise to a third conservative type, best represented by Theodore Roosevelt, whose immense popularity and influence made his ideas far more important to his generation than those of the Adamses. He shared with them a distaste for plutocracy and thought most big industrialists were narrow-minded, obtuse, and greedy. Unlike them, however, he thrust himself into public life, loved war, craved military distinction, and sought an imperial future for the United States. Born wealthy and never compelled to make his own living, he admired the aristocratic virtues and felt a sense of noblesse oblige toward the lower classes.

There was perhaps just one point on which advocates of these three quite different types of conservatism could agree: that socialism and communism represented a severe and growing threat to their world and that it would be a formidable enemy in the twentieth century.

CAPITALIST CONSERVATIVES

It may seem paradoxical to describe the intellectual defenders of capitalism, a world-changing system, as conservative. It is sometimes appropriate, however, because by the late nineteenth century they were writing under pressure from socialists to their left, men who wanted a yet more drastic transformation, including the abolition of private property and the creation of centralized economies. The paradox is heightened when we consider that William Graham Sumner, the foremost among these defenders, was resolutely antitraditionalist. He once wrote that "a man of good faith may come to the conviction sadly, but he must come to the conviction honestly, that the traditional doctrines and explanations of human life are worthless." Sumner—one of the founders of American sociology as well as a political economist—believed that politics, society, and economics should be studied coldly and scientifically, not as branches of Protestant morality. A sterling defender of free-market capitalism and a philosophical positivist, he strengthened the foundations of American libertarian conservatism.[1]

Sumner (1840–1910), ordained an Episcopal clergyman in 1867, soon found political and economic controversy much more to his taste than preaching the Gospel. He therefore left the ministry in 1872 to accept a professorship in political economy and social science at Yale, his alma mater, where he stayed for the rest of his life. Sumner developed an almost legendary reputation as a stimulating teacher and a fearless academic reformer. One former student wrote that "the majority of our teachers were mechanical and dull . . . but we came to [Sumner's] teaching with eager expectations and were never disappointed. He invited and loved intellectual resistance. Every sentence he spoke was a challenge." Moreover, "he used to enter the classroom as if he were pushing his way triumphantly through hostile forces; he had the air of a conqueror."[2]

Scientific method, from which one's personal preferences are rigorously excluded, seemed to Sumner the antidote to vagueness, conventional moralizing, and wishful thinking. The job of a political economist or sociologist was to lay bare the hard true facts. Not that he was calm about it. Another admirer wrote that despite his insistence on the impersonal scientific method, "Sumner never ceased to be a preacher," adding that he was "not so much an exhorter to morals as a denouncer of immorality." His scathing polemics show how completely he had internalized the New England sermon tradition of the jeremiad, even though he now preached it in secular guise. Scientific method, as he understood it, was thoroughly empirical and antimetaphysical. Having studied philosophy and theology as a young man, he turned against both. He told a

Yale faculty meeting, when it was considering hiring a new philosophy professor: "Philosophy is in every way as bad as astrology. It is a complete fake," he added, and should be removed from the Yale curriculum as an anachronism. "We might just as well have professors of alchemy or fortune-telling or palmistry."[3]

Among the hard facts Sumner's students learned was that the human struggle to live is perpetual and difficult and that it leads to unequal outcomes. Enlightenment ideas about natural rights and the essential equality of men—not based on science—were fallacious. Inequality was real, natural, and inevitable, the result of a constant struggle for survival, against nature and against one another. "If we do not like the survival of the fittest we have only one possible alternative and that is the survival of the unfittest. The former is the law of civilization; the latter is the law of anti-civilization."[4]

Capital, he wrote, is the accumulated good of social developments made over the generations, and its existence makes further progress possible. Capitalists and inventors are the central figures in civilization and are *benefactors* of the rest of humankind. If a nineteenth-century man bought a spade for one dollar, for example, he would be able to dig or farm far more effectively than his ancestors who dug only with sticks, yet most of the advantage of using the spade came to him free of charge, as part of the accumulated capital of his civilization. So "it is the utmost folly to denounce capital. To do so is to undermine civilization, for capital is the first requisite of every social gain."[5]

Sumner favored free trade and, indeed, a laissez-faire approach to as many areas of life as possible. Warning against government intervention in society, he argued that legislation on behalf of one group nearly always victimizes members of other groups, usually by forcing them to pay for it through taxation or by obstructing their access to the market. If the police should rescue a drunk from the gutter, for example, they and the courts and the prison to which the drunk was taken would all be paid for by "those who have resisted vice." He added: "It may shock you to hear me say it, but when you get over the shock it will do you good to think of it: a drunkard in the gutter is just where he ought to be. Nature is working away at him to get him out of the way." Compassion was all very well in the narrow domestic sphere, Sumner agreed, but it ought not to be the basis of government policy.[6]

Sumner eulogized "The Forgotten Man": "Who is the Forgotten Man? He is the clean, quiet, virtuous, domestic citizen, who pays his debts and his taxes and is never heard of out of his little circle. Yet who is there in the society of a civilized state who deserves to be remembered and considered by the legislator and statesman before this man?" The Forgotten Men's hard work, punctuality, sobriety, and self-discipline made them the most valuable part of the population.[7]

One of the most pernicious forms of government intervention, as Sumner saw it, and one of the most damaging to the Forgotten Man, was the protective tariff. In criticizing tariffs in the name of free trade he showed that he was by no means a mere flack for the Republican Party or for the business interests of his day, most of which at that stage favored high tariffs as a way of excluding foreign competitors. As obstacles to free trade, he reasoned, tariffs enrich one group (the manufacturers) at the expense of another (customers who are now forced to pay more for their goods). At the same time, they distort the economy and make it less efficient than it would have been, by discouraging citizens from undertaking the work to which their country is naturally best suited. In the 1880s and 1890s, when land was still plentiful and labor relatively scarce, America should not have been dedicating so much of its labor and capital to manufacturing; it was doing so only because of the distortions introduced by the tariff.[8]

Harsh with selfish businessmen, Sumner was even harsher with idealistic reformers. He denounced the most popular reform advocates of his day, like Henry George ("a half-educated apostle of the millennium"), as utopians whose proposals to remedy the social crisis of the 1880s and 1890s were nonsensical or vicious. Similarly he considered the growing socialist movement at the turn of the century mendacious, a threat to civilization itself: "The old classical civilization fell under an eruption of barbarians from without. It is possible that our new civilization may perish by an explosion from within." All these reform ideas, and socialism most of all, he wrote, shared the false first premise that people are equal, and the false hope that social engineering according to blueprints can transform society. On the contrary, he answered, civilization thrives on inequality, and the more it advances the greater the inequalities will become, *but from them everybody will benefit*. Only by going backward "to a status in which all are equally miserable" would civilization become less unequal.[9]

Sumner, like so many figures in this book, was conservative only in a paradoxical way, being a defender of classical liberal ideas and a forerunner of twentieth-century libertarians. He denied the idea of intrinsic human rights, left no place for God in his mature writings, and accepted the sweeping away of old forms by new enterprises as right and necessary in the constant struggle against nature. Mid-twentieth-century historians like Richard Hofstadter and Robert Green McCloskey regarded him as an exemplar of Social Darwinism, as though he relished the struggle of all against all. Robert Bannister and other revisionists have recently offered a corrective to that view. Bannister writes that "although he defended private property and individual enterprise, he did not celebrate a struggle for existence or believe that Darwinism (or any other -ism) justified the dog-eat-dog struggle of modern America." As Bannister sees it, Sumner merely refused to pretend that the world was kindly and scorned those who did.[10]

Whether or not the Darwinist label fits, it is certainly true that Sumner's ideas enjoyed widespread support among the business and political elite of his era. The Supreme Court, influenced particularly by the thinking of Justice Stephen J. Field (1816–99), created a sympathetic legal environment for laissez-faire businessmen by regularly striking down state and federal reform legislation that tried to limit workers' hours, wages, and working conditions. The conservatism of the post–Civil War judges, says one constitutional scholar, was indicated by their concern "primarily with protecting the property rights and vested interests of big business and with the defense of the prevailing economic and social order against agrarian and dissident reformers." In *Lochner v. New York* (1905), a celebrated example of this approach, the Court found a state law limiting bakery employees to ten hours' work per day to be unconstitutional because it violated freedom of contract. McCloskey observes: "The 'liberty' enshrined in the Constitution now can be recognized as a euphemism for entrepreneurial privilege. And the notion of 'equality,' for constitutional purposes, had become the amiable fiction that the employer and the unorganized worker stand as equals at the bargaining table. The originally humanistic doctrines of liberal democracy had been refashioned as pillars of the new conservatism." From the late nineteenth century right through to the Supreme Court "packing" crisis of 1937, the judiciary inhibited political regulation of economic activity on behalf of Sumnerian principles.[11]

Among the captains of industry who benefited from this legal situation the most articulate was Andrew Carnegie (1835–1919). A poor Scottish immigrant, his eventual domination of the American iron and steel industry made him one of the richest men in the world. He became a prolific writer too, justifying his wealth and his way of acquiring it while explaining how it ought to be spent. Carnegie was as dismissive of religion, tradition, and hierarchy as Sumner, and he saw American democracy as a vast improvement over European monarchy, aristocracy, and hereditary privilege. It was, as he saw it, a world in which all people had a chance to make fortunes by the exercise of their merits, as opposed to a world in which the accident of birth foreordained their occupations, class position, and destiny. But Carnegie was no egalitarian—he knew, like Sumner, that market competition led to vast inequalities of outcome. This inequality was, he argued, the motor of social progress, and he dreaded the possibility that communism or socialism might destroy it. While speaking up for the rights of all in a democracy, therefore, he did not shrink from using the courts and the repressive power of the state to defeat a bitter strike at his Homestead steel plant in 1892.[12]

Believing that society as a whole progresses through the unimpeded exercise of entrepreneurial capitalism, he regarded the acquisition of fortunes by the most skilled businessmen as an entirely 'natural' process. But Carnegie had an uneasy conscience. He also believed that men who made great fortunes, such as himself, had a duty to distribute their wealth benevolently, so as to advance the community as a whole. He thought it shameful for a man to die rich and approved the introduction of high death duties. This was, oddly, a version of the old aristocratic doctrine of noblesse oblige in a new guise. "The elitist implication of the idea that the millionaire must distribute his wealth during his own lifetime is unmistakable," says one critical commentator. By the time of his death, in 1919, he had almost certainly given away $350 million, for the endowment of libraries, colleges, church organs, and research institutes.[13]

THE CONSERVATIVE MUGWUMPS

Many other late nineteenth-century writers shared Carnegie's and Sumner's view that certain iron laws of nature, including economic laws, could not be overcome by human contrivance and that it was folly to tamper with them. Among them was a group of patrician Northerners who had stood with Lincoln and the Union in the Civil War but who became progressively disillusioned by the events of the Gilded Age. Remembered as the mugwumps, they came from prosperous urban homes, had been well educated in America and abroad, and shared a high sense of civic rectitude. Some experimented with radicalism; others took a conservative turn. These conservative mugwumps—including James Russell Lowell, Charles Eliot Norton, E. L. Godkin, and George William Curtis—were writers and editors for the Northern press. They were sickened by the deterioration of public morality and the political corruption of the 1870s and 1880s and feared that mass immigration from Europe would destroy America's tradition of civic republican virtue. Their own class seemed to be threatened by the new vulgar rich on one side, and by the ignorant swarming poor on the other.[14]

E. L. Godkin (1831–1902), an Irish Protestant, had immigrated to America in the mid-1850s, having already established himself as a capable journalist in Britain. He was one of the founding editors of the *Nation,* a highbrow periodical founded in the 1860s in New York, which for the next few decades spoke authoritatively on politics and high culture. A classical liberal in the mold of John Stuart Mill, Godkin opposed schemes of state intervention in the economy with Sumner-like energy. He campaigned vigorously against protective tariffs, for example, which he regarded as morally degrading and economically disruptive. Once protective tariffs were introduced, the economy was distorted and enterprises sprang up that could not have prospered without politicians' help. Knowing as much, their owners lobbied hard for higher tariffs in their own areas to get as much advantage over their foreign competitors as possible. In this way the economy became politicized on behalf of special interests while forcing consumers to pay more.[15]

The politicization of tariffs was particularly alarming to Godkin because America was now a mass democracy in which many comparatively poor men served in Congress. Their poverty made them vulnerable to bribery by corporate lobbyists. Abandoning tariffs would therefore have a moral as well as an economic significance. "The way to arm them [Congressmen] against temptation is to leave them as little as possible to sell of the things which capitalists are eager to buy." So long as lobbying for tariff favors persisted, workers in protected industries, seeing that their employers were buying political favors, had every incentive to do likewise, seeking legislation to promote trade unions. But unions were un-American. Godkin shared the view of his friend William Curtis that "trades-unions have never yet learned that their tyranny is as bad, and often much worse than, that of capital."[16]

Godkin had a similar objection to currency manipulation. He steadfastly opposed the Greenback movement of the 1870s and the Free Silver movement of the 1880s and 1890s, each of which was designed to create inflation. In his view, politically induced inflation was a form of fraud under cover of law, permitting debtors to avoid genuine repayment of their debts and pitching the entire process into the hands of corruptible legislators. In ancient days adulteration of money, or coin clipping, was a shameful expedient. "That it was a fraudulent device and that it was a thing if possible to be concealed, nobody ever denied." But now, in the Democratic campaign of 1896, in which candidate William Jennings Bryan sought the votes of Southern and Western farmers with a promise of "free silver," it was an openly avowed policy objective. Godkin was horrified. "Until it is well established that the currency will not come up as a question to be settled by the popular vote at every presidential election, there cannot be any industrial or commercial peace or tranquility."[17]

Local as well as national political issues troubled the mugwumps, showing some of them, at least, to be reformers, albeit of a very conservative kind. The nation's great cities, including New York, Philadelphia, and Boston, where most of them lived, were governed in the decades after the Civil War by immigrant political rings under the spoils system. Politics, in this system, was an opportunity not to exhibit one's republican virtue but to get rich, accept bribes, speculate in municipal lands, and help out your family and friends at the expense of the taxpayers.[18]

George William Curtis (1824–92) devoted his mature years to ending the spoils system. President Grant appointed him chair of a commission for the reform of the civil service in 1871; in this position Curtis proposed legislation to institute competitive examinations for civil service positions, ensuring that civic administrative work would be done by the best-educated and most qualified men, not by those with the right ethnic and political connections. It dismayed him to see that many members of the elite avoided politics, leaving it in the hands of "selfish and ignorant, or crafty and venal men."[19]

Curtis, despite his hatred of bad government, did not condemn democracy itself. Like his fellow mugwumps, however, he believed it should give rise to leadership by the virtuous elite, not by ordinary citizens. The educated leader "has faith enough in the people to appeal to them *against* themselves, for he knows that the cardinal condition of popular government is the ability of the people to see and correct their own errors." It was therefore the duty of such educated gentlemen as themselves, said Curtis, to run for office while refusing to pander to the voters' base instincts. The entire history of humankind, including the history of America, he added, affirmed that every element of progress had been achieved by the work of highly educated men.[20]

James Russell Lowell (1819–91) agreed with Curtis and Godkin that democracy was desirable only if it led to the election of a virtuous elite. Godkin said of Lowell that "he lived in an earlier republic of the mind, in which the legislation was done by first-class men, whom the people elected and followed. In a republic in which the multitude told the legislators what to do, he never really was at home." Lowell, the grand old man of American literature by the Gilded Age, was appointed U. S. minister to Spain by President Hayes (1877–81), and U. S. minister to Britain by presidents Garfield and Arthur (1881–85). Popular in both countries, he made occasional statements on politics, of which the most famous was an address in Birmingham, England, in 1884, which shows his eagerness to defend democracy on the one hand, but to circumscribe it on the other.[21]

Defending democracy at a time when Britain was contemplating the step of enlarging the suffrage to include urban workingmen, Lowell argued that it is far better to risk giving the vote to the masses than to let their grievances accumulate without a legitimate political outlet. He went on, however, to say that democracy was threatened in America's vast new cities; on the one side by the plutocrats with their irresponsible, corrupt, and vulgar wealth, on the other side by the ignorant mob of uneducated immigrant voters who lacked all sense of civic virtue and restraint. A firm advocate of Anglo-American friendship, Lowell regarded the American Constitution as the embodiment of good British principles. Rightly understood, he said, the American system no less than the British promotes the human instinct to admire and emulate superiority and should enable America, like Britain, to develop a hereditary elite in which high culture can be nurtured.[22]

The "good government" reformers of the Gilded Age often identified Irish Catholics and other immigrants as threats to their civilization. Those who did not oppose immigration outright agonized over its consequences. The first problem was immigrants' ignorance. Curtis, speaking in Concord, Massachusetts, in 1875, on the centenary of "the shot heard round the world," and in the presence of President Grant, Ralph Waldo Emerson, and other VIPs, noted that the immigrant population of Massachusetts was now far greater than the whole population of the state had been a hundred years before. "This enormous influx of foreigners has added an immense ignorance and entire unfamiliarity with republican ideas and habits to the voting class. It has brought other political traditions, other languages and other religious faiths. It has introduced powerful and organized influences not friendly to the republican principle of freedom of thought and action."[23]

Ignorant Catholic immigrants were bad enough; immigrant radicals were even worse, and the mugwumps feared a rising tide of socialism as the century neared its end. From Europe, wrote Godkin, had come socialist and anarchist ideas, a subject of rapidly growing concern in the era of great railroad strikes (1877, 1886, and 1894), the Haymarket Riot (1886), and the Homestead Strike (1892). The "state-managed laborer of Europe," when he found himself out of work, "declines to take care of himself in the old American fashion." Instead, "he looks about and asks his fellow-citizens, sullenly, if not menacingly, what they are going to do about it."[24]

Despite these strictures against immigrants, the conservative mugwumps nevertheless loved Europe. The Europe they loved, however, was a half-idealized place, the home of Civilization, with a capital C. It was the place from which came Chaucer, Dante, Shakespeare, Michelangelo, and Beethoven, the towering figures whose works enriched and ennobled life. It was not the Europe from which came Italian peasants, Jewish radicals, and the Irish, "with hatred for their home government bred in their very bones." Before America could take its place among the fully civilized nations of the world, they believed, it must assimilate the teaching of the great European culture makers and make comparable achievements of its own.[25]

To none of the group was this special Europe more important than to Charles Eliot Norton (1827–1908), the youthful author of an antebellum book criticizing utopian theories of liberty and democracy (see Chap. 3). As he matured, he befriended nearly all the leading British Victorian writers, including Thomas Carlyle, Matthew Arnold, John Stuart Mill, George Eliot, and John Ruskin, made a close study of medieval architecture, and become an expert on Renaissance art. Norton's best biographer describes him as "the most influential progenitor of the humanities in American education and scholarship" and "probably the pre-eminent cultural critic in the United States," adding that he was "a linchpin in the Anglo-American intellectual nexus that shaped high culture in Victorian America." Harvard, under the presidency of his cousin Charles W. Eliot, created for him its first professorship in the History of Fine Art, a position he held from 1874 to 1897. Skeptical about progress and about the achievements of his own era, he romanticized earlier ages, writing in a characteristic letter to a friend, "I should like to transfer myself for a time into the comparative tranquility of the eighteenth century, and to draw leisurely breath, to enjoy a meditative pause out of hearing of the steam whistle, undisturbed by the fretful interruptions of electric wires."[26]

Although he wrote no great books, he influenced the writing of many and contributed to the building of many cultural institutions. He was an early patron and promoter of William Dean Howells, Henry James, and Edith Wharton. Like his friend Longfellow, Norton translated Dante—irreverent Harvard students nicknamed his three daughters "Paradiso," "Purgatorio," and "Inferno." Norton also founded the Dante Society, the Boston Society of Arts and Crafts, and the Archaeological Institute of America. The historian Martin Green describes him as the most important cultural figure in the Boston of his era, an "aristocrat in a plutocracy." Lawrence Levine, in a similar judgment, traces his role in defining "highbrow" culture as something akin to a religious substitute for the privileged and educated classes.[27]

Was the spread of higher education enough to secure for America a position in the high civilization of the West? As an old man, Norton became progressively gloomier. Visits to Europe reminded him that his vision of it was at least partly idealized. "In Europe I could not but feel with pain the ill wrought by the progress of democracy—the destruction of old shrines, the disregard of beauty, the decline in personal distinction, the falling off in manners." Back in America he was horrified by the rise of aggressive nationalism, the jingoism of the 1890s that led to the Spanish-American War. To Leslie Stephen, one of his oldest friends (and the father of Virginia Woolf), he wrote in 1896: "The rise of democracy to power in America and Europe is not, as has been hoped, to be a safeguard of peace and civilization. It is the rise of the uncivilized, whom no school education can suffice to provide with intelligence and reason. It looks as if the world were entering on a new stage of experience, unlike anything heretofore, in which there must be a new discipline of suffering to fit men for the new conditions. I fear that America is beginning a long course of error and wrong, and is likely to become more and more a power for disturbance and barbarism." Later that year, he added in another letter to the same friend: "I can understand the feeling of a Roman as he saw the Empire breaking down and civilization dying out."[28]

TRADITIONALISTS

Most Americans in the post–Civil War generation—though often anxious at the rate of change—took pleasure and pride in the transformation of their world. No wonder. They were prospering because of it. A minority, by contrast, grieved at the passing of an older world and looked for ways to preserve or revive its characteristic ways of thinking and acting. The antimaterialist and nostalgic conservatism that they initiated became an increasingly important element of American conservative thought from then on, never dominant but always offering a counterpoint to the material concerns of their classical liberal brethren.[29]

Among the most famous American writers to become enamored of the Middle Ages were Henry Adams (1838–1918) and his younger brother, Brooks (1848–1927), grandsons of President John Quincy Adams. Burdened by family history, they felt themselves unequal to the task of carrying on the Adams tradition of public service. Politically they were insignificant; Oliver Wendell Holmes said that Henry Adams would have undertaken a life of public service only if it were "handed to him on a silver platter." They are, however, important figures in American intellectual history as traditionalist conservatives or antimodernists.[30]

Brooks Adams published *The Law of Civilization and Decay* in 1895, the first attempt by an American author to theorize about the entire course of history and its meaning. In it he argued that history is cyclical and that the vast forces that lead to the creation of great civilizations eventually undermine them. Civilizations, he claimed, begin from centers that command military force, intense piety, and striking artistic originality; their dominant emotion is *fear.* As they spread, however, they give rise to greater security, enabling fear to be replaced by greed. Bankers, usurers, and capitalists come to dominate, but they lack the creative vitality needed to maintain the structure of civilization. Degeneration sets in and the civilization falls into decline, becoming vulnerable to barbarian invasions. It happened to Rome, and, Adams implied, it will happen to Western Civilization also. In fact it will be worse this time because now we lack a supply of vigorous primitive peoples—barbarians—to generate the necessary energy for another cycle of the process.[31]

The emotional high point of *The Law* comes in his chapters on the Middle Ages. A creative form of fear governed the period and gave rise to courage, piety, daring, and phenomenal feats in cathedral architecture. The First Crusade, in Brooks Adams's telling, was one of the most glorious and selfless undertakings in the history of humankind. "In that age of faith no such mighty stimulant could inflame the human brain as a march to Jerusalem. A crusade was no vulgar war for a vulgar prize but an alliance with the supernatural for the conquest of talismans whose possession was tantamount to omnipotence. [Pope] Urban's words at Clermont, when he first preached the holy war, have lost their meaning now but they burned like fire into the hearts of his listeners then, for he promised them glory on earth and felicity in heaven. . . . So the crusaders rode out to fight, the originals of the fairy knights, clad in impenetrable armor, mounted on miraculous horses, armed with resistless swords, and bearing charmed lives." Once again, however, greed gradually displaced piety and courage, eroding old virtues and making men cowardly, complacent, and grasping. The later crusades sprang from baser motives: the Reformation was more a matter of seizing church property than searching for religious purification. If the crusader was the emblematic figure of the Middle Ages, the banker had become the emblem of the nineteenth century. Capitalists, as Brooks Adams told it, were too blinkered to realize that they were contriving their own ultimate destruction. Democracy, meanwhile, was degenerate, not constructive. It encouraged citizens to make demands on their rulers rather than to hunger for self-sacrifice.[32]

These conclusions were strikingly at odds with the themes of his predecessors in interpreting world history. Edward Gibbon, author of

The Decline and Fall of the Roman Empire, had blamed Christianity for undermining the Roman Empire; Brooks Adams saw usury as the culprit. The Whig tradition in historical writing, influential on both sides of the Atlantic in the work of Thomas Macauley and George Bancroft, argued for a steady upward trend of civilization, in wealth, civility, and achievement; it did not anticipate an eventual decline. American writers like John Fiske had added an optimistic gloss to Darwinian biology to create the idea of progressive evolution, which also had a steadily upward trajectory. Even Marxism, another great nineteenth-century theory of history, argued for stages of civilization, each one achieved through revolution but more advanced than its predecessor, while promising an idyllic outcome to history. Adams's grim promise of a return to barbarism seemed, to his critics, dismayingly gloomy. Theodore Roosevelt, for example, admired the book but denied the inevitability of decline and degeneration.[33]

Brooks Adams's brother, Henry, helped Brooks complete *The Law* but learned a lot from it too. Until then his own historical writing had been empirical rather than philosophical; now he too began to search for the meaning of history as a whole and to think of it as a scientific enterprise. Like Brooks he regarded the accumulation of wealth as vulgar and degrading. Rich through inheritance, he had no need to scramble for money like thousands of his contemporaries. He despised the captains of industry and the great new bankers, a dislike that in his work took on a vivid anti-Jewish coloration. In response to the financial crisis of the early 1890s he wrote: "I am myself more than ever at odds with my time. I detest it, and everything that belongs to it, and live only in the wish to see the end of it, with all its infernal Jewry."[34]

Searching for a superior alternative to his own world, Henry joined Brooks in identifying the Middle Ages as a supreme moment in human creativity, perfectly embodied in the great French cathedrals. In *Mont St. Michel and Chartres* (1904), an admiring account of two among them, he juxtaposed the beauties of architecture made in the name of God and the Virgin Mary against the grim aesthetics of the nineteenth century. He observed parallels in the buildings, poetry, philosophy, and theology of the medieval era, juxtaposing them against those of the degraded modern era. "Our age has lost much of its ear for poetry, as it has its eye for color and line, and its taste for war and worship, wine and women. Not one man in a hundred thousand could now feel what the eleventh century felt in those verses of the *Chanson [de Roland]*." Like his brother, Henry saw the First Crusade as a moment of supreme accomplishment, "the most interesting event in European history. Never has the western world shown anything like the energy and unity with which she then flung herself on the East."[35]

An immense display of Adams's erudition, his *Mont Saint Michel and Chartres* was nevertheless as much a work of wishful thinking as of real history—Adams exaggerated the unity of the Middle Ages and the spiritual power of the Virgin Mary, saying little about the ambitious and worldly bishops who raised the cathedrals in the first place or the era's chronic fratricidal warfare. As one Adams biographer remarks, "All the raptures . . . the fervors of scholarship, the bravura flourishes of drama with which he evoked the spirit of the bygone age were an elaborate rhetoric of condemnation of his own age." Characteristically he could rhapsodize about the beauty and power of the Virgin Mary without ever considering conversion to Catholicism.[36]

In 1907, Adams, then sixty-nine, published another odd book, *The Education of Henry Adams,* which has become a great conservative classic. It is part autobiography, part lament for civilization in decline, and part attempt to explain scientifically what he saw as a rapidly deteriorating world. It exhibits a steady skepticism about democracy, denies outright that the world is undergoing a beneficial form of progress, and expresses the fear that the crushing centralization of the plutocrats is going to be followed by the even-more-stifling centralization of the trades unions and socialists. *Education*'s most famous chapter, "The Dynamo and the Virgin," contrasts the Virgin Mary of the cathedrals with the great electricity generators he witnessed at the Paris Exposition in 1900. The dynamos were powerful and mysterious enough to tempt him to worship them. And yet not they but the Virgin represented "the highest energy ever known to man, the creator of four-fifths of his noblest art, exercising vastly more attraction over the human mind than all the steam-engines and dynamos ever dreamed of." He was sure that "all the steam in the world could not, like the Virgin, build Chartres."[37]

Many other intellectuals besides the Adams brothers admired the Middle Ages and strove to incorporate the best of their qualities into the modern world. The architect Ralph Adams Cram (1863–1942) was one.

Raised in New Hampshire on a strong diet of Matthew Arnold, Thomas Carlyle, and John Ruskin, Cram moved to Boston for an architectural apprenticeship in 1881 and developed a taste for medieval styles. He detested the "ignorant and savage bigotry of the Protestant Revolution" and reviled the memory of the Protestant iconoclasts, among whom the statue-smashing Oliver Cromwell and his New Model Army of the 1640s and 1650s were odiously representative.[38]

As Cram told it, there was something intrinsically conservative about architecture. First, it was durable, far outlasting the builders. Second, the survival of great old buildings gave later generations a glimpse of the superior civilizations that had made them. Third, these buildings stood in silent judgment over newer and worse generations. "Feudal and Catholic France," for example, had vanished, and by the twentieth century the land had become the "prey of political gangsters, profiteers, and atheists," but "Chartres and Bourges and Albi remain intact to proclaim the life that inspired them and that sometime might be again." In the same way the marvelous cathedrals, parish churches, castles, abbeys and manors of England stood, quietly rebuking the "ruin wrought by the eighth Henry and Cromwell and the industrialists of the nineteenth century."[39]

Cram established his own company and competed for commissions, making a breakthrough with a major project at the Military Academy, West Point. From there he went on to design and build numerous churches, culminating in a commission for the Cathedral of St. John the Divine in New York. He also enjoyed a twenty-five-year reign as chief architect at Princeton University, where his Graduate School, a set of beautiful dormitory quadrangles, and his magnificent Memorial Chapel dominate the surroundings. Always a prolific writer on architecture, eager to reconcile his architectural aesthetics with his religion, Cram argued that Gothic style had been abruptly cut off at the time of the Reformation for religious reasons but that its vitality could be recovered and continued. Denying, therefore, that his Gothic buildings represented mere antiquarianism, he saw them as the logical development of a great living tradition that surpassed the point it had reached in the early sixteenth century.[40]

Just as the right building promotes the right faith, said Cram, so an ugly or mutilated architectural form bespeaks a sick society. It was no coincidence, in his view, that American architecture should have become repulsive at exactly the same time as American politics. From 1830 to 1880, he argued, there was no good building in America, and this period coincided with the era of Jacksonian democracy, a vulgar and tawdry descent from the virtue and dignity of the early aristocratic republic. Did that indicate that the improvement of art and architecture after 1880 signaled a healthier society? No, merely that the arts had become fashionable and that a large, wealthy, and fickle public would for the moment give its money for styles that happened to be good.[41]

The Adams brothers and Cram revered the heritage of the Middle Ages and used it as a stick with which to beat their own era. Veneration of a place so distant in space and time made theirs a paradoxical kind of traditionalism, especially since they emphasized its interruption or destruction by the Reformation. Their contemporary Barrett Wendell (1855–1921), on the other hand, thought of America as part of an Anglo-American civilization that had enjoyed a long continuous life and was still a vital reality. In 1900 Wendell published *A Literary History of America,* the first general study of its kind, tracing American writers' debts to a rich English heritage and explaining the new and distinctly American elements of their work between the first colonial settlements and his own day. One of the pioneers of American literary criticism, he was at the same time a passionate Anglophile, traveled to England as often as possible, lectured at Cambridge, and wept when he heard the news of Queen Victoria's death. He took for himself the English ideal of the gentleman.[42]

In the mid-1890s Wendell, a Harvard professor, became increasingly concerned that this civilization—a dynamic but ultimately fragile thing—was in danger and that Britain and America faced common hazards. Among the threats unsettling their world was the sheer sweeping power of industrialization, "our incredible control of natural forces—steam, electricity, and applied mechanics." These great forces, as impressive to him as they were to Henry Adams, had suddenly created an era "as new as that of fire, of the wheel, of metal."[43]

Equally threatening to Wendell was the cult of democracy that had risen with industrialization and the rise of statist liberals and socialists in politics. To confront the crisis, what resources did America, or Anglo-America, have to offer? One was its tradition of political stability and moderation, qualities echoed in its rich literary tradition. A second was the resourcefulness of its elite, the gentlemen. They must find a way to preserve benign inequalities in society and hold back the wave of ignorant mass democracy. In a letter to a close English friend, written in 1895, Wendell outlined what seemed to him the alternatives: "Democracy, in old world or new, seems little better than a caricature of government. Power, wherever it resides, seems bound to develop the hateful traits of human nature—tyranny, dishonesty, petty baseness, corruption. In a government of the better classes, at least those traits are balanced by certain external graces and dignity, and often by some sense of personal consequence. . . . In any democracy they are at their worst." A third resource was the racial strength of the Anglo-Saxons. Like many contemporaries Wendell feared that great waves of immigrants would swamp the once distinct racial stock that had built up an English-speaking civilization on this side of the Atlantic. In a letter of 1905 he spoke of the "racial agony in which we are being strangled by invading aliens."[44]

Others in their generation turned to different moments of European history, sometimes for philosophical insight but sometimes simply as collectors. Henry Adams, for example, was a friend of Bernard Berenson (1865–1959), a leading art historian and connoisseur, who spent much of his life traveling through Europe, studying art, authenticating expensive Old Master paintings against the hazards of fraud, and making purchases on behalf of wealthy American clients and museums. In the late nineteenth and early twentieth centuries many of the richest Americans began building collections of European art and artifacts—creating the foundations of such galleries as the Frick, the Guggenheim, and the Morgan Library. The most vivid personality in this group was Isabella Stewart Gardner (1840–1924), who built an Italian Renaissance palace in Boston's Fenway and crammed it full of precious European paintings, sculptures, and tapestries. These collectors were not, in most cases, conservative writers, but by their actions they made the case for the continuity of European civilization on this side of the Atlantic, and its art as something to be cherished by Americans rather than something to be repudiated as symbolic of the decadent Old World.[45]

No one made a more articulate statement of their case than Henry James (1843–1916). The premier American novelist of his generation, he spent most of his adult life in Europe, traveling restlessly between England, France, and Italy and favoring the ancient centers of civilization, London, Paris, Rome, and Venice. He claimed that only there could he find adequate materials for the writing of first-rate fiction. Europe, after all, had a long unbroken past, well-developed classes and castes, and a venerable architectural tradition. How raw and primitive the United States seemed to him by comparison.[46]

When James did return to examine the United States in 1904, for the first time in nearly twenty-five years, his visit led to the composition of *The American Scene* (1907), a book brimming with impressions and insights. Determined to give his native land the benefit of the doubt, he praised its vigor, energy, creativity and rapidly rising standard of living. At the same time, he found a jarring lack of manners, deference, and cultivation in its people, and he deplored the impact of mass immigration on East Coast cities. Of the New York skyscrapers (which had not been there when he last visited), he said they looked horribly temporary; they were monuments solely to cupidity and destined to be replaced by even bigger and greedier ones. "They never begin to speak to you in the manner of the builded majesties of the world as we have heretofore known such . . . with the authority of things of permanence or even of things of long duration." Worse, they now rose insultingly above the beautiful Gothic spire of Trinity Church, leaving it "caged and dishonored." James ended his survey by asking, doubtfully, whether America's old virtues could withstand the impact of mass immigration and greedy industrialization.[47]

THE ROOSEVELT GENERATION

Although the mugwumps and traditionalists felt excluded from politics, young Theodore Roosevelt (1858–1918) was determined to participate, even though it meant getting his hands dirty among the Tammany machine men of New York. A larger-than-life figure almost from the start, he was blessed with material advantages at birth and overcame physical weakness as a teenager with a vigorous training regimen. His dandyish appearance at the New York state legislature in Albany provoked laughter when he arrived as a freshman legislator, but he soon showed he was a force to be reckoned with in the state's political life.[48]

Whether Roosevelt was a conservative depends, as always, upon one's definition, but a survey of his ideas about politics and about life more broadly presents strong evidence in favor of the idea. Even as he became a "progressive" leader as president and as presidential challenger in

1912, he had in view the preservation of traditions that rapid technical and social changes had threatened. He was one of the first American politicians to recognize the long-term threat of socialism and to take measures to head it off by judicious concessions. Always passionately opposed to socialism, he nevertheless favored extending the federal government's social and economic reach, to restrain capitalist abuses, and to protect workers from the vagaries of the business cycle. He often expressed anger at the "dull, purblind folly" of the industrialists and their "greed and arrogance" toward workers, which itself had the effect of increasing the attraction of socialism. The historian John Milton Cooper describes him as the "far-seeing, broadminded, dynamic leader of a conservative party," whose role was "to make his party bend and adapt to change and discontent."[49]

He exhibited many conservative qualities. He was, first, an elitist, believing strongly in the right of the elite to rule and its superiority over the masses. Inheriting his father's fortune at the age of twenty, he never had to worry about earning an income and disdained materialism with the hauteur of an aristocrat. He had an aristocrat's well-developed sense of noblesse oblige as well, recognizing that his position imposed on him responsibilities for those less fortunate.[50]

Second, he despised radicals and utopians, both in his own day and in history. In books about the early republic he honored the memory of Alexander Hamilton and the Federalists and scorned Jeffersonians. He believed that William Jennings Bryan's free silver campaign of 1896 "threatened [a] frightful disaster" that would "plunge all our people into conditions far worse than any of those for which he sought a remedy." Much worse, anarchism was a direct and terrifying threat to civilization itself. Roosevelt hated anarchists before 1901 (he favored lining up the Haymarket anarchists against a wall and shooting them) and, not surprisingly, hated them all the more after Leon Czolgosz shot and killed President McKinley in 1901. He saw the act as "a crime against free government, a thousand times worse than any murder of a private individual could be," adding that "we should war with relentless efficiency not only against anarchists but against all active and passive sympathizers with anarchists."[51]

Third, he believed in the ennobling character of violence. His historical writings consistently glorified warriors and demeaned pacifists. He feared that in times of peace and in a wealthy industrial society it was dangerously easy for men to lose the martial virtues and to neglect what he called the "strenuous life." He was delighted when America declared war against Spain in 1898. Relinquishing his job as assistant secretary of the navy, he raised a regiment that mixed cowboys with friends from Harvard and Wall Street, the famous "Rough Riders," leading them to Cuba and to victory in the Battle of San Juan Hill. He exposed himself to enemy fire, expected his officers to take heavier casualties than his men, and gloried in the dangers of the campaign. There would always be wars, Roosevelt believed. Pacifists horrified him, partly because they were indulging what seemed to him wishful thinking and partly because they seemed eager to rid humanity of the very manly and warlike qualities he valued and wanted to preserve.[52]

Fourth, he believed that society, no matter how complex and interdependent it became, still rested on the old individual virtues of fidelity, self-reliance, hard work, and personal bravery. Consider the opening of his autobiography:

> There is need to develop all the virtues that have the state for their sphere of action; but these virtues are as dust in a windy street unless back of them lie the strong and tender virtues of a family life based on the love of the one man for the one woman and on their joyous and fearless acceptance of their common obligation to the children that are theirs. There must be the keenest sense of duty, and with it must go the job of living; there must be shame at the thought of shirking the hard work of the world, and at the same time delight in the many-sided beauty of life. With soul of flame and temper of steel we must act as our coolest judgment bids us. We must exercise the largest charity toward the wrongdoer that is compatible with relentless war against the wrong-doing.

As president he advocated federal regulation of industries as a way of forestalling both the tyranny of monopolists and the rise of American socialism, each of which he saw as threats to the endurance of these personal qualities.[53]

A new element of American elitism in the late nineteenth century was the development of scientific racism, a blend of Manifest Destiny and Darwinian biology. Its advocates argued that the Anglo-Saxons (the group to which they themselves belonged) had been singled out by destiny, biology, or God as the supreme race. They were the world's racial elite, they had built a civilization superior to all others, they were exceptionally gifted in politics, and they should now dominate the rest of the world, bringing its blessings to backward and benighted people everywhere. It was a view shared by such influential figures as Rudyard Kipling in England, Cecil Rhodes in South Africa, and Roosevelt in the United States, all of whom believed the English-speaking peoples shared a special destiny and duty to rule the world.[54]

"Race" at the turn of the twentieth century was not a matter merely of black and white. The debate over whether to restrict immigration, which gathered force in the late nineteenth and early twentieth centuries, and in which Roosevelt took an interest, was also conducted in the language of race. Such authors on the issue as Francis Amasa Walker (1840–97) and William Z. Ripley (1867–1941) spoke of the different "races" of Europeans and offered scientific (or rather, pseudoscientific) support to the idea that races ought not to mix. They argued that the United States no longer benefited from immigration because new arrivals now came less from England, Scandinavia, and Germany, the Nordic countries, than from what they believed to be the racially inferior stocks of Southern and Eastern Europe. The birthrate among disheartened Anglo-Saxons in the face of this invasion, said Walker, had declined dangerously.[55]

Henry Cabot Lodge (1850–1924), one of Roosevelt's closest friends and political allies, shared their concern. He had studied medieval history under Henry Adams and later became a powerful U.S. Senator for Massachusetts between the 1890s and the 1920s. He believed that "no other people ever displayed political talents of so high an order as that derived from Anglo-Saxon stock" and in the 1890s campaigned against the "importation of the cheapest, lowest, and most ignorant labor of other countries." In Lodge's view, "More precious than the forms of government are the mental and moral qualities which make what we call our race. While those stand unimpaired all is safe. When those decline all is imperiled. They are exposed to but a single danger, and that is by changing the quality of our race and citizenship through the wholesale infusion of races whose traditions and inheritances, whose thoughts and beliefs, are wholly alien to ours and with whom we have never been assimilated or even been associated with in the past." Lodge linked the assassination of President McKinley, and anarchism generally, to the immigration question—the assassin Czolgosz was the son of a Polish newcomer. Such individuals, he wrote, "are the enemies of government, society, and patriotism."[56]

Roosevelt shared this general outlook, though was not so outspoken on the immigration issue as Lodge. His experience in the hurly-burly of New York politics showed him that immigrants came in all shapes and sizes; he was less of a racial purist than Lodge or than such later Nordic advocates as Madison Grant, author of *The Passing of the Great Race* (1916). But he was also unsentimental on racial questions. He had no doubt, for example, that the displacement of the Plains Indians in the 1860s and 1870s was necessary and justified. As a Dakota rancher in the 1880s he occupied lands that just ten years earlier had witnessed conflicts between pioneering frontiersmen and "a set of treacherous, revengeful, and fiendishly cruel savages." Now that the Indians had been defeated, he asserted, each should be given 160 acres of farmland, in accordance with the Homestead Act, or be left to take his chances as a laborer. If he would not work, he should be left "to perish from the face of the earth."[57]

In the same way, Roosevelt believed it right to conquer the old Spanish colonies and put an American empire in their place until the natives were ready for self-government, because the Anglo-Saxons would rule better than the Spaniards, displacing degeneracy with the civilized virtues, including honest administration and Protestantism. He saw empire building as a way of reviving the martial virtues that might otherwise atrophy in comfortable, commercial America. In his account of the Spanish-American War he evoked the idea that the war brought out the neglected fighting spirit of the ancient races from whom today's Anglo-Saxons were descended. "We drew recruits," he wrote of the Rough Riders, "from among men . . . in whose veins the blood stirred with the same impulse which once sent the Vikings over sea." He took it for granted, incidentally, that African Americans were racially inferior and that, as soldiers, they must be led by white officers.[58]

Among Roosevelt's and Lodge's like-minded friends was Alfred Thayer Mahan, author of *The Influence of Sea Power upon History, 1660–1783*

(1890). Mahan (1840–1914), a lecturer at the Naval War College in Newport, Rhode Island, theorized about naval warfare as a branch of politics in its widest geopolitical context. His book asked: why did Britain win its long succession of eighteenth-century wars against France? His answer was that superior sea power had assured British ascendancy, enabling it to dominate home waters and a growing empire, controlling maritime access and the sea lanes between its dispersed colonies. Like his political friends, Mahan believed that there would always be wars, that human nature made conflict inevitable, and that the way to national security came from possession of overwhelming force and readiness to use it.[59]

Soon after publishing *The Influence of Sea Power* to respectful American reviews, Mahan was ordered back to sea. Many navy old-timers doubted the usefulness of the Naval War College, and his commanding officer remarked, "It is not the business of a naval officer to write books." His voyage on the USS *Chicago,* however, turned into a triumphal procession once it reached Britain. The British admiralty, the prime minister, the queen, and the universities all acclaimed him as the man who had fully explained to Britain, for the first time, the reasons for its own imperial triumph. He became the first man ever to be awarded honorary doctorates from Oxford and Cambridge in the same week. Being lionized in Britain elevated his reputation back in America and from then on, Mahan was America's naval and geopolitical guru. Numerous later books, of the same high quality and clear-sightedness as the first, consolidated his reputation. He influenced not only American naval developments but also the decision of Germany and Japan to develop major naval forces, with immense consequences for the twentieth century.[60]

In 1899 and 1907, Mahan was an American delegate to conferences at The Hague designed to promote international peace. He took an unsentimental, open-eyed approach to the conference process, warning his colleagues not to be led into wishful thinking. "The cause of universal peace," he wrote, "will not be advanced but retarded by neglecting diligently and calmly to consider facts, to look them straight in the face; to see things as they are, and not merely as one would wish to see them now." He made a persuasive argument *against* international arbitration. In his view it was never going to replace war because "there is an absolute indisposition, an instinctive revolt, against signing away, beforehand, the national conscience, by a promise that any other arbiter than itself shall be accepted in questions of the future, the import of which cannot yet be discerned." Nations, like individuals, have consciences and ultimately cannot act against them. He even urged the U.S. delegates to vote *against* a motion outlawing poison-gas shells. After all, "the reproach of cruelty and perfidy addressed against these supposed shells was equally uttered formerly against firearms and torpedoes, both of which are now employed without scruple. Until we knew the effects of such asphyxiating shells there was no saying whether they would be more or less merciful than missiles now permitted." Better to develop them and then decide on their consequences than to neglect them and risk an adversary getting a tactical advantage by manufacturing them secretly. Andrew Dixon White, his colleague, was dismayed at first but later accepted Mahan's logic, writing that "his views have

vented any lapse into senti-

s and this stern, severe, ac-

but soon regretted it and

n he was clearly rethink-

most nineteenth-century

ır democracy. Ever since

nen of conservative tem-

norant, volatile, and sub-

that forced candidates to

nts. TR's life experience,

› trust the good sense of

anarchy, and plutocracy.

ace of democracy in the

twentieth century owes much to him. Rejected by the Republican Party, he ran an independent campaign as a Progressive, or "Bull Moose," candidate. His platform, the "New Nationalism," drew heavily on the ideas of Herbert Croly's *Promise of American Life* (1909), arguing a stronger role for the federal government as a counterweight to private economic power.[62]

His split from the Republican Party in 1912, however, and his enthusiasm for direct democracy occasioned bitterness and the sundering of old friendships. Barrett Wendell wrote that "his self-confidence and his general recklessness of speech are such that I conceive him personally to be untrustworthy as a friend and unmanageable as an ally. He is Caesar; and is not quite sure that he is not God." Many of the Republicans who condemned him thought of themselves as much more responsible conservatives than he, carrying on the older tradition. Ever since the start of his presidency, corporate leaders and bankers like J. P. Morgan had deplored Roosevelt's cultivation of popularity at their expense; they bridled at his description of them as "malefactors of great wealth." Their supporters in Congress, the standpat or Old Guard Republicans, opposed his measures to extend the reach of the federal government and his embrace of popular democracy.[63]

Another group of conservatives had supported him in the White House but drew the line at his defection in 1912. One was Henry Cabot Lodge. Another was Elihu Root (1845–1937), Roosevelt's secretary of war (1901–4) and secretary of state (1905–9), a brilliant and widely respected lawyer who, under slightly different circumstances, would have taken his turn at the White House. "Order was his passion," says Root's biographer, so he broke with TR and stayed loyal to Taft and the Republican regulars in 1912. A firm believer in representative government, as embodied in the Constitution, Root was dismayed by the Progressive Era shift toward direct democracy. He thought of votes for women as an attack on American womanhood and domesticity. As a lawyer, he opposed the movement for the election and recall of judges. In his view the judiciary must be *insulated* from, not exposed to, the vagaries of popular opinion. As a U. S. Senator (1909–15) he opposed the constitutional amendment for the direct election of senators (who had until then been chosen by the state governments), regarding the measure not as an increase in citizens' rights but as an assault on the checks and balances written into the Constitution. Root resigned his seat in 1915 rather than face a campaign of the sort long familiar to members of the House of Representatives but previously unnecessary to members of the upper house. The liberal *New Republic* bade him good riddance that year with the remark that "he has lacked vision" and that "no man can lead a people who has his back to the future." Conservatives who think of the past as rich and complex, and of the future as thin and vague, might regard the remark not as an insult but as a compliment.[64]

Lodge, Roosevelt, and Root were active practical politicians; Sumner, the Adams brothers, Norton, and Godkin were writers; Carnegie was an entrepreneur; and Cram was an architect. Each in his way can be thought of as conservative, but they were clearly conservatives of several distinct types. They disagreed widely on the relationship between theory and practice, morality and practical politics, the continuity or discontinuity of their civilization with its predecessors, and the benefits and drawbacks of democracy.

The new defenders of capitalism, like Sumner and Carnegie, wanted to conserve a spectacularly productive economic system against both old-fashioned challengers like agrarian populism and new-fashioned challengers like socialism and communism. Philosophical materialists, they believed civilization rested on material achievements, the accumulation of capital, and the distribution of ever more ingenious inventions. To prosper, however, capitalism needed internal peace, the rule of law, and a legal interpretation of the Constitution sympathetic to industrial interests. It also needed a mobile and energetic work force, men and women not hemmed in by traditional or prescriptive roles and able to make contracts without the intervention of paternalistic government.

The conservative mugwumps and the traditionalists, by contrast, looked on their world not as an exhilarating achievement but as a descent into barbarism and hankered back to an earlier time—the pre–Civil War years of their youth—in which there was still room for hierarchy, deference, and restraint. Deploring the immorality of public life and the increasing dominance of immigrants in politics, they felt trapped between two threatening groups: the vulgar plutocrats on one side and the immigrant mob on the other. They thought of themselves as the representatives of an endangered civilization. The politics of currency manipulation and tariffs they regarded as flagrant appeals to immorality, seeming to confirm their fear that democracy without the guidance of a virtuous elite was mere demagogy.

Theodore Roosevelt was as much an elitist as the mugwumps and traditionalists, but he found the common people more trustworthy, honoring their instinctive good sense and their aversion to imported radicalism. He showed that it was possible to live according to the code of the aristocrat and the warrior even in an urbanized mass society, though he was disappointed at the reluctance of the nation to undertake a world-spanning imperial mission of the sort that befitted the Anglo-Saxons. Like Mahan and Lodge, he expected the twentieth century, like all previous centuries, to be an era of warfare and tried to ensure that the nation would be able to fight, when it came to the test, on advantageous terms.

CHAPTER SIX

Conservatism in the 1920s and 1930s

TWO WORLD-CHANGING EVENTS OF 1917 had profound effects on American conservatism. The first was America's entry into World War I, and the second the Russian Revolution. From the first flowed, eventually, the American commitment to the role of superpower, and from the second came the great polar antagonism of the Cold War. Fear of socialism and communism, a persistent theme in conservative literature in the late nineteenth and early twentieth centuries, crystallized in reaction to the Bolshevik Revolution but would not become an obsessive concern for American conservatives until after World War II. Of more immediate concern was whether America should play a greater role in global affairs and whether it should be willing to subordinate its sovereignty to such international organizations as the League of Nations. Henry Cabot Lodge devoted the last years of his career to making sure it did not. Isolationist politicians and writers took up his mantle in the 1930s in the hope of preventing American participation in World War II.

In the interwar years, meanwhile, conservatism continued to mean different things to different groups. In the Northeast the old protest against mass democracy and in favor of a refined high culture persisted in the work of the New Humanists, an intellectual coterie centered on Irving Babbitt and Paul Elmer More. Neither man was widely influential, but each wrote in defense of intellectual elitism and classical standards; their work would influence their conservative successors after World War II. In the South at the same time, the Nashville Agrarians expanded on Lost Cause themes to decry nearly every aspect of modernity and industrial society. In their imaginative universe, the South became a surrogate for all the conservative virtues, and the North a surrogate for all the progressive vices.

H. L. Mencken, placed geographically between the two groups in Baltimore, and far livelier than either, blended an appreciation for modernism and urban life with a caustic critique of political progressivism. Never backward-looking or defensive like the conservative traditionalists, the New Humanists, and the Agrarians, he felt at home in a complex industrial world, lacked religion and a sense of reverence, and was passionately intolerant of utopianism; he knew exactly how to make it look ridiculous. Albert Jay Nock had a similar outlook but lacked Mencken's flair for publicity and high spirits. In the New Deal years, whose politics both of them despised, Nock declared himself entirely out of place, a "superfluous man" in a world most of whose inhabitants, he said, could hardly be thought of as humans at all.

VERSAILLES AND THE LEAGUE OF NATIONS

As Germany's armies retreated in the fall of 1918 and the end of the fighting neared, President Woodrow Wilson argued for a conciliatory peace treaty based on the Fourteen Points. They embodied his promise that this was the war to end all wars, and the war to make the world safe for democracy. Senator Henry Cabot Lodge, the dominant conservative figure in the Senate, by contrast, wanted an unconditional surrender from the Germans and found his views in close accord with those of America's British and French allies. He did not share Wilson's view that war would now disappear from the world or that an international organization could replace force with arbitration. Lodge was jubilant when Germany sought an armistice on November 11, 1918. He called the outcome of the war "the greatest victory for righteousness the world has ever seen."[1]

Wilson presented the draft Treaty of Versailles to the Senate in 1919 after prolonged negotiation with the Allies in France. Lodge and other conservatives were dismayed by several points in the treaty. Central to their objections was the proposed League of Nations, which would be charged with resolving all future international disputes. Lodge argued that the United States would not and should not submit to international arbitration on future matters affecting its national interest. To do so would be to surrender national sovereignty. Pretending a willingness to do so would be an act of bad faith. He could foresee that not only the U.S. but most other nations, if confronted by a challenge to what they perceived as their vital interests, would balk. He regretted the "natural view of good people . . . who think that if you shout peace loud enough you will have peace, and who do not see the dangers involved in agreeing to a treaty which makes promises we know we shall not carry out." Then there was the question of immigration. Lodge was a leading advocate of immigration restriction, but migration was an issue that affected both the sending and the receiving nations. Should it be a question submitted to the League, or should America be able to decide on its own immigration policy? And what about the Monroe Doctrine? League intervention in the affairs of the Americas would abridge the doctrine at once. With these objections Lodge was revoicing a point made in 1907 by his old friend Alfred Mahan at The Hague. Peace comes not from an automatic appeal to arbitration but from possession of overwhelming force and the will to use it decisively in just causes. By this logic it is not only unwise to agree ahead of time to arbitration, but actually immoral.[2]

Lodge and his conservative allies did not oppose the treaty or the League outright, however, and they did recognize that there were some questions in international life for which arbitration might be suitable. They proposed a series of amendments and reservations to the treaty as the basis for renegotiation. Wilson was intransigent. In the prolonged wrangling that ensued, he tried to appeal to the public over the heads of the recalcitrant senators but suffered a stroke during a nationwide tour to promote the treaty. His party lost the election of 1920, and the United States declined to join the League of Nations. The League's impotence over the next decades vindicated Lodge's predictions. When it came to the point, it was unable to assert its authority against what member nations thought of as their vital national concerns. Worst of all it could do nothing to stop escalating Japanese, Italian, and German aggression in the 1930s, the prelude to World War II.[3]

Meanwhile the Russian Revolution of 1917 had overthrown first the czar and then the pro-Allied provisional government, bringing Lenin to power and detaching Russia from the war. Lenin and then Stalin undertook an emergency program of industrialization in the 1920s and 1930s to turn the Soviet Union from a backward agricultural empire into a major industrial nation. Internally they ruled without mercy, annihilating all opposition. Externally they created the Third International, designed to coordinate communist parties throughout the world and to promote worldwide revolution, with the promise of bringing capitalism to an end everywhere. American conservatives, who had feared socialism and communism since the French Revolution of 1848 and the Paris Commune of 1871, were horrified; they elaborated a critique of communism and polemicized against the ideology and against the Soviet nation that embodied it.[4]

The Russian Revolution was a turning point in the history of American conservatism. Throughout the nineteenth century the United States had been in many ways the world's revolutionary leader. After 1917, by contrast, it became, in the eyes of supporters and detractors alike, the world's *counterrevolutionary* leader, trying to forestall the triumph of a newer and more radical political and economic system. Another characteristic of American conservatism from then on was that it would receive a steady succession of new recruits from former communists, in revolt against the horrible reality behind an ideology that had at first attracted them.[5]

THE NEW HUMANISM

The conservative critique of communism developed only gradually. Conservatism in the 1920s bore witness, meanwhile, to a rearguard action on behalf of cultural and political elitism, renewed doubts about democracy, and a protest against the intellectual characteristics of modern American life. The most philosophically weighty reaction to modernism came from the new humanists, led by Irving Babbitt and Paul Elmer More.

Many of the distinctive works of twentieth-century modernism were published in the 1920s, from T. S. Eliot's "The Waste Land" and James Joyce's *Ulysses* to the novels of F. Scott Fitzgerald and Ernest Hemingway. Abstract art and modern music also established themselves in galleries and concert halls; Picasso and Stravinsky were recognized modernist masters by the early 1920s. In the same decade Freudian psychoanalysis gained respect and popular interest among the educated middle classes. Pragmatism challenged older approaches to philosophy, while behaviorist psychologists began to argue for understanding human beings as nothing more than complex, stimulus-driven mechanisms. Darwinism and relativism, which had done so much to undermine older theories of order and fixity, dominated intellectual life, while liberal and progressive ideas dominated political theory. More and Babbitt reacted against these developments.[6]

Babbitt (1865–1933) had been a student at Harvard under two of the best known mugwump intellectuals, James Russell Lowell and Charles Eliot Norton. An uprooted midwesterner, originally from Ohio, he threw himself into his studies with such intensity that his nickname among the other undergraduates was "the professor." In 1894 he was appointed professor of Romance Languages and Comparative Literature during the long presidency of Charles W. Eliot, which lasted from 1869 to 1909, filling the chair previously held by his teacher Lowell.[7]

Eliot, impressed by the German research universities, had introduced the elective system into American undergraduate education and tried to make the college more scientific, more specialized, and more vocational. Babbitt objected. His first book, *Literature and the American College* (1908), paid tribute to the influence of Norton and made the case for humanistic education and against specialization. In Babbitt's view, specialization warped young men's minds prematurely. He thought of education chiefly as a moral task—that of teaching students the absolute standards and values of civilization. It also required "forming the complete man" while keeping all the moral and intellectual faculties in balance. "Man has gained immensely in his grasp of facts," wrote Babbitt, "but in the meanwhile has become so immersed in their multiplicity as to lose that vision of the One by which his lower self was once overawed and restrained." This reference to the "lower self" embodied an idea that persists through all of Babbitt's work: that the lower or animal side of humans must be disciplined and restrained by the higher, or intellectual, element, through a conscious exercise of the will, what he called the "inner check."[8]

Babbitt disliked modern science not only because it tempted students to specialize but also because it had fostered the fallacious idea that human beings were essentially materialistic, part of nature, and could be understood naturalistically. Science tried to substitute a philosophical monism for the actual dualism proper to the understanding of humanity. Science, in other words, distorted and debased rather than clarified our understanding of humanity.[9]

Hardly less threatening than science and materialism, in his view, was that philosophers since the Renaissance, Rousseau above all, had underestimated the power of human depravity, proposed that men are intrinsically good, and explained evil not as a result of man's moral shortcomings but as a product of the societies in which they lived. Many scholars of Babbitt's own era, notably John Dewey, had been influenced by these ideas, implying that reform of society was more useful than reform of the individual. In successive works Babbitt tried to draw attention back to the individual struggle for mastery over one's own will and to remind readers that what Rousseau saw as the "state of nature" might better be thought of as barbarism.[10]

Not surprisingly, Babbitt was no celebrant of mass democracy. In *Democracy and Leadership* (1924) he argued that good leadership was as important in a democracy as in any other sort of society, but that it was harder to find. "Genuine leaders, good or bad, there will always be, and . . . democracy becomes a menace to civilization when it seeks to evade this truth. The notion in particular that a substitute for leadership may be found in numerical majorities that are supposed to reflect the 'general will' is only a pernicious conceit. In the long run democracy will be judged, no less than other forms of government, by the quality of its leaders, a quality that will depend in turn on the quality of their vision. Where there is no vision, we are told, the people perish; but where there is sham vision, they perish even faster." The temptation to demagogy, to giving the people what they wanted when they wanted, rather than subjecting them to the discipline of the inner check, had never been greater.[11]

Leaders should certainly not be an aristocracy of scientists or technocrats. Neither should they be an aristocracy of artists—too emotionally unrestrained. Neither should they be Nietzschean supermen, whose will to power was the exact opposite of the inner check. Self denial, as usual with Babbitt, was they key. In American history he honored the leadership tradition descending from Washington, Marshall, and Lincoln because it blended the protection of human freedom with the classical ideal of self-restraint, and of not always giving the masses what they wanted.

He correspondingly denigrated the Jeffersonian ideal of direct democracy and radical decentralization. Recent Progressive Era reforms, such as direct election of senators, the initiative, referendum, and recall, he deplored as further concessions to a radical conception of democracy that anyone with an awareness of human history could not justify. And he lamented the remorseless decline of standards in a world that accepted moral relativism and idolized the common man.[12]

Paul Elmer More (1864–1937), like Babbitt, believed in absolute moral and aesthetic standards, warned against excessive confidence in the possibilities of science and deplored the emotional overindulgence of the Romantics. He too believed in the supreme achievement of the ancient Greeks, who provided the best yardstick for measuring newer art and philosophy, and he too argued for philosophical dualism in the study of humankind. Although they were near contemporaries, More described Babbitt as the most important formative influence on his life. Shy and withdrawn, he lacked Babbitt's combative temperament and took criticism hard. He complained to friends that he was simultaneously the least read and most hated author in the United States. As a journalist and editor, and later as a professor at Princeton, he spent part of every year in a rural retreat at Shelburne, New Hampshire, after which he named the long series of critical books for which he is best remembered, *The Shelburne Essays*. They were sufficiently widely admired, despite his self-deprecating joke, to make him a potential Nobel Prize candidate in 1932.[13]

More's humanism, unlike Babbitt's, was explicitly Christian. Attracted early in life by Eastern philosophies and religions, he gradually came to believe that their denial of the ultimate reality of the earth (in Hindu asceticism, for example) led to a neglect of worldly things. The Christian tradition, by contrast, had found ways to encourage an interest in the world, along with an acknowledgement that the world was of proximate, rather than ultimate, significance. Always an anglophile, More admired the Anglican Church for its judicious mix of religious and political elements in a stable, conservative compound. What the state-church Anglicans got right, in his view, the American churches, especially those influenced by the Social Gospel movement, got wrong. They had confused the religious and the worldly virtues. Faith, hope, and charity were religious values, but they were no basis for social policy; here on earth, prudence, courage, and honor were much more necessary. Churches would contribute to the redemption of humankind not by undertaking social work but by creating "a sense of the soul's obligation to a supernatural power."[14]

As a political writer More was chary of democracy and looked for ways to nurture an aristocracy of talent well educated in the classics. He argued in *Aristocracy and Justice* (1915) that the leadership of a propertied elite was indispensable and made the startling claim that "the rights of property are more important than the right to life." A sympathetic biographer explains the assertion in this way: "Human nature, not property, is the cause of greed and injustice. Simple redistribution of property, then, would not make men happy, though it could destroy civilization as we know it. Mere life is a pretty primitive thing, and all that makes it worthwhile, from the simplest material necessity to the highest production of art, is associated with property. Therefore . . . 'to the civilized man the rights of property are more important than the right to life.' " This is, to be sure, a roundabout way of saying that life is best protected not by being the subject of a rights claim but by existing in a society that makes strong property claims. Even so, the sentence was almost gratuitously provocative, given the time and place.[15]

As a literary critic More was interested less in literary form and aesthetics than in the morality embodied in authors' works. He rated more highly writers whose moral effects were benign than those he regarded as wayward geniuses. The Greeks and the eighteenth-century classicists were, accordingly, his favorites. His blind spot, by contrast, was modern literature, and he could find almost nothing good to say of any twentieth-century writing. He dismissed John Dos Passos's *Manhattan Transfer* as "an explosion in a cesspool" and described modern music as "liquefied ugliness, a moral and aesthetic poison gas." Even Mark Twain came under the lash. *Tom Sawyer* might seem harmless enough to you and me, but to More this "victorious liar, lucky vagabond and cunning rebel to authority" was an immoral figure. Such books were "not only enfeebling in their effect on the mind, but actually perverting in their effect on character."[16]

More, like Babbitt, gathered a scattering of admirers. One of them, Norman Foerster (1887–1972), advanced the idea that the two of them were the nucleus of a coherent and growing movement. He published the anthology *Humanism and America* (1930), which included statements from each of them and representative essays in the humanist idiom from other educators and critics. True humanism had never been more necessary, wrote Foerster, than in an America where "the noise and whirl increase, the disillusion and depression deepen," and "the nightmare of Futility stalks before us." Babbitt's and More's work, he believed, would eventually be recognized as the greatest critical writing of the early twentieth century because of its determined preservation of timeless standards. It might, at first glance, seem different from that of the Renaissance humanists, he admitted, but humanism had to respond to new problems in new eras while drawing from the same well of inspiration. "In the Renaissance its great foe was mediaeval otherworldliness; today its great foe is this-worldliness, obsession with physical things and the instincts that bind us to the animal order—in a word, the many forms of naturism that have all but destroyed humane insight, discipline, and elevation." The impulse to preserve tradition and to recognize the distinctiveness of humans over the rest of creation remained the same.[17]

If *Humanism and America* nicely summarized the new humanist outlook, C. Hartley Grattan's *The Critique of Humanism* (1930) constituted a stinging rebuttal. The contributors to this counter-anthology, many of whose names are better remembered today than those of the new humanists themselves, included Edmund Wilson, Malcolm Cowley, Allen Tate, R. P. Blackmur, Yvor Winters, and Lewis Mumford. Some among them, including Grattan himself, a historian, made exactly the kind of exaggerated claims for science and scientific method that the humanists deplored and that today seem excessive. Others made more telling points, such as that the humanists appeared unrestrained in their call for restraint and were apparently devoid of the very intellectual humility for which they argued.[18]

The critics asked: Has the new humanism actually inspired any great, or even noteworthy works of art? Their answer was no. If humanism was to be a viable guide out of society's current woes, surely it would have to win the esteem and assent of creative writers, artists, and musicians, not just that of critics. Otherwise it would remain a sterile academic cult, "the exclusive property of a small sect of schoolmasters so fatuous that they do not hesitate to assign schoolmasters' A's, B's, and

C's in Humanism to 'Homer . . . Plato, Aristotle, Confucius, Buddha . . . [and] . . . Jesus.' " So indeed it seemed, on the strength of *Humanism and America,* which, they said, was nothing but carping criticism based on the unsubstantiated assertion, that the world was getting worse. The new humanists were, almost without exception, intolerant of modern literature and modern art, with no interest in such experiments as Joyce's *Ulysses.* They did not speak well even of Eliot's *The Waste Land,* the era's most famous poem, though its author was among their sympathizers. That they were attracting sympathizers and supporters showed merely that in a complex world "it saves a great deal of anxiety and mental effort, to bow one's head to a traditional authority."[19]

Central also to their criticism of the humanists was the charge of political and sociological naïvete. It was certainly true that art and literature had changed greatly in the two centuries since Rousseau, but that was because society itself had changed greatly. Literature and the values it reflects do not develop in a vacuum but in very particular social and political circumstances, yet the humanists made no comment about the wider world (other than that it was vulgar) and appeared to believe that a sheer act of will could cause humanity to be different, to be better, and to act on behalf of older values. "Instead of attempting to achieve a balance between the individual and the environment which, after all, is the true nature of the problem," wrote Grattan, Babbitt "ignores the environment entirely and concentrates on the individual." Such an approach was as bad as that of a fundamentalist preacher, differing from it "only in the fact that he does not promise a final resolution of all troubles in Heaven." The literary critic Malcolm Cowley added that Babbitt and More had not ranged very widely across their world, had not tried to explain its suffering, and could not hope to address the "millhands of New Bedford and Gastonia" or the "men who tighten a single screw in the automobiles that march along Mr. Ford's assembly belt." They were, in effect, faculty club snobs, carefully excluding all but a handful of the like-minded and disdainful of all that was new in their world.[20]

The new humanism suffered the loss of its two leaders in the 1930s and did not develop further as a movement, though its influence on subsequent conservative intellectuals, especially post–World War II traditionalists like Russell Kirk and Peter Viereck, would be profound. David Hoeveler, their best historian, gives a sense both of their strengths and of their shortcomings in a judicious summary: "With the exception of education they never grappled with the concrete in a manner that would have given flesh and blood to their critique of modern America. The humanists, however, did make an intelligent plea for the priorities of the gifted few and the enlarged arena for the exercise of their talents. In a nation much given to indiscriminate leveling in its official rhetoric, that plea required courage and merited more consideration than it received. But in the end, though the Humanists perceived and effectively outlined much of the problem of democracy, they scarcely began to solve it." He notes that some of their intellectual contemporaries, including the neoorthodox theologian Reinhold Niebuhr, were more successful than the humanists in finding practical applications for unconventional theories about the nature of humankind.[21]

THE SOUTHERN AGRARIANS

The new humanists were a Northeastern intellectual coterie. Another regional intellectual group of the late 1920s, also strongly conservative in outlook, was the Southern Agrarians, centered in Nashville. They too dreaded the effects of vulgar wealth and feared that it threatened the traditional Southern way of life. They published *I'll Take My Stand: The South and the Agrarian Tradition* (1930), which argued for holding on to the South's traditions and folkways and rejecting industrial modernity. This collection sounded many of the distinctive notes that would mark the Southern branch of the conservative movement for the next half-century.

The Agrarians were, like so many figures in American conservative history, a paradoxical group. Arguing for the superiority of farm life, they were intellectuals, not tillers of the earth, and they certainly could not be mistaken for the rural fundamentalists who had gathered around William Jennings Bryan at the Scopes Monkey Trial a few years before. Their leader, Allen Tate, liked the idea of being a farmer-fundamentalist but found in practice that he could get hold of a farm only with a gift from his rich urban brother and couldn't make it pay except by leaving all the actual work to a family of experienced tenant farmers. Three others among the twelve, John Crow Ransom, Donald Davidson, and Robert Penn Warren, were modernist poets like Tate and had been influenced by Ezra Pound and T. S. Eliot; they belonged to a self-conscious intellectual coterie at Vanderbilt University. The other eight were social scientists, historians, and journalists. In varying degrees they tried to reject earlier, wider loyalties (such as the modernist poetry journal *The Fugitive*) and to force themselves to embrace the idea of rural Southern simplicity.[22]

I'll Take My Stand begins with a manifesto, condemning industrial society as unnatural, unstable, and corrosive of tradition and virtue. It was a tragedy that the South had lost the Civil War, wrote the twelve, because that defeat had deprived the nation of a wisdom it could not learn from other sections. In its headlong pursuit of material wealth through industrialization, America was destroying its closeness to nature, the dignity of labor, the integrity of local communities, the mysterious sense of life intrinsic to religion, and the possibilities of real artistic achievement. "We . . . look upon the Communist menace as a menace indeed, but not as a Red one; because it is simply according to the blind drift of our industrial development to expect in America at last much the same economic system as that imposed by violence upon Russia in 1917." Like the American Marxists who enjoyed their greatest vogue in the 1930s, in other words, the Agrarians agreed that the economic base of society affects the cultural superstructure. Unlike the Marxists they were more impressed by the similarities of industrial capitalism to industrial communism than by the differences.[23]

The Agrarians thought of their program as one designed to restore a vigorous humanism, but they were unimpressed by the new humanist critique of modernity proposed at the same time by Babbitt and More; it was too abstract, too remote from the practical concerns of real life. "Genuine humanism was rooted in the agrarian life of the older South. . . . It was not an abstract 'moral check' derived from the classics. . . . We cannot recover our native humanism by adopting some standard of taste that is critical enough to question the contemporary arts but not critical enough to question the social and economic life which is their ground."[24]

John Crow Ransom, in the book's lead essay, set about overturning all the American pieties of his age. Progress is bad; it brutalizes us into constant motion with no apparent destination except perpetual change. Leisure is natural; hard work is alien, but only Southerners really know how to be leisurely; the frontier and the pioneer are aberrations, whereas the settled society is America's greatest achievement. American are obsessed with the "strange idea that the human destiny is not to secure an honorable peace with nature, but to wage an unrelenting war on nature." Above all America is not, or ought not to be, unique. It is part of European civilization and, at its Southern best, is like the old rustic squirearchy of England. Ransom, an Anglophile, had been a Rhodes Scholar and admired English rural life which "long ago came to terms with nature, fixed its roots . . . founded its comfortable institutions, secured its modest prosperity—and then willed the whole in perpetuity to the generations which should come after, in the ingenuous confidence that it would afford them all the essential human satisfactions."[25]

Where Ransom was vague about the details of Southern history, his colleague Frank Owsley, a historian, was specific. The irrepressible conflict of the nineteenth century, he wrote, had not been between Northern freedom and Southern slavery but between factory and farm, "the industrial and commercial civilization of the North and the agrarian civilization of the South." The Civil War in which it culminated had been a double act of Northern aggression, first against the South itself, then against the young minds of rising Southern generations. "The North defeated the South in war, crushed and humiliated it in peace, and waged against it a war of intellectual and spiritual conquest." Certain hard truths must now be recalled despite this double conquest. Liberation of the slaves, for example, had been economically disastrous to the South and dangerous, too, because Reconstruction gave the area over to the "three millions of former slaves, some of whom could still remember the taste of human flesh and the bulk of them hardly three generations removed from cannibalism."[26]

Owsley was openly a racial supremacist who accepted the idea that the races were too different, and the whites too superior, to live together in an open society. Robert Penn Warren, in a chapter devoted to the "negro question," entitled "The Briar Patch," was more circumspect. The twenty-five-year-old Warren, like Ransom, was a Rhodes Scholar and submitted his contribution from England. Admitting that racial prejudice was widespread in the South, he nevertheless reproached black radicals for looking forward to a time when segregation might end, since such a change would provoke violent social upheavals. In line with the book's themes he also denied that the coming of industrial work to the

South would improve blacks' prospects. It might easily worsen them, giving rise to the kind of race riots that had become common in Northern cities when blacks "scabbed" as strike breakers. Farming, on the other hand, was a slow but sure avenue of advancement for poor blacks and poor whites alike.[27]

Andrew Lytle, a Yale-educated dramatist, agreed with Warren that farming was the panacea for all Southerners. Farmers, moreover, should resist the temptation to become "progressive farmers," as government agencies and advertisers urged. They should not mechanize or industrialize their farms, which might look like the avenue to wealth but would actually mean giving themselves over to the enemies of farm life: the bankers, machinery salesmen, and mortgage brokers. After all, "a farm is not a place to growth wealthy; it is a place to grow corn." Lytle's highly sentimentalized portrait of Southern yeoman farmers' lives followed Owsley's pattern by lamenting the catastrophe of the Civil War, to which the shattering of the old elite and all subsequent evils could be traced. Anyone who valued independence should turn against machinery, which was debasing the farm, the hearth, and even the quality of human entertainment. Instead they should emulate their ancestors by producing at home all necessary goods and pleasures. Lytle, with advocacy of this kind, was making a profoundly unhistorical argument. The whole trajectory of American agricultural history had been away from subsistence farming and toward integration in the market. As he and his youthful fellow writers must have anticipated, the practical political effect of the Southern Agrarians was negligible.[28]

Support from a handful of Distributists did little to change the situation. Distributism was a movement inspired by the writings of G. K. Chesterton and Hilaire Belloc in England. Catholic traditionalists, they deplored the centralization of property ownership that seemed to them the chief economic fact of late nineteenth- and early twentieth-century England and the displacement of small, independent property holders by a plutocracy of great wealth. Distributism was the name given their project to return the population to rural districts, to enable ordinary folks once again to own and run their farms, and to turn away from the vast forces of industrial capitalism.[29]

Distributism, whatever its economic, philosophical and religious merits, never drew more than a few hundred supporters, and many of those it did attract were spectacular cranks, like the artist Eric Gill, who practiced incest while his family almost starved in a Distributist commune. Not all, however. Among its more level-headed American devotees was Herbert Agar (1897–1980), a New York–born and New Jersey–educated historian with a gift for colorful writing. Agar, after befriending Chesterton and living for six years among the English Distributists, returned to America in 1934. His book *The People's Choice* (1933), a history of the decline of the presidency in an era of mass democracy, had just won the Pulitzer Prize, making him a welcome recruit to the Agrarian cause. His portrait of Depression-stricken America, *Land of the Free* (1935), increased his reputation and led to the offer of professorships (declined) and an editorship at the *Louisville Courier-Journal* (accepted). The energetic Agar befriended Allen Tate in the hope that together they could create, perhaps as early as the 1936 election, a political reality out of what was, as yet, no more than a literary expression.[30]

Their political plans came to nothing, but Agar and Tate together edited a second volume of essays, *Who Owns America?* (1936), an Agrarian-Distributist attack on economic centralization. Eight of the twelve *I'll Take My Stand* writers contributed again, including Lyle Lanier, Frank Owsley, Donald Davidson, John Crow Ransom, Andrew Lytle, and Robert Penn Warren, but they were now joined by Northerners such as the Ohioan Willis Fisher and Britons such as the Catholic Distributists Douglas Jerrold and Hilaire Belloc. Agar declared that he was writing on behalf of the American dream of independence, permanence, stability, and equality. "Today that dream is derided by two groups: first by the communists . . . second, by the friends of Big Business, who dishonor the dream by saying that it has been realized, that it lies all about us today." In fact monopoly capitalism was the "antithesis of our ideal" because it confronted workers continually with a horrible blend of boredom, insecurity, and fear. This second book was less regional and oriented more toward economics than *I'll Take My Stand* and lacked the earlier collection's attention to the arts and culture.[31]

Reviewers pointed out that it was, for all its earnest marshalling of facts, utopian. It argued for the widespread redistribution of property without explaining how this property could be detached from its current owners, except by the kind of violent revolution the authors abhorred. Agar and Tate also had the misfortune to publish just as their erstwhile friend and supporter Seward Collins, editor of the *American Review,* declared himself a fascist and an admirer of Mussolini and Hitler. Agar and Tate emphatically disagreed with Collins's stance, but their work had appeared often in his journal, and this association cost their cause much of its remaining credibility.[32]

Personal disagreements between Agar and the other Southern Agrarians (who saw him as an interloping outsider) led to more complications. When a sympathetic philanthropist, Chauncy Stillman, offered to finance an Agrarian-Distributist journal, *Free America,* the Agrarians were determined that it should not be edited in New York, whereas the Distributists, who had won the sympathetic attention of Northern groups such as the Catholic Worker Movement, were equally reluctant to see it cross the Mason-Dixon Line. In any event, it began publication in 1937 with support only from the Northern Distributists. Until America entered World War II, the journal carried a wide variety of decentralist and Distributist plans and proposals but was tiny in circulation and insignificant in its effects.[33]

H. L. MENCKEN

A third expression of conservatism in the 1920s, very different in mood and tone from that of either the new humanists or the Agrarians, could be found in The *American Mercury,* a journal edited by H. L. Mencken from 1924 to 1933. It served up a steady diet of elitist views in a distinctively modern American idiom and specialized in ridiculing the era's pieties. This was a conservatism strong on tough-mindedness but weak, very weak, on reverence for tradition. Mencken (1880–1956), a Baltimore journalist and one of the two or three most popular American writers of the 1920s, belongs to the tradition of Sumner and the libertarians, whereas the humanists and Agrarians were Europe-oriented traditionalists.

His *American Mercury* mocked all forms of progressivism, social service, liberalism, and moral uplift, denounced the vestiges of Puritanism in American life, and took a skeptical, amused view of politics. Explaining and situating his journal's role, Mencken said that "there must be room in the middle for an educated Toryism—the true Disraelian brand. It exists everywhere but in the United States it has no voice." The audience he sought was one of intelligent, educated urbanites; for them he delighted in undermining reverence for American pieties, especially the nation's agrarian traditions.[34]

Mencken, German by descent and sympathies, had opposed American entry into World War I in 1917 and, as a result, lost much of the audience he had first built up as a critic at *The Smart Set*. The experience of being considered a possible enemy agent, and of being spied on at home, turned him sharply against government in general and nourished in him a special detestation of President Wilson. So did the triumph, in 1918, of Prohibition. He wrote: "Between Wilson and his brigades of informers, spies, volunteer detectives, perjurers and complaisant judges, and the Prohibitionists and their messianic delusion, the liberty of the citizen has pretty well vanished in America. In two or three years, if the thing goes on, every third American will be a spy upon his fellow citizens." He remained an outspoken critic of Prohibition throughout the twenties and early thirties.[35]

The new humanists loved America's Puritan heritage and sought to revive its "inner check." To Mencken, by contrast, Puritanism was despicable in both its religious form and its social consequences. He dismissed the new humanism as the "natural and inevitable refuge of all timorous and third-rate men," and More and Babbitt as authors of "vague and witless blather." He was also a ruthless critic of organized religion, especially evangelical Protestantism, as he showed in a caustic account of the Scopes Monkey Trial in Dayton, Tennessee, in 1925.[36]

Just as he denounced popular religious figures like William Jennings Bryan, so Mencken denounced the rituals of democratic politics. He saw democracy as a political system based on envy. It made mediocrities famous by encouraging them to flatter the "mob." He was as reluctant as Shakespeare's Coriolanus to speak well of common folk. "The existence of most human beings is of absolutely no significance to history or to human progress. They live and die as anonymously and as nearly uselessly as so many bullfrogs or houseflies. They are, at best, undifferentiated slaves upon an endless assembly line, and at worst they are robots who leave their mark upon time only by occasionally falling into the machinery, and so incommoding their betters." He also rejected as a romantic fallacy the idea that "there is a mystical merit, an esoteric and ineradicable rectitude, in the man at the bottom of the scale." The idea was, in fact, the delusion of upper-class sentimentalists but was constantly belied as "stale Christian bilge" to anyone who knew the lower classes firsthand.[37]

If democracy was bad, socialism was much worse. It was based on two delusions about human nature: first, that people were equal, and second, that they were selfless. "A Socialist is simply a man suffering from an overwhelming compulsion to believe what is not true." Mencken wrote that Eugene Debs, the long-time Socialist Party leader and presidential candidate, was "unquestionably wrong, both in his naïve belief in the Marxian rumble-bumble and in his sentimental opposition to war." But at least Debs was "honest, and a gentleman." The Bolsheviks who had come to power in the new Soviet Union were much worse. "If [Communism] manages to survive, the Russian masses will be . . . enslaved beyond hope of redemption; they will also be convinced that their slavery is an heroic and even swell estate; they will be slaves by conviction as well as in fact."[38]

Not being a practical politician, Mencken did not feel obliged to provide alternatives, but it is clear from scattered remarks that he favored government by an aristocratic elite. Aristocracies, as he told it, are born to rule, do not share the claustrophobic fears of the masses, offer leadership in war, and are creative and broad-minded. America had begun to develop an aristocracy in the Old South, he argued, only to have it annihilated in the Civil War. The Northern business plutocracy that rose afterward was *not* an aristocracy. Its position was based on money alone—individuals of great wealth were really just members of the ignorant mob who happened to have gotten rich.[39]

Mencken's popularity depended on the widespread prosperity of the 1920s. He flattered middle-class readers into believing that they, like him, were urbane and sophisticated, no longer trammeled by old religious and social superstitions. His vogue declined in the 1930s, however, when many of his opinions came to seem objectionable. His mockery of the common people seemed much less palatable in the Great Depression when they were broke, unemployed, and terribly vulnerable. Besides, Mencken was as dismissive about President Franklin Roosevelt, the popular central political figure of the 1930s, as he had been about presidents Harding and Coolidge.

THE GREAT DEPRESSION AND THE NEW DEAL

Herbert Hoover (1874–1964) won the presidential election of 1928 and was inaugurated in the spring of 1929. Later that year he was forced to react to the Wall Street Crash and then to the catastrophic downward economic spiral that followed. His reaction seemed inadequate to most voters, and they pushed him brusquely out of the White House in the general election of 1932. Roosevelt's New Deal, in the ensuing years, established a far greater role for the federal government than ever before and brought it to bear directly on businesses and citizens in the states. An overwhelming reelection victory in 1936 emboldened Roosevelt to continue the experiment.

The New Deal was innovative in at least five ways. First, it provided federal relief and work programs. Second, it ratcheted up federal supervision and regulation of businesses, creating the Securities and Exchange Commission to oversee Wall Street and urging all businesses to collaborate according to the codes of the National Recovery Administration—a procedure that previously would have been illegal under the Sherman Anti-Trust Act. Third, it put the federal government directly into business, building dams and electricity generators under the guidance of the Tennessee Valley Authority. Fourth, it paid subsidies to farmers, under the Agricultural Adjustment Act, to restrict output as a way of raising prices. And fifth, it assured trade unions a permanent and legally protected role in the economy under the terms of the Wagner Act.[40]

The program was controversial at the time, and it has been controversial ever since. Some historians understand the New Deal as a coordinated plan to rescue American capitalism, others regard it as a set of ad hoc experiments to find ways of reducing unemployment and stimulating recovery, and still others regard it as a project to transform permanently the balance of power between state and federal governments, augmenting government control over all aspects of national life. It certainly marked a transformation in the meaning of liberalism. Until then the term *liberal* had connoted giving citizens the greatest possible liberty to pursue their own concerns while minimizing government. From the New Deal onward, liberalism came to mean assigning an ever *larger* role to government in promoting equality and protecting citizens' health, welfare, education, employment, and access to justice.[41]

Conservatives from both major parties were shocked at FDR's willingness to transform the traditional balance of power between state and the federal governments, at his readiness to create deficits by spending more money than taxation could raise annually, and at the idea that the federal government might, under some circumstances, offer direct relief to unemployed citizens. Opponents of the New Deal rallied around Hoover, who became a conservative standard-bearer in the 1930s. He was an heir of the Progressive movement rather than a member of the Republican Old Guard, however, and had been closer to Wilson than to Lodge on the Versailles and League questions in 1919 and 1920. A self-made mining engineer and entrepreneur, he had distinguished himself during and after World War I as a formidably efficient humanitarian, bringing food aid to millions of starving people in Central and Eastern Europe. He was by far the most widely traveled of all presidents and had seen, firsthand, the horrific human impact of war and revolution. Despite all this, he was in person shy and reserved, lacking the lively gregariousness and charisma of most successful politicians; he had found the electoral office of president much less to his liking than earlier administrative appointments.[42]

A year after leaving office, Hoover published *The Challenge to Liberty* (1934), a wide-ranging attack on the New Deal and its philosophical presuppositions. Roosevelt's programs were not expressions of liberalism, he argued, but an *attack* on the foundations of liberalism, the "great philosophy of society." Why? Because human liberty, the central tenet of liberalism, could survive only in a society where citizens were not coerced by government regulation and freely made their own economic decisions. The industry codes of the National Recovery Administration were therefore assaults on liberty. True liberals should dedicate themselves to preserving liberty even against government policies, like FDR's, which claimed a benign intent.[43]

Hoover regarded the centralization of power in the New Deal as a sinister departure from American tradition, likening it to the centralization of power then taking place in fascist Italy and Nazi Germany. He reminded audiences that assaults on liberty often start innocuously. "In Central Europe the march of Socialist or Fascist dictatorships and their destruction of liberty did not set out with guns and armies," he told the Republican convention of 1936. "Dictators began their ascent to the seats of power through the elections provided by liberal institutions. . . . They offered the mirage of Utopia to those in distress. They flung the poison of class hatred." To his audience, many of them stung by FDR's scapegoating of the rich and by what they saw as his creation of false hopes among the poor, the parallels seemed obvious.[44]

"The American people should thank Almighty God for the Constitution and the Supreme Court," declared Hoover in 1936, by which time the Court had overturned some of the most far-reaching New Deal legislation. No wonder he was alarmed anew, after FDR's second inauguration, by the president's "court-packing" plan. Roosevelt proposed to add new members to the Court, up to a maximum of fifteen, whenever a sitting justice reached the age of seventy. To Hoover this proposal was a barefaced attempt to politicize the court in FDR's favor and further evidence of his incipient dictatorship. "He wants [a Supreme Court] that will revise the Constitution so it will mean what he wishes it to mean." Hoover was heartened to discover that many Democrats, as well as his fellow Republicans, rose up in protest against the plan, forcing FDR to abandon it.[45]

In his speeches and writings throughout the 1930s Hoover spoke consistently for liberty, voluntarism, dispersed powers, self-help, and deference to American political traditions. His reputation as a Progressive from earlier decades, however, kept him at arm's length from another anti–New Deal group, the Liberty League. The League, founded in 1934 "to teach the necessity of respect for the rights of persons and property," and funded by DuPont, General Motors, and U.S. Steel, was never able to shake the reputation of being merely a rich businessmen's anti–New-Deal, anti-high-tax lobby. Roosevelt joked that it was the "millionaires' union," and Hoover also felt it was too obviously interested in preserving class privilege. One historian, noting the shift in meaning of the terms *liberal* and *conservative,* describes the Liberty League as the "mouthpiece of organized American conservatism" in the 1930s, whose role by then was to make "a defense of nineteenth-century individualism and liberalism." By the 1930s the defense of old-style or classical liberalism—the heritage of Adam Smith and John Stuart Mill—had become a form of conservatism.[46]

An early foreign policy initiative of the New Deal also alarmed Hoover and most other conservatives: the decision to give diplomatic recognition to the Soviet Union. Ever since the Russian Revolution the U.S. government had declined to normalize relations. Hoover, though he had been involved in feeding starving Russians in the early 1920s, refused to "lend respectability to a regime characterized by brutal oppression." In 1938 he made a tour of Europe and viewed with dismay the advance of dictatorships and the defeat of democracy. Of Stalin, who was then exterminating his former allies, the old Bolsheviks, Hoover wrote, "Marxian socialism is a dying faith. . . . The gigantic experiment in socialism in Russia is now devouring its own children and shedding rivers of blood." It, too, was becoming "a sort of Fascist regime."[47]

Hoover's value as a conservative standard-bearer was limited by the fact that he was widely blamed for the Depression (uprooted and homeless people called their shantytowns "Hoovervilles"). Robert Taft of Ohio, by contrast, was untainted by defeat. His anti–New Deal speeches beginning in 1935, and his election to the U.S. Senate in 1938, bore witness to a conservative recovery in politics. Taft (1889–1953) was the son of ex-president William Howard Taft. Sober, humorless, hard-working, and dedicated to the tradition of limited government and the free market, Taft was no more a typical politician than Hoover (even a sympathetic biographer says that his speeches, full of statistics, were "clumsy, dry, and disputatious"), but he rose quickly to leadership of Senate Republicans through sheer ability and hard work, often in alliance with conservative Southern Democrats.[48]

Taft agreed with Hoover that the New Deal was alien to American tradition and was philosophically akin to the European dictatorships. The idea of a centrally directed economy, toward which the U.S. seemed to be moving, made impossible demands on the men running it, even if they were selfless and dedicated. It was, Taft declared in an early speech, "absolutely contrary to the whole American theory on which this country was founded, and which has actually made it the most prosperous country in the world. It is inconsistent with democratic government. . . . Communism, Fascism, and Hitlerism have destroyed a system like ours in many European countries, and substituted a form of despotic socialism. . . . As far as we can judge, socialism will not work. There is no man and no group of men intelligent enough to coordinate and control the infinitely numerous and complex problems involved in the production, consumption, and daily lives of one hundred and twenty million individualistic and educated people." The federal government's development as a major and permanent part of the economy seemed to him particularly odious. The Tennessee Valley Authority, for example, was a government-owned business competing directly with private companies in several states, but it had an unfair advantage over them because it was backed by all the coercive power of the central government. To the extent that the New Deal aimed to replace the free market with a planned economy it was anathema.[49]

ALBERT JAY NOCK AND RALPH ADAMS CRAM IN THE 1930S

Albert Jay Nock (1870–1945) is to the 1930s what Mencken was to the 1920s. A caustic humorist, an iconoclast, and an elitist who despised democracy, he came to think of himself as a member of the "remnant," the handful of truly civilized men whose fate was to live among the half-educated barbarians of mass society. In the early 1920s Nock had been editor of the short-lived weekly magazine *The Freeman* (1920–24). It was nonpartisan and included a distinguished roster of contributors from all points on the political compass, including Van Wyck Brooks, Lewis Mumford, Bertrand Russell, John Dos Passos, Charles Beard, and Thorstein Veblen. If their contributions shared a common ideal, it was in the importance and dignity of the individual.[50]

Once *The Freeman* went out of business, Nock began writing for Mencken's *American Mercury*. As his biographer says, "His piquant use of English, combining earthy vernacular with eloquent Victorianisms, and his command of the hot flush and hostile snort, perfectly suited the *Mercury*." The rapid growth of the federal government in the 1930s prompted him to write a book-length attack on statism, which he believed to be menacing Europe and America alike. The result, *Our Enemy the State* (1935), argued that intervention by the state, even if benign in intention, is always coercive against citizens, always economically unproductive, and always dangerous to liberty. It has become a classic for American libertarians.[51]

A few years later Nock followed up with an intellectual autobiography, *Memoirs of a Superflous Man* (1943). It offers a vivid, outrageous, and amusing summary of his ideas about politics, economics, education, and religion from the vantage point of old age, and it, too, has attained cult status among conservatives. William F. Buckley, Jr., read it as a Connecticut schoolboy and at once declared it to be his favorite book. The crucial moment in Nock's political education came, he writes, when he read an *American Mercury* article by the architect Ralph Adams Cram, "Why We Do Not Behave Like Human Beings," which saved him from a growing tendency to hate nearly everybody. It showed him that most "creatures having the physical attributes which put them in the category of *homo sapiens*" are not really people at all: "They are merely the subhuman raw material out of which the occasional human being is produced." "Since then," he continued, "I have found myself quite unable either to hate anybody or to lose patience with anybody." After all, "one has a great affection for one's dogs, even when one sees them reveling in tastes and smells that are unspeakably odious." But that doesn't make one hate the dogs or try to change them—that's just the way they are. Likewise with the masses around him.[52]

Memoirs of a Superfluous Man expects of its readers a good knowledge of the classics and cites witticisms in Greek, Latin, and medieval French without translation. It presupposes familiarity with Rabelais's *Gargantua and Pantagruel* and the complete works of Matthew Arnold, Henry David Thoreau, and Herbert Spencer. Like the new humanism it exalts the classics and denigrates contemporary literature for what Nock saw as its excessive preoccupation with contemporary social problems. Astonishingly uninformative about Nock's actual life (he makes no mention of having been married, nor of having two sons, nor of his years in the clergy), it makes the argument that the mid-twentieth century has no place for a man of his abilities and beliefs; that he is in every way superfluous. Nock took on most of the interwar era's conventional beliefs and inverted them. He denied, for example, that universal literacy was desirable. On the contrary, it had the effect of degrading intellectual standards and impoverishing the quality of literature. Gresham's Law (that bad money in circulation drives out the good) was as applicable to literature as to currency. "Within my lifetime the country became largely literate, thus opening up an immense market made up of persons who were unable to read but . . . were able to pass literary produce through their minds. As this market widened, the satisfaction of it became increasingly profitable, and therefore the best energies of publishers, dragooned under the iron hand of Gresham's law, were bent that way." Universal literacy was also bad, Nock added, because it increased the reach and potency of advertising and propaganda: "It enables scoundrels to beset, dishevel and debauch such intelligence as is in the power of the vast majority of mankind to exercise," enabling "mediocrity and sub-mediocrity to run rampant, to the detriment of both intelligence and taste."[53]

The masses, then, had sullied literature. What about politics? As a child Nock's family had lived for a while in Brooklyn, and his first exposure to democratic politics was at the "Wigwam" of the nearby Tammany Hall machine. Witnessing its workings taught him, Nock wrote, that democratic politics are vulgar, debased, and disgusting. "A decent person could find no place in politics . . . for the forces of ignorance, brutality and indecency would outnumber him ten to one." Elections were spectacles in which greedy candidates ("dreadful swine") pandered to the masses' prejudices in exchange for their votes, a process lubricated by bribes and booze. Nor was politicians' actual work any more edifying. The principal work of Congress now was forcibly to extract money from ordinary citizens and give it to favored clients and corporations. The process was parasitic, abusive of liberty, and unproductive.[54]

Ralph Adams Cram, the Gothic architect whom we met in chapter 5 and whose essay "Why We Do Not Behave like Human Beings" had such a profound effect on Nock, was an equally outspoken critic of mass democracy. Nineteenth-century Americans, wrote Cram in this essay, had falsely believed that society moves forward and upward implacably by a process of progressive evolution, such that the "just plain man [of today] was equal to, if not better than the great few of past ages." They were wrong! On the contrary, said Cram, the greatest achievements in human history were the *earliest,* not the most recent, and were always the achievements of a tiny minority. The vast majority was scarcely different from the ancient Neolithic rabble, "mammals of unpleasant habits, indifferently covered with hair" who "dwelt untidily in caves." History, Cram continued, was for the most part a "bloody riot of cruelty, greed, and lust," extenuated only by the handful of brilliant men and women whom history honored—he listed thirty names including Plato, Buddha, Confucius, Dante, Leonardo, Shakespeare, Washington, and John Adams. In other words, "we do not behave like human beings because most of us do not fall within that classification." Further, "they of the great list behave like our ideal of the human being; they of the ignominious sub-stratum do not, because they are not."[55]

Cram admired the "old selective aristocratic Republic" that America had once been, "controlled and directed by men of tradition, education, inherited culture and exalted ideals." This elite had "produced such noble instruments of government as the Constitution of the United States and, for a certain length of time . . . it fulfilled the high anticipations of its creators." That republic had, tragically, suffered "destruction at the hands of the new forces that had been let loose through the election of Andrew Jackson, and that . . . hold control even until today." Advocates of mass democracy had deluded themselves with ideas of human equality and human perfectibility, with catastrophic consequences. Now a vast but ignorant proletariat was coming to power; its most unscrupulous members had risen to wealth as captains of industry, but they were as ignorant of real culture and beauty as their poor factory-worker brethren. No wonder the world was in crisis.[56]

In his own area of expertise, architecture and the related arts, Cram was an articulate critic of modernism. Admitting that some modern artists had brilliantly captured the spirit of their age (he mentioned Matisse, Cézanne, and Rodin), he lamented that so many of their imitators had picked up what was the worst rather than the best of their innovations, and in doing so had cut off the lifeline of continuity with the long tradition of Western art. He thought of art not as the work of individual artistic geniuses but as the representation of a society's spirit. "Art is . . . an expression not of the personal reactions of highly specialized individuals but of something that is almost communal, even racial, in its nature. This is true; if it were not I should reject it as my subject for I have scant sympathy with that entirely modern view of art which makes the artist a rebel against constituted society, an abnormal phenomenon, feeding upon his inner self, cut off from the life of his fellows, and issuing his aesthetic manifestos in flaming defiance. . . . Not so did the art of Greece, of Byzantium, of the Middle Ages come into being and relate itself to life." In architecture as in painting some modern works were excellent—he gave the example of the Empire State Building. Too many others, alas, were monumental but soulless. Egotistical architects, besotted with the idea of their own genius, asserted themselves without consideration for the setting or the human scale of their work. Most skyscrapers "have nothing to do with man; their scarps and tall cliffs crush him and his soul." To Cram, as to Henry James, skyscrapers were a potent symbol of America at its worst.[57]

In 1936, at the age of seventy, Cram published his autobiography, ending it with a lament for the sickness of his society, "capitalistic, industrial, technocratic, materialistic." The world was disfigured by "Dictatorships, New Deals, Totalitarian States [and] Proletarian Autocracies," all of which, under the leadership of "second rate proletarian minds" like Hitler's, were making the world worse, not better. His only consolation was that the human spirit would eventually re-create civilization. Artists, meanwhile, must endeavor to prevent the transition from this dying civilization to the new one from taking as long, and involving so much wretchedness, as had the transition from Rome to the high Middle Ages.[58]

EUROPEAN PROBLEMS

The new humanists, the Southern Agrarians, and the traditionalists all took for granted that the United States was part of a venerable European civilization. George Santayana took the same view, while making the further, humbling point that America was in many respects a cultural backwater with only the most cramped and limited understanding of this civilization's riches and resources. Like Mencken he thought of Puritanism more as a burden than a blessing—the enemy of real civilization. Early in the century, Santayana, Spanish by birth but American by education, had been a philosophy professor at Harvard (a faculty colleague of Irving Babbitt). Wealthy through inheritance and through successful writing, he was able to give up his post in 1912, after which he lived mainly in Europe, while continuing to make shrewd observations about the American scene.[59]

In Santayana's *The Last Puritan* (1936), a superb novel set in pre–World War I America, his protagonist Oliver Arden is weighed down by an overdeveloped sense of duty, which poisons most of his relationships with others. Successful as a student and athlete, and rich, too, he ought to be the ideal young American, but the burden of a Puritan heritage, embodied in the character of his repulsive mother, inhibits him at every turn. His ineffectual father knew what he was letting himself in for on marrying her and reflected: "I don't ask to be happy: I want to be at peace. If I must let some Juggernaut car crush my bones, let it be the old homely steamroller of traditional Puritanism. From earliest childhood I know its crunching sound." This Puritanism is no longer a matter of religion (the family are atheists), just a matter of life-destroying routine that has become utterly selfish. Santayana, like Henry James a few years before, depicted Europeans as more cultivated, more cynical, and better equipped to understand, enjoy, and exploit their world. His two European characters, Jim Darnley and Mario Van Der Weyer, like Oliver but find him priggish and intolerant; readers are tempted to sympathize with them despite their lack of scruples.[60]

But Europe in the early 1930s, however, had problems of its own much more serious than the burden of Puritanism. A second Spanish writer of the era to win a wide conservative audience was Jose Ortega y Gasset, author of *The Revolt of the Masses* (1930; English translation, 1932). Ortega, a philosophy professor in Madrid and a member of Parliament in the frail Spanish republic of the early 1930s, viewed with alarm the growing influence of the masses, men and women who, he said, did not understand their world, even while thoughtlessly enjoying it, and who did not care to excel. These apathetic and undisciplined masses were degrading culture and transforming the structure of Europe by displacing the aristocracies that historically had provided leadership and discipline. They demoralized the old regimes, making them vulnerable to dictatorial revolutions, as the rise of Stalin and Mussolini made only too clear. Ortega's *Revolt of the Masses* was to become a vital text for post–World War II American conservatives and anticommunists.[61]

The Great Depression and the apparent failure of liberal capitalism prompted many Americans to consider radical alternatives in the 1930s and to wonder whether the new European panaceas might work on this side of the Atlantic. Communism and fascism both attracted interest. The American Communist Party, though always small, was more active and influential in that decade than in any other. Meanwhile, as John Diggins has shown in his study of the American response to Mussolini, Americans were trying to work out what fascism was. As we look back to the 1930s with knowledge of what happened in the 1940s, we are likely to be dismayed to discover that some Americans were attracted to fascism. But, as Diggins says, the term was vague and protean, especially in the 1920s and early 1930s. To some it looked like a militant form of anti-communism, to others its economics marked a revival of the old guild system, and to yet others it was chiefly a way of asserting national pride in the face of the Great Depression.[62]

American conservatives of various types speculated that Italy's experiment might offer a viable solution to America's crisis. Albert Jay Nock was totally opposed to it, as an attack on liberty and free enterprise. Seward Collins, editor of the *American Review*, on the other hand, warmly embraced it as the only adequate response to emergency conditions. Irving Babbitt speculated that America might need a Mussolini of its own to forestall the rise of an American Lenin. The Edmund Burke scholar and Catholic convert Ross Hoffman, who visited Rome in the mid-1930s, was briefly attracted to fascism. He feared that America's "anti-authoritarian principles" had "brought about the wreckage of modern society" and that a "constructive revolution in behalf of authority, order and justice" was now essential.[63]

America's most enthusiastic advocate of fascism was Lawrence Dennis (1893–1977), a World War I army veteran and economic journalist. He explained why in his book *The Coming American Fascism* (1936). He believed the New Deal had not gone far enough in centralizing the economy. Complete centralization and rational economic planning could be achieved *without* the communist resort to class warfare. Banks and corporations ought to be nationalized, members of Congress should represent different vocations rather than different geographical areas, and sharply progressive taxation should be instituted to reduce social inequalities. A skilled elite would manage the whole process, ensuring that America achieved full employment and economic self-sufficiency. The book enjoyed respectful reviews, even in such responsible papers as the *New York Times*, partly because this version of fascism was not blighted by racism, conspiracy theories, or aggressive expansionism. Whether there was anything conservative about Dennis's program, however, is doubtful. He thought of fascism, and of Hitler's National Socialism, as statist movements of the political left.[64]

Nazi aggression in Central Europe soon discredited Lawrence Dennis's advocacy of fascism for America. It also prompted debate among America's scattered and poorly organized conservatives. Many of them, including such leaders as Hoover and Taft, believed that if a new European war broke out, America should remain neutral. Their view had a long American lineage, dating back to Washington's farewell address, the early republic's disengagement from European power struggles, and its decision not to participate in the League of Nations after World War I.[65]

Hitler's terrifying increase in power, however, changed the geopolitical landscape. The Nazi conquest of Poland, Denmark, Norway, Holland, Belgium, and France in quick succession in 1939 and 1940 prompted some conservative isolationists to have second thoughts. Herbert Agar was one. From being a leading advocate of small-government and Distributist-style decentralization in the mid-1930s, he had come by 1940 to believe that the future of civilization itself was at stake and that only the timely use of American power against the Nazis could save it. He joined the interventionists.[66]

Other conservative isolationists stuck to their principles between 1939 and 1941 and founded the America First Committee, an anti-intervention pressure group. Their best-known spokesman was the aviator Charles Lindbergh, who damaged the political credibility of his cause by making an anti-Semitic speech in the fall of 1941. Their leading sympathizers in Congress were Senator Robert Taft and Congressman Hamilton Fish. Taft pointed out that World War I had *not* been the war to end all wars and had not made the world safe for democracy. It had, to the contrary, led to the creation of "more extreme dictatorships than the world had seen for many days." Taft, already dismayed by the rapid growth of federal power under the New Deal, believed that America, by joining the war, would complete the transformation of the Roosevelt presidency into a dictatorship. To win, America might have to succumb to "an absolute arbitrary government in Washington," whereby the federal government would "take over business and regulate every detail of private and commercial life."[67]

The isolationists were certainly not indifferent to the European crisis. They agreed that victory for Hitler in Europe would be deeply regrettable, but, for America at least, it would not be mortal—the military technology for a transatlantic invasion did not exist. Better to see Hitler victorious than to see America itself first transformed into a dictatorship. The libertarian historian Justin Raimondo remarks: "The isolationist old right represented a distinctly *American* phenomenon which owed nothing to the Old World, and was, in all essential ways, the exact opposite of its European counterpart. It was a nationalism of an unprecedented kind, based not on blood and soil and the need to expand but on a tendency toward introversion, an impulse to draw back from the world and its endless quarrels."[68]

In the decades between the world wars, as earlier, American conservatism took various forms. In an age of modernism and relativism, it tended toward moral absolutism and tried to reassert older standards of right and wrong. The new humanists rejected science for its restricted theory of knowledge and abandoned philosophical materialism in favor of a dualism that understood humans as eternally at war against their own lower nature. They asserted absolute moral and aesthetic standards, preached self-denial, and invoked the austere classical ideal of the balanced, self-restraining individual. The Southern Agrarians were absolutists too. They equated the South with all they considered good: the earth, farming, religion, leisure, and the wisdom that comes from the experience of defeat. The North, by contrast, was in their eyes a personification of all that was shallow, false, and destructive; a zone of industry, finance, frenetic activity, relativism, and the delusion of progress. Neither group, despite the eloquence of their rhetoric, had anything to offer by way of a political program.

Mencken, by contrast, was a modern conservative and was as ready as William Graham Sumner to do away with tradition. He was impatient with everything rural, scoffed at traditional American religion for its tendency to anti-intellectualism and sentimentality, and was fully reconciled to a world of experts, machines, and cities. An unabashed elitist, he thought most citizens too stupid to play a significant role in public life and berated them for clinging to old superstitions and unexamined Puritan prejudices. Cram and Nock, likewise, saw far more harm than good springing from popular democracy and denied categorically the idea of human equality.

Different again was the conservatism of the anti–New Deal politicians. Hoover and Taft both came from the Progressive wing of the Republican Party but saw in FDR's innovations a grave threat to American constitutional government. The centralization of federal power, they feared, would undermine citizens' economic and political independence while giving too much coercive authority to bureaucrats. Roosevelt's court-packing plan of 1937 was especially ominous to Hoover; he saw it as a direct attack on judicial independence and perhaps as the prelude to a

European-style dictatorship. From our vantage point, it is clear that FDR was no Mussolini, but in a world where democracies were failing everywhere and dictators rising, Republican alarms were perhaps understandable. No wonder some conservative isolationists opposed American entry into World War II out of fear that it would enable Roosevelt to complete his subversion of balanced government and make himself an American-style dictator.

CHAPTER SEVEN

The New Conservatism, 1945–1964

THE TRIUMPH OF WORLD WAR II was the defeat of Nazi Germany and Imperial Japan. The tragedy of World War II was that the only way to defeat one ruthless tyrant, Hitler, was by forming an alliance with another, Stalin. The Anglo-American-Soviet alliance during the war was full of strains and mutual suspicions. No sooner had the Allies overthrown the Third Reich than they began to fall out. Stalin believed that the Americans had betrayed him by postponing the Second Front (D-Day), finally engaging on continental Europe only in the summer of 1944, by which time German and Russian armies had been locked in lethal combat for three years. American policy makers, conversely, believed that the Stalin who had made an alliance of convenience with Hitler in 1939 was not a "free world" leader to be trusted and that he had deceived them at Yalta, falsely promising to restore self-determination and democracy in the lands his armies liberated from German occupation. They watched with dismay as he colonized and impoverished Eastern Europe in 1945–46, snuffing out all political opposition and installing puppet regimes. So quickly did relations between the victors sour that no general treaty ever settled the war's remaining issues. Hot war against Germany turned rapidly into cold war against the Soviet Union.

The war had borne witness to a profound transformation inside the United States. After years of Depression-era unemployment, the economy had boomed, generating tens of thousands of high-wage jobs, sending the unemployment rate to record low levels, drawing millions of women into manufacturing work for the first time, and greatly expanding government control and surveillance of the economy. The great fear for nearly all Americans as the war ended was that Depression conditions would return.

Only after World War II did a genuine American conservative movement come into existence, the word *conservative* now being used proudly and self-consciously. It brought together a variety of interests and enthusiasms, of which militant anticommunism, free-market libertarianism, social and religious traditionalism, and opposition to statist liberalism were the most important. Scattered, few in number, almost as philosophically divided as the predecessors from whom they drew inspiration, the new conservatives might never have become a coherent group, still less have converted their ideas into political action, had it not been for the leadership of an exceptional young writer and editor, William F. Buckley, Jr. (b. 1925). In 1955 he founded *National Review* and turned it into a gathering place for conservatives of many different styles and temperaments. He publicized conservatism there, in books, and in a syndicated newspaper column, becoming a first-rate debater and television speaker. By 1960 he had made himself the face and voice of American conservatism.[1]

LIBERTARIANS

At first the conservative movement depended on a few individuals and the books they wrote, eight or ten of which have remained from mid-century almost to the present on nearly every conservative's reading list. First came Friedrich von Hayek's *The Road to Serfdom* (1944), a surprise best seller in Britain, then an even better seller in America. Hayek (1899–1992) had been born and raised in Vienna, had fought in World War I with the Austro-Hungarian Army, and had become a professor of economics at the London School of Economics from 1931. Alarmed at the rise of government intervention in the economies of the Western democracies, he wrote *The Road to Serfdom* during World War II as a philosophical defense of free-market capitalism.[2]

Fascism and Nazism, he argued, were forms of economic collectivism and grew logically out of socialism, which had been authoritarian from the outset. Hitler's National Socialism, in other words, really was a type of socialism, a movement of the left, not the right. No wonder so many prominent fascist leaders, like Mussolini in Italy and Oswald Mosley in Britain, had begun their political careers as leftists before making the switch. Fascists and Nazis, like socialists and communists, aimed to consign all economic initiatives to state planners. Central economic planning, however, prevented entrepreneurship, reduced innovation, and stifled creativity. It also drastically curtailed ordinary citizens' freedom.[3]

Denying that some malign quality in the German people had led to Nazism, Hayek insisted that the logic of socialism, which had been developing there since the late nineteenth century, led straight to this kind of total politics. Let Britain and America make sure that it did not also happen to them; otherwise, men and women of goodwill would unwittingly subvert the "basic ideas on which Western civilization has been built." Economic freedom, Hayek believed, was the precondition of all other freedoms. Societies that rewarded individual initiative had made phenomenal accomplishments in science and technology over the last three hundred years, as well as vastly enriching themselves.[4]

Hayek conceded that government should play a limited role in enforcing contracts, regulating hours of work, and safeguarding workplaces. It should not, however, try to plan production and distribution, and it certainly should not try to prevent competition. The British government imposed far-reaching controls on industry during World War II, as he was writing the book, while the American government extended regulations established during the New Deal. Continue these trends, Hayek lamented, and you will soon live like the German and Russian people under totalitarianism, a form of modern serfdom.[5]

But is it not vexing to submit to the invisible hand of the market, to forces you cannot fully understand? Yes, said Hayek; hence the perennial temptation to seek a rational alternative. The reality of this alternative, however, means submitting to the power of others, which is not better but worse. All of history shows us that people are always self-interested, so that life in a planned society gives power to the planners to govern as *they* see fit. No matter their protestations of selflessness and high-mindedness, they will plan what *they* see as the good society and then impose it on those around them, at the cost of freedom. Life in a planned society, moreover, is morally degrading. Collectivism takes away individuals' opportunity to demonstrate their moral integrity. All the great Anglo-Saxon virtues—independence, self-reliance, initiative, voluntarism, tolerance of difference, and suspicion of power—would disappear under collectivism. Already in the 1940s Britain had begun to despise the qualities and virtues for which it had long been most admired abroad.[6]

Hayek had studied in Vienna under Ludwig von Mises (1883–1973); the two of them made up the core of the American branch of the Vienna School, which aimed to revive the reputation of free-market capitalism in the face of Marxism. As early as 1922, in *Socialism,* Von Mises had argued that socialist economies cannot work, because without a free market there are no genuine prices. Prices reflect fluctuations in supply and demand and act as a way of allocating resources toward or away from certain economic activities. Without them, economic planners are reduced to guessing which commodities are in high demand and which are overabundant, and they cannot possibly have access to enough information, quickly enough, to make appropriate decisions. Socialism is bound, accordingly, to be both inefficient and autocratic.[7]

Von Mises, like Hayek, went into exile when the Nazis took over Austria. Jewish by descent, he was regarded as a curiosity among his contemporaries. Hayek remarked that "a Jewish intellectual who justified capitalism appeared to most as some sort of monstrosity, something unnatural, which could not be categorized and with which one did not know how to deal." He went first to Geneva, where he worked from 1934 until 1940, and then to the United States. From 1945 until the end of his life he worked at the business school of New York University. There he published his nine-hundred-page magnum opus, *Human Action* (1949), arguing on a plane of high abstraction for the superiority of free-market capitalism.[8]

Human Action was the kind of book that made converts and turned some readers into true believers—one critic described it as the "capitalist manifesto." It claimed to encompass the study not just of traditional economics, but of everything germane to human life—hence its title. Von Mises wrote that what until now we have called economics ought to be renamed "praxeology" and should include all forms of human behavior.

Modern economics had made the breakthrough: it "converted the theory of market prices into a general theory of human choice."

> It is the science of every kind of human action. Choosing determines all human decisions. In making his choice man chooses not only between various material things and services. All human values are offered for option. All ends, and all means, both material and ideal issues, the sublime and the base, the noble and the ignoble, are ranged in a single row and subjected to a decision which picks out one thing and sets aside another. Nothing that men aim at or want remains outside of this arrangement into a unique scale of gradation and preference. . . . No treatment of economic problems proper can avoid starting from acts of choice; economics becomes a part, although hitherto the best elaborated part, of a more universal science, praxeology.

Like William Graham Sumner, moreover, von Mises insisted that it was susceptible to scientific exactitude. But his was a different kind of science from those undertaken in laboratories, because human choices were not confined solely to material things. "It cannot be denied that the demand for goods is widely influenced by metaphysical, religious, and ethical considerations, by aesthetic value judgments, by customs, habits, prejudices, tradition, changing fashions, and many other things." Skeptical of historicism, von Mises emphasized the timeless truths of the laws of classical economics.[9]

As relations between the United States and the Soviet Union deteriorated at the close of World War II, Hayek and von Mises sought out the scholars and journalists in Western Europe and America who seemed to them most likely to work for the preservation of democracy and capitalism. Convening a meeting in Switzerland, the group spent ten days discussing the central issue of their era; ways to resist the double threat of communism abroad and creeping socialism at home. Their statement read: "The central values of civilization are in danger. Over large stretches of the earth's surface the essential conditions of human dignity and freedom have already disappeared. In others they are under constant menace from the development of current tendencies of policy. The position of the individual and the voluntary group are progressively undermined by extensions of arbitrary power. Even the most precious possession of Western Man, freedom of thought and expression, is threatened by the spread of creeds which, claiming the privilege of tolerance when in the position of a minority, seek only to establish a position of power in which they can suppress and obliterate all views but their own." Among the Americans present were two economists destined to have a far-reaching impact on the conservative revival, Milton Friedman and George Stigler, each of whom would later win a Nobel Prize. Naming themselves the "Mont Pelerin Society," after the mountain on whose slopes they met, the group persisted in the following decades as a blue-ribbon club of Cold War conservative intellectuals.[10]

The Vienna School won disciples in America as young economists and political philosophers gathered around von Mises and Hayek. One of the most striking and original of these followers was Murray Rothbard (1926–2005), a secular Jew from New York. He joined von Mises's seminar at New York University and wrote that *Human Action* was "a work of monumental grandeur" that "deserves a lifetime of study." He recalled later that at informal gatherings von Mises would tell his students, "Don't be afraid to speak up. Remember, whatever you say about the subject and however wrong it might be, the same thing has already been said by some eminent economist."[11]

Like Hayek and von Mises, Rothbard thought of government as an enemy and was, accordingly, dismayed by the continued growth of the federal government in the late 1940s and early 1950s. Whereas many new conservatives took the view that support for a large state was now an unfortunate necessity, for Cold War reasons, Rothbard denied it. Doubting that the Soviet Union had aggressive designs on the United States, doubting that America should be entangled in foreign alliances like NATO, disgusted by the military draft and the Korean War, he felt that the first shackles of serfdom were already being forged.[12]

Rothbard, like many young conservatives then and later, made contact with the novelist Ayn Rand (1905–82), author of *The Fountainhead* (1943). Rand, a strong-minded Russian émigré, believed that history advances thanks to the work of brilliant capitalist individualists, whose destiny is to struggle against a parasitic majority of bureaucrats, socialists, conventional thinkers, and drones.[13] She lived in New York, surrounded in the 1950s by a group of young disciples. Most were callow youths smitten by her vision of a capitalist utopia, but a few were, or became, major figures in their own right, such as Alan Greenspan, subsequently chairman of the Federal Reserve Board. Publication of her second blockbuster, *Atlas Shrugged* (1957), which went straight to the top of the best-seller lists, increased her fame and her monumental self-esteem. Describing her philosophy as "Objectivism," regarding herself in all seriousness as the greatest living thinker in the world, and reluctant to give credit to any other philosopher, she expected the unquestioning obedience and deference of all comers. She wrote essays with titles like "The Virtue of Selfishness," thought of herself as rigorously and uniquely logical, yet had a wide array of eccentric interests: tango dancing, heavy smoking, jewelry in the shape of dollar signs, and sexual privileges for superior beings, such as herself.[14]

For half a century now readers, especially teenage boys, have loved *Atlas Shrugged,* whose powerful, purposeful characters give you the sense that with enough willpower anything is possible. (This feeling is brilliantly expressed—and then exploded—in Tobias Wolff's novel *Old School* [2004.]) Its plot is riveting. One by one the great business leaders are disappearing from the American scene, and a puzzling question circulates among those left behind: "Who is John Galt?" After hundreds of pages, bristling with passion, brilliance, lust, and mystery, you learn that Galt is the leader of a capitalist counterculture hidden deep in the Rocky Mountains, biding his time until the rest of the world realizes that it is helpless without great entrepreneurs. Eventually he will lead the entrepreneurs back to command a society that has foundered without them. His great speech explaining and justifying this plan, itself more than a hundred pages long, climaxes the novel. By now *Atlas Shrugged,* like *The Fountainhead,* has sold more than five million copies. Although widely mocked and parodied it provided a steady stream of converts to libertarianism and to the new conservatism.[15]

Rothbard wrote Rand a fan letter after reading it, saying he had never previously thought much of fiction as a vehicle for advancing social theories, but now he understood how powerful it could be, adding that *Atlas Shrugged* was surely the greatest novel ever written. Rand accepted such praise as her due but then expected Rothbard to fall in line with all her ideas, never mind that he was already a Ph.D. in economics, far more widely read and intellectually astute than she. She denounced him for being married to a practicing Christian and then criticized him for not smoking. "Cigarettes were pro-life and pro-man since they were manufactured by productive capitalists for human enjoyment." When he balked in the face of her imperious demands, she excommunicated him.[16]

TRADITIONALISTS

Libertarianism was an important part of postwar conservatism. Another element, very different in mood and priorities, was cultural traditionalism. It carried on the work of the new humanists and a longer tradition stretching back to Charles Eliot Norton, George Ticknor, and John Adams. The deep fund of wisdom available to us from classical, Hebrew, and Christian sources from long before the Reformation and the settlement of America was more vital than ever, said traditionalists.

Richard Weaver, a literature professor at the University of Chicago, gave an early expression of this impulse in *Ideas Have Consequences* (1948). His point of view could not have been more different from that of the libertarians. He saw single-minded free-market fanatics, indeed, as one of the symptoms of a sick society. The world is not getting better and better, as nearly everyone seems to suppose, said Weaver, whose education had included a stint with the Southern Agrarians at Nashville and a doctoral degree in Southern history from Louisiana State University. To the contrary, it is getting worse, as the recent catastrophic war ought to have made obvious. His own proposed title for the book, *The Fearful Descent,* would have given a clearer idea of its theme, though the alternative, urged by his publisher, was also apposite. Weaver, a philosophical idealist, assumed that the explanation for the decline of civilization must be sought in the realm of ideas. What people thought and the way they justified themselves was the way to understand what they did in and to their world. The fact that they thought it was getting better was itself a sign of their capacity for self-deception.[17]

Had there been, at some time in the foregoing centuries, a wrong turn in the road that led to the contemporary delusions that now seemed so widespread? Weaver argued that the crucial moment had come in the Middle Ages, in a dispute between the scholastic realists and nominalists. The realists accepted Plato's idea that there are ideal forms or universals, to which the particular things in the world are mere approximations.

William of Occam (d. 1349), by contrast, was one of the scholastic nominalists who challenged this idea, proposing instead that things in the world come first and that our general names for them are merely organizational conveniences rather than an expression of higher realities. This was no mere semantic quibble: "The issue ultimately involved is whether there is a source of truth higher than, and independent of, man; and the answer to the question is decisive for one's view of the nature and destiny of humankind. The practical result of nominalist philosophy is to banish the reality which is perceived by the intellect and to posit as reality that which is perceived by the senses. With this change in the affirmation of what is real, the whole orientation of culture takes a turn, and we are on the road to modern empiricism." The denial of universals, Weaver added, means "the denial of everything transcending experience," which in turn annihilates the possibility of absolute truth. Western thought since William of Occam had turned to understanding the world itself—by the method of what we call science—rather than the higher reality that encloses and embraces the world. In this line of thought echoes of Irving Babbitt were strong.[18]

Weaver thought of the Christian Middle Ages as a time of intellectual unity, one that understood that the purpose of civilization was the glorification of God. Our commerce- and science-ridden society, by contrast, made itself odious with its obsessive pursuit of money and scientific knowledge, which could be achieved only by specialization and fragmentation. Specialization was pernicious because it came at the expense of letting go of the possibility of unified knowledge. He cited approvingly King Philip of Macedon's reproach to his son Alexander (that is, Alexander the Great), who as a young man was an excellent flute player: "Are you not ashamed, son, to play so well?" Nowhere was Weaver more shocking to many contemporaries—or more strongly reminiscent of his new humanist predecessors—than in his contemptuous disregard for the scientific specialist, whom he described as "an essentially ridiculous figure" whose work was a form of "escape and moral defeatism."[19]

The medieval scholastic doctors had grasped for the unity of all knowledge and were recognized as leaders. Their successors, a little later in European and early American history, were the class of *gentlemen* who also disdained specialization of knowledge while accepting the duty and responsibility of leadership. That class, too, was now rapidly disappearing in a society that (crazily, in Weaver's opinion) resisted the aristocratic ideal. In place of aristocracy had grown up a belief in human equality. But egalitarianism, in Weaver's view, was an almost entirely destructive force. Social stability presupposed hierarchy, he said, and healthy societies should value the benign hierarchy of fraternity far more than the individualism that comes with equality. "The comity of people in groups large or small rests not upon the chimerical notion of equality but upon fraternity, a concept which long antedates it in history because it goes immeasurably deeper in human sentiment. The ancient feeling of brotherhood carries obligations of which equality knows nothing. It calls for respect and protection, for brotherhood is status in family, and family is by nature hierarchical. It demands patience with little brother and it may sternly exact duty of big brother. It places people in a network of sentiment, not of rights." Indeed, "fraternity directs attention to others, equality to self, and the passion for equality is simultaneous with the growth of egotism." Societies most dedicated to equality, like contemporary America, were therefore the most selfish, envious, and resentful.[20]

The only American example of a benevolent aristocratic society of the sort Weaver favored had been the Old South, with its "Ciceronian tradition of eloquent wisdom." It had, he believed, been leisured, aristocratic, learned, dedicated to remnants of the ancient truth. Tragically, this society had been defeated in the Civil War and had then turned to "commerce and technology in its economy and to the dialectic of New England and Germany in its educational endeavors." Only a recovery of the old wisdom of scholastic realism, recognition that there is an absolute truth, and a revival of piety and hierarchy, could now rescue a foundering world.[21]

Weaver had studied with John Crowe Ransom, was familiar with the work of the other Southern Agrarians, yet wrote in an idiom that Catholic traditionalists were as likely to recognize as Jeffersonian Southerners. The historian Paul Murphy argues that Weaver is a bridge from the regional critique of the Southern Agrarians to the wider case for traditionalism that became central to postwar conservatism. Another critic, John Attarian, writes that the book showed that American conservatism need not be a utilitarian or pragmatic affair; that it could have a "strongly Catholic flavor"; and that conservatives might think of themselves as "aristocrats defending a humane civilization against mass man."[22]

One of Weaver's early admirers was Russell Kirk (1918–94), son of a Michigan train driver. A recently demobilized World War II army veteran, he had spent the war years as a sergeant on a chemical and biological weapons-testing base in the southwestern desert. Struggling in the late 1940s to run the Red Cedar Bookshop in East Lansing, while working as an instructor at Michigan State University, Kirk invited Weaver to speak there; the two became friends, despite temperamental differences. Kirk himself, a few years later, wrote a great book of his own, *The Conservative Mind* (1953), which joined Weaver's *Ideas Have Consequences* in defense of tradition and in asserting that Cold War America should heed the ancient wisdom of Europe.[23]

A wonderful mix of intellectual history and literary mythmaking, *The Conservative Mind* traces (or perhaps creates) a conservative lineage in the English-speaking world from Edmund Burke in the 1780s down to T. S. Eliot in Kirk's day. Kirk did more than any other writer at midcentury to devise a conservative family tree, over which his intellectual heirs have argued ever since. By opting for the lineage of Burke, he wrote, he had decided to exclude from the tradition various English-language authoritarians, antidemocrats, and antiparliamentarians. He also excluded all classical liberals and libertarians. Conservatism, as he saw it, was entirely compatible with constitutional republicanism and democracy. To the objection that the American system, at least, was based in revolution, Kirk responded with the old Federalist retort that the American Revolution was "a conservative reaction, in the English political tradition, against royal innovation."[24]

Kirk tried to summarize the essential features of conservatism. It was "not a fixed and immutable body of dogma" and was constantly changing in response to new historical contingencies. Nevertheless it was possible to make several confident generalizations. First, conservatism was the "preservation of the ancient moral traditions of humanity." He added: "Conservatives respect the wisdom of their ancestors. . . . They are dubious of wholesale alteration. They think society is a spiritual reality, possessing an eternal life but a delicate constitution." Like Weaver, Kirk believed in private property, benign social hierarchy, and the need for an aristocracy. He, too, disliked egalitarianism and thought that "political problems, at bottom, are religious and moral problems."[25]

What did conservatives most fear? Kirk noted five great rivals to Burkean wisdom over the last two centuries: "the rationalism of the *philosophes,* the romantic emancipation of Rousseau and his allies, the utilitarianism of the Benthamites, the positivism of Comte's school, and the collectivistic materialism of Marx and other socialists." All five had been fatally contaminated by the belief in the perfectibility of humankind, all denied the reality of original sin, and all favored economic and political equality. Tradition, in their view, had not been a rich accumulated heritage of wisdom but something to be swept into the dustbin of history.[26]

The Conservative Mind skipped lightly over some historical elements of the past two centuries, such as American slavery and the Civil War, but it made a brilliant case for social hierarchy, deference, reverence for tradition, and anti-utopianism. Its heroes were Burke, John Adams, Calhoun, Henry Adams, and Irving Babbitt. There was room in Kirk's conservative tradition for capitalism, but Kirk, like Weaver, cautioned that the free market alone was an inadequate foundation for a stable society. Shared moral and religious principles and a sense of community restraint were more important.[27]

Kirk wrote much of *The Conservative Mind* in Scotland—it was his doctoral thesis at the University of St. Andrews. Unlike most dissertations, however, it was well written, passionate, and did not follow the rule about clearly separating the author's voice from that of his subject. Often Kirk veered over from exposition to advocacy, merging his voice with that of his ostensible subjects. "Nature has furnished society with the materials for an aristocracy, which the wisely conducted state will recognize and honor—always reserving, however, a counterpoise to aristocratic ambition. Just as it is a fact of nature that the mass of men are ill qualified for the exercise of political power, so it is written in the eternal constitution of things that a few men, from various causes, are mentally and physically and spiritually suited for social leadership. The state which rejects their services is doomed to stagnation or destruction." Kirk made no effort to hide the fact that he was writing a manifesto for Burkean conservatism as well as an analysis of its history.[28]

Kirk found the Spartan conditions of postwar Scotland, with its rationing and lack of motor vehicles, preferable to the materialist orgy then getting under way in America. Much to his surprise *The Conservative*

Mind enjoyed enthusiastic reviews across much of the American media and made him so much money that he was able to abandon his academic career at Michigan State University (which he referred to as "Behemoth U.") and make a living for himself as an independent writer.[29] Settling in the northern Michigan village of Mecosta, where he had family ties, Kirk became the guru of the traditionalist branch of the conservative movement from then until his death, in the early 1990s. He worked hard on cultivating himself as an exemplar of the old virtues, did not drive a car, used an old mechanical typewriter well into the age of computers, published ghost stories, read tarot cards, was delighted to have his home compared to Elrond's "Rivendell" in Tolkien's *Lord of the Rings,* took in strays and wanderers, declined appointments in the Nixon and Reagan administrations, and kept up a vast correspondence in self-consciously ornate and archaic prose.[30]

Other writers joined Weaver and Kirk in advancing the conservative cause and linking it more explicitly to older European themes. Eric Voegelin, another central European, was one; he had known von Hayek and von Mises in the 1920s and, like them, was forced to flee Nazi Germany. In 1938 he moved to America, where he found work at Louisiana State University. He, too, found the antecedents of current woes in the Middle Ages. Whereas Weaver blamed William of Occam for a fatal wrong turning, Voegelin in *The New Science of Politics* (1952) blamed Joachim of Flora, an apocalyptic prophet of the late twelfth century. As Voegelin saw it, Joachim had tried to "immanentize the eschaton." In other words, he had tried to bring heavenly events down to the earth and to forecast a historical timetable for the stages of history, the end of the world, and the Second Coming of Christ. The scheme in Joachim's hands was openly religious, comprising the age of the Father, the age of the Son, and the age of the Holy Spirit, conforming to the pattern of the Holy Trinity. Since then, however, the idea had been secularized into a wide array of three-phase stages of history, such as "ancient, medieval, and modern," or the Marxist version, which spoke of the age of primitive accumulation, the age of the bourgeoisie, and the age of proletarian revolution and the withering away of the state that would bring history to its triumphant climax. The besetting temptation was Gnosticism, the belief that divine perfection could be achieved here on earth, which in practice led to tyranny. Young conservative activists who had grappled with Voegelin's opaque prose sometimes sported lapel badges that read: "Don't immanentize the eschaton!"[31]

Even writers not usually associated with conservative politics wrote works in a clearly conservative and traditionalist idiom during the late 1940s and early 1950s. Walter Lippmann, for example, one of the two or three best-known figures in the history of twentieth-century American journalism, published *Essays in the Public Philosophy* in 1954, arguing that the nation ought more openly to affirm its adherence to the ancient principles of natural law. A socialist in his youth, Lippmann had been disillusioned by the events of mid-century. He felt that popular sovereignty without the restraint of tradition had led to the catastrophes of Nazism and Stalinism, that popular democracy had degraded the republic, and that public opinion was almost invariably misguided or wrong. The attraction of natural law, a set of principles embedded in nature itself, was that it was immune to temporary popular enthusiasms. "A large plural society cannot be governed without recognizing that, transcending its plural interests, there is a rational order with a superior common law. This common law is 'natural' in the sense that it can be discovered by any rational mind, that it is not the willful and arbitrary positive command of the sovereign power. This is the necessary assumption, without which it is impossible for different peoples with their competing interests to live together in peace and freedom within one community." The ancients had understood this point and Thomas Aquinas had reformulated it in the Middle Ages. It was embodied in the American Constitution too, but modern theorists of democracy, and much worse the twentieth-century's totalitarians, had denied it. Lippmann, like Weaver and Kirk, was exploring intellectual resources from the Catholic tradition without being Catholic himself. His biographer notes that he was attracted to Catholicism less by the sacraments than by "the sense it conveyed of communion in a moral order above the whims of transient majorities and the dictates of tyrants."[32]

In the same way Peter Viereck, never a politically active conservative, wrote a respectful study of traditionalist conservatism in the same years. Viereck, a professor and poet at Mount Holyoke College, argued like Weaver and Kirk for the traditional virtues and for the accumulated heritage of our civilization. "Christianity is the needed time-capsule conserving and fusing the four ancestries of western man: the stern moral commandments and social justice of Judaism; the love for beauty and for untrammeled intellectual speculation of the free Hellenic mind; the Roman Empire's universalism, and its exaltation of law; and the Aristotelianism, Thomism, and antinominalism included in the Middle Ages. . . . Society is ever fusing them in new proportions to meet the ever-shifting emphasis on morality, beauty, intellect, legalism, or universality. To some degree all must be present. The razor's edge tension of the delicate and vulnerable balance between them is perhaps what goads western man to greatness and gives him his creativity, his élan." Humanity, wrote Viereck, is not perfectible, humans are brutes when not restrained by civilization, and education must be so formed that it can pass along the complex, precious, and fragile heritage to each new generation.[33]

ANTICOMMUNISTS

A third element in the development of postwar conservatism, along with libertarianism and traditionalism, was anticommunism. The phrase Weaver's editor had persuaded him to use as his title, *Ideas Have Consequences,* became one of the great truisms of the new conservative movement. No one explained the consequences of ideas more vividly than Whittaker Chambers (1901–61) in his dramatic autobiography *Witness* (1952). Even though he wrote the book as an anticommunist polemic, few English-language writers ever did a better job of explaining the immense attractiveness of communism as a selfless cause. As you read, he draws you in to share the thrill he felt as a young man in joining the Communist Party to participate in its world-changing mission. Selected by Soviet agents to work in espionage, Chambers became a courier in the 1930s, receiving information from secret American communists inside the New Deal agencies and passing it on to his contact at the Soviet Embassy.[34]

Learning of Stalin's brutal purges in the late 1930s, however, Chambers began to understand that communism represented not the highest achievement of civilization but its antithesis. "The Purge, like the Communist-Nazi pact later on, was the true measure of Stalin as a revolutionary statesman. That was the horror of the Purge—that acting as a Communist Stalin could have taken no other course, so long as he believed he was right. In that fact lay the evidence that Communism is absolutely evil. The human horror was not evil, it was the sad consequence of evil. It was Communism that was evil, and the more truly a man acted in its spirit and interest, the more certainly he perpetuated evil." Aghast, severing himself from the movement and in fear of assassination, he found that government security agencies did not even act on the information he had given them, the names of his fellow spies, even though he possessed microfilms that proved his claims. After 1945, however, with the onset of the Cold War, his old charges resurfaced. They led to the dramatic trial and conviction of Alger Hiss, the privileged New Deal bureaucrat who had been his most eminent contact in the 1930s. Chambers wrote that, in joining the anticommunist side in the great battle for civilization, he was probably joining the side destined to lose, but that nevertheless he must go down fighting. Over this captivating and melodramatic book hangs a sense of doom and dread, of civilization about to founder.[35]

Many other former communists ended up in the conservative movement. Max Eastman (1883–1969), the former Greenwich Village radical and editor of the socialist journal *The Masses,* was one of the first to be disillusioned by the Soviet Union. Having traveled there in the early 1920s, he quickly realized that it was becoming a repressive tyranny rather than a workers' paradise. Others took longer to realize the error of their ways. For some the decisive moment of disillusionment came with Stalin's extermination of the kulaks; or the show trials and executions of the Old Bolsheviks; or the way Stalin ordered communists in the Spanish Civil War to attack all others on the Republican side rather than fight with them, thus hastening the victory of Franco; or the supremely cynical Hitler-Stalin Pact of 1939, which obliged all American communists to express active approval of the joint Nazi-Soviet invasion of Poland. These ex-communists turned anticommunists included Will Herberg, who became a prominent religious sociologist, James Burnham, a foreign policy analyst, the novelist John Dos Passos, and the journalists Freda Utley, Louis Budenz, and Frank Meyer.[36]

NATIONAL REVIEW

William F. Buckley (1925–2008) brought together these three intellectual concerns: traditionalism, libertarianism, and anticommunism. Having served as an army officer at the end of World War II and as editor of the *Yale Daily News* as a postwar undergraduate, he was rich, confident, outspoken, and an excellent debater. His first book, *God and Man at Yale* (1951), was the precocious manifesto of a new college graduate. It argued that Yale had forgotten about the God in whose name it had been founded and turned its back on capitalism, the economic system that had kept it going ever since. Yale had become, instead, the home of economic collectivism and agnostic or atheistic humanism. Moreover, these two changes were connected. "I believe that the duel between Christianity and atheism is the most important in the world. I further believe that the struggle between individualism and collectivism is the same struggle reproduced at another level." Buckley, the son of a Catholic millionaire, made the case for restoring capitalism and Christianity as central themes in the college curriculum. He also took issue with the doctrine of academic freedom, which sheltered a faculty whose views were at odds with those of the society that protected them. Arguing that academic freedom should be construed much more narrowly, and with reference only to their research and writing, Buckley challenged professors' right to teach their beliefs, unless they were those of the society at large and enjoyed the university's explicit approval. The book was greeted with a chorus of indignant liberal reviews, one of which, by McGeorge Bundy, described him as a "twisted and ignorant young man."[37]

His next book, *McCarthy and His Enemies* (1954), written in collaboration with his brother-in-law, L. Brent Bozell (1926–97), was unlikely to make him any new liberal friends. It was the only even remotely plausible defense of the Wisconsin senator ever written. At a time when liberal intellectuals regarded McCarthyism as a scourge of Spanish Inquisition–like vileness, Buckley and Bozell depicted it as just another case of politics as usual. McCarthy, they said, is simply making the most of a handy issue, communism, in his appeal to the voters and is willing to play rhetorical tricks on his adversaries. He may be a blunt instrument and even a bully, but about the big question he is right: America is at war with international communism. It is a terrifyingly insidious war; one in which the enemy seeks to undermine us from within, by taking advantage of the safeguards provided by our Constitution. In the face of such an enemy, tough measures are necessary, a point McCarthy understands better than most of his colleagues on Capitol Hill.[38]

Buckley demonstrated in these books a fluent and entertaining style along with a gift for upending the conventional wisdom. Undeterred by ferocious criticism from the political center and left, he then set about gathering the individuals and the money to launch a conservative journal and brought out the first issue of *National Review* in November 1955. His aim was to set up a big tent, bringing in as many types of conservative as possible, and to keep them together despite their differences. He was aware that *Human Events* (founded in 1944), one of the few right-wing magazines already in circulation, had suffered a grave internal fracture between anti–Cold War libertarians and pro–Cold War conservatives and was eager to prevent such a schism. The views held by Hayek, von Mises, Rothbard, Weaver, Chambers, and Kirk were all represented. Kirk himself declined to become an editor but agreed to be *National Review*'s commentator on education. (Kirk founded *Modern Age* two years later, a scholarly conservative quarterly less attuned to the news.) Numerous ex-communists worked for *National Review,* including James Burnham, Willi Schlamm (Buckley's cofounder), Eugene Lyons, Frank Meyer, and eventually Whittaker Chambers. The only group conspicuous by its absence was the old isolationists; from the outset the journal was so militant in its anticommunism that it rejected the idea of letting the rest of the world go its own way. This decision in turn put *National Review* in the paradoxical position of hating big government in all areas except the one in which it was becoming biggest of all, defense.[39]

National Review had two clear adversaries: communism abroad and liberalism at home. It was well edited, bright, amusing, and provocative, carrying on the assault against the liberal elite that Buckley had begun in his early books. It made a memorable impression on readers. Patrick J. Buchanan (b. 1938), later a significant figure in the movement, wrote that when he first read a copy in 1960 he agreed with everything in it and was delighted by its iconoclastic style. "James Burnham, Frank Meyer, Russell Kirk, Whittaker Chambers, Jon Chamberlain, and Bill Buckley not only believed as I had come to believe, they wrote with passion, insight, and authority. Not content to contradict what passed for the conventional wisdom, they lampooned and ridiculed it. They did not politely disagree with the Liberal Establishment; they lacerated it." He added that "it is difficult to exaggerate the debt conservatives of my generation owe *National Review*" because it was their only source of "political and intellectual sustenance," and it showed, by its style, that conservatism did not have to mean "stuffy, orthodox Republican stand-pat-ism."[40]

Buckley capitalized on his journal's early success by writing his own conservative manifesto, *Up from Liberalism* (1959). Contemporary liberalism, as he described it, was philosophically incoherent, lacked moral foundations, suppressed individual freedom, and fetishized doubt rather than standing firm on the certain truths of civilization. Liberals "tend to believe that the human being is perfectible and social progress predictable, and that the instrument for effecting the two is reason; that truths are transitory and empirically determined; that equality is desirable and attainable through the action of state power; that social and individual differences, if they are not rational, are objectionable and should be scientifically eliminated; that all peoples and societies should strive to organize themselves upon a rationalist and scientific paradigm." Liberalism was a menace because it constantly justified the enlargement of the state and its intrusion into previously private areas of citizens' lives. We must, Buckley concluded, "bring down the thing called liberalism, which is powerful but decadent; and salvage a thing called conservatism, which is weak but viable."[41]

Buckley was particularly distressed by the fact that President Eisenhower, the Republican president who dominated the politics of the 1950s, was not offering a proper conservative alternative. On the contrary, Eisenhower had accepted nearly all the legacy of New Deal liberalism, whereas he should have attempted to roll it back and shrink the size of the federal government. Failing to do so meant undermining the traditional self-reliance of the American people, by leading them to expect that the government would support them if they did not support themselves. "It was the dominating ambition of Eisenhower's Modern Republicanism to govern in such fashion as to more or less please more or less everybody. Such governments must shrink from principle: because principles have edges, principles cut; and blood is drawn, and people get hurt. And who would hurt anyone in an age of modulation? . . . [His] leadership consists of giving the people everything they want—and, if they are caught not wanting enough, reminding them of all the things they should be wanting (except the right things)." Such government also meant heavier taxes, more bureaucratic intrusion into citizens' everyday life, and an erosion of traditional liberties. Buckley had been strongly influenced by Albert Jay Nock's

Our Enemy the State and was dismayed to see GOP politicians accepting the idea of large-scale state paternalism.[42]

Eisenhower had also accepted the Cold War standoff and seemed willing to tolerate permanent coexistence, according to which each bloc policed its own side of the Iron Curtain. Buckley editorialized bitterly against Eisenhower when he failed to intervene on behalf of the anti-Soviet Hungarian revolutionaries in 1956, and even more bitterly when he invited the Soviet premier, Nikita Khrushchev, to visit America in 1959. Surely America should not accept permanent coexistence and should seek ways to reverse the communist advance. To a packed audience in Carnegie Hall, he compared Eisenhower's speech of welcome to Khrushchev with Neville Chamberlain's appeasement of Hitler before World War II—as a short-term expedient, based on wishful thinking, which would soon make the situation worse. Exactly how to carry on the Cold War, and whether even a nuclear war might be justified, became a point of complex internal politics among *National Review*'s editors.[43]

Buckley was a capable publicist for the emerging conservative movement and recognized the importance of drawing young activists into it. Soon after publishing *God and Man at Yale* he became a founding member, and first president, of the Intercollegiate Society of Individualists (1953), a libertarian student group that became a permanent part of the conservative movement (later transformed into the tradition-oriented Intercollegiate Studies Institute). He also offered his home in 1960 for the founding conference of Young Americans for Freedom (YAF), a youth group that was to nurture dozens of conservative writers, organizers, and politicians. One of his friends, M. Stanton Evans, a twenty-six-year-old *National Review* contributor, drafted the "Sharon Statement," the organization's declaration of principles. Another friend, Marvin Liebman, a conservative publicist who had helped raise the money for *National Review,* provided office space in New York and advice to the fledgling group and helped it publish its journal, *New Guard.* For much of the 1960s YAF was larger and more active than its counterpart on the left, Students for a Democratic Society.[44]

Quick to exploit new possibilities, talented as a conciliator among argumentative factions, Buckley also knew how, when necessary, to play the role of policeman, excluding unwanted company that could only harm the growing conservative cause. He decided that the conspiracy-minded

John Birch Society, so paranoid in its hunt for communists that it suspected even Eisenhower of being a communist, ought not to be included, though denouncing it cost him several hundred subscribers and financial contributors. Buckley also took the risk of excluding the *American Mercury,* now openly anti-Semitic, and the novelist Ayn Rand, despite the wild popularity of her novels. Whittaker Chambers, reviewing *Atlas Shrugged* for *National Review,* said her outlook was the antithesis of genuine conservatism, a frightful form of grasping materialist utopianism that showed nothing but contempt for tradition.[45]

James Burnham desperately wanted *National Review* to matter and to move close to the centers of power. Burnham, probably Buckley's closest friend and adviser in the first decade of the journal, was an urbane and privileged New Yorker, at home in high society. For twenty years a philosophy professor at New York University, he had also been a Trotskyist organizer and theorist in the 1930s. Shocked by Trotsky's willingness to defend the Hitler-Stalin Pact in 1939, however, he had become steadily more critical of Marxism. His first important political book, *The Managerial Revolution* (1941), was an analysis of the similarities among modern regimes, including the United States, Nazi Germany, and Soviet Russia. All of them, he argued, are run by bureaucratic elites, the nature of whose work is actually more significant than the different ideologies they ostensibly follow. All are self-interested, even when they pretend to be working in the interests of the nation or the "people." (This was an insight that American neoconservatives would later pick up in their analysis of the "new class.") He added in *The Machiavellians* (1943) that all societies, left and right, are run by elites and that the rhetoric of democracy is usually no more than a cynical cover for competing elites' ambitions. He was changing, during the war years, from an elitist of the left to an elitist of the right, and in the early Cold War years he contributed to shaping the American posture of militant anticommunism.[46]

A trilogy of Burnham's postwar books, *The Struggle for the World* (1947), *The Coming Defeat of Communism* (1950), and *Containment or Liberation* (1953), drew widespread interest and led to invitations to consult with the Central Intelligence Agency, such that he was probably a formulator of as well as a commentator on American policy. Central to his postwar outlook was the conviction that the Soviet Union and the United States could not enjoy a stable coexistence. The Soviet Union was relentlessly expansionist and would stop its encroachment into the free world only if prevented by force. The policy of containment outlined by George Kennan, and adopted first by President Truman and then by President Eisenhower, was inadequate. Far from putting intolerable pressure on the Soviet Union of the kind Burnham favored, it permitted the Russians to consolidate their hold on Eastern Europe. Instead of containment, the United States should be promoting *liberation*, dedicating all its ingenuity to destabilizing communist regimes, setting up governments in exile for Soviet satellites, and looking for military opportunities to liberate the "captive nations." Burnham's *National Review* column, entitled "The Third World War," neatly summarized his view of the world situation.[47]

Frank Meyer, like Burnham, had studied at Princeton and Oxford, going on from there to the London School of Economics. He had been a communist organizer, editor, and teacher throughout the Great Depression, first in London, then in Chicago. Separating from the Communist Party at the end of World War II and, like Whittaker Chambers, fearing that he might be assassinated, he lived nocturnally in a secluded farmhouse in upstate New York, reading conservative and anticommunist literature extensively while scratching a living out of work for *Freeman*, the *American Mercury*, and other magazines. He befriended Buckley and, after 1955, became the book review editor of *National Review* and author of its regular column "Principles and Heresies."[48]

Meyer gradually worked out a conservative "fusionist" position, explaining why seemingly opposed groups in the movement, free-market libertarians and traditionalists, actually needed each other and should work together. Free-market economics, he reasoned, generates wealth and prevents the concentration of too much power in the state. Its supporters are right to be concerned about protecting individual freedom. But they ought not to regard freedom as an end in itself—men must use their freedom to strive after virtue. This was a point the traditionalists understood well, but traditionalists had weaknesses too—they often seemed willing to accept irrationality and to settle for authoritarian government, forgetting that only people who are free can pursue virtue. Each group must therefore educate the other. That traditionalists and libertarians were in fact cooperating in the growing movement showed that they already had some appreciation for this insight, made all the more logical by their shared anticommunism.

Meyer tried to win contributions from both sides of the argument in his 1964 anthology *What Is Conservatism?* Not everyone was convinced. Libertarians criticized him from one side and Catholic traditionalists like L. Brent Bozell from the other, but as the 1960s progressed and threatening new adversaries appeared on the scene, fusionism became the standard wisdom, embodied in Meyer's later book *The Conservative Mainstream.*[49]

Along with these ex-communists, European exiles played an important role in *National Review*'s early years. The influence of von Hayek and von Mises strongly affected its views on economics. Two Hungarian intellectuals, Thomas Molnar and John Lukacs, each of whom had found college professorships in America, became regular and important contributors. Both men grieved at Soviet domination of their homeland, but their explanations of how to respond differed, revealing another area of dispute in the movement. For Molnar the great issue was the *ideology* of communism, whose philosophical fallacies he analyzed in depth. For Lukacs, by contrast, the problem was *Russia,* whose imperial ambitions were, in his view, more significant than the ideology through which it currently justified them.[50]

Lukacs and Molnar, like Buckley himself, were Roman Catholics. Catholicism was, in fact, a distinctive element in the new conservatism, which also strengthened its ties to European traditionalism. As we have seen, the Old Right had generally been Protestant, isolationist, and exceptionalist, taking the view that America was the antidote to decadent old Europe and that it should keep to itself. Catholic conservatives, by contrast, regarded America as an integral part of the "Christian West" and thought it should make common cause with the Christian nations of Europe under siege from communist barbarism.[51]

The strongly Catholic flavor of the movement made it unlikely to accept the libertarian philosophy, based as it was on the idea that society is a collection of atomized individuals interacting rationally. The Catholic tradition takes the family, rather than the individual, as the basic unit of society and, historically, had clearly separated earthly and divine affairs. One important new Catholic voice in the conservative movement of the late 1950s and early 1960s was that of Garry Wills (b. 1934), who began writing for *National Review* at the same time as he decided against a vocation in the priesthood. In a superb essay, "The Convenient State," written well before his thirtieth birthday, he invoked St. Augustine's *City of God* as an important primer on politics. The state ought to be primarily dedicated not to justice, he argued, but to the nourishment of community, through compromise and conciliation. It must be willing to settle for the imperfection of sinners rather than undertake perfectionist crusades. Did Catholic history offer suitable examples? No. Ironically the best theoretical statement of this view of politics could be found in the *Federalist,* and its best living embodiment in the history of the United States.[52]

The Catholics at *National Review* were already well attuned to the principle of ecumenism, regarding religion in general as a highly desirable asset in America's struggle against communism. They did not regard the election of John F. Kennedy in 1960 as a Catholic triumph so much as an unwelcome victory for liberalism. They were also irritated by a cluster of Supreme Court decisions in the Kennedy years that found Bible reading, prayer, and recitation of the Ten Commandments in public school classrooms to be violations of the First Amendment's establishment clause. Joining the clamor for a constitutional amendment to "put God back in the classroom," they regarded the decisions as a violation of American tradition—nondenominational prayers in schools were widespread at the time. They also argued that the decisions had the unwelcome effect of diminishing the clear religious element in the Cold War itself.[53]

L. Brent Bozell felt so strongly about the decisions that he decided to write a book-length critique of the Supreme Court under Chief Justice Earl Warren. The Warren Court had helped set in motion the civil rights movement. It had also made sweeping decisions in electoral reapportionment and had offered what conservatives thought of as excessive protections to alleged subversives. It seemed to Bozell, as it seemed to many conservatives of his generation, that the Court was exceeding its authority. Not content simply to adjudicate the constitutionality of statutes, it had begun to legislate from the bench. Bozell's *The Warren Revolution* (1966) was one of the first big conservative statements against judicial activism, and against the Court's apparent willingness to ignore the intentions of the Founding Fathers. This theme would dominate conservative legal scholarship from then until the end of the century. Of Warren's approach to judicial innovation and his scanting of the Founders' intent,

Bozell wrote, "A more explicit repudiation of the underlying assumptions of constitutional government can hardly be imagined."[54]

It was characteristic of *National Review* in the 1950s and early 1960s to be more agitated by Supreme Court activism than by racial segregation. During the Montgomery bus boycott of 1955–56, when *National Review* itself was just a few months old, it editorialized that the boycotters were entitled to withhold their custom if they didn't like the service provided and that the bus company should try to offer better service. That was the standard libertarian response to any customer boycott. More often, however, on Southern racial questions, *National Review* showed its traditionalist side by coming out in favor of states' rights and white supremacy. Criticizing the *Brown* decision as "one of the most brazen acts of judicial usurpation in our history . . . shoddy and illegal in analysis and invalid as sociology," it also warned against a drastic change in the mores and folkways of the South. Buckley editorialized, and later repeated in *Up from Liberalism,* that the educated and more "civilized" whites were better equipped, and therefore more entitled, to run society. "In the south the white community is entitled to put forward a claim to prevail politically because, for the time being anyway, the leaders of American civilization are white. . . . The problem is not biological but cultural and educational. The question the white community faces, then, is whether the claims of civilization (and of culture, community, regime) supersede those of universal suffrage. . . . A conservative feels a sympathy for the southern position which the liberal, applying his ideological abstractions ruthlessly, cannot feel. If the majority wills what is socially atavistic, then to thwart the majority may be the indicated, though concededly the undemocratic, course. It is more important for a community, wherever situated geographically, to affirm and live by civilized standards than to labor at the job of swelling the voting lists." James J. Kilpatrick, a leading segregationist and editor of the *Richmond News-Leader* continued to make the constitutional case for segregation into the early 1960s. *National Review* opposed passage of the Civil Rights Act (1964) and the Voting Rights Act (1965) because they represented extensions of federal power into political questions previously confined to the states.[55]

The intensity of liberal intellectuals' dislike and contempt for the new conservatives can be sensed from the first book-length study of the movement from outside, Daniel Bell's edited collection *The New American Right* (1955). Bell and his collaborators, Richard Hofstadter, Nathan Glazer, Seymour Martin Lipset, and others, understood the new conservatism more as a pathology than as a serious intellectual or political phenomenon; it needed to be *diagnosed* rather than interpreted. Using the insights of social psychology, they treated it as a reaction to the stresses of modern society, a juvenile effort to solve complex questions with simple nostrums. In one chapter the sociologist Seymour Martin Lipset argued that citizens moving to the radical right did so from fear that their social status was in decline and that they scapegoated as communists the forces they most feared. Lipset made ominous comparisons with Nazi recruitment techniques.[56]

In the same vein the historian Richard Hofstadter labeled the movement "pseudo-conservatism," explicable by its adherents' status anxiety rather than as a rational response to the national and international situation. Drawing on Theodor Adorno's *The Authoritarian Personality* (1950), he argued that they were, in many respects, the antithesis of "real" conservatives. By declining to engage the conservatives on the level of ideas, however, Bell's group forestalled the development of a real debate. Buckley was to some degree justified when he wrote in *Up from Liberalism* that liberal critics showed "consistent intemperance, insularity and irascibility" when it came to discussing conservatives. "The liberals' implicit premise is that intercredal dialogues are what one has with Communists, not conservatives, in relationship with whom normal laws of civilized discourse are suspended." Ironically Bell himself and many of his collaborators (notably Glazer and Lipset) were destined to rethink their ideas on many political questions in the 1960s and early 1970s. As "neoconservatives" they would become friends and allies of the conservatives whom, in the 1950s, they had scornfully pathologized.[57]

THE CHICAGO ECONOMISTS

As the new conservatives drew critical attention, a new generation of economists was strengthening the intellectual case for free-market capitalism. Two among them, both professors at the University of Chicago, were Milton Friedman and George Stigler. Confining their work almost entirely to academic and technical issues in the 1950s, each won a reputation for rigorous scholarship. Friends of Hayek, they had attended the inaugural meeting of the Mont Pèlerin Society and were sympathetic to the new conservative movement; only in the 1960s, however, did they begin the advocacy work that would make them, and Friedman in particular, household names. Whereas the Vienna school, especially von Mises, wrote mainly in abstract and philosophical terms, Friedman and Stigler were practical men, not satisfied with a theory until they had subjected it to rigorous testing in the real world, proving that the market really did what their theories said it would do. They had more insight than their Austrian colleagues into the actual, vastly complicated American economy of their era. Also, where the Austrians' presumptive challenge came from Marxism, the Chicago School's adversary was Keynesianism, which had come to dominate Anglo-American economics since the 1930s.[58]

Marx believed that capitalism was inherently unstable and that each swing of the business cycle would be more disastrous than its predecessor. He also believed that capitalism was, in its essence, exploitative and that it enriched the bourgeoisie by impoverishing the proletariat. The history of the American working class in the decades leading up to 1960 suggested, to the contrary, that workers were sharing in the era's general prosperity; factory workers lived well, began buying houses and cars of their own, and had never before enjoyed such abundance. Marxism found even fewer recruits among postwar American workers than it did among American economists. The falsification of its economic predictions, and the fact that Marxism and the Soviet Union were now, in the popular mind, synonymous, diminished its importance as an intellectual antagonist.[59]

John Maynard Keynes (1883–1946) could not be dismissed so easily. Like Marx he believed in the inherent instability of the market economy. Unlike Marx, however, Keynes was a supporter of capitalism and an admirer of its achievements. His observations in Britain during the 1920s and 1930s had convinced him that mature economies tend to underconsume. In recessions and depressions, accordingly, government should intervene, spend more money, going into deficit if necessary, in order stimulate demand and create jobs. In prosperous times it should compensate by raising taxes to restrain excessive growth, spending them to pay off deficits incurred during the lean years. Keynes's *General Theory,* published in 1936, gave theoretical support to interventionist government in general and the high spending New Deal in particular.[60]

In 1962 Friedman published *Capitalism and Freedom,* a short, lucid book written in lay terms that challenged the Keynesian orthodoxy. Friedman admitted that there was a proper role for government in the management of the economy, but a far smaller one than was advocated by Keynes. Government's job was, principally, he wrote, to create the rules and then to enforce them like an impartial umpire, ensuring that the market ran fairly and that businessmen honored their contracts. Beyond that, government intervention was more likely to obstruct than to benefit the economy. As his title suggested, capitalism and freedom went together, and both should be defended.[61]

The greatest merit of a free market, Friedman argued, is that it decentralizes power and creates a minimum of coercion. Entrepreneurs offer commodities that potential customers buy or reject according to their needs and tastes. The second great merit of the free market is that, historically, it has generated immense wealth for the industrial nations, showing (against the fears of earlier economists) that one nation's gain need not be another nation's loss. Capitalism, in other words, is a tide that has raised all boats and has done it with a high degree of voluntarism. Third, capitalism is far less discriminatory than other systems. The price mechanism tells you exactly what a commodity costs but doesn't tell you who made it or who can and cannot buy it. The system works best when there is no discrimination. Although (relative) poverty is not eliminated, capitalism generates the surpluses to alleviate it. All these benefits are threatened by government intrusion, which constricts freedom, restrains economic growth, and legislates in favor of some citizens at the expense of others (William Graham Sumner's old argument against tariffs).[62]

For the first time in a publicly accessible place Friedman put forward in *Capitalism and Freedom* some of the ideas for which he later became well known. The first was the idea of educational vouchers. Government runs schools badly, he argued, whereas private educators have competitive incentives to run them well. Each family with a school-age child should therefore be given a voucher equal to the amount previously spent by government on his or her education, redeemable at any school, private or public. Families would in effect vote with their vouchers, keeping in operation schools that delivered satisfactory education while driving bad schools out of business, just as they kept good businesses going in other areas of the economy by patronizing them.[63]

Friedman also advanced the idea of a negative income tax. Dismayed by America's growing array of antipoverty programs, about whose failure to cure poverty he had strong premonitions, he proposed sweeping them all away and replacing them with a scheme that would ensure a minimum money income to all families, with far less government intrusion into their spending habits. If a family had an income above the cutoff point of, say, five thousand dollars per year, it would pay taxes on every dollar above that line. If a family had an income below the cutoff point, it would receive a subsidy (or "negative tax") bringing its total income up to the designated figure. "The advantages of this arrangement are clear. It is directed specifically at the problem of poverty. It gives help in the form most useful to the individual, namely, cash. It is general and could be substituted for the host of special measures now in effect. It makes explicit the cost borne by society." Busybody government would diminish; families would have what they needed most: money.[64]

What about the problem of monopoly, which had been a political issue ever since the 1890s? Given a three-way choice of unregulated private monopoly, publicly owned monopoly, or government-regulated private monopoly, Friedman scandalized the conventional wisdom by claiming that the least bad was unregulated private monopoly. Friedman's empirical work had led him to conclude that corporations in a dominant market position generally do not abuse their position by charging artificially high prices or letting the quality of their goods deteriorate. Those who attempted it were soon challenged by new firms, taking advantage of new technologies, which operated more efficiently and undercut the would-be monopolist. In the contemporary American environment of rapid and continuous technological change, even large corporations had to stay up-to-date, efficient, and competitive. They had to act as though they were not able to command and manipulate the market.[65]

Friedman even had an answer to what was then the most important objection to free-market capitalism: that it had produced the Great Depression. On the contrary, he said, the Depression had been caused by the blundering of a branch of the government, the Federal Reserve, which had failed to react to a shrinkage in the money supply as banks collapsed. "The Great Depression in the United States, far from being a sign of the inherent instability of the private enterprise system, is a testament to how much harm can be done by mistakes on the part of a few men when they wield vast power over the monetary system of a country." This was also one of the principal themes of his *Monetary History of the United States (1963)*.[66]

In arguing against government regulation he was building on a discovery his colleague George Stigler had made. Stigler showed that regulators had almost no ability to influence the prices charged by the corporations they were established to regulate. In that case why did they exist? Because the corporations *wanted* regulators, as a form of political insurance. They soon learned that they could dominate the regulatory agencies, which henceforth would operate more in their interest than in the public interest that had justified their creation in the first place. In other words, regulation was not only costly but was also worse than useless. Stigler also showed that competition remained strong even in near-monopolistic situations where one or few firms dominated a market. Why? Because of the dominant firm's awareness that new firms will sense the opportunity to enter the market if they cease being as competitive as they would have been in a world with dozens of competitors. It was axiomatic to Stigler that monopolies are very rare and that, even when they exist, they won't last long. As he wrote of his and his colleagues' work: "A . . . main theme of the Chicago School of industrial organization is that it is virtually impossible to eliminate competition from economic life."[67]

THE GOLDWATER MOVEMENT

The new conservatives were not content to be merely an intellectual movement. Writers about politics, they aspired to change the American political landscape, which had been nearly devoid of eminent conservative figures since the death of Robert Taft in 1953. Thoroughly dissatisfied with President Eisenhower for his acceptance of the New Deal legacy and what they saw as his conciliatory approach to the Cold War, they sought a new political champion and found one in Barry Goldwater.

Goldwater (1909–98) was an Arizona businessman and World War II veteran who had won a U.S. Senate seat in 1952 and secured a second term in the election of 1958. Tall, handsome, strong, and outspoken, he was sympathetic to the outlook of the new conservative movement, opposing the Eisenhower administration's centrist domestic policy and its acceptance of containment in foreign policy. Conservatives began in 1959 to mention his name as a possible presidential candidate and encouraged him to outline his ideas in a book. Written for him by the hard-working L. Brent Bozell and published in June 1960, *The Conscience of a Conservative* condemned liberalism for its philosophical relativism and its political statism, then outlined the kind of conservatism *National Review* regarded as both possible and desirable for America. Farm subsidies would be discontinued, the income tax severely ratcheted down, and the federal government taken out of housing, education, and urban renewal schemes. Honoring the tradition of states' rights would leave Southern states to work out the racial question in their own way. In foreign policy, America would no longer restrict itself to preserving the status quo but would actively seek ways to roll back communism.[68]

The first print run of the book was ten thousand copies, which sold out quickly, as did many subsequent printings; this enthusiastic backing encouraged Goldwater to think more seriously about a run for the presidential nomination, contesting the presumptive 1960 Republican favorite, Vice-President Richard Nixon. Goldwater ran strongly enough to make his mark at the convention but not to be nominated. When Nixon lost to Kennedy that fall, Goldwater's star continued to rise, and over the next three years the book sold 3.5 million copies. One young enthusiast who loved it was Pat Buchanan. He said that to young conservatives like himself "*The Conscience of a Conservative* was our new testament. It contained the core beliefs of our political faith, it told us why we had failed, what we must do. We read it, memorized it, quoted it. . . . For those of us wandering in the arid desert of Eisenhower Republicanism it hit like a rifle shot." Other conservative books to make an immense impact at the same time were Phyllis Schlafly's *A Choice, Not an Echo* (1964), which urged the GOP to detach itself once and for all from the New Deal orthodoxy, and John Stormer's *None Dare Call It Treason* (1964), which argued the continuing danger of internal communist subversion.[69]

The conservative movement succeeded in winning the Republican nomination for Goldwater in 1964. Young conservatives at the GOP convention, held in the San Francisco Cow Palace, found it an exhilarating and unforgettable experience, but the bruising struggle inside the GOP among Goldwater , George Romney, and Nelson Rockefeller augured ill for the party's fortunes in November. Moderate Republicans were dismayed to have Goldwater as their candidate, and he did little to soothe their feelings when he made an uncharacteristically abrasive and ideological acceptance speech. Its peroration became famous, especially his declaration: "Extremism in the defense of liberty is no vice. Moderation in the pursuit of justice is no virtue." The Democratic governor of California told journalists that "Goldwater's acceptance speech had the stench of fascism. . . . All we needed to hear was 'Heil Hitler.' " That was outrageously unfair, but Goldwater had more or less encouraged opponents and journalists to call him a self-declared extremist.[70]

Probably no Republican could have won in 1964, least of all one as ideologically outspoken as Goldwater, who was reluctant to tailor his message to his different audiences and would not truckle to the special concerns of different ethnic or special-interest blocs. Godfrey Hodgson, a British journalist who followed the campaign, was amazed at the way Goldwater failed to follow the usual pattern of tailoring his remarks to fit his audience. He seemed to do almost the opposite, speaking against social security in Florida to large groups of retirees, speaking against federal cotton subsidies in Memphis, and denouncing the Tennessee Valley Authority to a crowd of TVA employees in Knoxville. Hodgson added that Goldwater "had a hard time making himself heard over the uproar of perhaps the most one-sided and unfair press coverage ever deployed in a presidential campaign." He lost catastrophically.[71]

Despite Goldwater's defeat, conservatism was far stronger intellectually and politically by 1965 than it had been twenty years earlier at war's end. *National Review* had brought together representatives of the main lines of conservative thought; traditionalists like Weaver and Kirk, libertarians like Rothbard and Friedman, and heirs of the new humanism and the Southern Agrarians. All were energized by fear of communism, and they benefited from an influx of former communists like Whittaker Chambers, Frank Meyer, and James Burnham, who added an intellectual sophistication and a sense of urgency to their work. The historian George Nash summarizes the significance of these years: "Conservatives had not constructed a unified philosophy satisfactory to all, and they probably never would. The philosophic gap between traditionalism, with its stress on the restraint of man's will and appetites, and libertarianism, with its zeal for individual freedom and (implicitly) *self*-assertion, remained wide. No amount of theoretical juggling could produce theoretical unity out of the positions of a Kirk and a Mises, a Meyer and a Bozell . . . and a Hayek. . . . [But] conservatism in America in the 1950s and 1960s was not, in its essence, a speculative or theoretical enterprise. It was an intellectual movement with definite political implications." On practical questions, conservatives of these different stripes shared a determination to fight against communism abroad, liberalism at home, and the growth of centralized state power. Despite media predictions that conservatism would disappear in the wake of Goldwater's defeat, it did not. Recovering quickly, it soon became stronger than ever before, both inside the Republican Party and in the nation at large, as America confronted the most turbulent domestic upheavals of the entire twentieth century.[72]

CHAPTER EIGHT

The Movement Gains Allies, 1964–1980

BETWEEN 1964 AND 1980 the Democratic New Deal coalition broke up. White Southerners, often socially conservative, began to vote Republican when black Southerners began to vote Democrat. Numerous blue-collar Northerners (the "hard hats" or, later, "Reagan Democrats") also switched parties in reaction to the era's political controversies over social, gender, and lifestyle issues. The upheavals of the late 1960s and early 1970s seemed politically radical at the time, but their long-term beneficiaries were conservatives. The conservative intellectual movement gained important allies in the sixties and seventies, the neoconservatives, former Cold War liberals who started to fear that society was deteriorating and becoming ungovernable. Together they offered a cogent analysis of the era's crises and became the theoretical branch of an electoral coalition that would dominate American politics for the remainder of the century.

By the 1960s conservatism was as much a matter of activism as of theorizing. Goldwater's 1964 defeat disappointed but did not discourage most conservatives. His nomination was an achievement to build on in the coming decades as they transformed the character of the Republican Party. The historian Donald Critchlow, in his biography of the Republican activist Phyllis Schlafly, traces the acute GOP faction fighting as conservatives took over key positions from moderate or liberal Republicans.

This shift was helped along by local citizen activism, as Lisa McGirr has shown in her study of anticommunists in Orange County, California. Even groups like the intellectually muddled John Birch Society (JBS), whose leaders believed that the United States was actually being run by communists, offered an experience in practical politics that would pay electoral dividends in the 1970s and 1980s. The historian Jonathan Schoenwald argues persuasively that the Goldwater campaign, the JBS, and the Young Americans for Freedom (YAF) created a conservative "movement culture" in the 1960s. No longer was conservatism solely the preserve of scattered writers and politicians but rather a nationwide movement developing real political muscles. William Buckley himself ran a lively campaign as Conservative candidate for mayor of New York in 1965; he lost but wrote an entertaining and perceptive book about the experience, which helped publicize conservative ideas. Five years later his brother, James, also running as a Conservative, won a seat in the U. S. Senate.[1]

RACIAL POLITICS

Guided by President Johnson, Congress passed the Civil Rights Act of 1964 and the Voting Rights Act of 1965, sweeping away nearly all vestiges of legalized racial segregation. America, ideally, should now have become a colorblind society. Almost at once, however, the federal agencies began to interpret the laws in a color-*conscious* way, creating affirmative action programs to give preference to African Americans, in an attempt to overcome a heritage of bias and discrimination. Conservatives admitted that, historically, African Americans had been the victims of discrimination, but most of them denounced affirmative action as the abandonment of individual rights in favor of a policy of group rights. A job candidate's qualifications ought to matter more, they believed, than the population group to which he or she happened to belong. They also saw the Civil Rights Act as another power grab by the federal government, under the sway of liberal ideology. "Almost every section of the [1964 Civil Rights] bill," wrote Frank Meyer, "is directed toward destroying the constitutional balance of power and centering control over the lives of citizens in the hands of the chosen instruments of Liberalism, the Executive and a subservient Supreme Judiciary."[2]

The civil rights movement, under the leadership of Martin Luther King, Jr., had made progress in its early years by carefully holding on to the moral high ground and by preaching a lesson of Christian nonviolence. Even so, many conservatives condemned it. Meyer noted that King's policy of nonviolence was not peaceful. Rather, it was designed to provoke segregationists until they *committed* acts of violence. Will Herberg, one of *National Review*'s ex-communists and a scholar of religion, wrote that King's methods violated Christian tradition. "The early Christians, under the teaching of the apostles, were enjoined to obey the laws of the state, a pagan state, mind you, whether they held these laws to be just or unjust. . . . Strange as it may seem to Dr. King, the very purpose of government is to make us obey laws of which we do not approve." Garry Wills, in a detailed analysis of King's now famous "Letter from Birmingham Jail" (1963), judged it intellectually feeble—it merely "reaches out toward anything that calls up noble emotions . . . and appropriates it without further thought."[3]

By 1965 a black leadership dispute had brought to the fore a more militant generation, less willing than King's Christians to turn the other cheek, willing not just to provoke violence but to fight back when attacked. If white conservatives had found King unsettling, they were terrified of Malcolm X, Stokely Carmichael, and H. Rap Brown and felt more justified in opposing them with strident calls for repression. Such leaders were "insurrectionists" whose revolutionary acts, "spearheaded by organized rioting masses," threatened the "destruction of the constitutional order." Inner city riots in Watts (Los Angeles) and many other American inner cities—including Newark, Washington, and Detroit—between 1964 and 1969 signaled to conservatives the breakdown of law and order. When King himself proposed "massive civil disobedience" and widespread "dislocations" in the summer of 1967, William Buckley argued that he should be met by repressive force. "Repression is an unpleasant instrument, but it is absolutely necessary for civilizations that believe in order and human rights. I wish to God Hitler and Lenin had been repressed."[4]

How should the racial crisis be eased? Conservatives answered, first, that it was surely a mistake for government to offer panaceas that it could not possibly deliver—it simply raised false hopes and made stark realities harder to bear. Frank Meyer argued that Booker T. Washington, the African American leader of the early twentieth century, had been right in his belief that "the Negro people will gain respect and status primarily on the basis of their achievement of economic and social skills and disciplines—a truth that hundreds of thousands of solid Negro families are demonstrating in our time." It was also necessary to abolish the minimum wage, which discouraged employers from creating entry-level jobs; rent control, since it distorted the housing market and made it harder rather than easier to find affordable homes; and trade unions' restrictive practices, whose effect was to keep young African Americans out of the workforce. In other words, general conservative economic reforms would benefit the whole population, blacks included, far more than targeted efforts to aid them.[5]

In the late 1960s many American conservative intellectuals changed their racial views considerably, disavowing former ideas. Some, such as James J. Kilpatrick, had been vocal supporters of segregation but now backed off from what was becoming a socially disgraceful point of view. Many, indeed, became retrospective champions of the 1964 colorblind standard, using it as a base from which to oppose affirmative action and busing. A few, including William Buckley, even argued that limited forms of positive discrimination might be permissible. During a complicated Brownsville, New York, teachers' strike in 1968, for example, he argued: "To appoint a black teacher because he is black is racist, granted. But we have reached a point in race relations where it becomes desirable to act consciously in such a way as to accede to such demands of the Negro community as are in the least way plausible. Negro control over the education of Negro children would appear to be one of these defensible objectives." By then he was doubtful that complete integration was possible and noted that black-pride and black-power advocates had abandoned it as a goal.[6]

The election of 1968 testified to stresses in the political system, brought on in part by the racial and urban crisis. George Wallace, governor of Alabama and a militant segregationist, ran a strong independent third-party campaign and won eight million votes. A populist, appealing to poor Southern whites, he also won the support of Northern working-class whites by denouncing radicals, students, and "pointy-headed intellectuals." Wallace told a journalist that "the people don't like this triflin' with their children, tellin' 'em which teachers have to teach in which schools, and bussing little boys and girls half across a city jus' to achieve 'the proper racial mix.' " His campaign demonstrated that as more African Americans voted and became influential in the Democratic Party, growing numbers of white ex-Democrats would abandon their traditional loyalty.[7]

Was Wallace a conservative? Frank Meyer denied it and said that as a populist he posed as much of a threat as ideological liberals. "While Liberalism stands for the imposition of utopian design upon the people because the Liberals know it is right, populism would substitute the tyranny of the majority over the individual, the pure will of 'the people,' untrammeled by considerations of freedom and virtue." More pragmatic conservatives like the Republican strategist Kevin Phillips saw the significance of the Wallace campaign and helped shape Richard Nixon's "southern strategy" in its shadow, predicting that the GOP could gain support from white Southerners. It was also the theme of Phillips's *The Emerging Republican Majority* (1969). Republican appeals to whites were usually coded, then and later, around issues of education and crime—outright racist declarations were no longer tolerable, though race clearly remained a strong motivator to voters.[8]

FOREIGN POLICY

Presidents Kennedy and Johnson escalated the American presence in Vietnam through the first half of the 1960s, and by 1965 American combat troops were directly engaged in fighting Viet Cong guerrillas and the North Vietnamese Army. The escalation was justified according to the containment doctrine and domino theory, by whose logic the spread of communism should be stopped wherever it appeared in the world, lest it gain strength from local victories and press on to world domination. This approach had been costly in lives and materiel during the Korean War but had worked. The American objective in Vietnam was similar; preserve the south without trying to conquer the north. By 1968 nearly half a million Americans were fighting in Vietnam.

National Review conservatives like James Burnham, Frank Meyer, William F. Buckley, Jr., and M. Stanton Evans believed in the domino theory but argued that the appropriate response was not to *contain* communism but to diminish and restrict it—dominos can fall both ways. Once America had committed troops and air power, they argued, it should aim to overpower and destroy the enemy. Burnham and Evans both wrote that Americans were being forced to fight with one hand tied behind their backs and that they should either seek victory or go home; a mere holding action that cost thousands of American lives was surely immoral. Burnham believed that America should bomb the cities of Hanoi and Haiphong, destroy North Vietnam's industries, break its dikes to interrupt food production, and use chemical, biological, and even nuclear weapons to achieve its objectives. If China entered the war, so much the better, since it still lacked nuclear capability and would fight against the Americans at a hopeless disadvantage.[9]

The war became progressively more unpopular inside the United States between 1965 and 1968, not least because young men were being drafted to fight in an unpopular cause and because casualty rates kept climbing. The draft presented conservatives with a dilemma. Their anticommunism pushed them toward favoring it as part of the all-out war on communism. Their libertarianism pushed them away from it, on grounds that it is an exercise of raw coercive power by the state. Frank Meyer, whose fusionist position was becoming the movement's orthodoxy by the mid-1960s, argued that the draft was justified only when the existence of society itself was at stake. "The principle of universal military obligation is justly derived from the constitution of civil society, without which no human freedom could exist. It is therefore one of the pillars of a free society. But since the enforcement of that obligation perforce limits temporarily the free choice of the citizen, a free state has the right to enforce it only when such enforcement is the sole way to defend the structure of freedom itself—that is, only in circumstances of paramount necessity." He seriously doubted whether it was justified for the less-than-total war in Vietnam.[10]

Conservatives were far from unanimous about Vietnam. L. Brent Bozell, who had written Goldwater's *Conscience of a Conservative* and *The Warren Revolution,* argued the conservative case against the war with growing fervor. A Catholic convert, he founded the conservative Catholic journal *Triumph* in 1966, aiming to combine the general political outlook of the new conservatives with a special attention to Catholic affairs. In his view, church teaching should take precedence over anticommunist ideology in the making of foreign policy. Catholic teaching in the "just war" tradition specified, among other things, noncombatants' immunity, but it was clear to Bozell that Vietnamese civilians, in constant danger from American troops as well as guerrillas, were dying in large numbers. Burnham's tough-minded advocacy of chemical weapons to starve out the enemy horrified him and prompted *Triumph* to split from *National Review.*[11]

Another source of division among the conservative writers was President Nixon's foreign policy innovations. His choice of Henry Kissinger, first as national security adviser, later as secretary of state, displeased the conservative Cold Warriors. Kissinger's adherence to the old European realpolitik tradition led him to assume that America could not prevail in the Cold War and that coexistence was a semipermanent condition. Kissinger moved toward a policy of détente in the early 1970s, hoping to ratchet down the dangerous and costly nuclear confrontation while disengaging from Vietnam. James Burnham regarded failure in Vietnam, negotiation of the first Strategic Arms Limitation Treaty (1972), and expressions of mutual goodwill between Soviet and American leaders as a failure of will by America, which would end in defeat. Another conservative activist, Phyllis Schlafly, wrote an impassioned eight-hundred-page attack on the secretary of state, *Kissinger on the Couch.*[12]

The most innovative element of the Nixon-Kissinger foreign policy was their decision to open diplomatic negotiations with the People's Republic of China (Mainland China), which the United States had treated as a pariah since Mao's victory over Chiang Kai-Shek in 1949. Conservatives were strongly represented in the remains of the "China Lobby," a group of military and diplomatic intellectuals who favored American support for Taiwan against Mao and were dismayed at the new initiative. When Nixon visited China early in 1972, Buckley was among the journalists who accompanied him, and he hated what he saw there. When Nixon toasted the Chinese leader, Buckley wrote that "the effect was as if Sir Hartley Shawcross had suddenly risen from the prosecutor's stand at Nuremberg [i.e., the Nazi war crimes trials at the end of World War II] and descended to embrace Goering and Goebbels and Doenitz and Hess, begging them to join with him in the making of a better world."[13]

LIBERTARIANISM

While the *Triumph* group dissented from the conservative foreign policy orthodoxy on religious grounds, libertarians dissented because they opposed all foreign adventures. The isolationist tradition of the Old Right had never disappeared completely, despite the powerful anticommunist consensus, and libertarians like Murray Rothbard still thought of the state itself as an enemy, to be resisted in all its claims on citizens. Washington, not Moscow or Beijing, was the place to watch with suspicious eyes.[14]

In Rothbard's view, *National Review* conservatives and mainstream Republicans exaggerated the Soviet menace as a way of justifying the arms race, heavy taxes, and an alarming increase in state power. In this way they had betrayed the old conservative small-government heritage. He was convinced that the Soviet economy was far weaker than most Sovietologists realized and that it was destined to collapse from its own internal contradictions. Meanwhile he was a vocal opponent of the draft.

Who shared these views? The growing New Left, whose ideas in those years Rothbard began to find persuasive. Rothbard, Leonard Liggio, and a handful of other libertarians, following the logic of these ideas, spent much of the late 1960s in the company of young leftists, even demonstrating in the streets against the war and working with revolutionary Maoists in the Peace and Freedom Party during 1968. The most colorful of their collaborators was Karl Hess (1923–94), another passionate antistatist but formerly a senior staffer of the Barry Goldwater presidential campaign. Hess wrote that Vietnam had made him realize that he could no longer remain part of the conservative movement: "Conservatives like me had spent our lives arguing against Federal power—with one exception. We trusted Washington with enormous powers to fight global Communism. We were wrong—as Taft foresaw when he opposed NATO. . . . Vietnam should remind all conservatives that whenever you put your faith in big government for *any* reason, sooner or later you end up as an apologist for mass murder." Together Rothbard and Hess edited the journal *Left and Right*, founded in 1965.[15]

Rothbard also contributed his "Confessions of a Right-Wing Liberal" to the radical journal *Ramparts* in 1968. His views had remained the same, he wrote, since the late 1940s, when he first became a libertarian, yet having once been denounced as a man of the "Neanderthal" right, he was now being condemned as part of the far left. The reason for this great shift was the fact that the American right had itself changed beyond recognition. In the 1940s it had opposed the Cold War, NATO, and intervention in Korea because it recognized militarism and conscription as "instruments of mass slavery and mass murder." But now it endorsed such commitments because of its obsessive anticommunism. Why had the right become internationalist and statist? First, because McCarthyism had mobilized the conservative masses in the name of anticommunism; second, because Buckley had been too willing to listen to the ex-communists who dominated his journal *National Review;* and third, because traditionalists like L. Brent Bozell and Russell Kirk (author of *The Conservative Mind*) did not regard personal liberty as the value most to be protected and promoted. Their "foul European conservatism" was the very thing America had rebelled against in the 1770s, yet "we have surrendered our libertarian birthright into the hands of those who yearn to restore the Golden Age of the Holy Inquisition." It was time, wrote Rothbard, "to wake up and rise up to restore our heritage."[16]

Among the young libertarians swept up in these odd shifts and alliances was Jerome Tuccille, whose insightful and entertaining memoir *It Usually Begins with Ayn Rand* (1972) is a forgotten gem about the Sixties experience. Tuccille described how he, like many other adolescent boys, many of them Jews and Catholics, first discovered libertarian politics as a substitute faith via their reading of Rand's novels. "The young crusader in search of a cause enters the world of *The Fountainhead* or *Atlas Shrugged* as though he were about to engage in unheard-of sexual delights for the first time. He has been warned beforehand. There is no need to search any further. The quest is over. Here is all the truth you've been looking for contained in these tightly packed pages of two gargantuan novels. He steps inside, cautiously at first, perhaps even skeptically, but before long he is swept away by the rampaging prose of the author and the heroic activities of her characters." Tuccille moved on from Rand to the Goldwater movement ("With a jaw like that he can't lose!") and to attempts to unite elements of the left and right against the Vietnam War. He recalls situations in which he, as an "anarcho-capitalist," addressed audiences made up of hippies and "anarcho-communists" on the merits of the free market and found himself in "a maelstrom of ideological furies representing every conceivable point along the starboard political spectrum."[17]

The unpopularity of the war and the continuing growth of government in the late 1960s prompted a wave of press interest in libertarianism and gave Rothbard the opportunity to publish his manifesto, *For a*

New Liberty (1973), with a major press, Macmillan. Well written and persuasive, it argued out the implications of his foundational beliefs that "War is Mass Murder, Conscription is Slavery, and Taxation is Robbery." The book's success coincided with the founding of the Libertarian Party, in 1972. From then on, it fielded candidates in elections nationwide, beginning with John Hospers (a philosophy professor at the University of Southern California), who ran for president in 1972. Membership and voting strength were tiny at first, and the party was plagued by utopians and hippies, who scared away potential middle-class members. Gradually, however, it grew to include slightly more than 1 percent of the electorate in the presidential election of 1980. Its think tank was the well-funded Cato Institute, founded in 1977. Like most third parties its leaders expected it not to win but to influence the political system and, if possible, to shift the grounds of debate in a libertarian direction. Strong personalities and sectarian squabbling—if nothing else—ensured that it would never reach very far as a practical political force.[18]

In 1974 libertarianism benefited from the publication of Robert Nozick's *Anarchy, State, and Utopia,* the most philosophically profound statement of its position thus far. Nozick (1938–2002), a Harvard professor, was writing in response to his colleague John Rawls's book *A Theory of Justice* (1971). Rawls had argued that inequalities in wealth are inherently unfair and that the state is justified in redistributing it, making transfers from more to less wealthy citizens. Nozick, by contrast, denied that economic inequality is necessarily a sign of injustice, because the human processes of wealth acquisition, enterprise, and deserving are so complex, and so dynamic over time. Any government attempting to redistribute what citizens happened to possess at any given moment would be tyrannically intrusive, violating everybody's rights all the time, but it was axiomatic to Nozick that "individuals have rights and there are things no person or group may do to them [without violating them]." Arguing that liberty is more important than equality, Nozick thought no more than a "night-watchman" state was justified.[19]

DOMESTIC UPHEAVAL

University campuses were transformed by a wave of campus rebellions in the 1960s, beginning with the Free Speech Movement at Berkeley in the fall of 1964. The Berkeley students demanded an end to restrictions on political activism on campus, and in the following years many other student groups pushed for an abolition of curfews and parietal rules and the introduction of coed dormitories. Some demanded more "relevant" courses; others argued for the abolition of grades or the right of students to grade their professors, as well as to be graded by them. At Columbia a demonstration urged the administration to transform its relations with the surrounding community; at Cornell a demonstration split down the middle on racial lines, as African American students, some armed with rifles, undertook an occupation of their own.

Conservatives reacted to these demonstrations with anger, directed, first, at the students themselves but, second, at the liberal faculty members and deans who seemed to them pathetically eager to mollify rather than discipline the students. These demonstrations, they wrote, threatened to annihilate the academy, which should be a place set apart from the bustle of society and dedicated to contemplation, detached study, and the passing on of society's accumulated wisdom. William Buckley, who had been a popular campus speaker for fifteen years by the late 1960s, increasingly found himself subjected to heckling and abuse from black radicals and members of Students for a Democratic Society (SDS). When, after being forced to abandon one campus speech, he asked his apologetic host why the majority of students tolerated such disruptions, the young man told him, "Last time we ejected one of these people the chancellor gave us hell. We just can't do anything, period. Especially not if they're black." Buckley reflected that university administrators ought to call the police on such occasions. "There is nothing at all wrong with the overwhelming majority of the students, whose intimidation is less the result of the raucous minority than the result of the intellectual and moral abdication of their faculty and deans." As in the inner cities, so on the campuses, sometimes law and order had to come first. "Policemen are, in certain circumstances, precisely the agents of civilization and humanity. Their availability is something that the forces of reason and enlightenment should celebrate, rather than deplore."[20]

Why was there so much student unrest? Russell Kirk believed that it was caused not by principled objection to real conditions on campus but by ennui and boredom. Always an unashamed elitist, Kirk thought far too many young people were going to college, where they really did not belong. The idea that college is right for everyone, he said, was the secular equivalent of the old Pelagian heresy—that everyone will go to heaven! Most young people, in his view, were intellectually unsuited to prolonged rigorous study. Those who did have the gift were discouraged when they witnessed the inevitable dilution of standards on American campuses and the frivolity of the curriculum. "American affluence and a fatuous social permissivism [have] turned out a college-age population often intellectually flaccid and insulated against the harsher aspects of the human condition—though sentimentally lachrymose whenever the 'underprivileged' or 'culturally deprived' [are] mentioned." The fact that campus enrollments were swelled by young men eager to avoid the Vietnam draft just made matters worse. Huge campuses like Berkeley were now just holding pens for "intellectually rootless" youth, "depersonalized by the vastness of the campus crowd."[21]

A youth culture flourished, not only on campuses but among the huge number of baby boomers in their teens and twenties. Its approach to life had an effect even on those reluctant to give up all the trappings of respectability; it revolutionized the appearance of young Americans. Just glance at college campus photographs from 1960 and then 1970. In the former the close-cropped men are wearing suits and ties, and the women twin sets and pearls beneath their permed hair. In the latter, men and women alike have long shaggy hair and wear bell-bottom jeans, brightly colored tie-dyed shirts, and loose sandals. Short-haired men still clinging to the old look can now be identified as young conservatives—some will be wearing lapel badges that read "Bomb Hanoi" or "Don't Immanentize the Eschaton." As Jerome Tuccille wrote, going to a YAF conference in the mid-1960s was "like entering a time capsule and being transported ten or fifteen years into the past. In an age of long hair, jeans, and love-beads it was a mind-blowing experience to . . . find yourself surrounded by a brigade of Pat Boones."[22]

By 1968, lack of progress in Vietnam, race riots, student demonstrations, and rising crime rates had brought many conservatives to fear imminent social collapse. The New Left was longing for it, the New Right was dreading it, and (said conservatives) the liberal leadership was to blame for it. Frank Meyer summarized: "In its surrender before Communism in Vietnam, as in its surrender before mobs in our cities and our universities, that leadership is no longer merely doing what it has done for 35 years, retreating before Communism abroad and steadily dismantling the Constitution at home. It is no longer merely governing with bad means to achieve bad ends. It is showing an inability to govern at all: abroad, betraying the most fundamental interests of the Republic, and at home letting the constituted power in its trust slip from its nerveless fingers into the possession of self-proclaimed 'representatives of the popular will,' who burn our cities, desecrate our universities, and occupy our capital." If there was a bright spot on the horizon, it came from the arrival of new allies, disillusioned Great Society liberals who soon came to be known as the neoconservatves.[23]

THE NEOCONSERVATIVES

Neoconservatism began in reaction to the era's urban, racial, and educational crises, among intellectuals alarmed at the direction of American liberal politics. Many of the first neoconservatives were social science professors at America's major universities, and they gave conservatism a stronger foothold in the academy than it had held hitherto. As professors and authority figures, they were sometimes the targets of student demonstrations in the 1960s, and they began to understand the *National Review* conservatives' concern that the academic traditions of stability and detachment were under threat. In some respects, however, they were at odds with the older conservatives on philosophical and practical grounds. Only gradually would the two movements converge, with profound consequences for each.[24]

Many of the neoconservatives, like many of the *National Review* group, were alumni of the pre–World War II left. The most famous of them, Irving Kristol (b. 1920), had been a Trotskyist in his student days at the City College of New York. Like the authors and editors of *Partisan Review,* his favorite journal in the 1930s, he took pride in his detachment from the Stalinist or communist left but spent many years as a Marxist. By the late 1940s and early 1950s, after wartime service in the army, Kristol had broken with the left and become an anticommunist, sharing much of the outlook common to Arthur Schlesinger, Jr., Reinhold Niebuhr, Morton White, and other Cold War liberals, the view elaborated in Schlesinger's influential book *The Vital Center* (1949). Unlike them he declined to condemn McCarthyism, an early augury of his move to the political right. Marxist-style class analysis continued to appear in his and his colleagues' work, however, as did the biting polemical writing style they had learned on the left.[25]

Neoconservatism was a movement dominated by Jewish and Catholic thinkers, the sons and grandsons of Eastern European immigrants. In the pages of *The Public Interest,* an intellectual and policy journal founded in 1965 by Kristol and the Harvard sociologist Daniel Bell (b. 1919), sociologists and urban studies specialists diagnosed urban problems and proposed practical ways to remedy them, in the hope that they could provide government departments with the best current data. Nathan Glazer, Daniel Patrick Moynihan, Seymour Martin Lipset, Aaron Wildavsky, and James Q. Wilson—all academics with government ties—were among its regular contributors. They did not think of themselves as conservatives of any kind at that point, and they tried, especially in the early years, to be as unideological as possible. They even declared in the inaugural issue that some readers would regard *The Public Interest* as "a middle-aged magazine for middle-aged readers." Bell had argued in *The End of Ideology* (1960) that pragmatic, down-to-earth problem solving was replacing the early twentieth-century's obsession with messianic ideologies. The *Public Interest* approach, accordingly, was to gather statistics on urban problems, analyze them objectively, by computer when possible, review proposed responses, and advocate those that proved most effective in practice. Only gradually did the authors realize that all the issues they addressed contained unavoidable moral elements; as they stressed this moral dimension their work began to take on a conservative coloration.[26]

Another important recruit in the late 1960s was Norman Podhoretz (b. 1930), editor since 1960 of *Commentary,* the journal of the American Jewish Committee. At first he took New Left writers seriously and promoted their work in *Commentary.* But Podhoretz was an iconoclast and contrarian. He blew the whistle on liberal pieties about race relations in "My Negro Problem, and Ours" (1963). Then, in the controversial autobiography *Making It* (1967), he implicitly attacked nearly all his left and liberal friends and associates. The book traced his rise from humble origins in Brooklyn to a position of wealth, power, and influence among American opinion makers. Glorifying material success and America's mainstream material values, it sneered at the cult of literary alienation and denigrated many of his intellectual peers. He had become determined, he wrote, to regard success as better than failure, wealth as better than poverty, and power as better than meekness, and to be defiantly proud of his success, as defined in middle-class terms. Reviewers of *Making It* (devotees of the world of literary alienation) panned it without mercy. Podhoretz retaliated by going to war against the left-liberal outlook, epitomized by his former friend Jason Epstein, editor of the *New York Review of Books*. *Commentary* in the late sixties and early seventies became the flagship journal of the neoconservatives.[27]

The "neocons," as they came to be known, brought a set of distinctive insights to their study of America. Among them was the idea of the "new class," an idea earlier sketched by James Burnham in *The Managerial Revolution* (1941). They argued that America's educated managers and bureaucrats should be thought of as a class that stood to gain by the expansion of the role of government. Members of this new class administered the rapidly expanding welfare bureaucracy, Medicare and Medicaid, and all the rest of the Great Society programs. They were the teachers and professors staffing America's rapidly expanding public educational sector too. The members of this new class, however, had different values and interests from those of business bureaucrats, to whom, at first glance, they seemed similar. Skeptical of the market economy, new class bureaucrats held a direct stake in the expansion of government programs—despite their claims of objectivity and expertise they were *not* disinterested parties. Many, moreover, had been educated in the modern humanities, which taught them to challenge their society's conventional wisdom. They represented, said the neoconservatives, the views of a rapidly growing "adversary culture," as likely to undermine as to uphold American standards, institutions, and principles. Their growing influence in society therefore threatened its core institutions and beliefs.[28]

As social observers at the time noticed, however, the adversary culture was paradoxical. Rock music and subversive literature might indeed be undermining the traditional virtues and verities, but how did ordinary citizens find out about them? Usually through advertisements and commercial promotions. In other words, at least part of the business community, far from being the polar antagonist of the adversary culture, was actively promoting it. Leftists of the 1960s described rock bands that signed lucrative recording contracts as sellouts who were being co-opted by the system. From the neoconservative point of view, it was the record companies that were selling out, by agreeing to promote music that criticized—and therefore apparently threatened—American values and traditions. They were, in other words, fulfilling the economist Joseph Schumpeter's old claim that capitalism carries the seeds of its own destruction.[29]

A related neoconservative idea, found especially in the work of Samuel Huntington, was that as more of the population became highly educated, society became progressively more ungovernable. The 1960s and early 1970s in America appeared to illustrate his point. Too many citizens standing up for their rights and demonstrating in the streets threatened to destabilize society into the indefinite future. Where generations of civics teachers had urged students to do their duty by voting, the neoconservatives raised the opposite possibility—perhaps stable democracies needed a higher level of citizen passivity and noninvolvement. Huntington was clearly looking at society from the point of view of the government rather than the citizenry. The neoconservatives all assumed that government was a job for the experts, specialists who could bring the greatest knowledge to bear and had a proper appreciation of complexity. Unlike populist reformers, they never resorted to simple cure-all nostrums, and in the late sixties and early seventies they rated stability as almost the highest political good. Marxists analyzed society in order to overthrow it. These ex-Marxists analyzed it in order to stabilize it.[30]

If the idea of the new class hinted at the neoconservatives' Marxist past, so did their promotion of the idea of an American underclass. Marx had called it the *lumpenproletariat* and his Victorian Tory contemporaries had called it the "mudsills" or the "dregs of society." Whatever the name, this was the group at the bottom of society, whose members were unable or unwilling to hold down steady jobs and who rejected the idea of deferred gratification.

Daniel Patrick Moynihan was an important early contributor to the underclass debate and later became a prominent neoconservative. He cowrote *Beyond the Melting Pot* (1963) with Nathan Glazer, a sociological classic on the persistence of ethnicity in the society and politics of New York City. Drawn from his Harvard professorship to work as an assistant secretary of labor in the Johnson administration, he then wrote an internal government memorandum in March 1965, "The Negro Family: The Case for National Action." It argued that the passage of antidiscrimination legislation alone was not enough to ensure upward social and economic mobility for African Americans. Black-family breakdown, single-parent families, and the widespread absence of working fathers had created what Moynihan described as a "tangle of pathologies," which were going to require a great deal of remedial government aid. As illegitimacy rates increased, said Moynihan, more young black men grew up in unstable family units without the presence of a strong male role model. They were likely to become members of a permanent underclass.[31]

Warmly received at first inside the Johnson administration and consonant with the interventionist mood of the Great Society, the Moynihan report was then leaked, provoking an outcry among black and leftist intellectuals who regarded it as insulting, abrasive to black dignity, and defective in understating the impact of racial discrimination. Moynihan, widely vilified, wrote a scorching rebuttal to these criticisms, but the experience had the effect of alienating him from many former colleagues. The riots of 1966 and 1967 had the same effect. Liberals, he wrote in 1967, must stop "defending and explaining away anything, however outrageous, which Negroes, individually and collectively, might do." They should also realize that their concern for preserving order made them logical allies with conservatives. At the same time, conservatives like Buckley and Meyer were beginning to regard Moynihan as a potential convert to their own point of view. Buckley wrote in October 1967 that Moynihan "is saying some of the most interesting things being said these days in public life, most strikingly that liberals have a good deal to learn from conservatives. . . . Anything we conservatives can do to help, just holler."[32]

The underclass theme, meanwhile, was developed by Edward Banfield (1916–99), another urban sociologist from Harvard, in *The Unheavenly City* (1970). Banfield shared Moynihan's view that culture, not prejudice, made inner-city progress difficult. Lower-class people, whether black or white, he argued, constituted about 5 percent of the urban population but caused most of its severe problems. They lacked the capacity for long-term planning and self-sacrifice, tended to live in the moment, and dropped out of school too early to be competitive in an increasingly technological world.

Their "preconventional morality" lured many to lives of crime, and they were sexually profligate, unable to create stable families. Unlike liberal optimists who believed (or who had believed until recently) that America's residual social problems could now be solved rationally one by one, Banfield thought they were probably here to stay. Among his suggestions for managing (as opposed to solving) them was that liberal intellectuals should discuss them less, because in the discussion, they created the impression that the problems were now going to be solved. Banfield dismissed the notion that the urban riots were rebellions. On the contrary, he wrote, they were opportunistic—fueled by the search for "fun and profit." The book was greeted by a firestorm of criticism from political and academic reviewers who questioned his methodology, his unexamined assumptions, and what some of them interpreted as his "blame the victim" approach. Conservatives, by contrast, lauded it as a work of genius. The historian George Nash identifies *The Unheavenly City* debate as one of the bridges that linked *National Review* conservatives and *Public Interest* neoconservatives at the start of the 1970s.[33]

Moynihan, Banfield, and others, in their analysis of the urban crisis, added a significant element to the neoconservative lexicon—the law of unintended consequences. Admitting that the intentions of the Great Society planners had been benign, they showed that the programs, as enacted, had had unforeseen side effects, creating perverse incentives that their architects had not anticipated and sometimes worsening the problems they were meant to remedy. Such effects, they added, *always* develop, and the more ambitious the program, the more likely it is to have unintended consequences whose ultimate effect will be more significant than its intended benefits. The implication was that government ought to be much less willing to undertake dramatic programs because it could never really know what it was getting into.[34]

The classic example was Aid to Families with Dependent Children (AFDC). Benign in intention, it was designed to ensure that poor single mothers would be able to care for themselves and their children, at least at the basic subsistence level. Among the unforeseen consequence, however, was that AFDC inadvertently provided poor women with an incentive to have children and *not* to marry, because married women were ineligible for the payments. Not marrying became a rational response to the program, even though "family breakdown" was already being described in government and the media as a national crisis. This observation did not mean that government should do nothing. The idea of bringing an end to poverty in America once and for all long remained an alluring prospect. The first neoconservatives were certainly not libertarians, for whom government action was virtually always wrong, but they were starting to recognize its limits.[35]

Why were most Americans *not* part of the underclass? How did citizens learn and sustain a sense of social morality? An atomized society of self-interested economic players could not nurture the virtues; neither could a totalitarian society. What could? Neoconservatives answered that "mediating institutions," standing halfway between the individual and the state, were all-important. When they thrived, the community would prosper. The family was the most important of these mediating institutions, followed by the church or synagogue, the voluntary association, and the ethnic group, all of which were based on the fact that humans are social animals with a disposition to fraternize with like-minded people. Moynihan and Glazer had shown in *Beyond the Melting Pot* that ethnic groups do not disappear. The neoconservative writer Michael Novak added, in *The Rise of the Unmeltable Ethnics* (1972), that their survival is highly desirable, a welcome counterweight to the corrosive standardization of contemporary life. Peter Berger and Richard Neuhaus, in *To Empower People* (1977), made a comparable point, seeing intermediate sources of belonging for citizens as keys to social health. In these and dozens of other works, on an apparently diverse array of topics, neoconservative writers stressed the importance of moral education in mediating institutions for the preservation of a good society.[36]

The existence of these mediating institutions and ethnic groups had implications for social policy. After all, one of the great projects of the 1960s was racial integration of education and the workforce. Neoconservatives were among the first to argue that outlawing racial discrimination, while good in itself, was by no means a guarantee that integration would follow. After all, members of families favor one another; so do the members of ethnic groups; so do the members of particular clubs and particular neighborhoods. As Moynihan and Glazer had shown, jobs in New York were passed on from father to son or cousin in a dense web of ethnic and family relations. Busing and affirmative action were designed to overcome these stubborn facts, but neoconservatives were quick to see that such policies had a destructive as well as a constructive aspect. Busing, in particular, broke down neighborhoods by carrying children away to distant schools and making parental participation in the life of their children's schools much more difficult. Neoconservative writers cautioned readers against the assumption that anyone who opposed busing or affirmative action was necessarily a barefaced racist; more likely they were citizens eager to defend their local traditions and their family and kin group's aspirations.[37]

The neoconservatives' social thought was steadily anti-utopian. They believed that aspiring to create a perfect society leads to intolerant or repressive measures. Already in 1971 Nathan Glazer was writing about the "limits of social policy," pointing out how many issues were simply beyond the reach of government programs. Surely, he wrote, it was better to have lower expectations and to accept imperfect realities, while maintaining traditional standards of decency and not making unrealistic promises.[38]

NEOCONSERVATIVES AND FOREIGN POLICY

In the 1970s neoconservatives were as anti-utopian about foreign policy as they were about domestic affairs. Wars, they believed, are going to happen now and in the future, just as they have always happened in the past. Belligerence and the urge to dominate are intrinsic to human nature. Nations, accordingly, must prepare themselves to fight on the most favorable possible terms. At the same time, American tradition and history demonstrate that wars can sometimes improve a political situation, can, for example, lead to the liberation of slaves (the American Civil War) or rescue Europe from Nazi thralldom (World War II). They came to believe, accordingly, that fighting on behalf of American principles could be both necessary and honorable.

Most of them had been "vital center" Democrats in the 1950s and 1960s, firm believers in a strong anticommunist and anti-Soviet foreign policy. Many of them admitted by 1970 that America should disengage from Vietnam, but they did not think the essential issues of the Cold War had changed. They continued to believe that Soviet communism was their great antagonist and the greatest threat to American security and that the policy of containment enunciated early in the Cold War should be maintained. They were dismayed to see the McGovern wing of the Democratic Party (George McGovern was the Democratic presidential candidate in 1972) favoring a retreat into isolationism. Norman Podhoretz's "Making the World Safe for Communism" (1975) argued that the policy of détente was a retreat from necessary confrontation and was paving the way to surrender. Liberalism under FDR, Truman, Kennedy, and Johnson had been a fighting faith, he continued, and so it should be still. Invoking the memory of Woodrow Wilson, Podhoretz declared that it was right "to use American power to make the world safe for democracy."[39]

An important foreign policy question for many neoconservatives was the survival of Israel. From the moment of its birth in 1948 Israel had been ringed by hostile Arab nations that denied its right to exist and wanted to destroy it if possible. Israel, accordingly, had had to fight for its life from the beginning and could never let down its guard. By analogy the neoconservatives believed that America, too, must be ready to fight for its life against an implacable foe and prepare carefully for the eventuality. Failure to do so would be unpardonably naïve, as would be hoping or expecting that war and the prospect of war might cease. The Soviet threat to America was perhaps less immediate than the Arab threat to Israel, but the principle was the same in both cases. Israel was more than just a metaphor or analogy, however. Many neoconservatives were Jewish, and the condition of Israel concerned them deeply. They took pride in Israel's victories in the wars of 1967 and 1973 and tried to ensure continued American support for Israel. The anti-Zionist criticism of other American Jews, such as Noam Chomsky and I. F. Stone, enraged them. They also disliked the Carter administration, elected in 1976, because it seemed to them insufficiently pro-Israel.[40]

American self-confidence had reached a low ebb by the mid-1970s, thanks to an odious combination of economic stagnation, inflation, defeat in Vietnam, and the protracted Watergate crisis. One of the first public figures to work at reviving confidence was Daniel Patrick Moynihan, whom President Ford appointed his ambassador to the United Nations in 1975. He challenged denunciations of American imperialism by Third World countries, which had become part of the UN's standard rhetoric by then, and avowed the superiority of America over communism. When the Ugandan dictator Idi Amin sponsored a resolution that "Zionism is a Form of Racism and Racial Discrimination," Moynihan, in a speech that Podhoretz had helped him write, denounced him as a "racist murderer" on the floor of the General Assembly. This swashbuckling and patriotic rhetoric in a place famous for its muted hypocrisy made Moynihan a popular figure and enabled him to run successfully in 1976 for a U.S. Senate seat from New York.[41]

Reviving confidence in America as an actor in world politics seemed essential to neoconservatives in the 1970s, not least because American deterrence policy depended on convincing the Russians that America really would defend itself with nuclear weapons if it came to the point. Nuclear-arms limitation talks were, therefore, hazardous. The Nixon administration negotiated the first Strategic Arms Limitation Treaty (SALT I), which Congress ratified in 1972. The Ford and Carter administrations of the mid- to late 1970s carried on another round of negotiations, and Carter was ready to sign SALT II in 1979. The treaties' supporters, including the CIA's "Team A," took the view that mutually assured destruction (MAD) gave both sides an incentive to economize in the area of new weapon development, since each side was already capable of annihilating the other. Neoconservatives, however, preferred the report of "Team B," a group of Sovietologists appointed by CIA director George Bush to offer a second opinion. Their study of Soviet weapons development and strategic doctrine convinced them that the Russians looked on nuclear weapons as eminently usable and potentially as war-winning devices. They also claimed to detect a massive Soviet arms buildup.[42]

Team B leaders included Richard Perle, Richard Pipes, Paul Wolfowitz, and Paul Nitze, articulate advocates of the neoconservative view that the Cold War was as dangerous as ever and that America ought not to be content merely with a policy of coexistence. Nitze (1907–2004) was among the founders, in 1976, of the Committee on the Present Danger, a pressure group designed to "help promote a better understanding of the main problems confronting our foreign policy, based on a disciplined effort to gather the facts and a sustained discussion of their significance for our national security and survival." In an early statement the committee declared that the Soviet Union "has been enlarging and improving both its strategic and conventional military forces far more rapidly than the United States and its allies" and that "Soviet expansionism threatens to destroy the world balance of forces on which the survival of freedom depends." Their view, accordingly, was that the Soviets would sign the SALT II treaty only if they perceived it as giving themselves a strategic advantage in the Cold War. If it *did* give them an advantage, of course the United States ought not to sign. In any event, the Team B view prevailed because the Soviet invasion of Afghanistan in 1979 led to a sharp deterioration of American-Soviet relations.[43]

As the Cold War heated up again in the late 1970s, some neoconservatives retrospectively revised their views about Vietnam. The war had finally ended when Saigon fell to a North Vietnamese Army attack in 1975. Southern Vietnamese who had worked for the old regime or for the Americans were shipped off to jungle "re-education" camps or killed. Tens of thousands of desperate refugees, the "boat people," set sail in unseaworthy vessels to get away from the tyrannical new regime. Witnessing these developments some neoconservatives chided themselves for their earlier outspokenness against the war. Perhaps, they wrote, they had been wrong in opposing the war during the 1960s. Perhaps the nation had been right to shoulder the sacrifice of such a war if the alternative was this ruthless tyranny. Peter Berger (b. 1929), previously an antiwar writer and activist, wrote that "I was wrong and so were all those who thought as I did. . . . Contrary to what most members (including myself) of the antiwar movement expected, the peoples of Indochina have, since 1975, been subjected to suffering far worse than anything that was inflicted upon them by the United States." Norman Podhoretz reconsidered the war in *Why We Were in Vietnam* (1982) and admitted that he, too, had been "facile in failing to take the full measure of what an American defeat would cost."[44]

In the ensuing decades neoconservatives, both intellectually and practically, were to play an ever increasing role in American conservatism in foreign and domestic affairs. Peter Steinfels, author of the first analytical study of the group, wrote of them in 1979: "Hundreds of books have been written on the political developments of the sixties. . . . Yet oddly enough the decade's most enduring legacy to American politics may be the outlook forged in reaction to sixties turbulence, an outlook fierce in its attachment to political and cultural moderation, committed to stability as the prerequisite for justice rather than the other way around, pessimistic about the possibilities for long-range, or even short-range change in America, and imbued with a foreboding sense of our civilization's decline." It was a prophetic comment. By the early 1990s neoconservative voices would dominate the political right.[45]

FEMINISM AND ITS ANTAGONISTS

Many innovations of the sixties and early seventies lasted no more than a year or two, but a few had lasting consequences. The women's movement is a case in point. Betty Friedan's *The Feminine Mystique* (1963) was a surprise best seller and prompted her to create the National Organization for Women in 1966. It argued that gender discrimination in employment and the law was unjust, that all careers should be open to women, and that women and men should receive equal pay for equal work. It campaigned for the abolition of invidious discrimination in employment. Radical feminism, growing up inside the student and antiwar movements, began almost at once to build on these foundations but went further, arguing that a society now known to have been poisoned by racism was also poisoned by "sexism" (then a neologism), that women collectively were victimized by men collectively, and that a radical restructuring of gender relations was necessary.

If one group of women, the feminists, thought they were the victims of discrimination, wrongly condemned to the status of second-class citizens, another group, conservatives, felt that feminism was misguided and would worsen rather than improve American women's situation. Midge Decter (b. 1927), an energetic neoconservative controversialist (and the wife of Norman Podhoretz), wrote extensively on the issue in the early 1970s. In "The Liberated Woman" (1970) she noted that young middle-class women enjoyed more material advantages and greater security than any others in history. Their claim to be victims was therefore ludicrous on its face. Women also benefited from the same social freedoms as men, being equally free to marry or to pursue careers, or both. Feminism, as Decter saw it, was an infantile form of status seeking among the already privileged, so that its alleged similarity to the black freedom struggle was completely bogus. Developing the theme at book length in *The New Chastity* (1972), Decter argued that the women's movement was essentially similar to the youth movement of the 1960s, part of "a terror-ridden refusal to be hooked into the . . . ecological chain of birthing, growing, and dying. It is the demand, in other words, to remain children." Arlene Croce, a *National*

Review alumna now writing for *Commentary*, agreed. She offered a witheringly dismissive survey of feminist literature and philosophy. The work of Kate Millett, Shulamith Firestone, and even Betty Friedan, she said, was childishly petulant, usually linked to clumsy advocacy of utopian socialism and profoundly inaccurate about the nature of men's and women's experience. "Feminism is a solipsistic haven, a place in the psyche where all the bad and bitter feelings unite, where unbearable personal failures are rationalized by a belief in failures in society."[46]

The politics of feminism came to a head over the Equal Rights Amendment (ERA). Passed by Congress in 1972, the amendment specified that "equality of rights under the law shall not be denied or abridged by the United States or by any State on account of sex," adding that Congress was empowered to intervene where necessary to enforce this principle. At first, state governments acted quickly to ratify the amendment, and advocates of the ERA felt confident that the necessary three-quarters of the states (thirty-eight) would soon be secured.

Phyllis Schlafly (b. 1924), a conservative Catholic writer and Republican activist from St. Louis, previously concerned mainly with anticommunism, campaigned to stop the amendment. She built an effective grassroots lobby, StopERA, to campaign against it. In the essay "What's Wrong with 'Equal Rights' for Women?" (1972) she explained why. The family, she wrote, is the basic institution of society in Judeo-Christian tradition, and it depends on different but complementary roles for men, women, and children. Women are essentially nurturers and need to be legally supported and protected in raising their children. What had really liberated American women was not feminism but the labor-saving technologies invented over the past century and distributed by free-market capitalism. The ERA, far from helping women, would deny them the protection long afforded them by special labor legislation, would expose them to the military draft, and would increase the intrusion of the federal government into their lives. Feminism, in her view was "anti-family, anti-children, and pro-abortion. . . . women's libbers view the home as a prison and the wife and mother as a slave."[47]

When state legislatures gathered to debate ratification of the ERA, they began to find crowds of energetic antifeminist women chanting slogans at the State House, while their offices were bombarded with correspondence hostile to the amendment. As Schlafly's biographer notes, this was the first time in American history that large numbers of conservative women had rallied to protest a domestic political reform. The monthly *Phyllis Schlafly Report* kept StopERA chapters in touch with one another and publicized effective lobbying techniques while its inexhaustible author, the mother of six children, worked her way through law school. One by one state governments began to yield to this lobbying pressure, declining to endorse the amendment—several even rescinded their ratifications. In consequence, the seven-year ratification period and an extension both expired without the necessary thirty-eight states giving their consent. The amendment never did become part of the American Constitution, and the triumphant Schlafly went on to write *The Power of the Positive Woman* (1977), a vindication of traditional gender roles.[48]

The social transformations of the 1960s and 1970s generated other new forms of political conflict. None was more inflammatory than abortion. Radical feminists claimed that all issues relating to their sexuality and reproduction should be dealt with by women themselves and that women ought not to have to defer to the expertise of a largely male-dominated medical profession. They should be entitled, they said, to abortion on demand. It was not clear at first that this issue would involve conservatives, certainly not that it would become a flashpoint for bitter controversy. William Buckley even suggested, in a 1965 article, that conservatives should take a libertarian view of the issue and let people decide for themselves. As a Catholic he accepted his church's teaching against abortion, but he recognized that different people had different views on the subject.[49]

L. Brent Bozell, the editor of *Triumph* magazine, had already dissented from the *National Review* conservatives' line on Vietnam. In 1970 the rift between Bozell and Buckley widened when Bozell led what was probably America's first antiabortion demonstration. Learning that a clinic at the George Washington University Hospital in Washington, D.C., was the site of abortions, he and a group of Catholic traditionalists marched in procession against the clinic, bearing a cross and other Christian icons, calling themselves the "Sons of Thunder" and chanting "Viva Cristo Rey" (long live Christ the King). They scuffled with law enforcement officers, smashed windows, and got themselves arrested. The District of Columbia police, familiar with left-wing militants after countless demonstrations, did not realize that these demonstrators were right-wingers or that their clothes honored the Carlist militia, monarchists from the Spanish Civil War, not Che Guevara. Bozell insisted the demonstration was justified; Buckley deplored it as a silly parody of leftist street theater.[50]

From the early 1970s on, abortion became an increasingly contentious issue. The Supreme Court's decision in *Roe v. Wade* (1973), however, astonished even advocates of a liberalized abortion policy. It horrified opponents. The 7-2 majority decision, which overturned laws in all fifty states, declared that the constitutional right to privacy, first discovered by the court only eight years previously in *Griswold v. Connecticut,* protected the decision of women, if pregnant, as to whether to have an abortion. In the first three months of a pregnancy the right was declared to be almost absolute; restrictions applied with increasing rigor for the second and third trimesters. The decision, written by Justice Blackmun, has become one of the most notorious of the twentieth century, lauded by pro-choice advocates, reviled by pro-lifers.[51]

Justices Rehnquist and White, dissenting, pointed out that abortions are surgical procedures, that they happen in public hospitals, that they require the services of doctors and nurses, and therefore cannot possibly be regarded as private. Neither could the dissenters find anything in the Constitution to justify the procedure. White wrote: "The Court simply fashions and announces a new constitutional right for pregnant mothers and, with scarcely any reason or authority for its action, invests that right with sufficient substance to override most existing state abortion statutes. The upshot is that the people and legislatures of the 50 states are constitutionally disentitled to weigh the relative importance of the continued existence and development of the fetus, on the one hand, against a spectrum of possible impacts on the mother, on the other hand." White described the decision not as a matter of constitutional interpretation but as "an exercise of raw judicial power," which was "improvident and extravagant."[52]

First into the field to protest *Roe v. Wade* were Catholic conservatives, led by James McFadden. McFadden (1930–98), another friend of William Buckley and a long-time staff member of *National Review,* recalled hearing about the *Roe* decision with the same intensity as a later generation of Americans recalled hearing about the attack on the World Trade Center. It was, he said, his "road to Damascus," a life-changing event that horrified him and led him to devote all his energy to reversing it. He founded a new journal, *Human Life Review*, in 1975. It began as a single-issue antiabortion journal, but with the passage of time began to incorporate other bioethical controversies too, taking a fervently prolife position in all of them.[53]

As it developed, the conservative critique of *Roe v. Wade* advanced on two fronts. One was moral, a straightforward declaration that a fetus is a human being and that to destroy it is therefore to take a human life. The strongest analogies, widely employed by such prolife writers as Joseph Sobran and John T. Noonan, were to slavery, which had wrongly denied the humanity of an entire category of people, and with the Holocaust, in which millions of people had been annihilated not because of what they had done but because of what they *were*. If the first critique was moral, the second was legal. Conservative legal critics like Noonan and Charles Rice argued that *Roe v. Wade*, like the school prayer cases of the 1960s, was an example of judicial activism, of judges *deciding* what the law should be rather than impartially testing the law against preexisting constitutional standards. The Supreme Court, yet again, had usurped Congress's legislative function.[54]

Perhaps no single event had more lasting consequences for the shape of American politics in the thirty years following the decision than *Roe v. Wade*. By 1980 the Republicans had positioned themselves as the more sympathetic of the two major parties to the antiabortion cause, but party strategists knew that their big tent also contained millions of voters who were pro-choice, just as the Democrats sheltered millions of prolifers. The election-campaign rhetoric of GOP candidates often included fire-breathing denunciations of the "baby-killers," but Republicans in Congress and the White House put little or none of their energy into legislating against, or seeking a constitutional amendment affecting, abortion. This was one of the many areas in which conservatives in power, during the 1980s, were to find themselves not only genuinely divided but also forced to make practical concessions to political realities.

THE NEW CHRISTIAN RIGHT

In the late 1970s evangelical Protestants joined pro-life Catholics in protesting abortion. They also joined campaigns against a wide range of social and lifestyle issues that had arisen out of the 1960s and 1970s.

Disengaged from organized politics since the 1920s, seeking to convert souls to Christ one by one rather than to transform society, evangelicals reentered the conservative political arena in the 1970s and played an important role in the presidential election campaign of 1980. Their principal theorist was Francis Schaeffer, a grizzled and bearded guru who lived in a Swiss mountain retreat called L'Abri, where Protestant pilgrims from America went to seek out his wisdom. Behind him, in turn, stood a distinguished lineage of such Dutch Calvinist theologians as Abraham Kuyper. Schaeffer wrote a book and hosted a television series, *How Should We Then Live?* (1976), designed to counter two television blockbusters of that era: Kenneth Clark's *Civilisation* (1969) and Jacob Bronowski's *The Ascent of Man* (1973). Clark and Bronowski took what Schaeffer called a "secular humanist" approach to the history of humankind and the progress of civilization. They denigrated Christianity, he said, and had substituted a materialist for a spiritual vision of life.[55]

In books, lectures, and articles of the 1970s Schaeffer hammered away at the theme that evangelicals could no longer afford to turn their backs on the world, because to do so was to leave it in the hands of the secular humanists, whose contempt for the Christian verities was epitomized by *Roe v. Wade*. By 1980 more than a million legalized abortions per year were being performed in America: a new Holocaust. "Sixty years ago could we have imagined that unborn children would be killed by the millions here in our own country? Or that we would have no freedom of speech when it comes to speaking of God and biblical truth in our public schools? Or that every form of sexual perversion would be promoted by the entertainment media? Or that marriage, raising children, and family life would be objects of attack? Sadly we must say that very few Christians have understood the battle that we are in. Very few have taken a strong and courageous stand against the world spirit of this age as it destroys our culture and the Christian ethos that once shaped our country." Schaeffer also believed that American evangelicalism suffered from an excess of emotionalism and that it was intellectually undernourished. Billy Graham–style revivalism, he argued, was all very well, but it created a temporary euphoria that brought only shallow conversions; becoming a Christian should engage the head as well as the heart.[56]

Schaeffer's was the principal theoretical voice behind the group of ministers and conservative activists who created a new political organization in the late 1970s, the Moral Majority. Led by the Reverend Jerry Falwell, a charismatic Baptist minister from Lynchburg, Virginia, and supported by Richard Viguerie, one of the pioneers of conservative direct-mail fund-raising campaigns, it brought out the evangelical vote in 1980 on behalf of Republican candidate Ronald Reagan. Was America in the midst of a moral crisis in the late 1970s? The claim could certainly be heard from many sides, and it was true that a rapid succession of jarring social changes had taken place very recently. The stigma against pre- and extramarital sex had disappeared among large sections of the middle class; recreational drug use was widespread; crime rates and divorce rates were rising. Moral Majority's supporters saw themselves as last-ditch defenders against social breakdown, chaos, and evil, whereas its critics treated the movement as a cynical Republican grab for votes and power.[57]

GEORGE WILL

In the 1970s a new generation of conservative political writers matured, the most noteworthy of whom was George Will. Born in 1941, the son of an Illinois philosophy professor, Will began his career as an academic, earning a Princeton Ph.D. in political philosophy and teaching in the late sixties at Michigan State University (the campus Russell Kirk had so disliked) and then at the University of Toronto. He moved to Washington in 1970, however, to work for a Republican senator, Gordon Allott of Colorado.[58]

In Washington, Will established himself as a stimulating and controversial conservative writer, working as *National Review*'s Capitol Hill correspondent between 1972 and 1978. He began a political column in the *Washington Post* in 1974 and helped to separate *National Review* from President Nixon by his outspoken articles on the worsening Watergate crisis. In 1976 he began a regular column in *Newsweek* as well, demonstrating the mainstream media's increased willingness in that decade to employ ideological conservatives. In 1977 he reached the journalist's nirvana by winning a Pulitzer Prize for political commentary. Stylistically he favored a lofty Anglophile tone (sometimes with echoes of the young William Buckley) and encouraged comparisons of himself to Alexander

Pope, Jonathan Swift, Samuel Johnson, and Benjamin Disraeli. He was, however, careful to leaven the highbrow tone and to assert his full-blooded Americanness with entertaining stories about baseball.[59]

Will contributed to the intellectual convergence of various strands in the conservative movement but perhaps also to the marginalization of the libertarians, whose views he dismissed as "decayed Jeffersonianism characterized by a frivolous hostility to the state." He believed that the role of government was to promote virtue in citizens and to nurture a sense of civic community. Citizens should certainly enjoy as much freedom as possible, but government *did* have claims on them, extending even to the sacrifice of their lives in times of war and national emergency. Statecraft, in other words, was not just a matter of appointing judges, adjusting taxes, assigning tariffs, and then leaving citizens alone as much as possible; it was, in addition, "soulcraft," the attempt to shape their minds and ideals while promoting civic virtue. He elaborated this idea at book length in *Statecraft as Soulcraft* (1983). "It is generally considered obvious that government should not, indeed cannot, legislate morality. But in fact it does so, frequently; it should do so more often; and it never does anything more important. By the legislation of morality I mean the enactment of laws and implementation of policies that proscribe, mandate, regulate or subsidize behavior that will, over time, have the predictable effect of nurturing, bolstering or altering habits, dispositions and values on a broad scale." Invoking the wisdom of classical rather than modern exemplars, Will believed that much contemporary conservatism was intellectually too thin. "The United States needs a real conservatism, characterized by a concern to cultivate the best persons and the best in persons. It should express renewed appreciation for the ennobling functions of government."[60]

What did that mean in practice? Among other things it led Will to argue against laws upholding gay rights. "The notion that no form of sexuality is more natural, more *right,* than any other is . . . a facet of the repudiation of the doctrine of natural right on which Western society rests." On the other hand, it caused him to favor seat-belt laws and federal imposition of improved gas-mileage requirements on Detroit automakers, because government must not consider citizens simply as consumers with the right to decide such things for themselves. No, government has "a duty to look far down the road and consider the interests of citizens yet unborn." Will was unpredictable enough on the policy questions of the day to supply plenty of thought-provoking columns while always structuring them around bedrock principles of communitarian conservatism.[61]

The 1960s and 1970s witnessed the maturing of the conservative movement. *National Review* conservatives found common ground with neoconservatives on domestic policy issues, despite their earlier antipathies. Both groups feared the era's racial upheavals and the street activism that came first with the civil rights movement and then with black power. Both hated the New Left, the cult of political spontaneity, and the youth culture. They deplored the radicalization of higher education and the tendency of university administrations to appease rather than confront riotous students. Sometimes, they said, repression is absolutely necessary in the interest of preserving society and civilization. They were dismissive of the new feminism, even regarding it in some cases as a form of infantile reluctance to accept the hard biological realities of gender difference.

Journalists coined the phrase "generation gap" in the 1960s to describe the split between young radicals, born in the baby boom, and their parents, who had been born and raised in the Depression and had fought in World War II. New conservatives and neoconservatives alike took sides emphatically with the older generation—their contemporaries—against what to them looked like a rabble of young ingrates.

Their convergence was made easier by a shared anticommunist stance in foreign policy and a shared skepticism about détente. In their view the Soviet Union was, and would remain, an extremely dangerous adversary, dedicated to the victory of communism and the annihilation of capitalism. There might be strategic advantages to opening diplomatic relations with China, but American leaders ought not to deceive themselves into thinking that permanent coexistence with any group of communists was either possible or desirable. Nuclear weapons were valuable, and America must maintain the credibility of its threat to use them if deterrence was to succeed. Even the Vietnam War, source of the most sundering disagreements in the 1960s, came to appear to most conservatives, after the fact, as a defensible attempt to prevent the spread of communism.

Conservatism as a political movement took further strides through the decision of evangelical leaders to lead their flocks into electoral politics, after decades of quietism. Opposition to legalized abortion was the decisive issue here; it motivated fundamentalists to enter what they saw as an almost demonic political arena that sanctioned the killing of children. The New Christian Right was always intellectually weak, but its impassioned voters brought an immense amount of energy and big numbers into elections at every level, permanently redefining the American political landscape.

CHAPTER NINE

The Reagan Revolution and the Climax of the Cold War

CONSERVATIVES FELT EXHILARATED by Ronald Reagan's election victory in 1980. Would he now enact their long-awaited transformation of American politics? No, because different conservatives wanted different things, and to gratify one group would be to disappoint others. He could not simultaneously legislate on behalf of family cohesion and roll back the heavy hand of government. Neither could he slash federal expenditures and taxes while elevating America's military might to impose unbearable pressure on the Soviet Union.

The 1980s was a decade of triumph and dismay for American conservatives. Not only did the movement have to find a way to deal with its different constituent groups, it also discovered a new breach: between those for whom ideas were all important and those for whom power mattered most. Conservative members of Congress, raised on the movement's ideas, did not merely throw them aside as irrelevant, but neither could they enact them into law, especially when they contradicted their constituents' taste for pork and threatened their own reelection prospects. For intellectuals, getting the ideas straight matters most, but the American political system has checks and balances; it thrives on compromise, the trading of favors, and incremental changes. Conservatives in the GOP often had to sound militant while being careful to act moderately.

Emmett Tyrrell, editor of the *American Spectator,* writing about the Reagan Revolution a decade later, noted the irony that Irving Kristol and the other leading neoconservative intellectuals, despite their intense interest in the issues, had little knowledge of how politics worked from day to day, no interest in the charity balls and couture designers who swept into Washington, and no familiarity with the "country club Republicans" who were the party's heart and soul. "In an elemental way [the country clubbers] are conservative, but it is a conservatism governed by inertia."[1]

There was, however, one important point of contact between the intellectuals and the politicians: the conservative think tanks, which proliferated in the 1970s and 1980s. Some, such as the Hoover Institution at Stanford University, which specialized in foreign-policy questions, offered their fellows plenty of latitude for independent thought, and publication according to academic standards and timetables. Others, particularly those inside the Washington Beltway, became an extension of the conservative lobbying apparatus, supplying position papers, speeches, and draft legislation to members of Congress. They were less intent on intellectual work for its own sake than on effecting political changes. Among the most significant were the American Enterprise Institute (founded in 1943 but tiny until the 1970s), the Heritage Foundation (1973), and the Cato Institute (1977).[2]

The think tanks in turn depended for their funding on an array of conservative foundations, most of which were the creations of successful business leaders. First into the field was the Colorado brewer Joseph Coors; followed by Richard Mellon Scaife, heir to a banking fortune; David and Charles Koch, sons of an oil entrepreneur; Lynde and Harry Bradley, owners of an electronics company; John Olin, a chemicals and munitions magnate; and many others. By 1990 these men had paid tens of millions of dollars to the conservative think tanks and related conservative causes, making them far stronger and wealthier than those on the left. They also subsidized an array of journals and publishing ventures. Their cumulative effect was to create a pipeline so that conservative ideas would find their way into Republican policy initiatives of the 1980s and 1990s.[3]

FOREIGN POLICY

President Reagan did not want to continue his predecessors' policy of peaceful coexistence with the Soviet Union. The détente mood of the

1970s had, in any event, been shattered when Russian armies overran Afghanistan in the last year of the Carter administration. Before long Soviet troops were struggling in their efforts to prop up the Afghan Marxist regime. Extremely rough terrain, poor communications, a tradition of tribal independence, and the spread of militant Islamic fundamentalism all helped the antigovernment rebels. America refused to participate in the Moscow Olympic Games, suspended grain shipments to the Soviet Union, and sent military aid and advisers to anti-Soviet groups like the Taliban. The American press began referring to Afghanistan as the Soviets' Vietnam.[4]

In a speech to evangelical leaders in Orlando Reagan denounced the Soviet Union as the "Evil Empire." The phrase struck different listeners in different ways. It fed the evangelicals' apocalyptic approach to politics but alarmed advocates of détente, as well as America's European allies, by suggesting that Reagan believed war against this evil was both possible and necessary. On the other hand, it delighted conservatives who believed that "an 'evil empire' is precisely what the Soviet Union actually is," with its persecutions, its "comprehensive lying, the ongoing war against poetry, art, religion and all forms of free thought."[5]

To put pressure on the Evil Empire, Reagan presided over the biggest peacetime arms buildup in American history. He authorized the deployment of a new generation of nuclear missiles, even though they violated the unratified SALT II Treaty and inaugurated research and development for the Strategic Defense Initiative, which held out the possibility of defensive nuclear weapons orbiting the earth.[6]

He took these assertive moves despite the revival of a popular antinuclear movement. Conservative intellectuals in the 1950s had had no doubt that nuclear weapons were necessary to combat the Soviet menace, but influential sections of society had always felt uneasy about the policy. The American Catholic bishops' pastoral letter *The Challenge of Peace: God's Promise and Our Response* (1983) posed in acute form the great dilemma of nuclear weapons. How can a society claiming to honor a merciful and loving God, and His Son who sacrificed His life for us, defend itself with the threat of annihilating millions of people? Reinhold Niebuhr had raised the question in his classic *The Irony of American History* (1952), and the bishops raised it again, urging a rapid modification of America's defense policy. Other churches joined in with comparable letters and statements of their own.[7]

Michael Novak (b. 1933), a Catholic neoconservative, wrote an answer to the bishops, *Moral Clarity in the Nuclear Age* (1983), which used the same principles as had the bishops—that is, the Catholic tradition of "just war"—but came to different conclusions. The whole point of nuclear weapons, said Novak, was that they achieved maximum effect with minimum damage. The adversary's knowledge of their destructive power and fear of retaliation prevented it from taking aggressive action, and so preserved the peace. In other words, America was *using* its nuclear weapons all the time by *not* firing them. They thus perfectly fulfilled the "proportionality" principle of just-war tradition by achieving a good end without excessive destruction. Novak warned, however, that the whole deterrence structure would be destabilized if the Soviet adversary ever started to believe that, when it came to the point, America might *not* launch a counterstrike. Paradoxically, then, the antinuclear movement was actually increasing the danger of a nuclear weapons exchange! William F. Buckley, Jr. ,was so impressed by the cogency of Novak's argumentation, and regarded the issue as so important, that he devoted an entire issue of *National Review* to Novak's text.[8]

While this nuclear weapons imbroglio was heating up, Midge Decter founded the Committee for the Free World (1981), an intellectuals' pressure group designed to publicize the "rising menace of totalitarian barbarism" and to keep the pressure on Reagan to live up to his rhetoric. It was funded by three conservative foundations, Scaife, Olin, and Smith-Richardson. Decter, Norman Podhoretz, and other neoconservative hawks like Walter Laqueur feared that Reagan was, when it came to the point, not militant enough, fears that increased as the eighties continued and he became more interested in arms control. They were impatient with the compromises of practical politics, such as Reagan's decision to resume grain sales to the Russians and his cautious approach to the Solidarity movement that challenged Polish communism.[9]

What about other world conflicts? Reagan's ambassador to the United Nations, Jeane Kirkpatrick (1926–2006), formerly a professor of political science at Georgetown University and a scholar at the American

Enterprise Institute, had drawn the new president's attention with a *Commentary* article, "Dictatorships and Double Standards" (1979), which made a distinction between authoritarian and totalitarian regimes. According to Kirkpatrick, it was possible for an authoritarian regime to evolve toward respect for human rights, a prospect that made American support and collaboration acceptable. Totalitarian regimes, by contrast, were incapable of such changes and must be opposed at all costs. "There is no instance of a revolutionary 'socialist' or Communist society being democratized [but] right-wing autocracies do sometimes evolve into democracies—given time, propitious economic, social, and political circumstances, talented leaders and a strong indigenous demand for representative government." Spain and Portugal in the 1970s were cases in point.[10]

Reagan took a new approach to Central American and Caribbean affairs with this distinction in mind. He and Kirkpatrick believed that the Carter administration had deluded itself with the idea that the area need no longer be thought of in Cold War terms. Cuban and Soviet proxies, exploiting what they interpreted as an admission of American weakness, were gaining in the area, threatening pro-U.S. regimes and undermining America's strategic and security interests. Carter's globalism, she wrote, "denies the realities of culture, character, geography, economics and history in favor of a vague, abstract universalism." Reagan threw his support to the Contras, an alliance of forces in Nicaragua opposing the Marxist Sandinista regime. He also supported the pro-American regime in El Salvador despite its record of human rights abuses and its apparent cooperation with assassins who shot down the archbishop of San Salvador in his own cathedral. The rights and wrongs of Reagan's Latin America policy created bitter controversy throughout the 1980s and was perhaps the issue for which the American left condemned the president most harshly.[11]

NEW DEFENDERS OF CAPITALISM

In the late 1970s the economist Milton Friedman, who had won the Nobel Prize in 1976, hosted a public television series, *Free to Choose.* The program elaborated many of the insights he had laid down in *Capitalism and Freedom* (1962) and illustrated these points with anecdotes from the economic history of the 1960s and 1970. A book based on the series became a great best seller, the number one nonfiction book in America of 1980. Translated into twenty languages, it also circulated illegally in communist Eastern Europe. By then Friedman was a household name. He was a regular columnist in *Newsweek,* where he challenged the conventional economic wisdom week after week, gaining what was surely a bigger mainstream audience than any other advocate of libertarian ideas. He believed that the chronic inflation of the 1970s, the decade's great economic problem, was chiefly attributable to uncontrolled growth in the money supply. "Financing government spending by increasing the quantity of money is often extremely attractive to both the President and members of Congress. It enables them to . . . [provide] goodies for their constituents, without having to vote for taxes to pay for them, and without having to borrow from the public."[12]

Politicians, always jittery about reelection, understood that to follow Friedman's advice on this and other matters, intervening in the economy less, abolishing the minimum wage, and terminating major government programs would be electorally catastrophic, even if benign in the long run. Meanwhile, business leaders, even though they often spoke up for the free market in general, did not want to lose their array of government-conferred advantages, many of which sheltered them from the icy winds of real competition. They grumbled about high tax rates but lobbied to maintain high tariffs. As Friedman noted, "Few US industries sing the praises of free enterprise more loudly than the oil industry. Yet few industries rely so heavily on special government favors."[13]

In the late 1970s and early 1980s the neoconservative intellectuals, who until then had devoted relatively little of their time to economics, began to study it more attentively, subjecting it to the same scrutiny they had earlier given to race, education, urban decay, and poverty. Doggedly they challenged the stereotypes—that capitalism appeals to human greed, that it exploits the working majority to enrich the minority, and that the marketplace is an impersonal mechanism, an "invisible hand."

The two economists whose names came to be associated with "Reaganomics" were Arthur Laffer (b. 1940) and Robert Mundell (b. 1932). They suggested to conservatives that the relationship between taxes and government revenue was paradoxical. When tax rates rise slightly, national revenue rises, but when tax rates rise sharply, revenue no longer keeps pace and eventually begins to tail off. Why? If the tax rate is zero, obviously, the government will never get any revenue, no matter how productive the economy. If, on the other hand, the tax rate is 100 percent, the government will also get nothing because no one will have any incentive to work. The "Laffer Curve" demonstrates what happens to the relationship between tax rate and revenue between these extremes. A rate of 10 percent, for example, will give the government a revenue amounting to one-tenth of national income, leaving a healthy 90 percent for private economic actors and offering them plenty of incentives to work hard and get rich. When tax rates rise from a low starting point, said Laffer, revenue will rise too, but beyond a certain point, increases in the tax rate lead not to increases in revenue but to declines, because high tax rates give the producers of wealth less and less incentive to work. They also tempt producers to hide their economic activity in a tax-free black market or to search for tax shelters. Counterinstinctual yet true: raising the tax rate can mean *shrinking* government's income. High tax rates also mean, Laffer added, slow economic growth, stagnation, and unemployment. On the other hand, decreasing rates can have the effect of *increasing* revenue in that citizens have a stronger incentive, knowing they'll be principal beneficiaries of their own hard work. Cheating is no longer worth the risk, and the economy moves into high gear, which benefits everyone.[14]

A theory that promised economic growth, more tax revenue, lower tax rates, and more freedom to citizens was of course politically alluring, all the more so when presented in graspable form by three talented popularizers, Irving Kristol, Jude Wanniski (1936–2005), and George Gilder (b. 1939). Wanniski's *The Way the World Works* (1979) made the case for supply-side economics in an approachable lay language full of homely analogies. He even argued that we are, in effect, hardwired to the economic insight embodied in the Laffer curve. Babies, for example, before they can walk or talk, let alone read, know all about it. They know that if they never cry they will not attract mother's attention (the zero-zero point), but they also quickly learn that if they cry all the time mother will again learn to pay no attention (the zero-100 point). Instead, they learn to cry *sometimes,* skillfully calibrating their use of tears to maximize maternal attention. That is, they locate the point on the Laffer Curve that maximizes revenue (mother's attention) and appreciate that it can sometimes be achieved by crying *less.*[15]

Irving Kristol first encountered supply-side theory in 1974. Already an influential figure, widely respected on many points of the political spectrum, and acknowledged as the neoconservatives' unofficial leader, Kristol introduced Laffer to Robert Bartley of the *Wall Street Journal,* to Congressman Jack Kemp, and to other influential conservative opinion makers and politicians, ensuring that his ideas would gain a respectful hearing in high places. He also gathered his own articles on economics and business (most of them from the *Wall Street Journal*) into an anthology, *Two Cheers for Capitalism* (1979). Capitalism needs only two cheers, he said (paraphrasing E. M. Forster's "two cheers for democracy"), because it is not a beautiful thing in itself, merely a system that works well in practice. "Capitalism is the least romantic conception of a public order that the human mind has ever conceived. . . . What previous cultures would have called 'the domestic virtues' are what capitalism prizes most in its citizens: prudence, diligence, trustworthiness, and an ambition largely channeled toward 'bettering one's condition.' " He recognized that the system's lack of glamour and its resolutely anti-utopian approach to life led a section of every generation to reject it—hence the anti-big-business animus of popular culture in the 1970s. The business community and the defenders of capitalism, he cautioned, now needed to work harder at demonstrating the real merits of their system rather than yielding cultural ground to the growing chorus of populist, New Left, and new class critics.[16]

George Gilder, in his best seller *Wealth and Poverty* (1981), added the third cheer for capitalism that Kristol had withheld. Perhaps no book has ever expressed more admiration and excitement about capitalists—it bubbles with pleasure. Gilder described entrepreneurs not as self-interested individuals but as altruists. The risks they took in investing, he said, provided not only jobs but also products and services that must benefit the rest of society; otherwise they would not prosper. Entrepreneurs were like the ambitious young males in primitive tribes who give parties and distribute gifts—hoping but never knowing for sure that other members of the tribe will reciprocate. When entrepreneurs or investors make their initial outlay, they cannot be sure they will succeed (after all, most businesses do not), so they are, in effect, *giving* to the rest of society. The commodities and goods entrepreneurs have created (or "given") over the last three centuries have improved human life immeasurably.[17]

Gilder added that wealth is constantly in circulation; fortunes are always being lost as well as won: lost especially by those who inherited rather than earned their money. Why? Because the world is so unpredictable! The fatal mistake of socialist bureaucracies (and of companies that got too big and complacent to stay competitive) was to believe that demand could be known and supply organized to match. "Socialism presumes that we already know most of what we need to know to accomplish our national goals. Capitalism is based on the idea that we live in a world of unfathomable complexity, ignorance, and peril, and that we cannot possibly prevail over our difficulties without constant efforts of initiative, sympathy, discovery, and love. . . . The ultimate strength and crucial weakness of both capitalism and democracy are their reliance on individual creativity and courage, leadership and morality, intuition and faith. But there is no alternative except mediocrity and stagnation." As Gilder tells it, life under capitalism is a constant adventure, as each new generation's most daring risk takers find ways to improve the community and enrich themselves into the bargain; nothing is more valuable to society than its most wealthy members.[18]

There is, moreover, a great difference between riches and wealth; the first can be a mere accumulation of money, whereas the second is actively producing new goods. Like other neoconservatives, Gilder argued that wealth is more a matter of cultural and moral attitudes than of material possessions. Possession of an asset alone does not ensure that it will become wealth. If exploited for short-term gain, indeed, it can make a bad situation worse rather than better by discouraging the kind of self-discipline necessary for genuine wealth creation. At a time (pre-Thatcher) when the British economy was famously dysfunctional, Gilder wrote that the apparent windfall of its North Sea oil and gas reserves might be a case in point: "Will this oil be seen later as a 'curse in disguise' which prevents Britain from recovering from its real losses: the declining productivity of its work force and the slackness of its management? Oil, like a neutron bomb, could end by destroying the real wealth of the land—the morale and ingenuity of its people—and leave standing only the sterile structures of an advanced industrial economy, ruled by a bloated and increasingly oppressive bureaucracy, trained only in the barren arts of redistributing bonanzas." He also denied that the famous old "invisible hand" metaphor was useful. To the contrary, capitalism was all about particular people making particular decisions in particular places, "the quite visible and aggressive hand of management and entrepreneurship."[19]

Building on the work of Wanniski, Kristol, and Gilder, Michael Novak's *The Spirit of Democratic Capitalism* (1982) added a theological element to this new defense of capitalism. Novak's early writing on capitalism emphasized that it was essentially a means to make money, scarcely engaging people's higher and nobler faculties but nonetheless desirable. In a 1979 essay he even speculated that the paradox of capitalism was comparable to the paradox of Christianity itself. "Capitalist ideology . . . follows the paradox of Isaiah and of Christ, that redemption should come in the most unlikely spot, through the weakest and poorest of persons, as in the carpenter from a very poor and undeveloped part of the Roman Empire. In a related way, capitalist thinkers discovered the dynamic energy to change the face of history not where it might be expected, in human nobility, grandeur, and moral consciousness, but in human self-interest. In the pettiest and narrowest and meanest part of human behavior lies the source of creative energy." Early Christians had had to struggle to overcome the idea that the Messiah had such humble origins. Skeptics about capitalism had to struggle to overcome the idea that such a productive system should originate in such an unlovely zone of humanity.[20]

In the ensuing years Novak became more upbeat about the moral quality of capitalism; *The Spirit of Democratic Capitalism* (1982) was his mature statement on the whole issue. Now denying, like Gilder, that capitalism appeals chiefly to individual greed, Novak argued that, empirically, it has more often stimulated men to provide for their *families* and is replete with examples of self-sacrifice and a quasi-religious dedication to human improvement. In general, wrote Novak, entrepreneurs become rich not to spend money on themselves but to improve conditions and prospects for their children and descendants. Capitalism is based on self-interest, then, only if you accept an extremely broad definition of self-interest, which includes "religious and moral interests, artistic and scientific interests, and interests in justice and peace. . . . It is part of the function of a free economy to provide the abundance which breaks the chains of the mere struggle for subsistence, and to permit individual persons to 'find themselves,' indeed to define themselves through the interests they choose to make central to their lives."[21]

Novak specified, however, that capitalism alone was not enough; to thrive it must be accompanied by political democracy and a pluralistic liberal culture. Capitalism works best when information circulates freely and easily, when the regime in which it operates is legitimate and has the support of the population, and when all citizens contribute to setting and adjusting the rules by which it operates. The book ended with a challenge to theologians, chiefly those in his own Catholic church (the book's dedication was "in homage to Pope John Paul II"), but to others as well, to embrace democratic capitalism. Until now, he wrote, theologians had not studied economics carefully enough to be able to write intelligently about it and had been too easily taken in by the old bromide that capitalism was about selfishness, and socialism about selflessness. Some writers in his theological tradition had recently developed a form of quasi-Marxist liberation theology, whose outcome in practice, said Novak, would be an odious mixture of tyranny and poverty. "Just as the Catholic tradition has something to teach America," he concluded, "so also American democratic capitalism has some new things to add to the Catholic tradition."[22]

Capitalism, as all these writers agreed, not only provides superior products at lower cost; it also creates a counterweight to government power. Friedman, Novak, and the other conservative writers, still in the thick of the world struggle against communism, feared the unchecked growth of the monster state and saw in business a necessary counterweight. Evidence from the Soviet Union had taught nearly everyone by the 1980s that a centrally planned economy was hopelessly inefficient; the conservatives added that government, when it has the opportunity, adds oppression to inefficiency to enforce its will. Entrepreneurial capitalism, by contrast, helps keep state power at bay.[23]

THE ROBERT BORK AFFAIR

Robert Bork (b. 1927) was a distinguished but outspoken legal theorist, a former Yale law school professor, and a member of the conservative Federalist Society, whose members lamented the judicial activism of recent decades. He had been President Nixon's solicitor-general and was a judge on the United States Court of Appeals for the District of Columbia when President Reagan nominated him to the Supreme Court in 1987. The Senate hearings over his nomination marked a flashpoint in the era's conservative-liberal confrontations, mixing an exchange of philosophies with bitter personal and political recriminations. Liberal organizations mounted an alarmist public relations campaign to nix the appointment, claiming that Bork was a conservative extremist, that he opposed equal rights for all citizens, that he would roll back most of the social progress of recent decades, and that he was hostile to the abortion decision in *Roe v. Wade*. Even some of those groups who opposed the nomination, like *The New Republic,* admitted that "liberal interest groups stand accused, justly, of spreading hysteria about Robert Bork."[24]

Bork denied that he was an ultra-conservative. His book *The Tempting of America* (1990), written in the wake of his rejection, explained his "originalist" approach to the law. Judges on the bench, he said, must put the impartial interpretation of the law before everything. If a case presented a judge with a choice between established law, on the one hand, and his conception of social justice, on the other, he must choose the law. Failure to do so would soon undermine the rule of law itself. In interpreting the law, a judge must always attempt "to discern what those who made the law intended." Judges should do no more than study the original intent of legislators as well as that of the framers of the Constitution and should decide whether the two were compatible. If the law as it stood violated a new generation's sense of justice, legislatures, not the judiciary, should rewrite it.[25]

Unfortunately, said Bork, the rise of radical legal studies had tempted a generation of influential legal scholars to argue for their particular ideal of justice instead. "There is a remarkable consistency about these theorists. No matter the base from which they start, they all wind up in the same place, prescribing a new constitutional law that is much more egalitarian and socially permissive than either the actual Constitution or the legislative opinion of the American public." Their decisions would not have been enacted by legislatures whose members hoped to be reelected. In this way the judges made themselves an unelected second legislature and a threat to democracy. *Roe v. Wade* was a case in point. In Bork's view, the Constitution had absolutely nothing to say about abortion, and the issue should therefore remain in the hands of the state legislatures. "From the beginning of the Republic until that day, January 22, 1973, the moral question of what abortions should be lawful had been left entirely to state legislatures. The discovery this late in our history that the question was not one for democratic decision but one of constitutional law was . . . implausible. In the entire opinion there is not one line of explanation, not one sentence that qualifies as legal argument."[26]

The Supreme Court seat went instead to the relatively uncontroversial Anthony Kennedy. Another Supreme Court seat became available in 1991 with the retirement of Thurgood Marshall, the first African American justice. President George H. W. Bush, recognizing the symbolic importance of nominating another African American, chose Clarence Thomas (b. 1948), former head of the Equal Employment Opportunity Commission and an opponent of affirmative action. Thomas, admired by conservatives but bitterly denounced by many black activists as an Uncle Tom, prepared for contentious hearings on the Bork model. This time around, his defenders were better prepared for a tough fight while Thomas himself spoke much more circumspectly to the Senate Judiciary Committee and declined to comment on the legality of abortion altogether. When Anita Hill, one of Thomas's former colleagues, alleged before the Senate Judiciary Committee that he had sexually harassed her, conservative investigators went into high gear in an attempt to refute the charges and to depict her as vindictive. The full Senate, unconvinced by the evidence she provided to support her allegations, narrowly approved of Thomas, who took his seat on the Court.[27]

CULTURE WARS I

Conservative intellectuals in the 1980s faced a paradox; they were winning in the struggle for political power and making gains toward their economic and foreign policy goals, but felt they were losing in the struggle for civilization. Most of them believed that America was continuing to deteriorate culturally and that each new generation was more ignorant, less well educated, less self-disciplined, and ruder than its predecessor. The legacy of the sexual revolution continued to vex many of them. Social conservatives, particularly those in the newly active Christian Right, were dismayed by the ubiquity of sexual themes in films, music, and television, the high rates of sexual activity before and outside of marriage, and the growing acceptance of homosexuality as a lifestyle choice in many parts of society. Above all, they were horrified by the number of abortions—one million or more most years—taking place in America. For this combination of problems they blamed the philosophy of secular humanism. Conservatives with a less religious outlook shared some of these concerns but emphasized their adverse economic and psychological effects rather than the affront they gave to God. Both groups saw education as the battleground of American culture. If American children and young adults learned different things, in different ways, perhaps they could restore the old ways.[28]

Allan Bloom's *Closing of the American Mind* (1987) was the era's most famous expression of conservative concerns about education. Bloom (1930–92), a philosophy professor at the University of Chicago who had studied under Leo Strauss, believed devoutly in that university's Great Books tradition. In his view the elite members of every generation could learn from Plato, the Bible, Shakespeare, and Hegel and should study them deeply for the great truths of life, discovering what is right and true and good. Bloom was dismayed by the decline of the Great Books, the cult of openness in American academia, and the vogue of cultural relativism among academics. To regard every society anthropologically, nonjudgmentally, did not seem to him an intellectually enlightened approach. Much better to study them in the same way one studied the great texts, not contextually but in light of absolute standards.[29]

Bloom, like his teacher Strauss (1899–1973), did not entirely believe in the value of historical study, at least not if it was done in a historicist way. He believed it was a mistake for historians to explain historical events and phenomena with reference to their context (a method absolutely central to most academic historians of the late twentieth century). Instead they should explain them in light of their closeness to, or remoteness from, the absolute values of civilization. The university curriculum, he believed, ought not to be susceptible to transient moods, and it certainly ought not be utilitarian. The faculty's job was not to prepare young men and women to fit into roles in contemporary society. If anything it should teach them how to resist the blandishments of their world and to conform to the judgment of their civilization's great tradition. This role required courage, austerity, and detachment in teachers, along with an intimate acquaintance with the tradition in all its richness.

The reality was completely otherwise. Bloom had been a professor at Cornell University in the late 1960s and had witnessed firsthand the administration and faculty yield to threats and intimidation from armed and radicalized black activists on campus. The Cornell uprising had been, in Bloom's view, a disgraceful spectacle, convincing him that the university's leaders had lacked both courage and integrity.[30]

Bloom also offered an unflattering portrait of contemporary youth culture, much of which served to *dis*qualify even the University of Chicago's elite undergraduates. In a chapter on music that became notorious, he argued that teenagers' obsession with rock music was equally an obsession with sex, because "young people know that rock has the beat of sexual intercourse." Rarely did they read—he believed most were profoundly unlearned—but they certainly saturated themselves in this brutal music.

> Picture a thirteen-year-old boy sitting in the living room of his family home doing his math assignment while wearing his Walkman headphones or watching MTV. He enjoys the liberties hard won over the centuries by the alliance of philosophic genius and political heroism, consecrated by the blood of martyrs; he is provided with comfort and leisure by the most productive economy ever known to mankind. Science has penetrated the secrets of nature in order to provide him with the marvelous, lifelike electronic sound and image reproduction he is enjoying. And in what does progress culminate? A pubescent child whose body throbs with orgasmic rhythms; whose feelings are made articulate in hymns to the joys of onanism or the killing of parents; whose ambition is to win fame and wealth imitating the drag-queen who makes the music. In short, life is made into a nonstop, commercially prepackaged masturbational fantasy.

Just because such things were now familiar did not make them reasonable or defensible. "People of future civilizations will wonder at this and find it as incomprehensible as we do the caste system, witch-burning, harems, cannibalism, and gladiatorial combats."[31]

To his amazement his book became a great best seller, making him suddenly a rich man. He became something of a cultural guru in the remaining five years of his life, giving the commencement address at Harvard in 1988 (which he began with the words: "My Fellow Elitists"). That so many people had bought and studied *The Closing* could, of course, be taken as evidence that the American mind was not really as closed as he had supposed; his success might even have disproved his own hypothesis. The book's wild success remains a puzzle, however. Written in a dense, unforgiving style, packed with references to Plato, Rousseau, Tocqueville, Nietzsche, Heidegger, and other philosophers, it requires a great deal of sustained attention. Some commentators raised the possibility that it might well be one of the most *bought* books of its era rather than one of the most *read*. [32]

In any event, from inside the indicted universities arose a howl of rage to match Bloom's cry of woe. His popularity with the wider American audience was certainly not matched inside the ivy walls—academic reviewers vilified Bloom for sexism, racism, elitism, cultural imperialism, insensitivity to minorities, and an attempt to stifle pluralism and multiculturalism. One critic, alarmed by Bloom's denigration of historicism and anthropological method, judged that *The Closing* "cannot be taken seriously" because it was the "bilious output of an anti-modern, anti-democratic, anti-intellectual mind." Another noted that Bloom's stinging critique of mass culture was just a warmed-over staple of conservative rhetoric that "has been with us since the Enlightenment." Bloom had no real interest in democracy, only in the welfare of an exceptional intellectual elite. His "hyperbolic tirade" was made on behalf of a "frankly aristocratic vision" of society and scarcely masked his yearning "for the return of a more rigidly stratified civilization in which the crowd is contained within the land of the marketplace and its pleasures are confined to the rituals of the carnival." A third critic noted that Bloom, after his passage on students, which was "parlor psychologizing of a truly lamentable sort," favored a return to the "good old Great Books approach" but that "by offering no advice on how to implement such a curriculum pedagogically, he forfeits his claim to sympathy, hugging his noble failure instead of dirtying his hands trying to show us how an elite course of instruction might function in a democratic society."[33]

More temperate and more democratic than Bloom was E. D. Hirsch (b. 1928), a professor of English at the University of Virginia, whose *Cultural Literacy* (1987) lamented the decline of a universal American culture. In former days, Hirsch believed, all educated Americans had learned a more or less common body of knowledge and had been able to deploy relevant parts of it when they met or worked together. Such knowledge gave all who possessed it great advantages. Increasingly, however, education based on theories of relevance and syllabi based on the experiences and the literature of neglected and victimized groups had broken down this informal common curriculum. When young Americans sought work and upward economic mobility, however, Hirsch argued that those who had been educated in the new way would be, so to speak, culturally illiterate and would face serious obstacles; they simply would not understand what they were being told by their employers. Those who still possessed the older knowledge and understood the cultural references, by contrast, would be at a great advantage. Where Bloom had led readers through an exhausting philosophical obstacle course, Hirsch offered merely a sixty-five-page list of the things every culturally literate person should know a bit about, a list that was later expanded into a dictionary. On their own the items looked odd and disconnected: "fiscal policy, Fish or cut bait, fission, nuclear, fits and starts, Fitzgerald, Ella, Fitzgerald, F. Scott, fjord, flapper," and so on. Whatever the merits of his choices and exclusions, Hirsch favored giving young citizens the smattering of the historical learning that Bloom deplored. He also favored giving it to all of them.[34]

Hirsch, like Bloom, made a fortune. He, too, was vulnerable to charges of elitism, however, because of his assertion that certain ideas and concepts, along with certain authors, events, and traditions, were central to American culture and others only marginal. His critics on the left pointed out that these cultural markers were themselves the residue and symbols of historic struggles over power, but that Hirsch unself-critically gave himself over to validating the process by which they had triumphed over other possibilities. Surely, they added, education and intellectual life involved digging beneath the surface to find out *how* these cultural effects had come about and giving previously silenced historical voices the chance to speak again. His claim to be helping the disadvantaged, in other words, was really a covert attempt to "colonize" them.[35]

Bloom and Hirsch, neither of whom was entirely comfortable with the conservative label, were so successful that they helped inspire a wave of more openly conservative analyses of American education. Charles

Sykes's *Prof-Scam* (1988) and *The Hollow Men* (1990) argued that the American tenure system, created to protect academic freedom, had become an excuse for professorial idleness and the worst kind of specialist inbreeding; that professors fobbed off the actual teaching onto graduate students whenever possible; and that the modern-day curriculum was as "denuded of value as if it had . . . been created by a curriculum committee of Vandals with doctorates." Peter Shaw's *The War Against the Intellect* (1989) deplored the rise of victim groups as objects of study in the humanities and the triumph of emotion over intellectual rigor, while Martin Anderson's *Impostors in the Temple* (1992) asserted that greedy, empire-building administrators and negligent tenured faculty made modern universities a "witches' brew of incompetence, timidity, and neglect."[36]

None of these indictments was more controversial than Roger Kimball's *Tenured Radicals* (1990). As he told it, political radicals from the 1960s, having failed in their initial hope of overthrowing society directly, had now adopted a devious long-term strategy. Gaining doctoral degrees in the humanities and social sciences, they had won tenure at the nation's major universities. From these secure positions they were now teaching revolution to new generations of students, revolution as much cultural as political. They were attacking all the old verities of Western civilization and deliberately corroding their students' understanding of their heritage. Feminism, Afrocentrism, deconstructionism, poststructuralism, gay studies, and the new historicism, many of the new academic methods, might seem very different from one another to their practitioners, but "when seen from the perspective of the tradition they are seeking to subvert—the tradition of high culture embodied in the classics of Western art and thought—they exhibit a remarkable unity of purpose. Their object is nothing less than the destruction of the values, methods, and goals of traditional humanistic study." Moreover, said Kimball, the tenured radicals had stifled academic freedom under a blanket of academic political correctness, which prevented the genuinely free play of ideas on all issues related to race, gender, sexuality, disability, and formal artistic standards.[37]

Kimball (b. 1953), like Bloom, was dismayed by the radical academics' attack on the idea of absolute standards of excellence and by their claim that there is no objective truth. Leading critics like Jacques Derrida,

Fredric Jameson, Frank Lentricchia, and Elaine Showalter, he wrote, denigrate classic texts and play games with the language itself, while assaulting a distinguished and humane tradition of literary criticism in their obscure jargon. Kimball noted that when, in 1987, one of the deconstructionists' darlings, Paul de Man, had been exposed as a former Nazi sympathizer and collaborator, many of them had rallied to his defense on grounds of his intrinsic brilliance rather than admit an odious point of contact between writing and the hard outside world.[38]

While the grown-ups debated the condition of American education and intellectual life, a new generation of conservative college students began to take initiatives of its own, founding student journals to challenge academic orthodoxy. One of the first of these journals, the *Dartmouth Review,* aimed to do locally the kind of work *National Review* was doing nationwide. It enjoyed financial support from foundations sympathetic to the conservative cause. An unrelenting critic of political correctness on campus, it mocked the era's campus platitudes and shibboleths, scorned feminism, polemicized against affirmative action, and wrote hostile and ridiculing stories about radical professors. One of its series of stories, about an African American music professor who delivered abusive racial harangues in class, finally forced the man into retirement.[39]

Its writers and editors were adolescents, their antics sometimes juvenile and tasteless. Admitting they sometimes crossed the boundaries of good taste, the *Dartmouth Review* group justified their excesses on the grounds that they confronted a strongly entrenched, intolerant, and sometimes hypocritical university culture that needed to be shocked into self-consciousness. Under these circumstances the restraint and decorum of traditional conservatism would not work. "The dilemma can be stated this way. Typically, the conservative attempts to conserve, to hold on to the values of the existing society. But . . . what if the existing society is inherently hostile to conservative beliefs? It is foolish for a conservative to attempt to conserve that culture. Rather, he must seek to undermine it, to thwart it, to destroy it at the root level. This means that the conservative must . . . be philosophically conservative but temperamentally radical. That is what we at the *Dartmouth Review* quickly understood." The paper upset one college official so much that he attacked the editor, Ben Hart, by biting him. Conservative students at dozens of other campuses followed the Dartmouth lead, founding a cluster of newspapers that enabled young writers to gain their first experience in reporting and polemics. Ann Coulter (b. 1961), later a confrontational conservative muckraker, started out at the *Cornell Review.*[40]

Culture wars and the rights and wrongs of political correctness began on college campuses but had wider implications. The journal *New Criterion,* founded in 1982, used conservative criteria to defend high culture—as traditionally defined—against postmodernism and against the breakdown of taste and judgment. Its editor, Hilton Kramer (b. 1928), formerly the principal art critic of the *New York Times,* was similar to Allan Bloom in that he believed there were objective standards of artistic excellence that could be discerned by anyone who was sufficiently learned. These standards were, however, under attack from politicized advocates of art by women and disadvantaged minorities, art from the Third World, and art that was allegedly subversive. Standards were also under attack from a widespread democratic challenge to the old idea that distinctions among highbrow, middlebrow, and popular arts were defensible and legitimate.

In the 1950s populist conservatives had sometimes reacted to modern art with philistine spluttering. Kramer came at the subject much more subtly and with vastly more erudition. An enthusiast for high modernism and an admirer of American abstract expressionism, one of the dominant mid-twentieth-century American styles, he certainly was not the man to denounce such art as part of a Commie plot. The problem, as he saw it, lay not with modernism but with *post*modernism. After all, the artistic avant-garde and the bourgeoisie over the past century, despite countless clashes over the quality of art, had gradually developed aesthetic standards and criteria of judgment. Now, alas, irrelevant political criteria had elbowed their way into the art world, challenged the concept of a single standard of excellence, and subordinated aesthetic achievement to questions of political correctness.[41]

In an inaugural editorial, Kramer wrote that *New Criterion* looked back to the days "when criticism was more strictly concerned to distinguish achievement from failure, to identify and uphold a standard of quality, and to speak plainly and vigorously about the problems that beset the life of the arts and the life of the mind in our society." The prevailing aesthetic and artistic ideas of the 1960s, he added, were an "insidious assault on the mind," substituting sentimental radicalism for intelligent and critical thought. The art world had turned against capitalism, even though "capitalism, for all its many flaws, has proved to be the greatest safeguard of democratic institutions and artistic freedom that the world has given us." This journal's standard, its "new criterion," was to be nothing other than the truth on such matters. The journal flourished with consistently engaging writing, embracing a wide variety of views but with a generally conservative tendency. Regular contributors included Norman Podhoretz, Joseph Epstein, Robert Nisbet, Gertrude Himmelfarb (who was married to Irving Kristol), and Roger Kimball, with occasional appearances by such conservative eminences from abroad as the English conservative philosopher Roger Scruton.[42]

Art wars had political as well as aesthetic consequences, because some government agencies, notably the National Endowment for the Humanities (NEH) and the National Endowment for the Arts (NEA), funded scholarly and artistic projects. In 1989, for example, the Corcoran Gallery in Washington, D.C., planned a retrospective exhibition of photographs by Robert Mapplethorpe, who had recently died of AIDS. The show was underwritten in part by a grant from the NEA. Some of the images were of children in sexually provocative poses; others of men engaged in homoerotic and sadomasochistic activities. Protests by Jesse Helms and other conservative members of Congress, who regarded the show as pornographic, prompted the museum to withdraw it. That decision in turn led art-world intellectuals to decry "government censorship."

Hilton Kramer reacted to the news by criticizing the art world for its exaggerated self-esteem and for its moral obtuseness. First, he said, the issue was not censorship, because other galleries (private) remained free to show the photographs. Second, yes, the photographs were works of art, but that did not mean that the public (and its representatives) thereby lost the right to judge them, especially since it was being asked to pay for them. Third, "there is in the professional art world a sentimental attachment to the idea that art is at its best when it is most extreme and disruptive." Hence the acclaim for Andres Serrano's photograph of the crucified Christ "submerged in the artist's urine," which had also garnered federal dollars. *National Review,* agreeing with Kramer's view that the photographs were indeed art, also agreed that in itself that was no defense. The photographs "deliberately chose subjects that shock the normal sense of decency, and displayed them for the sake of their abstract form. [Mapplethorpe] counted on and exploited the dual reaction to create tension in the viewer; what is indecent and immoral becomes stunningly beautiful. And thus especially disturbing. But to pretend the obscenity isn't there—that it exists only in the dirty mind of Jesse Helms—is as false to the pictures as to deny their beauty."[43]

As the 1980s ended Kramer was convinced that an unprecedented crisis confronted the arts and humanities, especially in the universities. They had, he believed, given in to radical politics, forsaken their hard-won independence, and surrendered "to an ideology that has as its goal the complete destruction of the arts and the humanities as independent and autonomous fields of study." A two-pronged counterattack was therefore necessary; self-aware political conservatives should fight back against the radicals, but at the same time practitioners of high culture should never accept the ultimately political character of their work. Instead they must reassert the legitimacy of its transcendent cultural value. "The defense of art must not, in other words, be looked upon as a luxury of civilization—to be indulged in and supported when all else is serene and unchallenged—but as the very essence of our civilization."[44]

THE PALEOCONSERVATIVES

After years in opposition, the conservative movement had to adapt to being the new establishment. Inevitably disputes arose over how to enact the conservative agenda, disputes between theorists and practical politicians, on the one hand, and disputes among theorists, on the other. Should conservative intellectuals migrate to Washington and work for the federal government now that one of their own stood at the helm? Or should they maintain their old insistence that the federal government was already far too big and ought, above all, to be dismantled?

One dispute over job patronage symbolized a larger dispute between neoconservatives and traditionalists. Conservative traditionalists like Sam Francis, Clyde Wilson and Thomas Fleming, contributors to southern and midwestern conservative journals like *Southern Partisan* and *Chronicles of Culture*, hoped that M. E. Bradford (1934–93), the historian, literary critic, and literature professor at the University of Dallas, would be nominated by President Reagan to head the National Endowment for the Humanities. Leading neoconservatives such as Irving Kristol and *Newsweek* columnist George Will disagreed strongly. They pointed out that Bradford had worked for George Wallace's racist presidential campaign in 1968 and that he had denounced the first Republican president, Abraham Lincoln, as a tyrant. Their favored candidate, William Bennett (b. 1943), got the job instead, but in doing so he created a lasting legacy of bitterness within the conservative movement. The losers in this contest took up the title of "paleoconservatives," a term suggesting that they were holding true to the old (*paleo*) conservative principles, as against the pseudoliberal ideas of the *neo*conservatives. [45]

M. E. Bradford weighed more than 250 pounds, wore a broad-brimmed Stetson, and spoke with a strong Texas accent. He had studied at Vanderbilt under Donald Davidson, one of the original Southern Agrarians, and regarded their manifesto *I'll Take My Stand* as "a voice for the deepest sentiments of the people I have known best, a voice bringing into focus the largely prescriptive and anecdotal wisdom of the world 'where I was born and raised.' " Like the Agrarians he grieved at the destructive side of Southern modernization and hated corporate capitalism, political centralization, and the rhetoric of equality. Like Russell Kirk in *The Conservative Mind,* Bradford was not only a scholar of conservatism but a participant in the great controversies of his time. His writing was often impassioned and polemical.[46]

Bradford thought of America as a profoundly and essentially conservative country. The earliest settlers, he wrote, had sought landed property and aspired to the condition of gentlemen. Honoring the unwritten British constitution, they had surrounded themselves with institutions that promoted civil stability and the rule of law. These colonists enjoyed more than a century of "benign neglect" from the mother country. "The most English feature of this established order (until 1776)," wrote Bradford "was its legalism, its devotion to the Constitution and common law, and its dependence on lawyers. . . . Nothing could be more natural than that, once we lost one Constitution and Bill of Rights through revolution (an act based on elaborate Constitutional arguments) we established another Constitution and another Bill of Rights—or rather, several of both—as soon as possible. There is no way of understanding the origins of our fundamental law apart from eighteenth-century English constitutionalism, than which there is no doctrine more conservative." The colonists' religiosity completed the picture of this deeply rooted conservatism, because "Christian faith discouraged in the Fathers the modern tendency to seek salvation in politics, protected a private sphere, and discouraged men from divinizing the state." After the Revolution an increasing emphasis on equality had, unfortunately, distorted this old heritage. Originally, equality meant equal protection of the laws, but by the twentieth century it had come to mean belief in equality of opportunity and even equality of results. This far-reaching change, "based on a misunderstanding of our heritage from the Declaration of Independence and from the Christian promise that grace is available to all, threatens to swallow up our reverence for law, responsible character, moral principle, and inherited proscription." Conservatives must do what they could to forestall the tide of egalitarianism.[47]

Bradford, normally a jovial man, was indeed a passionate hater of Abraham Lincoln. His essay "The Lincoln Legacy, a Long View," depicted Lincoln not as a heroic leader and martyr but as something more like a dictatorial war criminal. By insisting on absolute victory over the Confederacy he had lengthened the Civil War and multiplied the death toll. He was an economic centralizer whose banking policy, tariffs, and subsidies to big corporations had sown the seeds of the disgraceful "great barbecue" that followed the Civil War. He had connived at the "rotten army contracts given to politically faithful crooks" and had lured immigrants to America with the promise of free land, "only to force them into the ranks of General Grant's meat grinder or into near slavery in the cities of the East." In domestic affairs he had granted himself virtually dictatorial powers, and he had destroyed the balance of powers in the Constitution, with grave and continuing consequences to the nation. Bradford hated not only the man but also the great monument erected to his memory in Washington, "where his oversized likeness is elevated above us like that of a deified Roman emperor."[48]

Bradford and his fellow paleoconservatives wanted to limit government power and restore states' rights, a program they justified with an appeal to the Founding Fathers. "[Our] task is to restore the federal republic at home. In order to carry out this task we will need the spirit of liberty that animated generations of our forefathers." Jefferson had understood, wrote Bradford's friend Clyde Wilson (b. 1941), that the temptations of power corrupt *everyone* and that no one can be trusted to decide for others. Yet America today, with its immense federal government and its activist judiciary, had concentrated power in a small, centralized group, becoming more an oligarchy than a democracy. Only by seizing power back from this oligarchy, reducing the scale of government, reasserting states' rights, and reverting to a regime of low taxation could citizens regain their freedom. Wilson, a professor at the University of South Carolina and editor of John Calhoun's papers, shared much of Calhoun's Southern patriotism and aversion to federal power.[49]

The fact that so many Americans currently acquiesced to the status quo, said the paleoconservatives, was a sign of their diminished virtue, as the Founders would have recognized at once. That is, they had accepted what the founders condemned as "luxury" (in today's terms, a high standard of living) in return for surrendering their autonomy. Accordingly, "the people must not only put limits on government. They must break their own dependence upon the corrupt system, give up the expectation that things will be done for them, and demand the return of our resources to ourselves, to dispose of in our own way."[50]

Some paleoconservatives, including Bradford and Wilson, were Southern traditionalists, whose journal *Southern Partisan* first saw the light of day in 1981. Eager to preserve the outlook of the Agrarians and Richard Weaver, they were dissatisfied with the "Yankee conservatism" of *National Review*. One of the founders recalled that in the early 1980s "there was no popular voice for the qualities and the values embodied in Southern history: the importance of family life, small communities, local government, honor and manners; the sacred value of the land; the need to nurture the religious roots of the Republic and to keep the old stories alive as a basis for renewal." Sometimes highbrow (the historian Eugene Genovese was a contributor), sometimes middlebrow, *Southern Partisan* devoted most of its pages to retrospectives on the Old South, the Civil War, and Southern literature, arguing that the South remained a neglected repository of wisdom for solving contemporary problems. Its standard rhetoric featured grievances against the North, home of the "ideologues and robber barons . . . who continue to make war on this region in the name of the modern shibboleths of 'equality' and 'progress.' " It was vulnerable to accusations of insensitivity on racial questions and of sentimentalizing the old slave South.[51]

Another group of paleoconservatives, similar in many respects to these Southerners, were heirs of the old prewar midwestern isolationists. Their journal *Chronicles* (originally *Chronicles of Culture*), founded in 1977, was funded by the Rockford Institute of Rockford, Illinois. It was skeptical equally of neoconservatives and of Eastern Establishment Republicans. Sam Francis (1947–2005), one regular *Chronicles* contributor, wrote an enthusiastic retrospective on McCarthyism in 1986, arguing that "the American right, if it is serious about wanting to preserve the nation and its social fabric and political culture . . . must continue to embrace Joe McCarthy and the kind of militant anti-liberal and antiestablishment movement that he was the first to express on a national scale." In the same year, its editor, Thomas Fleming, sounded nativist notes when he opposed large-scale immigration to America and what he saw as its corrupting cultural influence.[52]

The *Chronicles* group did not shy away from arguing—in an idiom Theodore Roosevelt would have recognized—that America was essentially an Anglo-Saxon nation and that it ought to restore the racially restrictive immigration policy it had had between the 1920s and the mid-1960s. Paul Gottfried (b. 1941), a participant in and historian of the group, noted that "Hamilton, Jefferson, Madison, Jay, and Franklin all spoke out against liberal immigration and warned against admitting into the new republic those who had come from cultures markedly different from the one they were entering." Another contributor, Chilton Williamson, agreed; he added that America ought not to permit large-scale immigration even if (as he doubted) it brought economic benefits. Why? Because the nation's cultural homogeneity was the basis of its greatness. He noted the paradox that by the late 1980s "it is considered 'humanitarian' to fret about population growth and its effects on the environment at the global . . . level but 'racist,' 'xenophobic,' 'uncompassionate,' and 'un-American' to worry about the population crisis as it immediately effects the United States, the only place in the world where we are in a position to do anything about it."[53]

As these assertions suggest, writers for *Chronicles* had no patience with the neoconservatives' idea that liberal democracy is, potentially, for everyone and that immigration does more good than harm. Their distaste for neoconservatives on immigration and other issues intensified as the eighties progressed. At a meeting of the Philadelphia Society in 1986, for example, usually a mild and decorous forum for the discussion and exchange of conservative ideas, a group of paleoconservatives denounced the neocons. One in particular, Stephen Tonsor, gave an impassioned tirade against what to him was the corrupting influence on the movement of these ex-leftists. "It is splendid when the town whore gets religion and joins the church. Now and then she makes a good choir director, but when she begins to tell the minister what he ought to say in his Sunday sermons, matters have been carried too far." Tonsor and his colleagues accused the neoconservatives of being far too complacent about the growth of the welfare state and of being "global democrats and secularists whose democratic universalism was reminiscent of Trotskyist utopianism."[54]

Neoconservatives reacted to such assertions with alarm, particularly when Sam Francis's attack on the "cultural and intellectual vanguards of the elite" with their "ethic of hedonism, immediate gratification, and cosmopolitan or universalist dispersion of concrete identities and loyalties" began to sound like the old rhetoric of anti-Semitism. Richard Neuhaus (b. 1936), director of the Center on Religion and Society, which was funded by the Rockford Institute, had become steadily more dissatisfied with *Chronicles'* attitudes during the preceding years and was seeking a way to separate his institution from Rockford. He deplored what he described as "the magazine's indulgence in nativism, and its increasingly shrill and mean-spirited war on conservatives who did not pass its ideological tests."[55]

In May 1989, a group of Rockford executives brought the dispute to a crisis by summarily ejecting Neuhaus from his New York offices. The mainstream media, hearing about an angry brouhaha on the right, gave the story extensive coverage, whose upshot was highly favorable to Neuhaus and damaging to the paleoconservatives. A major grant from the Bradley Foundation that had been supporting Neuhaus stayed with him rather than reverting to Rockford. Michael Joyce, of the Bradley Foundation compared the antagonists: "The Center and its publications are reflective of a forward-looking conservatism. They tend to favor markets and limited government as a way of spurring growth and improving democratic institutions. . . . Rockford, particularly its magazine *Chronicles,* is somewhat critical of free markets and spreading democracy. It looks back to agrarian society, small towns, religious values. It sees modern times as too secular, too democratic. There's a distrust of cities and of cultural pluralism, which they find partly responsible for social decay in American life." Neuhaus was convinced that *Chronicles* was anti-Semitic. He wrote later: "It is not only totalitarians who cannot stand Jews and Judaism. In this country we are familiar with a brand of conservatism that is marked by nativist and chauvinist sentiment. It advocates a form of cultural coherence that requires a clear line between 'us' and 'them,' " one that uses the "classical language of anti-Semitism" in a thinly coded condemnation of Jews. Neuhaus would emerge in the 1990s as leader of another branch of the movement, the "theoconservatives."[56]

The division between neoconservatives and paleoconservatives was both pragmatic and philosophical. Dan Himmelfarb, writing in *Commentary* in 1988, noted several real differences: the neoconservatives were the newcomers and more likely to be Jewish, more likely to be social scientists, and more tolerant of big government and overseas democratization projects. Paleos, conversely, were old-time conservatives, more likely to be Christian, more likely to be litterateurs and theologians, and less tolerant of big government and overseas adventures for democracy. "The fundamental difference" was something deeper, however. "Neoconservatives belong to the tradition of liberal-democratic modernity, the tradition of Montesquieu, Madison, and Tocqueville; paleoconservatives are the heirs to the Christian and aristocratic Middle Ages, to Augustine, Aquinas, and Hooker." Himmelfarb, clearly writing from the neocon side of the divide, went on to claim that his side's values were "explicitly American" and that those of the paleos were "fundamentally extra-American," dating far back to the Middle Ages and the ancient world. Luckily, he added, the two groups could often agree in practice, even if their reasons for favoring a conservative policy were distinct.[57]

In 1989, a meeting at Rockford later brought together the paleoconservative traditionalists and libertarians from the Ludwig von Mises Institute. The institute's principal figures were Llewelyn Rockwell and Murray Rothbard, the most gifted libertarian writer of his generation. Rothbard had suffered repeated disappointments in his relations with the Libertarian Party, recognizing that as long as libertarianism had a hippie, counterculture image, it would scare off middle-class voters, no matter how persuasive its ideas. He now welcomed the idea of trying to reestablish good relations with members of the Old Right, sympathized with Rockford in its dispute with Neuhaus, and denied the allegation that *Chronicles* was anti-Semitic (Rothbard was himself Jewish). The meeting gave birth to the John Randolph Club, named for Randolph of Roanoke (see Chap. 2), whose members by and large agreed on the need for radically reduced government, even though they differed on the question of protectionism and free markets. Among them were numerous talented polemical writers who were to constitute the brain trust of Pat Buchanan's bids for the presidency in 1992, 1996, and 2000.[58]

TWILIGHT OF THE COLD WAR

Might a change in the Soviet leadership lead to a change in the long Cold War standoff? Mikhail Gorbachev became Soviet premier in 1985 and soon made headlines with his policies of glasnost and perestroika, auguring greater economic and personal freedom behind the Iron Curtain. Anticommunist hard-liners like Podhoretz at *Commentary* and Buckley at *National Review* regarded these initiatives as just another set of hypocritical gestures, aimed at disarming world opinion. They were ideologically committed to the idea that reform inside a totalitarian system was simply impossible. As the historian John Ehrman notes, "Since 1970 Podhoretz had increasingly defined *Commentary*'s stands by a rigid opposition to any compromise or flexibility in foreign policy."[59]

Other conservative intellectuals, however, believed that Gorbachev was something genuinely different. This more flexible reaction appeared in Irving Kristol's new journal *The National Interest,* founded in 1985 with a grant of six hundred thousand dollars from the Olin Foundation. It, too, was a neoconservative vehicle, dedicated to providing the same sort of insights in foreign policy that its predecessor, *The Public Interest* had done in domestic affairs twenty years earlier. This time around, says the historian Gary Dorrien, "Kristol made no pretense of avoiding ideology." Its contributors included Kristol himself, Robert Tucker, Owen Harries, and Henry Rowen, who began gathering evidence to show that by the late 1980s the Soviet Union, far from being more powerful than ever before, was desperately weak internally, falling to pieces economically, and scarcely able even to feed its people.[60]

By 1989 the evidence of genuine and far-reaching change in the Soviet Union was becoming almost impossible to deny. Soviet authority was breaking down, borders to the West were opening, and finally the Berlin Wall itself, strongest symbol of the long Cold War standoff, crashed to the ground. Even the most skeptical conservatives were forced to acknowledge that that the long communist nightmare was ending, and they began, cautiously, to accept and take pleasure in the truth. Podhoretz, after a visit to Russia in the summer of 1989, admitted that free political debate was suddenly possible and that even at the highest levels, politicians were telling him that the countries of Eastern Europe could now regain their independence.[61]

Three consecutive Republican presidential victories and a pervasive conservative culture in Washington, D.C., marked the ascendancy of conservatism in the 1980s, as did the prosperity of conservative think tanks and journals. Differences among groups of conservative intellectuals, and difficulties in converting ideas into policies, prevented all of them from feeling vindicated in practice, but collectively they had certainly managed to restore the intellectual credibility and political viability of their philosophy. The 1980s was, strikingly, an era in which capitalism, which had been on the defensive throughout the twentieth century, attracted new intellectual champions and came to seem all the more effective, as communism, its great challenger, moldered its way to comprehensive failure throughout the Eastern bloc.

With capitalism secure and communism in retreat, conservatives moved increasingly in the late 1980s to the fighting of culture wars. As in earlier eras, one group, exemplified by Allan Bloom and Hilton Kramer, emphasized the continuing importance of high culture, classical standards, and the imperative of rigorous education of the leadership elite. Others, like E. D. Hirsch and the *Dartmouth Review* group, concentrated on reversing insidious long-term trends in mass culture and on university campuses.

Two sets of conservatives, meanwhile, felt conspicuously excluded from the new "Establishment" of the 1980s: libertarians and paleoconservatives. The libertarians had been unable to make electoral headway for their candidates, and their opposition to the military-industrial state marginalized them throughout the Cold War years. The paleoconservatives' apparent sympathy for the old Anglo-Saxon outlook, meanwhile, made them vulnerable to accusations of racial insensitivity, against which mainstream conservatives had, by the 1980s, managed largely to insulate themselves. Whatever their internal divisions, however, America's conservatives were united in celebrating the collapse of Soviet communism, the fall of the Berlin Wall, and end of the Cold War.

CHAPTER TEN

Conservatives After the Cold War, 1989–2001

TWO YEARS AFTER THE BERLIN WALL FELL, Germany was reunited and the Soviet Union dissolved. Russia lurched toward democracy while its old satellites became new self-governing post-Soviet states. The Cold War, a central fact of world politics for nearly half a century, had ended without the long-dreaded exchange of nuclear weapons. China, North Korea, and Cuba retained a vestigial loyalty to Marxism, but the old claim that sooner or later communism would conquer the world had completely evaporated.

Conservatives rejoiced, but the vanquishing of their great foe presented dilemmas as well as delights. After all, anticommunism had been the glue that held their movement together, and it now seemed possible that the many varieties of American conservatives, no longer sharing a common fear of the great Soviet bear, might follow different paths into the future. Would conservatism remain politically significant, or would it once again become the kind of theoretical concern it had often been before the Cold War, pursued by isolated intellectual coteries and far removed from the realities of power?

R. Emmett Tyrrell (b. 1943), editor of *American Spectator,* published *The Conservative Crack-Up* in 1992. It was a sequel to his book *The Liberal Crack-Up* (1984), which had argued for the complete intellectual bankruptcy and frivolity of American liberalism by the time of Reagan's election. The new book, part memoir and part analysis of the conservative movement, predicted decline and dispersal. Tyrrell argued that conservatives, though they had made some headway in electoral politics, had lost the battle for American culture, which remained in the grip of a liberal oligarchy. The conservative worldview, he added, had made virtually no impact on college campuses or in the major news media. No artists publicized conservative ideas; the White House had done nothing to cultivate an intellectual constituency, outside of narrowly political and policy-oriented writers. Now conservatism was in danger from its ostensible friends—shallow opportunists who had flooded Washington, voicing their conservative ideas. Other analysts also speculated that the conservative movement, having been called forth by the crisis conditions of the mid-twentieth century, might now disappear. Michael Lind, a disillusioned ex-conservative, wrote in 1996 that the conservative intellectual movement was hopelessly split between an elite intellectual minority and a vulgar populist mass.[1]

VISIONS OF THE FUTURE: FUKUYAMA AND HUNTINGTON

With the demise of communism, was the world becoming safer or more dangerous, more united or more divided? Ever since the 1960s the idea of the global village had been a shorthand way of referring to the proximity of the world's different peoples and the speed of communication between them. Were the different parts of the world in fact becoming more similar, or did proximity inflame irreconcilable differences? Two statements, both by imaginative neoconservative writers, drew opposite conclusions.

In "The End of History," a *National Interest* article written while Soviet communism was expiring in 1989, Francis Fukuyama (b. 1952), a State Department official, argued that the centuries-long conflict over how societies should be organized and governed was coming to an end with the triumph of liberal democracy. It had defeated the vestiges of monarchy earlier in the century, then fascism and Nazism, now communism. "The triumph of the West, of the Western *idea,* is evident . . . in the total exhaustion of viable systematic alternatives to Western liberalism." So far, to be sure, the victory was chiefly in the realm of ideas, but "there are powerful reasons for believing that [liberal democracy] is the ideal that will govern the material world *in the long run.*" Even before the Berlin Wall came down, Fukuyama saw that "Gorbachev has finally permitted people to say what they had privately understood for many years, namely, that the magical incantations of Marxism-Leninism, were nonsense."[2]

Were there any remaining legitimate challengers to liberal democracy in the world? Fukuyama examined religion and nationalism as possible rivals but rejected both. Religion answered to human cravings in the private sphere, but no religion offered a world-embracing political and economic system. In most cases, nationalism, too, was a negative aspiration—the desire for "independence *from* some other group or people"—and did not offer "anything like a comprehensive agenda for socio-economic organization." It often thrived in places whose people felt deprived of the blessings of liberal democracy. For the immediate future, conflict between nation-states would continue, and much of the world would still have to travel far before reaching the end point already arrived at by Western Europe and the United States. The long-term prognosis was nevertheless benign. Just as the nations of Western Europe no longer fought one another as they had done for centuries, the world would become more peaceful as it became more liberal democratic.[3]

Samuel Huntington (b. 1927), by contrast, a Harvard professor of politics, writing just four years later, foresaw a completely different future and one likely, if anything, to be more challenging and bloody than the twentieth century. A "clash of civilizations," he wrote, would be the next stage in the development of international relations. In early modern Europe great wars had been conflicts between kings and dynasties. After the French Revolution they were conflicts between nation-states. After the Russian Revolution they were conflicts between ideologies: communism, Nazism, and democratic capitalism, all taking place within Western civilization. Now, however, the world's different *civilizations* were coming into conflict: "The fundamental source of conflict in this new world will not be primarily ideological or primarily economic. The great divisions among humankind and the dominating source of conflict will be cultural."[4]

Ideologies are comparatively shallow, he continued, but civilizations are deep, "differentiated from each other by history, language, culture, tradition, and most important, religion. . . . These differences are the product of centuries. . . . They are far more fundamental than differences among political ideologies and political regimes." As economic modernization weakened old local identities, fundamentalist religion often took their place. Elites seeking to influence events in Islamic, Hindu, Confucian, and Russian contexts were becoming "de-westernized." It seemed to Huntington that wars within each of the civilizations were becoming less likely because of "civilizational rallying" but that conflicts between them were becoming more likely. The bloody fragmentation of southeastern Europe in the early 1990s was a case in point; Yugoslavia had stood on the borderline of Islam, Western Christian, and Orthodox Christian civilizations.[5]

Where Fukuyama had cautiously foreseen convergence on common standards, Huntington argued for increasing conflict and difference: "Western ideas of individualism, liberalism, constitutionalism, human rights, equality, liberty, the rule of law, democracy, free markets, the separation of church and state, often have little resonance in Islamic, Confucian, Japanese, Hindu, Buddhist, or Orthodox cultures." Besides, "the very notion that there could be a 'universal civilization' is a Western idea."[6]

The political implications of these contrasting views were profound. If Fukuyama was right, the world would gradually move toward liberal democracy with a corresponding diminution in conflict. If Huntington was right, efforts to encourage or impose liberal democracy would inflame resistance and conflict. The politics of the 1990s and early 2000s were complex and ambiguous enough to give both views encouragement at certain times, and discouragement at others. Certainly the collapse of the Soviet Union, the wave of post-Soviet democratizations in the 1990s, and the economic liberalization of China had a Fukuyamesque flavor. The Balkan wars of the 1990s and later the attack on the World Trade Center, on the other hand, seemed to confirm Huntington's gloomier forecast.

FOREIGN POLICY

America's first post–Cold War foreign policy crisis could itself be interpreted either way. It was also the conservative movement's first test of post–Cold War durability. Saddam Hussein, the Iraqi dictator, invaded Kuwait in the summer of 1990, making himself the dominant figure in the Arabian Gulf, with a menacing degree of control over the area's oil supply. President George H. W. Bush responded by building a United

Nations alliance against Hussein, which moved troops to the area and ordered Hussein to withdraw. In the fall of 1990 the United Nations tried to enforce its will through economic sanctions and diplomatic pressure, but when these methods failed, it switched early in 1991 to direct military force. The UN armies, with Americans fighting front and center, won an overwhelming and rapid victory, driving the Iraqi forces out of Kuwait in the space of a few days and killing thousands.[7]

American conservatives debated the war and the policy decisions surrounding it with their usual polemical energy. Right from the start much of the conservative mainstream supported President Bush's decision to intervene. Norman Podhoretz, editor of *Commentary,* argued that Saddam Hussein might justly be compared with Hitler: "When Hitler occupied the Rhineland in 1936, a moment which roughly corresponds to the invasion of Kuwait by Iraq, he had not yet attained to the level of evil Saddam Hussein has already reached in launching a pointless war against Iran that resulted in a million casualties, in using poison gas against his own Kurdish citizens, and in the grisly atrocities he has committed in Kuwait." Podhoretz added that early intervention against Hitler when he was weak would have saved millions of lives and a catastrophic war. The analogy, justifying President Bush's intervention, was clear. (It also offered a tantalizing premonition of the preemptive war doctrine that the second President Bush would later develop.)[8]

National Review, in similar vein, editorialized that "President Bush deserves the gratitude of all Americans for the courageous and visionary leadership" he showed. It added that attempts to discredit the war as "merely" for the sake of oil supplies were disingenuous. "Oil," wrote William Rusher, publisher of *National Review,* "is not only a vital energy source for modern nations; in addition, the petrochemical industry is the very foundation of huge areas of modern technology, from pharmaceuticals to plastics. No doubt science will some day free the world from its slavish dependence on oil, but for the foreseeable future its availability at reasonable prices is absolutely essential." That America was better able to supply its own oil needs than Japan and Western Europe, however, demonstrated that the American intervention in Kuwait was not solely self-interested but had in view international political stability and the welfare of the entire world economy.[9]

Delighted as they were by the quick and (on their side) nearly bloodless victory, some hawkish conservatives wanted to capitalize on success. They therefore deplored the president's decision not to topple Saddam Hussein while he had the chance, especially since there was evidence that the dictator was again trying to build himself a nuclear arsenal (Israel had preemptively bombed Iraq's nuclear facilities back in 1981). Bush's apparent faltering at the eleventh hour, said these hawks, was merely storing up trouble for later, trouble that would have to be resolved by another resort to arms. "Saddam's regime," wrote Angelo Codevilla in *Commentary,* "may be compared to a bacterial infection that has been treated with enough antibiotics to make the patient feel better but not enough to kill it. The patient has every reason to fear that in time the infection will become more virulent, and meet less resistance, than before." Sustaining the metaphor, he added: "By focusing on the Kuwaiti symptom rather than on the Iraqi disease, Bush put himself in the worst of positions." Hussein, meanwhile, crushed Kurdish and Shiite rebellions and restored his control over Iraq for the next twelve years.[10]

Despite their regrets over a job left unfinished, most conservative hawks believed that the war had rung down the curtain on the old Vietnam syndrome, the hesitancy Washington had felt about committing military forces overseas since its retreat from Southeast Asia eighteen years earlier. They noted with pride the effectiveness of American "smart" weapons, the vigor and high morale of the all-volunteer army, its low casualty rate, and its commanders' verve and dash. Norman Schwartzkopf ("Stormin' Norman") became the nation's first real military hero since Douglas MacArthur, in the early days of the Korean War, especially among conservatives. They also applauded the army's decision to keep reporters well away from the scene of the actual fighting, lest Vietnam-style journalism sow doubt in citizens' minds about the war's justifiability.[11]

Admiration for and advocacy of more aggression was only half the story, however. Another group of American conservatives, the paleoconservatives, thought that America had no business going to war in the Arabian Gulf and that vital American interests were not at stake there. Joseph Sobran (b. 1946), a senior editor at *National Review,* was alarmed at his fellow conservatives' enthusiasm for war. "With the end of the Cold War," he wrote, "conservatives ought to be redoubling their efforts to achieve the domestic goal of restoring a limited republic, not sacrificing this purpose to global empire." America was capable of achieving economic autonomy, he added, and faced no direct threat from Saddam Hussein, whom the media had made "our new Hitler of the month."[12]

Sobran and other antiwar paleoconservatives, for whom Patrick Buchanan quickly became the leading mouthpiece, argued that the end of the Cold War ought to have ended America's world-bestriding foreign role. Buchanan, a long-time Cold Warrior, who had earlier been a speechwriter for President Nixon and White House communications director for President Reagan, believed America should now resume something approaching its old isolationist foreign policy after what was, in effect, a fifty-year emergency brought on by the Nazi and Soviet threats.[13]

Buchanan's opposition to the war provoked controversy in the conservative movement, partly because he appeared to be reviving the "America First" approach of Charles Lindbergh and partly because he sometimes sounded anti-Semitic. Buchanan believed that American Jews and lobbyists for Israel had promoted a war that would benefit Israel more than America, even though the lives placed most at risk were those of Americans. As he expressed it: "There are only two groups beating the drums for war in the Middle East—the Israeli Defense Ministry and its amen corner in the United States." A few days later he called Congress "Israeli-occupied territory." If America went to war, the fighting and dying would be done by "kids with names like McAllister, Murphy, Gonzales, and Leroy Brown."[14]

Angry recriminations ensued, with extensive coverage in *Commentary* and *National Review,* eventuating in a book-length study of the affair by William Buckley. He reproached Buchanan for insensitivity but denied allegations of outright anti-Semitism made by Podhoretz and the *New York Times* editor A. M. Rosenthal. Buckley had played the role of alliance builder and reconciler for decades by then and was the grand old man among conservative intellectuals, but healing this rift was more than even he could manage. Animosities generated during the Gulf War persisted through the 1990s and aggravated a sharp intraconservative division.[15]

Buchanan's side favored no foreign entanglements and a form of economic nationalism, including high tariff barriers and immigration restriction. The fact that Buchanan ran for president in the elections of 1992, 1996 and 2000 meant that his proposals enjoyed plenty of publicity throughout the nineties. In 2002 the views of Buchananite paleoconservatives would be expressed in another new journal, *The American Conservative.* Buchananites argued that the neoconservative vision was a recipe for disaster. Based on Woodrow Wilson–style delusions about making the world safe for democracy, there was, they said, nothing conservative about it. If anything, it carried the whiff of the old internationalist Trotskyism that Irving Kristol and his friends had favored in their struggle against the Communist Party at City College of New York in the late 1930s.[16]

Meanwhile a new generation of neoconservatives, led by Irving Kristol's son, William (b. 1952), continued to press for an aggressive foreign policy. Kristol and Robert Kagan published *Present Dangers* in 2000, a representative anthology of their views. America should be using its supremacy more actively than ever, they said, shaping the world in its own image and to suit its own interests. Never before had it had such an opportunity, because never before had a condition of "unipolarity" existed, with one nation—the United States—incomparably stronger than all the others. American action against tyrannies would be welcomed around the world because the human yearning for democracy and freedom were universal. They aspired to American greatness, taking the old expansionist conservative Theodore Roosevelt as their model. "The present danger is that the United States, the world's dominant power, on whom the maintenance of international peace and the support of liberal democratic principles depends, will shrink its responsibilities and . . . allow the international order that it created and sustains to collapse."[17]

The *Present Dangers* group argued that, in the long run, passivity, or excessive attachment to the status quo, is immoral and costly. Using their favorite analogy they pointed out that early intervention against Hitler, and cultivation of the will to oppose him, would have forestalled World War II, saved millions of lives, and been relatively cheap. Perhaps there was at present not so imminent a threat to America as Hitler had been, but the proliferation of nuclear weapons and other weapons of mass destruction made waiting for threats to develop more dangerous than ever before. America should attack not only actual menaces but even nations and terrorist groups that might *become* menacing. Its policy should be forward and proactive.[18]

The group lobbied President Clinton hard (but unsuccessfully) to end Saddam Hussein's regime, continuing to think of the Iraqi situation as tragically unfinished business. Having befriended Ahmed Chalabi, head of the exiled Iraqi National Congress, they believed his argument that Iraq without Saddam could become a functioning democracy in the heart of the Middle East and serve as a benign example that would stimulate further democratization throughout the area. After the attack on the World Trade Center and the Pentagon in 2001 they would find a new president willing to adopt their plan.[19]

RELIGIOUS CONSERVATIVES

Jerry Falwell announced that the Moral Majority was closing shop in 1989. Financial troubles in the wake of the great evangelical scandals of the late 1980s had cut into the organization's resources, and its members felt disillusioned by the events of the past ten years. President Reagan, despite his courtship of the Christian Right, had done little or nothing to enact its programs and had not prioritized legislation or a constitutional amendment against abortion.[20]

Falwell would remain a luminous figure among conservative Christians into the next century, but for the moment his place in Christian politics was taken by Ralph Reed and the Christian Coalition. Their candidates and campaigns contributed to major Republican gains in the election of 1994 but as an intellectual force they were negligible. Thomas Fleming, a paleoconservative, lamented that while conservative evangelicals could sometimes be found trying to ban sexy and smutty books from local libraries, they were never found lobbying those same libraries to buy complete editions of the classics or the Church Fathers. The Bible itself, the theology of Francis Schaeffer, and occasional works of C. S. Lewis were about as far as any of them went. "If the library refused 100 requests for Goethe or Bishop Berkeley, then it would be time to accuse the library of censorship." But the churches, instead of "working to improve the common culture," were content "to rail against the immorality of the 'secular humanists.' " Fleming concluded: "After decades of efforts to ban nasty books, rate movies, and put warning labels on records, the Tipper Gores of America have contributed nothing, literally nothing positive to our culture."[21]

Evangelicals were not alone in bringing Christian principles to bear on contemporary politics. Catholics, always an important element of the Cold War conservative movement, became more significant than ever, thanks to Richard Neuhaus. He, like many of the neoconservatives, had made a long journey across the political spectrum since the 1960s, when he had been a militant young Lutheran pastor in the slums of Bedford-Stuyvesant. Enraged at the American role in Vietnam, he had, in those days, come very close to advocating revolutionary resistance. An augury of things to come, however, had been his early belief that abortion was a horrible sin and that the same humane imperative that drove American critics of the war should govern their view of the need to protect unborn babies at their most vulnerable moment.[22]

Increasingly sympathetic to the neoconservative critique of liberalism in the 1970s and 1980s, Neuhaus wrote two influential books in the Reagan years, *The Naked Public Square* (1984) and *The Catholic Moment* (1987). In the first he decried the secularization of America in recent decades, which had denied it a religious foundation on which citizens could take their moral bearings. The First Amendment, he argued, had never been meant to secularize America, merely to keep any one of the many competing churches from imposing its will on other Christians. The Supreme Court's recent decisions on prayer, sexuality, censorship, and abortion, however, had had the cumulative effect of endorsing a permissive, hedonistic, and explicitly nonreligious culture, while actively forestalling religious practices in public life. Without a transcendent point, Neuhaus argued, the public square became vulnerable to pseudoreligious impostors.[23]

In the second of these books, *The Catholic Moment,* Neuhaus, though a Lutheran, praised the Catholic Church for its conservative resources, both human and intellectual. Its philosophical tradition, balancing reason and revelation, its veneration for natural law, its just war tradition—these and the heritage of papal teachings embodied in encyclical letters made the Catholic Church well placed to combat the destructive tendencies of the age, especially since it had dropped much of its old defensive standoffishness at the Second Vatican Council. The 1980s, he wrote, was a time in which "the Roman Catholic Church in the world can and should be the lead church in proclaiming and exemplifying the Gospel" and the moment in which "the Roman Catholic Church in the United

States assumes its rightful role in the culture-forming task of constructing a religiously informed public philosophy for the American experiment in ordered liberty." The church must, however, keep liberation theology at arm's length—Neuhaus's heroes were Pope John Paul II and Cardinal Joseph Ratzinger (the future Pope Benedict XVI).[24]

Soon thereafter Neuhaus announced his own conversion to Catholicism (1990). Always a celibate, he quickly trained for and was ordained into the priesthood, but this change did not signal a withdrawal from public life. He had split from the Rockford Institute over its nativism and what he perceived as its anti-Semitism (see Chap. 9). He now launched *First Things*, an interfaith journal of religion and conservatism, blending the insights of Protestants, Catholics, and Jews. Among regular contributors to *First Things* were the Jewish scholar and rabbi David Novak and the former Watergate conspirator Charles Colson (b. 1931), now a born-again evangelical Christian. Neuhaus and Colson sought ways to unite Catholic and evangelical social conservatives, making a joint statement in 1994, titled "Evangelicals and Catholics Together," on their shared traditions and common interests.[25]

The *First Things* group, known as theoconservatives by their secular brethren, agreed with Christian Coalition evangelicals that victory over communism was only half the battle and that they must find ways to overcome decadence at home. America was in catastrophic moral decline, they said, especially in matters relating to sex. The breakdown of the taboo against pre- and extramarital sex, the epidemic of AIDS and other sexually transmitted diseases, the widespread incidence of abortion, the prevalence of one-parent families, and the proliferation of pornography were all evidence of social collapse. Making a bad situation worse, they added, the American judiciary seemed to be abetting rather than combating these developments. In November 1996 Neuhaus devoted an issue of *First Things* to a symposium, "The End of Democracy? The Judicial Usurpation of Politics."[26]

Conservatives had criticized judicial activism ever since the New Deal. In Neuhaus's view, the problem was getting worse, creating "an entrenched pattern of government by judges that is nothing less than the usurpation of politics." It was bad enough that unelected judges were taking important political decisions out of Congress's hands. Worse, their decisions were promoting immorality: "Law, as it is presently made by the judiciary, has declared its independence from morality. Indeed . . . morality—especially traditional morality, and most especially morality associated with religion—has been declared legally suspect and a threat to public order." In an America whose people had long expressed their faith in God and country, many now found they must choose God *or* country. And since divine imperatives trump earthly ones, it might be necessary to give up on the country itself. This was the conundrum the editors of *Triumph* had voiced in the early 1970s (see Chap. 8).[27]

One contributor to the symposium, the Princeton political scientist Robert George (b. 1955), invoked the encyclical *Evangelium Vitae* (1995) of Pope John Paul II on the need to combat the contemporary "culture of death" and John Paul's reminder that civil laws in violation of the natural law are invalid. If the Supreme Court directed pro-life citizens to stop their protests against abortion, therefore, Christians must not obey. "It is not merely that the claim of these justices to have found a pro-abortion 'mandate' in the Constitution is manifestly ludicrous. The value of constitutional democracy lies ultimately in its capacity to serve and secure the common good, which demands above all the protection of fundamental human rights. If the Constitution really did abandon the vulnerable to private acts of lethal violence, and, indeed, positively disempowered citizens from working through the democratic process to correct these injustices, then it would utterly lack the capacity to bind the consciences of citizens." Charles Colson, another contributor, investigated the sources in American tradition and in scripture for justified opposition to the "regime." He concluded that the church "would . . . have to separate herself and declare her independence, disavowing any moral legitimacy indirectly or unofficially provided for the state in the past. Through her teaching and preaching office, the church would need to expose the nature of the state's rebellion against God—in effect, bringing the state under the transcendent judgment of God."[28]

More secular conservatives were alarmed at this defiance and chastised the Neuhaus group for thinking out loud about detaching themselves from the United States and declaring it illegitimate. Gertrude Himmelfarb noted that slavery, disgraceful though it surely was, had not delegitimized the founding of America, and neither did abortion. John Leo warned that wild talk of revolution would simply play "into the hands of people who wish to lump us [conservatives] with cranks and violent extremists." William Bennett, the former secretary of education and drug czar in the Reagan and Bush administrations, respectively, added that America was uniquely blessed with a political system that *could* redress wrongs, through legislation or a constitutional amendment. "The elected representatives of this country are as responsive to the desires of the public as perhaps any legislative body ever; even if the Supreme Court undermines the popular will . . . the citizens of America have several means of responsible recourse available to them. And that is just one of the many crucial differences that separate America from Nazi Germany, a regime invoked a number of times in the symposium. I take the demoralization of America quite seriously. But the analogy to Nazi Germany is both wrong and regrettable." Midge Decter was even more indignant and rebuked Neuhaus and *First Things* for voicing "the kind of careless radicalism you and I not all that long ago prayed for our country to have put behind it." The problem was a cultural one, she added, derived from the fact that most citizens did *not* feel outraged by abortion, homosexual marriage, and euthanasia. The job of conservatives, accordingly, was to work at changing citizens' opinions, educating them about the horrible implications of these new phenomena. It was not to deny legitimacy to the government and the courts.[29]

CULTURE WARS II

Not just in politics but in cultural and educational affairs, the intense debates of the Cold War years persisted into the 1990s. In *The Long March* (2000), a sequel to *Tenured Radicals,* Roger Kimball attempted to diagnose the intellectual origins of 1960s radicalism and the baleful influence of that decade's public intellectuals. A sharply hostile analysis of Norman Mailer, Norman O. Brown, Susan Sontag, Allen Ginsberg, Abbie Hoffman, the Beatles, the Black Panthers, and other iconic figures of that period, *The Long March* describes the 1960s as "a protracted and spiritually convulsive detonation" that "tore apart, perhaps irrevocably, the moral and intellectual fabric of our society." The guardians of American culture in those years had abdicated their position, coming to favor immaturity over experience. The result was disastrous. "The idealization of youth has resulted not only in the spread of adolescent values and passions; it has also led to the eclipse of adult virtues like circumspection, responsibility, and restraint." Passion for its own sake had somehow come to be treated as necessarily a virtue, as had the cult of authenticity.[30]

Where had it all started? Kimball suggested that the rot had set in with the Beat poets of the 1950s: Kerouac, Ginzburg, Burroughs, and their friends, whose work "anticipated so many of the pathologies of the Sixties and after. Their programmatic anti-Americanism, their avid celebration of drug abuse, their squalid promiscuous sex lives, their pseudo-spirituality, their attack on rationality and their degradation of intellectual standards, their aggressive posturing; in all this and more the Beats were every bit as 'advanced' as any Sixties radical." To make matters worse their influence had affected *supporters* of bourgeois society as well as its adversaries, which appeared to confirm Kimball's fear that conservatives had won the era's political war yet were "conspicuous losers" in its culture war.[31]

Kimball challenged a familiar stereotype. Denying numerous historians' assertions that the 1950s were a decade of dreary conformity, the age of the "man in the gray flannel suit," he argued that this view was itself Beat propaganda that subsequent youth fads (and political groups like the New Left) had picked up to justify their own excesses. In fact, he argued, American culture in the 1950s had been "vibrantly alive . . . confident, prosperous, and dynamic," and the nation "had never offered young people more real freedom, economically, socially, or intellectually." This was a view, however, with which conservatives of that decade would not have agreed. They thought they were living in an age of degraded rubbish, as a glance at early copies of *National Review* can attest. Kimball was retrospectively glorifying the 1950s as a way of emphasizing what to him were the noxious qualities of the 1960s.[32]

Occasionally, conservative ideas about art, culture, and education had direct political consequences. In the 1990s, for example, a debate over national standards for historical study provoked a confrontation between conservative and liberal academics. Congress, reacting to widespread concern at declining standards in historical study, mandated the writing of a set of national history standards for schools. Lynne Cheney (b. 1941), conservative head of the National Endowment for the Humanities, asked the National Center for History in the Schools at the University of California at Los Angeles to undertake the task in 1992, which it did over the next two years, drawing collaborators from all over the country. UCLA professor Gary Nash headed the team of writers, who delivered their work in the fall of 1994. The standards they came up with, however, were not what conservatives had hoped for. Cheney herself, by then out of office, wrote in the *Wall Street Journal* an angry op-ed article against the committee, saying the project had been hijacked and perverted by advocates of political correctness. The new standards, in her view, were unpatriotic and gave too much attention to obscure figures in the nation's past while unfairly neglecting many of the great ones. Harriet Tubman was mentioned honorably six times, McCarthyism was condemned nineteen times, the Ku Klux Klan was condemned seventeen times, but the Constitutional Convention, Robert E. Lee, the Wright Brothers, Albert Einstein, and Thomas Edison shared not a single word among them! One proposed exercise for tenth and eleventh graders was to put John D. Rockefeller on trial "for knowingly and willfully participating in unethical, amoral business standards." The tendentious political correctness of these standards had the effect, Cheney believed, of advancing a radical political agenda while making it difficult for young Americans to take pride in their nation's heritage. The conservative columnist Charles Krauthammer (b. 1950) agreed. "The whole document strains to promote the achievements and highlight the victimization of the country's preferred minorities, while straining equally to degrade the achievements and highlight the flaws of the white males who ran the country for its first two centuries."[33]

Conservatives' anger over the content of the standards was only the beginning. They were equally impatient with Nash's ideas about how history should be studied in schools. "Let's let the kids out of the prison of facts, the prison of dates and names and places," said Nash, "and let's have them discuss really important momentous turning points in American history"; mock trials, debates, and children's own efforts to write history could make it all more enjoyable, he believed. Krauthammer demurred: "How can they discuss anything without first having mastered dates, facts, places, and events?" American children were still seriously deficient in reading and writing; "it was precisely the woeful lack of these tools, documented in the 1983 'Nation at Risk" report on American education that had sparked the drive for national standards in the first place."[34]

This controversy prompted the Senate to vote against accepting the standards. It ordered the committee to modify and resubmit them, which it did two years later. Most conservatives considered the second draft an improvement over the first, but *National Review* editorialized that it was still dominated by multiculturalism and "left-wing editorializing." Cheney, again writing in the *Wall Street Journal,* continued to find them objectionable and wished in retrospect that she had never inaugurated the project. If one state taught history poorly, she now realized, it could be set right by forty-nine others, but to have imperfect *national* standards would mean degradation on a nationwide scale.[35]

Nash, writing about the controversy later, was unapologetic, describing his conservative opponents as old-fashioned elitists. "Having put up half the money," he wrote of Lynne Cheney, "she believed she was entitled to the history standards she wanted, guidelines that would exalt traditional heroes, put a happy face on the American past, and broadcast the triumph of western civilization." Far from regarding his approach as one that highlighted victims and denigrated traditional heroes, Nash saw it as consonant with the social history revolution of the foregoing decades. History in a democracy should be the history of all the people, and the standards outlined "the vast dimensions of the human experience heretofore unnoticed. Why should a democratic people dedicated to equality not applaud the attention now given to the roles in history of women, African Americans, working people, religious denominations, and other groups relatively powerless in the formal political sense? . . . Is this the voice of 'political correctness' or a recognition of the link between a democratic society and a more historically complete and accurate rendering of the past?" Nash's book about the episode, *History on Trial* (2000), is written in a tone of wounded surprise, that of a reasonable man unexpectedly attacked without provocation. It reasserts the defensibility of writing American history as the story of oppressed groups struggling for inclusion. Cheney's own book about the affair, *Telling The Truth* (1995), depicts her as a guardian of civilization fighting for truth and common sense at the last barricade. As in so many of the era's cultural conflicts, two conflicting sets of principles were in direct contradiction, causing each side to accuse the other of bad faith.[36]

RACE AND CULTURE

During the 1970s and 1980s several African American writers had published studies of urban affairs, education, and affirmative action that supported the neoconservative point of view. The best-known among them was Thomas Sowell (b. 1930), who had earned a Ph.D. in economics at the University of Chicago under Milton Friedman and George Stigler. Others included the political scientist Alan Keyes, a Straussian, the economist Glen Loury, and the literary scholar Shelby Steele. They urged African Americans to wean themselves from dependence on government support, to abandon the group-rights approach to advancement, and to recognize that affirmative action taints its recipients and creates resentment among whites. Above all, said these conservatives, African Americans should not think of themselves as victims. The fact that a strong black middle class had developed since 1960 was evidence, they believed, that racism no longer stopped African Americans from prospering. Nothing would do more to help the black population now than lower taxes, less government, the free market, and school vouchers. Clarence Thomas, a Supreme Court justice since 1991, said that the writings of Sowell in particular had influenced the development of his ideas about race and politics.[37]

These African American conservatives were professors or think-tank fellows; they lacked a constituency among the black electorate. In fact a smaller percentage of blacks voted Republican in 1992 than in 1960. The intellectuals also endured harsh criticism from the black intellectual mainstream, including allegations that they had cynically sold out for personal gain. Benjamin Hooks, leader of the National Association for the Advancement of Colored People, described them as "a new breed of Uncle Tom . . . some of the biggest liars the world ever saw."[38]

This background, in addition to the disappointing aftermath of the War on Poverty, helps explain the passionate debate that surrounded two of the most controversial American books of the 1990s, Charles Murray and Richard Herrnstein's *The Bell Curve* (1994) and Dinesh D'Souza's *The End of Racism* (1995). Charles Murray (b. 1943) was already a conservative lightning rod. His book *Losing Ground* (1984) had argued that welfare programs, by encouraging dependency and illegitimacy, worsen poverty rather than alleviate it. The most emphatic assertion of the law of unintended consequences ever written, it ended with the claim that, if there had been no Great Society programs at all, poverty, urban crisis, and family breakdown would have diminished much more rapidly than they did in the 1960s and 1970s. The programs, in other words, had been worse than useless. Urban African Americans were not the beneficiaries of these programs but, in effect, their victims.[39]

Murray was not a man to shy away from controversy. *The Bell Curve,* written with the Harvard psychologist Richard Herrnstein (1930–1994), argued that intelligence is, at least in part, hereditary and that the range of intelligence among any group of people can be arranged along a bell curve, with a small "cognitive elite" at the top, a majority bunching densely in the middle, and a small intellectually weak group at the bottom. It also argued that the bell curve for the intelligence of white Americans is different from (and superior to) the bell curve for the intelligence of African Americans. Now that America was an acutely education-conscious country it was increasingly likely, said the authors, that smart men would marry smart women, fortifying and isolating the cognitive elite at the top. It was also likely that the least intelligent men and women would intermarry, or at least interbreed, creating a permanent underclass at the bottom. The gap between the achievements of the two sectors would widen, as would their wealth and their propensity for lawful conduct. Among the book's many noteworthy claims was that a permanent *white* underclass was developing, likely to exhibit the same pathologies as the black underclass.[40]

A firestorm of liberal and African American criticism greeted *The Bell Curve.* Although its argument was principally about class, the authors' assertion of a genetic component in intelligence, and a racial difference, deviated from social scientists' strong preference, in the foregoing decades, for regarding environmental factors as all-important. Hasty misreadings of the book could also give the impression that the authors were arguing for the permanent genetic superiority of whites over blacks.[41]

The Bell Curve gained a mixed reception among conservatives. A *National Review* symposium offered measured respect for the authors' thoroughness and for their willingness to break the taboo against hereditarian arguments in a racially sensitive area. Michael Barone saw the book as "an argument against racial discrimination," adding that it had merely confirmed a widely shared common-sense view that abilities in all endeavors are not distributed randomly across the entire population and that different groups excel in different activities. Ernest Van Den Haag agreed, noting that "God is not an egalitarian, much as Thomas Jefferson thought it 'self-evident' that He is. People are born unequally gifted. If they have equal opportunity to use their unequal gifts, major social inequalities are unavoidable." Glen Loury, a black conservative, demurred. The authors, he argued, seemed too fatalistic about their discoveries, implying that vast disparities among citizens were destined to become permanent. While accepting the legitimacy of hereditarian arguments, he thought they should also have included questions of character and spirit, issues on which conservatives ought to be particularly alert. Going further, Brigitte Berger saw the book as a bad case of "methodological fetishism" and felt the authors had fallen into the trap of assuming that IQ tests really did measure pure intelligence abstracted from the test takers' cultural situation, which she insisted was a fallacy.[42]

Conservatives reacted as much to the *Bell Curve* debate as to the book itself. Chester Finn, writing in *Commentary*, noted that "with exceptions that can be counted on one hand, most of *The Bell Curve*'s critics do not much seem to care whether what the book says is true." Instead, he argued, their objective was "to restore the taboos and to intimidate anyone else who would dare violate them again." The critics were exhibiting "political correctness in all its chilling power" and, he said, showing their awareness that the book threatened the institutional position of the new class. "We have elaborate institutional arrangements—and lots of professional careers and taxpayer dollars—riding on the proposition that nurture matters more" in the nature-nurture debate.[43]

Dinesh D'Souza's *The End of Racism* caused almost as much controversy, though it offered a cultural interpretation of the race problem in contrast to Murray and Herrnstein's genetic emphasis. Its author (born 1961) was an immigrant from India and a former editor of the conservative *Dartmouth Review*. After college he had written an enthusiastic biographical study of Jerry Falwell, worked briefly in the Reagan White House, and then joined up with Michael Novak as an editor of the Catholic neoconservative journal *Crisis*. His book *Illiberal Education* (1991) was an attack on political correctness and echoed many of the themes of Kimball's *Tenured Radicals*.[44]

The theme of his new one, *The End of Racism,* was that almost every element of the standard wisdom in America about race was wrong. It is not white racism that causes the problems of the black underclass, wrote D'Souza, but a dysfunctional black culture and African Americans' affinity for the most destructive elements of the general American culture. Unfortunately, he added, white intellectuals' embrace of cultural relativism inhibits them from making frank criticisms of blacks' self-destructive conduct. He endeavored to show with voluminous statistical evidence that white Americans' racial attitudes had changed dramatically since 1950, when racism *was* still a powerful force. Affirmative action and welfare programs, not racism, worsened the black community's problems, he added, by encouraging dependency on government and by substituting a group-rights approach for the economic individualism that had historically helped other populations thrive.[45]

In D'Souza's view, certain traditions in black culture, especially the tradition of male defiance and resistance, made African Americans particularly susceptible to destructive behavior and to a poor showing in the pursuit of success and helped explain high rates of criminality and imprisonment. Ranging far and wide and offering quirky insights on the history of slavery and scientific racism, D'Souza appeared in places to be arguing that black achievement depended on the abandonment of black culture. This was in fact the point on which he ended: "For generations, blacks have attempted to straighten their hair, lighten their skin, and pass for white. But what blacks need to do is to 'act white,' which is to say, to abandon idiotic Back-to-Africa schemes and embrace mainstream cultural norms, so that they can effectively compete with other groups."[46]

Liberal critics condemned *The End of Racism* in a succession of vitriolic reviews. Conservative critics, on the other hand, recognized the book's merits while pointing out flaws in some of the author's historical and analytical reasoning. Peter Brimelow, a *National Review* editor whose book *Alien Nation* urged drastic immigration restrictions, felt that D'-Souza had falsely simplified the issue to a black-white question at a time when America was becoming a complex multiracial society. Clifford Orwin, in *The Public Interest,* praised D'Souza for "debunking the notion that racism is the main obstacle facing blacks today" but pointed to flaws in his critique of cultural relativism. He also noted that D'Souza's description of the long ugly legacy of American race relations made his ultimate argument in favor of middle-class respectability facile and unconvincing.[47]

Black conservatives were also divided. Thomas Sowell, the most prominent in the group, described it as a "heartbreaking book, because the truth is heartbreaking." He added: "The fantasies and frauds of Afrocentric education, the cynical promotion of paranoia and polarization by the 'race merchants,' and the savage and barbaric crimes of ghetto hoodlums against their own people, are just part of the grim and bitter picture painted with meticulous care by D'Souza." Other black conservatives, by contrast, were indignant. Two of them, Glenn Loury and Robert Woodson, severed their links with the American Enterprise Institute, where D'Souza was now a fellow, and angrily refuted his claim that elements of black culture were barbaric. Woodson described the book as "degrading, dehumanizing, and damaging to low-income blacks," and all the more dangerous because it "interweaves bigotry with legitimate points that I and many other conservatives have been making for years."[48]

D'Souza, undeterred, countered that he was working in the tradition of Martin Luther King, Jr., on behalf of racial integration. Debating a Hasidic rabbi, who argued that the separation of distinct cultural groups was not necessarily a bad thing, D'Souza countered that the melting pot had worked for dozens of other immigrant groups and would work for African Americans too: "Just because heavy-handed and coercive policies such as busing and racial preferences have failed to reach the goal of integration, we need not conclude that the goal itself is undesirable." Integration would come in the wake of economic success, community discipline, and academic achievement.[49]

By the late 1990s a new generation of conservative intellectuals was making its mark in journalism, academia, and the foundations. William Kristol (nicknamed "Dan Quayle's Brain" for his work with George H. W. Bush's vice-president) was as important a figure in Washington as his father, Irving, had been in New York twenty years earlier. Norman Podhoretz's son John had joined Kristol at an influential new Washington journal, *The Weekly Standard* (founded 1995). Conservative commentators were working in the mainstream media, notably David Brooks, who graduated from the *Wall Street Journal* to the *Weekly Standard* and then, early in the new century, to the *New York Times,* and David Frum, a Yale- and Harvard-educated Canadian with a similar pedigree.

Frum's book *Dead Right* (1994) lamented the inability of conservatives in power during the Reagan-Bush years to cut government spending. Their failure, he argued, enabled citizens to act recklessly yet not to suffer the consequences of their actions. Frum, like Emmett Tyrell and Michael Lind a few years before, speculated grimly about whether, after its failures in the 1980s, the conservative movement had a future. The answer was that, despite its fractures, paradoxes, and contradictory impulses, it did have a future. This new generation was entrenched in influential places and found itself in a position to affect politics in the momentous years of the early twenty-first century—Frum himself became a speechwriter for the second George Bush.[50]

The events of the 1990s had demonstrated the durability of American conservatism. Internal divisions persisted, both intellectual (as with Huntington and Fukuyama's dispute about the nature of the new world order) and attitudinal (as with the dispute between Buchananites and Podhoretzites over anti-Semitism). As it analyzed a perceived condition of cultural breakdown, the movement was also becoming more explicitly religious, a trend personified in the work of Richard Neuhaus and the *First Things* group. The prominence of African American conservatives suggested a broader appeal than hitherto, though debates over *The Bell Curve* and *The End of Racism* kept racial controversy between conservatives and their adversaries at a very high temperature.

Conclusion

THE ATTACK ON THE WORLD TRADE CENTER and the Pentagon in September 2001 opened a new era in American political history. American armies invaded Afghanistan and Iraq, overthrew old regimes, and struggled to create new ones, along lines proposed by the contributors to William Kristol and Robert Kagan's *Present Dangers*. As I write these words, neither campaign has reached a satisfactory conclusion, and the wars have provoked a sharp debate among conservative intellectuals, as well as among their critics. Rather than attempt a detailed analysis of this most recent controversy, whose outcome remains so uncertain, I end this account with the end of the twentieth century. Passions run high, rhetoric escalates, and even points of information are so hotly disputed that it would be easy to mistake transient issues for themes of permanent significance.

The past two decades have witnessed a flood of historical and journalistic writing on conservatism, a flood that continues. Much of it has been ideologically motivated, trying to persuade readers to adopt particular definitions of conservatism, to take sides in the culture wars, and to see events from the vantage point of this or that faction or author. I hope this book, by contrast, can be of equal use to readers from all points on the political spectrum, as an explanation of the main themes of American conservative history and an introduction to some of its principal characters. My intention throughout has been to keep the rhetorical temperature as low as possible and to be descriptive rather than prescriptive.

Conservatism in American history has meant many different things. For some men and women, whom I have referred to here as the guardians of civilization, it was always a matter of securing for America a place in the high culture of Western Europe and of ensuring the education of a highly cultivated elite to sustain it through each new generation. For others, conservatism took the form of a nagging fear that equality and democracy, far from liberating the American people from the constraints of the Old World and turning them into something better in the New, would cause them to degenerate into barbarism and to suffer the politics of demagogy. Members of both these groups were more impressed by the striking outward facts of human inequality than by the abstract theory of human equality, even those like Theodore Roosevelt who thought elitism and democracy to be compatible. For yet others, conservatism was, chiefly, the defense free-market capitalism, even though, paradoxically, capitalism has probably done more to *change* the world in the past two centuries than anything else. From the late nineteenth century to the late twentieth, moreover, conservatism was also dedicated to preventing the rise and spread of socialism and communism, capitalism's most threatening challengers.

Certain conservative continuities can be traced through American history. The conservative *attitude,* to be found among many of the characters introduced here, was one of trusting to the past, to long-established patterns of thought and conduct, and of assuming that novelties were more likely to be dangerous than advantageous. What neoconservatives in the 1970s described as the law of unintended consequences was part of this attitude—the fear that reformers can intend good effects but accidentally cause bad ones, such that the evil outweighs the good. The attitude was, in part, a secularization of the idea of original sin, embodying the belief that there is a deep human propensity for evil, which is best kept in check by sticking to the tried and true, to ways of life that have stood the test of time. The conservative attitude also included a sense of veneration for old things, often religious but sometimes secularized, as in the veneration of the Founding Fathers by Daniel Webster and Abraham Lincoln.

All but the simplest conservatives understood, however, that social and political changes are facts of life and that attempts to prevent them altogether are doomed. They sought, accordingly, to manage changes incrementally, cautiously, and methodically, looking for analogies in earlier conditions and trusting more to historical examples than to theoretical aspirations. They were skeptical about contract theories of society (Hobbes, Locke, Rousseau), because they could find no historical examples of people living in its requisite prepolitical "state of nature."

The conservative attitude persisted, but the circumstances in which it operated differed. In the early republic, during the wars of the French Revolution, conservatives' inclination was to take the side of Britain, a politically stable, hierarchical society and constitutional monarchy, rather than that of Jacobin France, with its (to them) delusional rhetoric of liberty, equality, and fraternity. In the Old South it often meant accepting slavery, which could be justified equally by appeals to the Bible, to the ancient world, and to nearly all other societies of which they were aware. The attitude was one that shied away from bold or utopian schemes for social transformation but could at times require either strong central government in the face of severe threats (as during the Civil War or the late 1960s) or weak central government to forestall the perceived threat of despotism (as during the New Deal). The passage of time could also bring about odd reconfigurations, such as the elevation of Thomas Jefferson, once dreaded as a dangerous radical, into the hero of anti-big-government Southern conservatives in the twentieth century.

Sometimes conservatives were excessively pessimistic. It is hard to imagine how they would ever have begun the agitation against slavery in the nineteenth century or done away with racial segregation in the twentieth; it is equally hard to see how they would have imagined the creation of a society in which wealth was widespread, life expectancy was dramatically increased, and cases of illiteracy were regarded as a social problem rather than as an inevitable characteristic of life. At other times, however, their sense of unpleasant realities and human limitations gave them an advantage over their rivals. Conservatives never let themselves believe that a war might be fought "to end all wars" or "to make the world safe for democracy," never believed that a planned society could function efficiently or be compatible with individual liberty, and appreciated more readily than their liberal critics the actual benefits of industrial capitalism, whatever unlovely facets of human nature its workings might disclose.

In the mid-1950s Louis Hartz argued, in *The Liberal Tradition in America,* that liberalism on Lockean principles was effectively the sole political philosophy of American history and that the nation had never experienced significant ideological divisions. Individuals whose ideas I have here described as conservatives he treated merely as the inhabitants of one end of the liberal spectrum. *The Liberal Tradition* was an artifact of its time, appearing just before the new conservative movement became too important to ignore. Fifty years later, after self-identified conservative writers have made a distinct impression on American intellectual life, and after a succession of governments led by self-identified conservative politicians, it would be perverse to voice an argument like Hartz's. A wide array of historians has shown, in the intervening decades, that ideological divisions have been widespread and persistent. I hope I have been able to underline part of that new story here and to show that conservative ideas have, in fact, been important to virtually all the great issues and moments of American history.

NOTES

CHAPTER 1: THE FEDERALISTS

1. Albert Furtwangler, *The Authority of Publius: A Reading of the Federalist Papers* (Ithaca: Cornell University Press, 1984). New York *Daily Advertiser,* quoted in Ron Chernow, *Alexander Hamilton* (New York: Penguin, 2004), 43.
2. Chernow, *Hamilton,* 252. On inconsistencies among the authors, reflected in the Federalist, see Bernard Bailyn, *To Begin the World Anew: The Genius and Ambiguities of America's Founders* (New York: Knopf, 2003), 100–125.
3. Edward Mead Earle, ed., *The Federalist: A Commentary on the Constitution of the United States* (New York: Modern Library, n.d.); increased central power, 6–10, 23–25; limitations on power and terms of office, 50–52; indirect elections to Senate, 62–65; judiciary, 78–83; national defense, 2–5.
4. Federalist, No. 10, in Meade, *Federalist,* 53–62, quotation on 60.
5. Ibid., No. 45, in Meade, *Federalist,* 298–304, quotation on 303.
6. Ibid., No. 51, in Meade, *Federalist,* 335–41, quotation on 337.
7. On opponents of the Constitution, see Jackson T. Main, *The Antifederalists: Critics of the Constitution* (Chapel Hill: University of North Carolina Press, 1961). Richard Hofstadter, *The Idea of a Party System: The Rise of Legitimate Opposition in the United States, 1780–1840* (Berkeley: University of California Press, 1969).
8. On the conservative character of American politics after 1790, see Larry Tise, *The American Counterrevolution* (Mechanicsburg, Pa.: Stackpole, 1998). Samuel Eliot Morison, *Samuel Gray Otis, 1765–1848: The Urbane Federalist* (Boston: Houghton Mifflin, 1969), 87.
9. J. G. A. Pocock, *The Machiavellian Moment: Florentine Political Thought and the Atlantic Republican Tradition* (Princeton: Princeton University Press, 1975).

Bernard Bailyn, *Intellectual Origins of the American Revolution* (Cambridge: Harvard University Press, 1967). Richard Buel, *Securing the Revolution: Ideology in American Politics, 1789–1815* (Ithaca: Cornell University Press, 1972).

10. Gordon Wood, *The Creation of the American Republic* (New York: Norton, 1969), 593–615. John Malsberger, "The Political Thought of Fisher Ames," *Journal of the Early Republic* 2 (Spring 1982): 6.
11. Joseph J. Ellis, *Passionate Sage: The Character and Legacy of John Adams* (New York: Norton, 1993), 90, 149, 90.
12. Ellis, *Passionate Sage*, 165–73. See also David McCullough, *John Adams* (New York: Simon and Schuster, 2001), 374–79.
13. Paul Zall, ed., *Adams on Adams* (Lexington: University of Kentucky Press, 2004), 122–23.
14. Davie, quoted in David H. Fischer, *The Revolution of Conservatism: The Federalist Party in the Era of Jeffersonian Democracy* (New York: Harper and Row, 1965), 151.
15. Ames, quoted in Fischer, *Revolution of Conservatism*, 20. On "Phocion," see Linda Kerber, *Federalists in Dissent: Imagery and Ideology in Jeffersonian America* (Ithaca: Cornell University Press, 1970), 9; Fischer, *Revolution of Conservatism*, 50–72.
16. David Waldstreicher, "Federalism: The Styles of Politics and the Politics of Style," in Doron Ben-Atar and Barbara Oberg, eds., *Federalists Reconsidered* (Charlottesville: University Press of Virginia, 1998), 99–117.
17. Garry Wills, *Cincinnatus: George Washington and the Enlightenment* (Garden City: Doubleday, 1984); Kerber, *Federalists in Dissent*, 5.
18. Forrest McDonald, *Alexander Hamilton: A Biography* (New York: Norton, 1979), 117–62. On the historians' dispute over Hamilton, see James Kirby Martin, "Beyond the Good-Guys-Bad Guys Syndrome: Will the Real Alexander Hamilton Please Stand Up?" *Reviews in American History* 11 (March 1983): 51–54.
19. Chernow, *Hamilton*, 295–300, 321–30. McDonald, *Hamilton*, 163–88.
20. Doron Ben-Atar, "Alexander Hamilton's Alternative: Technology Piracy and the Report on Manufactures," in Ben-Atar and Oberg, *Federalists Reconsidered*, 41–60.
21. McDonald, *Hamilton*, 297–303.
22. Wood, *Creation of Republic*, 427–28. On tensions over established churches in the states, see James Beasley, "Emerging Republicanism and the Standing Order: The Appropriation Act Controversy in Connecticut, 1793–1795," *William and Mary Quarterly* 29 (October 1972): 587–610, and Jonathan D. Sassi, "The First Party Competition and Southern New England's Public Christianity," *Journal of the Early Republic* 21 (Summer 2001): 261–99.
23. Cobbett, quoted in David A. Wilson, ed., *William Cobbett: Peter Porcupine in America: Pamphlets on Republicanism and Revolution* (Ithaca: Cornell University Press, 1994), 10, 42. See also Tise, *American Counterrevolution*, 368–74.

24. On Jefferson and the French Revolution, see Merrill Peterson, *Thomas Jefferson and the New Nation* (New York: Oxford University Press, 1970), 376–84. Otis's *Eulogy on Alexander Hamilton* (1804), quoted in Samuel Eliot Morison, *Harrison Gray Otis: The Urbane Federalist* (Boston: Houghton Mifflin, 1969), 90.
25. Ames, quoted in Malsberger, "Political Thought of Ames," 11. Otis's letter to his wife, March 14, 1798, quoted in Morison, *Otis,* 105.
26. James F. Simon, *What Kind of a Nation?: Thomas Jefferson, John Marshall, and the Epic Struggle to Create a United States* (New York: Simon and Schuster, 2002), 52. Otis's "Wild Irish" speech, July 1797, quoted in Morison, *Otis,* 108. On the XYZ affair, see John C. Miller, *The Federalist Era* (New York: Harper, 1960), 210–12, 242–43; McCullough, *John Adams,* 495–98.
27. Peterson, *Jefferson,* 288–93. Drew McCoy, *The Elusive Republic: Political Economy in Jeffersonian America* (Chapel Hill: University of North Carolina Press, 1980), 13–17.
28. Sedgwick and Ames, quoted in Fischer, *Revolution of Conservatism,* 26–27. Dwight, quoted in Simon, *What Kind of Nation?,* 123.
29. Simon, *What Kind of Nation?,* 142.
30. Noah Webster's July Fourth Speech, New Haven, 1798, quoted in Kerber, *Federalists in Dissent,* 21. On the "Dusky Sally" rumors (which have since been confirmed by DNA evidence), see Peterson, *Jefferson,* which quotes this poem from the *Boston Gazette:* "Of all the damsels on the green/On mountain, or in valley,/A lass so luscious ne'er was seen/As Monticellian Sally" (708).
31. Ames, quoted in Malsberger, "Political Thought of Ames," 19; Plumer, quoted in Fischer, *Revolution of Conservatism,* 45. On the centrality of public opinion in the first party system, see Buel, *Securing the Revolution,* x–xi.
32. On the Federalist-Republican debate over Louisiana, see McCoy, *Elusive Republic,* 199–203. Ames, quoted in Andrew Cayton, "Radicals in the Western World: The Federalist Conquest of Trans-Appalachian North America," in Ben-Atar and Oberg, *Federalists Reconsidered,* 78. For Pickering and secession, see Robert Ernst, *Rufus King: American Federalist* (Chapel Hill: University of North Carolina Press, 1968), 280–82.
33. Peterson, *Jefferson,* 745–62. On Federalist opposition to the purchase, see Buel, *Securing the Revolution,* 265–66; and Richard G. Hewlett, "Josiah Quincy: Reform Mayor of Boston," *New England Quarterly* 24 (June 1951): 79.
34. Buel, *Securing the Revolution,* 271–89.
35. Ibid., 289–95.
36. John Adams to his son John Quincy, quoted in Paul C. Nagel, *John Quincy Adams: A Public Life, a Private Life* (New York: Knopf, 1997), 76. John Quincy. to his father, in Lynn Hudson Parson, *John Quincy Adams* (Madison, Wis.: Madison House, 1998), 63.
37. Nagel, *John Quincy Adams,* 126.
38. Watts, "Ministers, Misanthropes, and Mandarins," in Ben-Atar and Oberg, *Federalists Reconsidered,* 159.

39. Larry Tise, *Proslavery: A History of the Defense of Slavery in America, 1701–1840* (Athens: University of Georgia Press, 1987), 234–37. Kerber, *Federalists in Dissent,* 30–31. Paul Finkelman, "The Problem of Slavery in the Age of Federalism," in Ben-Atar and Oberg, *Federalists Reconsidered,* 135–56.
40. David Robarge, *A Chief Justice's Progress: John Marshall from Revolutionary Virginia to the Supreme Court* (Westport, Conn.: Greenwood, 2000).
41. Marshall, cited in Earl Warren, "Chief Justice Marshall, Expounder of the Constitution," in Jesse H. Choper, ed., *The Supreme Court and Its Justices* (Chicago: American Bar Association, 1987), 50.
42. Douglas Gordon, "John Marshall: A Judicial Pioneer," in Choper, *Supreme Court,* 30–47.
43. Leo Pfeffer, *This Honorable Court: A History of the United States Supreme Court* (Boston: Beacon, 1965), 89–94.
44. Robert McCloskey, *The American Supreme Court,* 4th ed. (Chicago: University of Chicago Press, 2005), 54.

CHAPTER 2: SOUTHERN CONSERVATISM

1. James Broussard, *The Southern Federalists: 1800–1816* (Baton Rouge: Louisiana State University Press, 1978). Adam Tate, *Conservatism and Southern Intellectuals: 1789–1861* (Columbia: University of Missouri Press, 2005), 3.
2. Peter Parish, *Slavery: History and Historians* (New York: Harper and Row, 1989), 20–21, 46–60.
3. Bertram Wyatt Brown, *Southern Honor* (New York: Oxford University Press, 1982), 31. Drew Faust, *A Sacred Circle: The Dilemma of the Intellectual in the Old South* (Baltimore: Johns Hopkins University Press, 1977), 47.
4. On Jefferson's slaves, see Merrill Peterson, *Thomas Jefferson and the New Nation* (New York: Oxford University Press, 1970), 28. On entrepreneurial slaveholders, see Parish, *Slavery,* 45–47. On post-1830 intellectual shift, see Larry Tise, *Proslavery: A History of the Defense of Slavery in America* (Athens: University of Georgia Press, 1987), 323–46.
5. Forrest McDonald, *States' Rights and the Union: Imperium in Imperio, 1776–1876* (Lawrence: University of Kansas Press, 2000), 41–43.
6. On the life and work of Taylor, see Adam Tate, *Conservatism and Southern Intellectuals, 1789–1861: Liberty: Tradition, and the Good Society* (Columbia: University of Missouri Press, 2005), Norman Risjord, *The Old Republicans: Southern Conservatism in the Age of Jefferson* (New York: Columbia University Press, 1965), and Robert Shalhope, *John Taylor of Caroline: Pastoral Republican* (Columbia: University of South Carolina Press, 1980).
7. On the life and work of Randolph, see Tate, *Conservatism;* Risjord, *Old Republicans;* Russell Kirk, *John Randolph of Roanoke* (Chicago: University of Chicago Press, 1951); and Robert Dawidoff, *The Education of John Randolph* (New York: Norton, 1979). George Ticknor's description of Randolph is from William Cabell Bruce, *John Randolph of Roanoke,* 2 vols. (New York: Putnam's, 1922), 2:599–600. On his dress and horses, see William W. Freehling, *The Road to*

Disunion: I, Secessionists at Bay, 1776–1854 (New York: Oxford University Press, 1990), 171. For the duel, see Gerald W. Johnson, *Randolph of Roanoke: A Political Fantastic* (New York: Minton Balch, 1929), 243–45.

8. *Arator*, quoted in Shalhope, *Taylor*, 134. On Hamiltonian politics, ibid., 74–75, and Tate, *Conservatism*, 14–15, Kirk, *Randolph*, 86.
9. Tate, *Conservatism*, 57. Kirk, *Randolph*, 93, 66.
10. Risjord, *Old Republicans*, 19. Tate, *Conservatism*, 64–69.
11. Kirk, *Randolph*, 93.
12. Ibid., 35. Russell Kirk, *The Conservative Mind: From Burke to Eliot*, 3d ed. (1953. Chicago: Henry Regnery, 1960), 172.
13. Kirk, *Randolph*, 140. Tate, *Conservatism*, 40.
14. Freehling, *Road to Disunion*, 150–56.
15. Tate, *Conservatism*, 70–74.
16. Biographical information on Calhoun is based on Irving Bartlett, *John C. Calhoun* (New York: Norton, 1993), and Richard Current, *John C. Calhoun* (New York: Washington Square Press, 1966). On Calhoun and republicanism, see Lacy Ford, "Republican Ideology in a Slave Society: The Political Economy of John C. Calhoun," *Journal of Southern History* 54 (1988): 405–24, quotation on 422. Richard Hofstadter, *The American Political Tradition and the Men Who Made It* (1948. New York: Vintage, 1989), 90. Kirk, *Conservative Mind*, 208–9.
17. Bartlett, *Calhoun*, 142–48.
18. John C. Calhoun, "South Carolina Exposition and Protest," in H. Lee Cheek, Jr., ed., *John C. Calhoun: Selected Writings and Speeches* (Chicago: Regnery, 2003). Bartlett, *Calhoun*, 150–51. For the context of this controversy and for Calhoun's confrontation with Daniel Webster, see Chap.3. John Niven, *John C. Calhoun and the Price of Union* (Baton Rouge: Louisiana State University Press, 1988), 180–84. Bartlett, *Calhoun*, 182.
19. Hofstadter, *American Political Tradition*, 111–13. Bartlett, *Calhoun*, 353–54.
20. Bartlett, *Calhoun*, 191–200.
21. Kirk, *Randolph*, 79.
22. Bartlett, *Calhoun*, 350–52.
23. John L. Thomas, ed., introduction to *John C. Calhoun: A Profile* (New York: Hill and Wang, 1968), vii–x. Bartlett, *Calhoun*, 353–55.
24. Current, *Calhoun*, 54. Bartlett, *Calhoun*, 355–59.
25. Martin Goldman, *Nat Turner and the Southampton Revolt of 1831* (New York: Watts, 1992). Sean Wilentz, *The Rise of American Democracy* (New York: Norton, 2005), 331–41.
26. Kirk, *Randolph*, 113. Hofstadter, *American Political Tradition*, 103. Bartlett, *Calhoun*, 362.
27. William Harper, "Memoir on Slavery," in Drew Faust, ed., *The Ideology of Slavery: Proslavery Thought in the Antebellum South* (Baton Rouge: Louisiana State University Press, 1981), 81.
28. See esp. Michael O'Brien, *Conjectures of Order: Intellectual Life and the*

American South, 1810–1860, 2 vols. (Chapel Hill: University of North Carolina Press, 2004); Faust, *Sacred Circle;* Eugene Genovese and Elizabeth Fox-Genovese, *The Mind of the Master Class* (New York: Cambridge University Press, 2005). On the historiography of slavery, see also Parish, *Slavery.*

29. Bartlett, *Calhoun,* 218.
30. William Sumner Jenkins, *Proslavery Thought in the Old South* (Chapel Hill: University of North Carolina Press, 1935). Bartlett, *Calhoun,* 311. Oakes, *Ruling Race,* 201.
31. Thornton Stringfellow, "A Brief Examination of Scripture Testimony on the Institution of Slavery," in Faust, *Ideology of Slavery,* 138–67.
32. Eugene Genovese, "James Henley Thornwell," in *The Southern Front: History and Politics in the Cultural War* (Columbia: University of Missouri Press, 1995), 34, 37.
33. Eugene Genovese and Elizabeth Fox-Genovese, "The Culture of the Old South," in Genovese, *Southern Front,* 59.
34. Faust, *Sacred Circle,* 119–21.
35. James Henry Hammond, "Letter to an English Abolitionist," in Faust, *Ideology of Slavery,* 170–205; see in particular 184–85. Eugene Genovese, *The World the Slaveholders Made* (New York: Pantheon, 1969), 179.
36. Eugene Genovese, *The Slaveholder's Dilemma: Freedom and Progress in Southern Conservative Thought, 1820–1860* (Columbia: University of South Carolina Press, 1992), 37.
37. Bartlett, *Calhoun,* 227.
38. C. Vann Woodward, introduction to Fitzhugh, *Cannibals All!* (1857/1959), at www.faculty.fairfield.edu/faculty/hodgson/Course/city/fitzhugh/george.html. On criticism of Fitzhugh by other proslavery writers, see Faust, *Sacred Circle,* 127. By contrast Calhoun explicitly denied any allegiance to Filmer. See Ford, "Republican Ideology," 422.
39. Kirk, *Randolph,* 109. Eugene Genovese, *Western Civilization Through Slaveholding Eyes: The Social and Historical Thought of Thomas Roderick Dew* (New Orleans: Graduate School of Tulane University, 1986), 11. Tise, *Proslavery,* 73.
40. Genovese, *Mind of the Master Class,* 250–56. Genovese, "Higher Education in the Defense of Slave Society," in *Southern Front,* 92–113, quotation on 92. Genovese, "Higher Education," 93.
41. James Oakes, "From Republicanism to Liberalism: Ideological Change and the Crisis of the Old South," *American Quarterly* 37 (1985): 555–71. Genovese and Fox-Genovese, "Culture of the Old South," in *Southern Front,* 57.
42. James Oakes, *The Ruling Race: A History of American Slaveholders* (1982. New York: Norton, 1988), 192–224, quotations on 193–94, 205.
43. Drew G. Faust, *James Henry Hammond and the Old South: A Design for Mastery* (Baton Rouge: Louisiana State University Press, 1982), 54, 287. Tate, *Conservatism,* 146.

CHAPTER 3: NORTHERN ANTEBELLUM CONSERVATISM AND THE WHIGS

1. Sean Wilentz, *The Rise of American Democracy: Jefferson to Lincoln* (New York: Norton, 2005), 312–13.
2. Thomas Payne Govan, *Nicholas Biddle: Nationalist and Public Banker, 1786–1844* (Chicago: University of Chicago Press, 1959), 78–111. Wilentz, *American Democracy,* 365.
3. Michael F. Holt, *The Rise and Fall of the American Whig Party: Jacksonian Politics and the Onset of the Civil War* (New York: Oxford University Press, 1999), 15–17. Govan, *Nicholas Biddle,* 130. Wilentz, *American Democracy,* 366, 370.
4. Govan, *Nicholas Biddle,* 199–206. Wilentz, *American Democracy,* 371. Clement Eaton, *Henry Clay and the Art of American Politics* (Boston: Little Brown, 1957), 106–7.
5. John Ashworth, *Agrarians and Aristocrats: Party Political Ideology in the United States, 1837–1846* (Atlantic Highlands, N.J.: Humanities Press, 1983), 7–51.
6. Ashworth, *Agrarians and Aristocrats,* 52–84, quotation on 69; Sean Wilentz, *American Democracy,* 485–93.
7. Daniel Walker Howe, *The Political Culture of the American Whigs* (Chicago: University of Chicago Press, 1979), 236–37.
8. Howe, *Political Culture,* 87–88. Alfred Cave, *An American Conservative in the Age of Jackson: The Political and Social Thought of Calvin Colton* (Fort Worth: Texas Christian University Press, 1969), 19–20.
9. Cave, *American Conservative,* 14.
10. Ibid., 20–21, 24, 43.
11. Ibid., 29–35.
12. Howe, *Political Culture,* 225–37. Thomas E. Woods, ed., *The Political Writings of Rufus Choate* (Washington, D.C.: Regnery, 2002), 1–12, 38–40.
13. Choate, "The Position and Functions of the American Bar, as an Element of Conservatism in the State," in Woods, *Political Writings,* 189–209, quotation on 192.
14. Howe, *Political Culture,* 108–21, quotations on 111, 112.
15. On Clay and his great contemporaries, see Merrill Peterson, *The Great Triumvirate: Webster, Clay, and Calhoun* (New York: Oxford University Press, 1987). Clay, quoted in Howe, *Political Culture,* 123.
16. Michael Lind, *What Lincoln Believed* (New York: Doubleday, 2004), 69–115.
17. Peterson, *Great Triumvirate.* Howe, *Political Ideology,* 210–25. Carl Prince and Seth Taylor, "Daniel Webster, the Boston Associates, and the U. S. Government's Role in the Industrializing Process," *Journal of the Early Republic* 2 (Fall 1982):, 283–99.
18. George Hillard, ed., *Life and Letters of George Ticknor* (Boston: James Osgood, 1877), vol. 1, 330. Story, quoted in William Rehnquist, foreword to *Daniel Webster: The Completest Man,* Kenneth E. Shewmaker, ed. (Hanover, N.H.: University Press of New England, 1990), xiii.

19. Irving H. Bartlett, *Daniel Webster* (New York: Norton, 1978), 119–20, 6.
20. George Pierson, *Tocqueville and Beaumont in America* (New York: Oxford University Press, 1938).
21. Alexis de Tocqueville, *Democracy in America,* ed. Philips Bradley, 2 vols. (1835. New York: Vintage, 1990), 1:8.
22. Ibid., 1:46–60, 94–97.
23. Ibid., 1:52, 2:225.
24. Ibid., 1:136, 414.
25. Ibid., 1:53–54.
26. Biographical summary is based on Frank Freidel, *Francis Lieber: Nineteenth-Century Liberal* (Gloucester, Mass.: Peter Smith, 1968), 135; and Bernard Edward Brown, *American Conservatives: The Political Thought of Francis Lieber and John W. Burgess* (New York: Columbia University Press, 1951).
27. Freidel, *Francis Lieber,* 145. Brown, *American Conservatives,* 46.
28. Brown, *American Conservatives,* 26–57.
29. Ibid., 65. Freidel, *Francis Lieber,* 152.
30. Freidel, *Francis Lieber,* 133, 292, 251.
31. Merle Curti, "The Impact of the Revolutions of 1848 on American Thought," *Proceedings of the American Philosophical Society* 93 (June 10, 1949): 209–15.
32. James Turner, *The Liberal Education of Charles Eliot Norton* (Baltimore: Johns Hopkins University Press, 1999), 117. Richard C. Rohrs, "American Critics of the French Revolution of 1848," *Journal of the Early Republic* 14 (Autumn 1994): 359–77, quotations on 363, 367, 369.
33. Curti, "Impact of the Revolutions," 212. Holt, *Rise and Fall,* 693–94. Howard Jones, "Daniel Webster, the Diplomatist," in Kenneth E. Shewmaker, ed., *Daniel Webster: The Completest Man* (Hanover, N.H.: University Press of New England, 1990), 221–22.
34. Martin Green, *The Problem of Boston: Some Readings in Cultural History* (New York: Norton, 1966), 80–101, quotation on 91. Ticknor, quoted in Warner Berthoff, "George Ticknor," *Harvard Magazine,* January–February 2005, 47–48.
35. Samuel Eliot Morison, *Three Centuries of Harvard* (Cambridge: Harvard University Press, 1936), 225–37.
36. Green, *Problem of Boston,* 88–92.
37. Irving H. Bartlett, "Edward Everett Reconsidered," *New England Quarterly* 69 (September 1996), 426–60.
38. Garry Wills, *Cincinnatus: George Washington and the Enlightenment* (Garden City: Doubleday, 1984). Meyer Reinhold, *Classica Americana: The Greek and Roman Heritage in the United States* (Detroit: Wayne State University Press, 1984).
39. Bartlett, "Everett," 435, 441.
40. Ibid., 449. Morison, *Three Centuries,* 275–79.
41. Bartlett, "Everett," 459.
42. Thomas Bender, *New York Intellect* (New York: Knopf, 1987), 120, 129.

Carleton Mabee, *The American Leonardo: A Life of Samuel B. Morse* (New York: Knopf, 1943), 162–80.

CHAPTER 4: CONSERVATISM AND THE CIVIL WAR

1. James Turner, *The Liberal Education of Charles Eliot Norton* (Baltimore: Johns Hopkins University Press, 1999), 166. Laura Wood Roper, *FLO: A Biography of Frederick Law Olmsted* (Baltimore: Johns Hopkins University Press), 92.
2. Frank Freidel, *Francis Lieber: Nineteenth-Century Liberal* (Baton Rouge: Louisiana State University Press), 255. Howard Doughty, *Francis Parkman* (New York: Macmillan, 1962), 400.
3. Bellows, quoted in George Frederickson, *The Inner Civil War: Northern Intellectuals and the Crisis of the Union* (1965. New York: Harper Torchbooks, 1968), 27.
4. Robert Bruce Mullin, *The Puritan as Yankee: A Life of Horace Bushnell* (Grand Rapids: Eerdman's, 2002), 105–18, quotation on 117.
5. Turner, *Liberal Education,* 115–16. Frederickson, *Inner Civil War,* 28.
6. Frederickson, *Inner Civil War,* 56.
7. Paul Varg, *Edward Everett: The Intellectual in the Turmoil of Politics* (Selinsgrove: Susquehanna University Press, 1992), 183, 186, 192.
8. Freidel, *Francis Lieber,* 299. Fredrickson, *Inner Civil War,* 55–56.
9. Francis Parkman to the *Boston Daily Advertiser,* September 4, 1861, in Wilbur Jacobs, ed., *Letters of Francis Parkman* (Norman: University of Oklahoma Press, 1960), 141–43. On the life of Parkman, see Robert Gale, *Francis Parkman* (New York: Twayne, 1973).
10. Parkman to Mary Dwight Parkman, September 27, 1862, in Jacobs, *Letters,* 153. Parkman to *Boston Daily Advertiser,* January 8, 1862, ibid., 145.
11. Parkman to *Boston Daily Advertiser,* June 30, 1863, in Jacobs, *Letters,* 159.
12. Fredrickson, *Inner Civil War,* 55–56. Louis Auchincloss, ed., *The Hone and Strong Diaries of Old Manhattan* (New York: Abbeville Press, 1989), 161.
13. Fredrickson, *Inner Civil War,* 98–107.
14. Henry W. Bellows, *Unconditional Loyalty* (New York: Anson D. F. Randolph, 1863), 5, 14.
15. Charles Chauncey Binney, *The Life of Horace Binney with Selections from His Letters* (1903. Freeport, N.Y.: Books for Libraries Press, 1972), 336–37. Freidel, *Lieber,* 310–11.
16. Mullin, *Puritan as Yankee,* 220. Turner, *Liberal Education,* 168–70.
17. For a favorable judgment of Lincoln as conservative, see Harry Jaffa, *A New Birth of Freedom: Abraham Lincoln and the Coming of the Civil War* (Lanham, Md.: Rowman and Littlefield, 2000). For harsher evaluations, see Edmund Wilson, *Patriotic Gore: Studies in the Literature of the American Civil War* (New York: Oxford University Press, 1962), where he is compared to Bismarck and Lenin as the builder of a tyrannical state; and M. E. Bradford, "The Lincoln Legacy, A Long View," *Modern Age* 24 (1980): 355–63.
18. Biographical summary based on David Donald, *Lincoln* (New York: Simon

and Schuster, 1995), and Michael Lind, *What Lincoln Believed* (New York: Doubleday, 2004), 60–61.

19. Lind, *What Lincoln Believed,* 112.
20. Harry Jaffa, new preface to his *Crisis of the House Divided: An Interpretation of the Issues in the Lincoln-Douglas Debates* (Chicago: University of Chicago Press, 1982), v.
21. Eric Foner, *Free Soil, Free Labor, Free Men: The Ideology of the Republican Party Before the Civil War* (New York: Oxford University Press, 1970), 216–19.
22. Lind, *What Lincoln Believed,* 200, 183–85, 194.
23. Garry Wills, *Lincoln at Gettysburg: The Words That Remade America* (New York: Simon and Schuster, 1992). Allen Guelzo, *Abraham Lincoln, Redeemer President* (Grand Rapids: Eerdman's, 1999), 369–75.
24. Guelzo, *Abraham Lincoln,* 419–20. Jaffa, *Crisis of the House Divided,* 190–91.
25. Lind, *What Lincoln Believed,* 173, 175–80.
26. Mark Neely, Jr., *The Last Best Hope of Earth: Abraham Lincoln and the Promise of America* (Cambridge: Harvard University Press, 1993), 117.
27. Howard C. Perkins, "The Defense of Slavery in the Northern Press on the Eve of the Civil War," *Journal of Southern History* 9 (November 1943): 501–31.
28. Douglas Fermer, *James Gordon Bennett and the New York Herald* (London: Royal Historical Society, 1986), 62, 65–68.
29. Fermer, *James Gordon Bennett,* 168, 194.
30. Forrest McDonald, *States' Rights and the Union: Imperium in Imperio, 1776–1876* (Lawrence: University of Kansas Press, 2000), 194–99.
31. Dan Monroe and Bruce Tap, *Shapers of the Great Debate on the Civil War* (Westport, Conn.: Greenwood, 2005), 314.
32. Frank Klement, *The Limits of Dissent: Clement Vallandigham and the Civil War* (Lexington: University of Kentucky Press, 1970), 163–64. Pendleton, cited in Jean H. Baker, *Affairs of Party: The Political Culture of Northern Democrats in the Mid-Nineteenth Century* (Ithaca: Cornell University Press, 1983), 162. See also Jennifer L. Weber, *Copperheads: The Rise and Fall of Lincoln's Opponents in the North* (New York: Oxford University Press, 2006), 95–100.
33. Russell Kirk, *The Conservative Mind* (1953. Chicago: Henry Regnery, 1967), 283.
34. Arlin Turner, *Nathaniel Hawthorne: A Biography* (New York: Oxford University Press, 1980), 363.
35. Turner, *Hawthorne,* 364–66. Nathaniel Hawthorne, "Chiefly About War Matters," *Atlantic Monthly,* April 1862, 48–49.
36. Hawthorne, "War Matters," 56, 49.
37. Arthur Schlesinger, Jr., *Orestes Brownson: A Pilgrim's Progress* (Boston: Little Brown, 1939). Patrick Allitt, *Catholic Converts: British and American Intellectuals Turn to Rome* (Ithaca: Cornell University Press, 1997), 64–67.
38. Orestes Brownson, *The American Republic: Its Constitution, Tendencies, and Destiny,* with an introduction by Peter A. Lawler (1865. Wilmington, Del.: ISI Books, 2003), 239.

39. Ibid., 44.
40. Ibid., 91–99, 140–44.
41. Ibid., 221–23, 231–32.
42. Ibid., 106–7, 194, 199–200.
43. For an elaboration of the church-state question, see Peter Lawler, introduction to Brownson, *American Republic,* xli–xlii, and Gregory Butler, *In Search of the American Spirit: The Political Philosophy of Orestes Brownson* (Carbondale: Southern Illinois University Press, 1992), 163–92. Brownson, *American Republic,* 264.
44. William C. Davis, *A Government of Our Own: The Making of the Confederacy* (New York: Free Press, 1994), 1–30.
45. Charles B. Dew, *Apostles of Disunion: Southern Secession Commissioners and the Causes of the Civil War* (Charlottesville: University Press of Virginia, 2001), 37–50.
46. William C. Davis, *Jefferson Davis: The Man and His Hour* (New York: HarperCollins, 1991), 301–21.
47. Carl Degler, *The Other South: Southern Dissenters in the Nineteenth Century* (New York: Harper and Row, 1974), 128, 130.
48. Emory Thomas, "Reckoning with Rebels," in *The Old South in the Crucible of War,* Harry P. Owens and James J. Cooke, eds. (Jackson: University of Mississippi Press, 1983), 8, 7.
49. Drew G. Faust, *The Creation of Confederate Nationalism* (Baton Rouge: Louisiana State University Press, 1988), 22–40, quotation on 29, "Yankees or the Devil," 39.
50. Faust, *Creation,* 11, 13.
51. Bruce Levine, "The Inexorable Logic of Events," in *Half Slave, Half Free: The Roots of Civil War* (New York: Hill and Wang, 1992), 225–42.
52. Faust, *Creation,* 72.
53. Paul Escott, "The Failure of Confederate Nationalism," in Owens and Cooke, *Old South,* 19, 190. Faust, *Creation,* 17–18.
54. Gaines M. Foster, *Ghosts of the Confederacy: Defeat, the Lost Cause, and the Emergence of the New South: 1865–1913* (New York: Oxford University Press, 1987), 11–35.
55. Alexander Stephens, *A Constitutional View of the Late War Between the States,* 2 vols. (Philadelphia, Pa.: National Publication Co., 1868–1870). Rudolph Von Abele, *Alexander H. Stephens* (New York: Knopf, 1946), 270–76.
56. Pollard, cited in Rollin Osterweis, *The Myth of the Lost Cause* (Hamden, Conn.: Archon Books, 1973), 12. See also Jack P. Maddex, "Pollard's *The Lost Cause Regained:* A Mask for Southern Accommodation," *Journal of Southern History* 40 (November 1974): 595–612. Maddex shows that Pollard was an opportunist whose political opinions shifted with the tide in the late 1860s and early 1870s. Nevertheless, Pollard's *Lost Cause* and *Lost Cause Regained* (1868), were immensely influential in creating the vocabulary and general principles of Lost Cause ideology.

57. Robert L. Dabney, *A Defense of Virginia, and Through Her, of The South, in Recent and Pending Contests Against the Sectional Party* (New York: E. J. Hale, 1867). Charles Reagan Wilson, *Baptized in Blood* (Athens: University of Georgia Press, 1980). James Wert, "James Longstreet and the Lost Cause," in Gary Gallagher and Alan Nolan, eds., *The Myth of the Lost Cause and Civil War History* (Bloomington: Indiana University Press, 2000), 128–43.
58. Osterweis, *Myth of the Lost Cause,* 123.
59. Ibid., 16–23, 25.
60. Thomas, "Reckoning with Rebels," 13. Escott, "Failure of Confederate Nationalism," 27.
61. Osterweis, *Myth of the Lost Cause,* 41–47.
62. Raymond B. Nixon, *Henry Grady: Spokesman of the New South* (New York: Russell and Russell, 1943).
63. Osterweis comments: "By his refusal to abandon the glamorous appeal of 'the footsore Confederate soldier, in his faded gray jacket, plodding homeward after Appomattox,' Grady helped to make the Myth of the Lost Cause acceptable to the very men who had destroyed the Old South" (*Myth of the Lost Cause,* 131).
64. Nolan, "The Anatomy of the Myth," in Gallagher and Nolan, *Myth,* 28.

CHAPTER 5: CONSERVATISM AFTER THE CIVIL WAR

1. Summary of Sumner's life in the following passage is based on Maurice R. Davie, *William Graham Sumner* (New York: Thomas Crowell, 1963); Bruce Curtis, *William Graham Sumner* (Boston: Twayne, 1981), "antitraditionalist" quotation on 65; Robert Green McCloskey, *American Conservatism in the Age of Enterprise* (New York: Harper and Row, 1951); and Robert C. Bannister, ed., *On Liberty, Society, and Politics: The Essential Essays of William Graham Sumner* (Indianapolis: Liberty Fund, 1992), ix–xxxix.
2. William Lyon Phelps, introduction to William Graham Sumner, *Folkways: A Study of the Sociological Importance of Usages, Manners, Customes, Mores, and Morals* (1906. New York: Blaidsell, 1965), ix–x.
3. Albert G. Keller, preface to Albert G. Keller and Maurice Davie, eds., *Essays of William Graham Sumner,* 2 vols. (New Haven: Yale University Press, 1934), 2:xii. Phelps, introduction to Sumner, *Folkways,* xi.
4. W. G. Sumner, "The Influence of Commercial Crises on Opinions about Economic Doctrines," in Keller and Davie, *Essays* 2:56.
5. W. G. Sumner, "Socialism," in Bannister, *On Liberty,* 161–62, 166.
6. Ibid., "The Forgotten Man," 212.
7. Ibid.
8. Ibid., "The Argument Against Protective Taxes," 110–26.
9. Curtis, *Sumner,* 105. Sumner, quoted in Ross, *Origins,* 87. Sumner, "Socialism," 174.
10. Bannister, foreword to *On Liberty,* xxxv.
11. Alfred Kelly and Winfred Harbison, *The American Constitution: Its Origins and*

Development, 4th ed. (New York: Norton, 1970), 519. McCloskey, *American Conservatism,* 84.

12. Andrew Carnegie, *Autobiography* (Boston: Northeastern University Press, 1985). Herbert Gutman, "Protestantism and the American Labor Movement," in *Work Culture and Society in Industrializing America* (New York: Vintage, 1977), 104–5. Harold Livesay, *Andrew Carnegie and the Rise of Big Business* (New York: Addison Wesley, 1999).
13. Andrew Carnegie, "Wealth," *North American Review* 391 (June 1889): 653–64. McCloskey, *American Conservatism,* 166.
14. David M. Tucker, *Mugwumps: Public Moralists of the Gilded Age* (Columbia: University of Missouri Press, 1998). Gerald W. McFarland, "The New York Mugwumps of 1884: A Profile," *Political Science Quarterly* 78 (March 1963): 40–58. Thomas Bender, *New York Intellect* (New York: Knopf, 1987), 169–205. On their reputation among historians, see Geoffrey Blodgett, "The Mugwump Reputation, 1870 to the Present," *Journal of American History* 66 (March 1980): 867–87.
15. Biographical summary is based on William Armstrong, *E. L. Godkin: A Biography* (Albany: SUNY Press, 1978). E. L. Godkin, "The Economic Man," in Morton Keller, ed., *Problems of Modern Democracy: Political and Economic Essays* (Cambridge: Harvard University Press, 1966), 156–79, quotation on 174. In his view the only defensible tariff was one designed to raise revenue, where a definite sum of money to be raised could be fixed, without endless quibbling over relative advantages to this or that corporation. E. L. Godkin, "Some Political Aspects of the Tariff," in Keller, *Problems,* 98–122, quotation on 113.
16. Godkin, "Some Political Aspects," in Keller, *Problems,* 110. Curtis, quoted in Gordon Milne, *George William Curtis and the Genteel Tradition* (Bloomington: Indiana University Press, 1956), 236.
17. E. L. Godkin, "The Political Situation in 1896," in Keller, *Problems,* 249–74, quotation on 259.
18. On machine politics in New York, for example, see Alexander B. Callow, *The Tweed Ring* (New York: Oxford University Press, 1966).
19. Curtis, "The Public Duty of Educated Men," quoted in McFarland, "New York Mugwumps," 43.
20. George W. Curtis, "The Leadership of Educated Men," in Charles Eliot Norton, ed., *Orations and Addresses of George William Curtis, 3 vols.* (New York: Harper and Bros., 1894), 1:315–36.
21. Biographical summary is based on Edward Wagenknecht, *James Russell Lowell: Portrait of a Many-Sided Man* (New York: Oxford University Press, 1971). E. L. Godkin, "Duty of Educated Men in a Democracy," in Keller, *Problems,* 199–224, quotation on 201.
22. James Russell Lowell, "Democracy," in William Smith Clark II, ed., *Lowell: Essays, Poems, and Letters* (New York: Odyssey Press, 1948), 143–67. See also Martin Duberman, *James Russell Lowell* (Boston: Houghton Mifflin, 1966),

332–34. Norton to Lowell, November 16, 1884, in Sara Norton and M. DeWolfe Howe, eds., *Letters of Charles Eliot Norton,* 2 vols. (Boston: Houghton Mifflin, 1913), 2:166.

23. George William Curtis, "Centennial Celebration of the Concord Fight," in Norton, *Orations* 87–121, quotation on 114.
24. Godkin, "Some Political Aspects of the Tariff," 117.
25. E. L. Godkin, "Criminal Politics," in Keller, *Problems,* 123–55, quotation on 129.
26. Biographical information based on James Turner, *The Liberal Education of Charles Eliot Norton* (Baltimore: Johns Hopkins University Press, 1999). Arthur Sedgwick, "Words of a Contemporary," printed as an appendix in Norton, *Letters,* 2:439. Turner, *Liberal Education,* xi. Norton to Mountstuart Grant-Duff, September 1, 1890, Norton, *Letters,* 2:201.
27. Martin Green, *The Problem of Boston: Some Readings in Cultural History* (New York: Norton, 1966), 122. Lawrence Levine, *Highbrow/Lowbrow: The Emergence of Cultural Hierarchy in America* (Cambridge: Harvard University Press, 1988), 176–77, 214–15.
28. Norton to Edward Lee-Childe, September 29, 1883, in Norton, *Letters,* 2:156. Norton to Leslie Stephen, January 8, 1896, ibid., 2:236–37. Norton to Leslie Stephen, March 20, 1896, ibid., 2:241.
29. Jackson Lears, *No Place of Grace: Anti-Modernism and the Transformation of American Culture, 1880–1920* (New York: Pantheon, 1981).
30. Biographical summaries based on Ernest Samuels, *Henry Adams* (Cambridge: Harvard University Press, 1989), and Thornton Anderson, *Brooks Adams, Constructive Conservative* (Ithaca: Cornell University Press, 1951). Holmes quotation from Samuels, *Henry Adams,* 326.
31. Brooks Adams, *The Law of Civilization and Decay,* Charles Beard, ed. (1895. New York: Knopf, 1943), 333.
32. Adams, *Law of Civilization,* 123.
33. Herbert Butterfield, *The Whig Interpretation of History* (London: G. Bell, and Sons, 1931). Milton Berman, *John Fiske: The Evolution of a Popularizer* (Cambridge: Harvard University Press, 1961). Gregor McLennan, *Marxism and the Methodologies of History* (London: Verso, 1981). Roosevelt's review of Adams is quoted in Charles Beard's introduction to Adams, *Law of Civilization,* 44–47.
34. Samuels, *Henry Adams,* 296.
35. Henry Adams, *Mont Saint Michel and Chartres,* in *Novels, Mont Saint Michel, The Education* (New York: Library of America, 1983), 368, 371.
36. Samuels, *Henry Adams,* 362.
37. Henry Adams, *The Education of Henry Adams,* in *Novels, Mont Saint Michael and The Education,* 715–1181, quotations on 1071, 1074.
38. Cram, in his autobiography, describes a series of meetings with Adams in which he finally convinced him to publish the book to a wider audience. Ralph Adams Cram, *My Life in Architecture* (Boston: Little Brown, 1936),

226–28, 186. On his attitudes, see also "I had always instinctively hated the three great revolutions—Protestant, Cromwellian, and French," ibid., 130.

39. Ibid., 260–61, 261.
40. Ibid., 72–73, 176.
41. Ibid., 265
42. Mark De Wolfe Howe, *Barrett Wendell and His Letters* (Boston: Atlantic Monthly Press, 1924), 185. Barrett Wendell, *A Literary History of America* (New York: Scribner's, 1900). Wendell to Sir Robert White-Thomson, January 23, 1901, in Howe, *Letters,* 139: "I found myself today literally moved to tears for the loss of her [Queen Victoria]."
43. Howe, *Letters,* 137, 198.
44. Ibid., 112–13, 162.
45. Ernest Samuels, *Bernard Berenson: The Making of a Connoisseur* (Cambridge: Harvard University Press, 1979), and Samuels, *Bernard Berenson: The Making of a Legend* (Cambridge: Harvard University Press, 1987). Douglas Shand-Tucci, *The Art of Scandal: The Life and Times of Isabella Stewart Gardner* (New York: HarperCollins, 1997).
46. Leon Edel, *Henry James, A Life* (New York: Harper and Row, 1985).
47. Henry James, *The American Scene* (1907. New York: Horizon Press, 1967), 77–78.
48. Biographical information in this passage is based on Kathleen Dalton, *Theodore Roosevelt: A Strenuous Life* (New York: Knopf, 2002), John Milton Cooper, *The Warrior and the Priest* (Cambridge: Harvard University Press, 1983); Nathan Miller, *Theodore Roosevelt: A Life* (New York: William Morrow, 1992); and Theodore Roosevelt, *An Autobiography* (1913. New York: Scribner's, 1920). Quotations are from Cooper, *Warrior,* 11, 27.
49. Roosevelt, *Autobiography,* 486–501. Miller, *Roosevelt,* 452. Cooper, *Warrior,* 82.
50. Dalton, *Roosevelt,* 67–71 (father's death), 300–13 (political morality).
51. Roosevelt, *Gouverneur Morris* (Boston: Houghton Mifflin, 1888). Miller, *Roosevelt,* 191. Roosevelt, *Autobiography,* 273 (on Bryan). Dalton, *Roosevelt,* 150–54 (Riis and urban reform). Henry Cabot Lodge, ed., *Selections from the Correspondence of Theodore Roosevelt and Henry Cabot Lodge, 1884–1918,* 2 vols. (New York: Scribner's, 1925), 1:500.
52. Theodore Roosevelt, "The Strenuous Life," in Robert Bridges, ed., *The Roosevelt Book* (New York: Scribner's 1909), 21–29. Dalton, *Roosevelt,* 165–80, and Theodore Roosevelt, *The Rough Riders* (1899. New York: Modern Library, 1999).
53. Roosevelt, *Autobiography,* vii–viii.
54. On scientific racism, see Mark Haller, *Eugenics: Hereditarian Attitudes in American Thought* (New Brunswick: Rutgers University Press, 1963); Matthew Pratt Guterl, *The Color of Race in America, 1900–1940* (Cambridge: Harvard University Press, 2001); and Stephen Jay Gould, *The Mismeasure of Man* (New York: Norton, 1981).
55. Haller, *Eugenics,* 50–57. John Higham, *Strangers in the Land: Patterns of American Nativism 1860–1925* (1963. New York: Atheneum, 1965), 142–43.

56. Widenor, *Lodge,* 7. Karl Schriftgiesser, *The Gentleman from Massachusetts: Henry Cabot Lodge* (Boston: Little Brown, 1944), 116–17. Lodge, *Correspondence of Roosevelt and Lodge,* 1:504–5.
57. On Madison Grant, see Matthew Pratt Guterl, *The Color of Race in America: 1900–1940* (Cambridge: Harvard University Press, 2001), 14–67. Theodore Roosevelt, *Hunting Trips of a Ranchman,* in *Hunting Trips of a Ranchman and the Wilderness Hunter* (New York: Modern Library, 1996), 26.
58. Miller, *Roosevelt,* 252–56. Roosevelt, *Autobiography,* 502–10; Roosevelt, *Rough Riders,* 8, 87–88.
59. Richard W. Turk, *The Ambiguous Relationship: Theodore Roosevelt and Alfred Thayer Mahan* (Westport, Conn.: Greenwood, 1897). Charles Carlisle Taylor, *The Life of Admiral Mahan* (New York: George Doran, 1920). Alfred Thayer Mahan, *The Influence of Sea Power upon History, 1660–1783* (1890. Boston: Little Brown, 1916). Alfred Thayer Mahan, *From Sail to Steam* (New York: Harper and Bros., 1907), 282.
60. Taylor, *Mahan,* 57–77. This first biographer was himself an Englishman who was quick to recognize and admire the significance of Mahan's work.
61. Mahan, "The Peace Conference and the Moral Aspect of War," in his *Lessons of the War with Spain and Other Articles* (Boston: Little Brown, 1899), 207–38, quotation on 219. Taylor, *Mahan,* 94–95, 100.
62. Herbert Croly, *The Promise of American Life* (1909. Hamden, Conn.: Archon, 1963).
63. Barrett Wendell to Mrs. Wheelock (his daughter), February 26, 1912, in Howe, *Letters,* 245.
64. Richard W. Leopold, *Elihu Root and the Conservative Tradition* (Boston: Little Brown, 1954), 9, 75–76, 7.

CHAPTER 6: CONSERVATISM IN THE 1920S AND 1930S

1. John A. Garraty, *Henry Cabot Lodge: A Biography* (New York: Knopf, 1953), 343.
2. Garraty, *Lodge,* 346, 352. Philip Jessup, *Elihu Root* (New York: Dodd, Mead, 1938), 2:383–411.
3. Garraty, *Lodge,* 357–82. August Heckscher, *Woodrow Wilson* (New York: Scribner, 1991), 581–639.
4. Richard Pipes, *A Concise History of the Russian Revolution* (New York: Knopf, 1995). Markku Ruotsila, *British and American Anticommunism Before the Cold War* (London: Frank Cass, 2001), 3–21.
5. The classic account of these events is Robert K. Murray, *Red Scare: A Study in National Hysteria, 1919–1920* (Minneapolis: University of Minnesota Press, 1955). On Debs, see Ernest Freeberg, *Democracy's Prisoner* (Cambridge: Harvard University Press, 2008). On ex-communists in the Conservative movement, see John Diggins, *Up from Communism: Conservative Odysseys in American Intellectual History* (New York: Harper and Row, 1975).
6. On aspects of American cultural and intellectual life in the 1920s and early

1930s, see Richard Perry, *Intellectual Life in America: A History* (New York: Franklin Watts, 1984), 319–76.

7. Biographical details based on Thomas R. Nevin, *Irving Babbitt: An Intellectual Study* (Chapel Hill: University of North Carolina Press, 1984), and Stephen Brennan, *Irving Babbitt* (Boston: Twayne, 1987).
8. Irving Babbitt, *Literature and the American College,* Russell Kirk, ed. (1908. Washington, D.C.: National Humanities Institute, 1986), 80, 86.
9. Irving Nevin, *Irving Babbitt* (London: Constable, 1924), 15–16.
10. David Hoeveler, "Babbitt and Contemporary Conservative Thought in America," in George Panichas and Claes Ryn, eds., *Irving Babbitt in Our Time* (Washington, D.C.: Catholic University of America Press, 1986), 177–99.
11. Irving Babbitt, *Democracy and Leadership* (London: Constable, 1924), 16.
12. Ibid., 239–64.
13. Biographical information on More is based on Francis X. Duggan, *Paul Elmer More* (New York: Twayne, 1966). Paul Elmer More, *Aristocracy and Justice: Shelburne Essays,* 9th ser. (New York: Houghton Mifflin, 1915), 136. Duggan, *More,* 29. David Hoeveler, *The New Humanism: A Critique of Modern America* (Charlottesville: University of Virginia Press, 1977), 14
14. Duggan, *More,* 68–70.
15. Ibid., 80–81, 83.
16. More, quoted in Arthur Hazard Dakin, *Paul Elmer More* (Princeton: Princeton University Press, 1960), 298. Duggan, *More,* 57.
17. Norman Foerster, ed., *Humanism and America: Essays on the Outlook of Modern Civilization* (New York: Farrar and Reinhart, 1930), v, x.
18. C. Hartley Grattan, "The New Humanism and the Scientific Attitude, in Grattan, ed., *The Critique of Humanism: A Symposium* (New York: Brewer and Warren, 1930), 3–36.
19. Edmund Wilson, "Notes on Babbitt and More," in Grattan, *Critique of Humanism,* 48. Henry Hazlitt, "Humanism and Value," ibid., 88.
20. Grattan, "New Humanism," in Grattan, *Critique of Humanism,* 7–8, 28. Malcolm Cowley, "Humanizing Society," ibid., 68.
21. Hoeveler, *The New Humanism,* 150–51.
22. Biographical information from Daniel Singal, *The War Within: From Victorian to Modernist Thought in the South, 1919–1945* (Chapel Hill: University of North Carolina Press, 1982), on Tate, 233–60; on *Fugitive,* 198–202.
23. Twelve Southerners, *I'll Take My Stand: The South and the Agrarian Tradition* (1930. New York: Harper and Row, 1962), xxiii–xxiv.
24. Ibid., xxvi.
25. John Crowe Ransom, "Reconstructed but Unregenerate," in ibid., 7, 5.
26. Frank Owsley, "The Irrepressible Conflict," in ibid., 74, 66, 62.
27. Robert Penn Warren, "The Briar Patch," in ibid., 246–64. Warren had grown up in Guthrie, Kentucky, scene of the "Black Patch War" between competing groups of tobacco farmers. Members of his family had also been involved in feuds and violent confrontations in the aftermath of the Civil

War, incidents that had led him to dread social upheaval (Singal, *War Within,* 346).

28. Andrew Lytle, "The Hind Tit," in Twelve Southerners, *I'll Take My Stand,* 205. On the realities of Southern agriculture, see Pete Daniel, *Standing at the Crossroads: Southern Life in the Twentieth Century* (New York: Hill and Wang, 1986), 4–13, 82–87.
29. Patrick Allitt, *Catholic Converts: British and American Intellectuals Turn to Rome* (Ithaca: Cornell University Press, 1997), 206–10.
30. Herbert Agar, *The People's Choice, From Washington to Harding: A Study in Democracy* (New York: Houghton Mifflin, 1933). Agar, *Land of the Free* (Boston: Houghton Mifflin, 1935). On Agar's career, see Daniel Spillman, "Herbert Agar and the Task of American Conservatism: Biography of a Twentieth-Century Intellectual," seminar paper, Emory University, 2006.
31. Herbert Agar and Allen Tate, eds., *Who Owns America? A New Declaration of Independence* (Boston: Houghton Mifflin, 1936), viii.
32. Spillman, "Herbert Agar," 43–52.
33. Ibid., 53–58.
34. Robert Muccigrosso, "American Mercury," in Ronald Lora and William H. Longton, eds., *The Conservative Press in Twentieth-Century America* (Westport, Conn.: Greenwood, 1999), 243–52.
35. Terry Teachout, *The Skeptic: The Life of H. L. Mencken* (New York: HarperCollins, *2002),* 144–45.
36. Charles Fecher, *Mencken: A Study of His Thought* (New York: Knopf, 1978), 234.
37. Teachout, *Skeptic,* 16. H. L. Mencken, *Notes on Democracy* (1926. New York: Octagon, 1977), 3–4.
38. Fecher, *Mencken,* 185–87.
39. H. L. Mencken, "The National Letters," in *Prejudices,* 2d ser. (New York: Knopf, 1920), 9–101. Fecher, *Mencken,* 187–92.
40. Summary of the New Deal programs is based on David M. Kennedy, *Freedom from Fear: The American People in Depression and War, 1929–1945* (New York: Oxford University Press, 1999), 131–59, 249–87.
41. On the historians' debate about the New Deal, see Morton Keller, "The New Deal, A New Look," *Polity* 31 (Summer 1999): 657–63.
42. Biographical summary based on David Burner, *Herbert Hoover: A Public Life* (New York: Knopf, 1979).
43. Herbert Hoover, *The Challenge to Liberty* (New York: Scribner, 1934), 6, 82.
44. George Nash, "The Social Philosophy of Herbert Hoover," in Lee Nash, ed., *Understanding Herbert Hoover: Ten Perspectives* (Stanford: Hoover Institution Press, 1987), 27–41. Herbert Hoover, "Crisis to Free Men," in *American Ideals Versus the New Deal* (New York: Scribner, 1936), 5.
45. On Franklin Roosevelt and the Supreme Court, see Kennedy, *Freedom from Fear,* 325–36. Herbert Hoover, "Hands off the Supreme Court," in his *Addresses upon the American Road* (New York: Scribner's, 1938), 233.

46. Herbert Hoover, *Challenge to Liberty* (New York: Scribner's, 1934). Frederick Rudolph, "The American Liberty League, 1934–1940," *American Historical Review* 56 (October 1950): 19–33, quotations on 21, 20. George Wolfskill, *The Revolt of the Conservatives: A History of the American Liberty League* (Boston: Houghton Mifflin, 1962).
47. Robert Paul Browder, *The Origins of Soviet-American Diplomacy* (Princeton: Princeton University Press, 1953), 39–41. Hoover, "Foreign Policies for America," in *Addresses,* 317.
48. Biographical summary based on James T. Patterson, *Mr. Republican: A Biography of Robert A. Taft* (Boston: Houghton Mifflin, 1972), 166.
49. Russell Kirk and James McClellan, *The Political Principles of Robert A. Taft* (New York: Fleet Press, 1967), 13 (quotation), 24–27 (TVA), 16 (planned economy).
50. Nock's biographer Michael Wreszin demonstrates that in the 1920s Nock was more optimistic about ordinary citizens' abilities than Mencken and that the two sparred over this question. Only in the 1930s did Nock begin to see himself as part of the Remnant. Michael Wreszin, *The Superfluous Anarchist: Albert Jay Nock* (Providence: Brown University Press, 1972), 19–52, 60–63. Francis Neilson, "The Story of The Freeman," *American Journal of Economics and Sociology* 6 supp. (October 1946): 3–53.
51. Wreszin, *Superfluous Anarchist,* 82, 127, 129. Albert Jay Nock, *Our Enemy, the State* (New York: William Morrow, 1935).
52. Albert Jay Nock, *Memoirs of a Superfluous Man* (New York: Harper and Bros., 1943), 13, 137. John Judis, *William F. Buckley, Jr., Patron Saint of the Conservatives* (New York: Simon and Schuster, 1988), 44–46. Nock, *Memoirs,* 138–39.
53. Nock, *Memoirs,* 41, 49.
54. Ibid., 52.
55. Ralph Adams Cram, "Why We Do Not Behave Like Human Beings," in *Convictions and Controversies* (Boston: Marshall Jones, 1935), 140, 143, 149, 150. On Cram's earlier life and work, see Chap. 5; Douglas Shand-Tucci, *Ralph Adams Cram: Boston Bohemian* (Amherst: University of Massachusetts Press, 1995); Shand-Tucci, *Ralph Adams Cram: An Architect's Four Quests* (Amherst: University of Massachusetts Press, 2005); and Michael D. Clark, *The American Discovery of Tradition: 1865–1942* (Baton Rouge: Louisiana State University Press, 2005), 116–61.
56. Cram, "Challengers of Democracy," 127, 115, 124, and "Fulfillment," 95, in *Convictions and Controversies.*
57. Cram, "Ordeal by Beauty," in *Convictions and Controversies,* 2. Cram, *My Life in Architecture* (Boston: Little Brown, 1936), 282. Cram, "Radio City—and After," in *Convictions and Controversies,* 40.
58. Cram, *My Life in Architecture,* 292–94.
59. Biographical sketch based on John McCormick, *George Santayana: A Biography* (New York: Knopf, 1987).

60. George Santayana, *The Last Puritan* (New York: Scribner's, 1936), 62.
61. Biographical sketch based on Rockwell Gray, *The Imperative of Modernity: An Intellectual Biography of Jose Ortega y Gasset* (Berkeley: University of California Press, 1989).
62. Harvey Klehr, *The Heyday of American Communism* (New York: Basic, 1984). John P. Diggins, *Mussolini and Fascism: The View from America* (Princeton: Princeton University Press, 1972).
63. Hoffman, quoted in Albert E. Stone, Jr., "Seward Collins and the American Review: Experiment in Pro-Fascism," *American Quarterly* 12 (Spring 1960): 6. On the variety of American conservatives' and right-wingers' reactions, see Diggins, *Mussolini and Fascism,* 206–11.
64. Ronald Radosh, *Prophets on the Right: Profiles of Conservative Critics of American Globalism* (New York: Simon and Schuster, 1975), 275–96. Justus Doenecke, "Weekly Foreign Letter," in Lora and Longton, *Conservative Press,* 281–94.
65. Patterson, *Mr. Republican,* 196–202. Burner, *Hoover,* 332–34. Kennedy, *Freedom from Fear,* 385–89. Frank Hanighen and H. C. Engelbrecht, *Merchants of Death: A Study of the International Armament Industry* (New York: Dodd and Mead, 1934).
66. Richard W. Fox, *Reinhold Niebuhr: A Biography* (San Francisco: Harper and Row, 1985), 193–201. Spillman, "Herbert Agar," 63–72.
67. Radosh, *Prophets on the Right,* 120–21.
68. Ibid., 128. On reluctance to aid the British Empire, see Justus Doenecke, *Storm on the Horizon: The Challenge to American Intervention* (Lanham, Md.: Rowman and Littlefield, 2000), 203–11. Justin Raimondo, *Reclaiming the American Right: The Lost Legacy of the Conservative Movement* (Burlingame, Calif.: Center for Libertarian Studies, 1993), 52.

CHAPTER 7: THE NEW CONSERVATISM, 1945–1964

1. By now an extensive literature on the movement exists. The first and still the single best study of it is George Nash, *The Conservative Intellectual Movement in America Since 1945* (1976. New York: Basic, 1979). See also John Judis, *William F. Buckley, Jr., Patron Saint of the Conservatives* (New York: Simon and Schuster, 1988); Patrick Allitt, *Catholic Intellectuals and Conservative Politics in America, 1950–1985* (Ithaca: Cornell University Press, 1993); Michael Miles, *The Odyssey of the American Right* (New York: Oxford University Press, 1980); Paul Gottfried, *The Conservative Movement,* rev. ed. (New York: Twayne, 1993); Lee Edwards, *The Conservative Revolution: The Movement That Remade America* (New York: Free Press, 1999); and John Micklethwait and Adrian Wooldridge, *The Right Nation: Conservative Power in America* (New York: Penguin, 2004).
2. Biographical summary of Hayek is based on Alan Ebenstein, *Friedrich Hayek: A Biography* (New York: Palgrave, 2001). F. A. Hayek, *The Road to Serfdom* (Chicago: University of Chicago Press, 1994).

3. Hayek, *Road to Serfdom,* 43–87.
4. Ibid., 12, 13–15.
5. Ibid., 37–42.
6. Ibid., 147–49.
7. Biographical information on von Mises is based on Murray Rothbard, *Ludwig von Mises: Scholar, Creator, Hero* (Auburn, Ala.: Ludwig von Mises Institute, 1988). On *Socialism,* see Richard Ebeling, "Ludwig von Mises: The Political Economist of Liberty," in Gary Wolfram, ed., *Great Economists of the Twentieth Century* (Hillsdale, Mich.: Hillsdale College Press, 2006), 15–33.
8. Kenneth R. Hoover, *Economics as Ideology: Keynes, Laski, Hayek and the Creation of Contemporary Politics* (Lanham, Md.: Rowman and Littlefield, 2003), 73. Ludwig von Mises, *Human Action* (New Haven: Yale University Press, 1949).
9. Seymour Harris, quoted in Nash, *Conservative Intellectual Movement,* 13. Von Mises, *Human Action,* 3, 234.
10. Mark Skousen, *Vienna and Chicago: Friends or Foes* (Washington, D.C.: Regnery, 2005), 2. Nash, *Conservative Intellectual Movement,* 26–28, quotation on 26.
11. Justin Raimondo, *An Enemy of the State: The Life of Murray Rothbard* (New York: Prometheus, 2000), 52, 51.
12. Ibid., *Enemy of the State,* 69–81.
13. Ayn Rand, *The Fountainhead* (Indianapolis: Bobbs Merrill, 1943). On her life, see Barbara Branden, *The Passion of Ayn Rand* (Garden City: Doubleday, 1986). On her significance to the conservative movement, see Jennifer Byrne, "Goddess of the Market: Ayn Rand and the American Right, 1930–1980," Ph.D. diss., University of California, Berkeley, 2005. Rothbard, *Enemy of the State,* 109–12.
14. Ayn Rand, *Atlas Shrugged* (New York: Random House, 1957). Jerome Tuccille, *Alan Shrugged: The Life and Times of Alan Greenspan, the World's Most Powerful Banker* (Hoboken: John Wiley, 2002). Tuccille details Greenspan's long friendship with Rand, which ended only at her death, in 1982. On teenagers' infatuation with her vision, see also Tuccille's *It Usually Begins with Ayn Rand* (New York: Stein and Day, 1971).
15. Tobias Wolfe, *Old School* (New York: Knopf, 2003). Byrne, "Goddess of the Market," 2. Byrne's persuasive work makes the argument that intellectual snobbery on the left and right has led scholars to underestimate the influence of Rand in drawing recruits to conservatism.
16. Raimondo, *Enemy of the State,* 117–25. Tuccille, *It Usually Begins,* 32.
17. On Weaver's life and work, see Fred Douglas Young, *Richard M. Weaver, 1910–1963: A Life of the Mind* (Columbia: University of Missouri Press, 1995). Nash, *Conservative Intellectual Movement,* 36–43.
18. Richard Weaver, *Ideas Have Consequences* (Chicago: University of Chicago Press, 1948), 3–4.
19. Ibid., 56, 57.

20. Ibid., 41–42.
21. Ibid., 55.
22. Paul V. Murphy, *The Rebuke of History: The Southern Agrarians and American Conservative Thought* (Chapel Hill: University of North Carolina Press, 2001), 151–78. John Attarian, "Illuminating Richard Weaver's Ideas," *Modern Age* 41 (Fall 1999): 348.
23. Russell Kirk, *The Sword of Imagination: Memoirs of a Half-Century of Literary Conflict* (Grand Rapids: Eerdman's, 1995), 79–82.
24. Russell Kirk, *The Conservative Mind: From Burke to Eliot* (1953. Chicago: Regnery Gateway, 1967), 4–5.
25. Ibid., 6, 7.
26. Ibid., 8.
27. Ibid., 540–41.
28. Kirk, *Sword of Imagination,* 85–91, 133–37. Kirk, *Conservative Mind,* 70.
29. Nash, *Conservative Intellectual Movement,* 69–76.
30. Kirk, *Sword of Imagination.* Wesley McDonald, *Russell Kirk and the Age of Ideology* (Columbia: University of Missouri Press, 2004), ix–xiv.
31. Eric Voegelin, *The New Science of Politics: An Introduction* (Chicago: University of Chicago Press, 1952), 110–13, 117–21. Nash, *Conservative Intellectual Movement,* 49–50.
32. Walter Lippmann, *Essays in the Public Philosophy* (1955. New Brunswick: Transaction Press, 1989), 106–7. On Lippmann, see Ronald Steele, *Walter Lippmann and the American Century* (Boston: Little Brown, 1980), 492.
33. Peter Viereck, *Conservatism Revisited* (1949. New York: Free Press, 1962), 46–47.
34. Whittaker Chambers, *Witness* (New York: Random House, 1952). Sam Tanenhaus, *Whittaker Chambers: A Biography* (New York: Random House, 1997).
35. Chambers, *Witness,* 1–22, quotation on 79. Tanenhaus, *Whittaker Chambers,* 339–442 (on the trials).
36. On Eastman, Burnham, Dos Passos, and Herberg, see John P. Diggins, *Up from Communism: Conservative Odysseys in American Intellectual History* (New York: Harper and Row, 1975). Kevin J. Smant, *Principles and Heresies: Frank Meyer and the Shaping of the American Conservative Movement* (Wilmington, Del.: ISI Books, 2002).
37. Biographical summary based on Judis, *Buckley.* William F. Buckley, Jr., *God and Man at Yale: The Superstitions of "Academic Freedom"* (Chicago: Henry Regnery, 1951), xii–xiii. On reception of *God and Man,* see Judis, *Buckley,* 92–98, and Nash, *Conservative Intellectual Movement,* 30–33, 140–41.
38. William F. Buckley and L. Brent Bozell, *McCarthy and His Enemies* (Chicago: Henry Regnery, 1954). Judis, *Buckley,* 104–14.
39. Judis, *Buckley,* 113–42. Kirk, *Sword of Imagination,* 187–88, 190–208. On *Human Events,* see Scott Rubish, "Human Events," in Bruce Frohnen et al., eds., *American Conservatism: An Encyclopedia* (Wilmington, Del.: ISI Books, 2006), 410–11.

40. Patrick J. Buchanan, *Right from the Beginning* (Boston: Little Brown, 1988), 218, 221.
41. William F. Buckley, Jr., *Up from Liberalism* (1959. New York: Bantam, 1968), 7, xvii.
42. Buckley, *Up from Liberalism,* 84–85. Judis, *Buckley,* 44–46.
43. Allitt, *Catholic Conservatives,* 68.
44. Nash, *Conservative Intellectual Movement,* 290, 305. Judis, *Buckley,* 188–90. Marvin Liebman, *Coming Out Conservative: An Autobiography* (San Francisco: Chronicle, 1992), 150–56. See also John Andrew, *The Other Side of the Sixties: Young Americans for Freedom and the Rise of Conservative Politics* (New Brunswick: Rutgers University Press, 1997).
45. Judis, *Buckley,* 193–200 (on John Birch Society), 173–74 (on *American Mercury*). Nash, *Conservative Intellectual Movement,*156–59 (on Rand).
46. Biographical summary based on Daniel Kelly, *James Burnham and the Struggle for the World* (Wilmington, Del.: ISI Books, 2002), 94–98 (on *Managerial Revolution),* 105–13 (on *The Machiavellians).*
47. Kelly, *James Burnham,* 121–47, 175–80. Garry Dorrien, *The Neoconservative Mind: Politics, Culture and the War of Ideology* (Philadelphia: Temple University Press, 1993), 23–63.
48. Smant, *Principles and Heresies,* 1–20.
49. Nash, *Conservative Intellectual Movement,* 171–80. Smant, *Principles and Heresies,* 49–52. Frank Meyer, ed., *What Is Conservatism?* (New York: Holt, Reinhart and Winston, 1964). Meyer, *The Conservative Mainstream* (New Rochelle: Arlington House, 1969).
50. Allitt, *Catholic Intellectuals,* 204–42.
51. Ibid., 16–82.
52. Garry Wills, "The Convenient State," in William F. Buckley, Jr., ed., *Did You Ever See a Dream Walking? American Conservative Thought in the Twentieth Century* (Indianapolis: Bobbs Merrill, 1970), 7–37. Allitt, *Catholic Intellectuals,* 246–52. Garry Wills, *Confessions of a Conservative* (Garden City: Doubleday, 1979), 49–59.
53. Allitt, *Catholic Intellectuals,* 84–89 (Kennedy campaign); 106–10 (Supreme Court and religion).
54. L. Brent Bozell, *The Warren Revolution: Reflections on the Consensus Society* (New Rochelle: Arlington House, 1966), 54. See also Allitt, *Catholic Intellectuals,* 142–44.
55. Untitled editorial, *National Review,* March 14, 1956, 6 (Montgomery). Editorial, "Segregation and Democracy," ibid., January 25, 1956, 5 (*Brown* case). Buckley, *Up from Liberalism,* 111–12 (civilization and states rights).
56. Seymour M. Lipset, "The Sources of the 'Radical Right,' " in Daniel Bell, ed., *The Radical Right* (*The New American Right* [1955] expanded and updated; Garden City: Anchor Doubleday, 1964), 307–71.
57. Richard Hofstadter, "The Pseudo-Conservative Revolt," in Bell, *Radical Right,* 74–95, quotation on 76. Buckley, *Up from Liberalism,* 22.

58. Mark Skousen, *Vienna and Chicago: Friends or Foes?* (Washington, D.C.: Regnery, 2005). Eamonn Butler, *Milton Friedman, A Guide to His Economic Thought* (New York: Universe, 1985). Nash, *Conservative Intellectual Movement,* 284–91
59. Mark Skousen, *The Making of Modern Economics* (Armonk, N.Y.: Sharpe, 2001), 155–64.
60. Ibid., 366–410.
61. Milton Friedman, *Capitalism and Freedom* (Chicago: University of Chicago Press, 1962), 22–36.
62. Ibid., 13 (noncoerciveness), 108–18 (nondiscrimination), 190–95 (poverty).
63. Ibid., 85–107.
64. Ibid., 192.
65. Ibid., 119–36.
66. Friedman, quoted in Nash, *Conservative Intellectual Movement,* 287. Milton Friedman and Anna J. Schwartz, *A Monetary History of the United States, 1867–1960* (Princeton: Princeton University Press, 1963).
67. Skousen, *Vienna and Chicago,* 84. George Stigler, *Memoirs of an Unregulated Economist* (New York: Basic, 1985), 164.
68. Robert Alan Goldberg, *Barry Goldwater* (New Haven: Yale University Press, 1995), 138–57. Barry Goldwater, *The Conscience of a Conservative* (1960. Princeton: Princeton University Press, 2007).
69. Buchanan, quoted in Goldberg, *Goldwater,* 139. Donald Critchlow, "Conservatism Reconsidered: Phyllis Schlafly and Grassroots Conservatism," in David Farber and Jeff Roche, eds., *The Conservative Sixties* (New York: Peter Lang, 2003), 110.
70. Goldberg, *Barry Goldwater,* 204–7; Nash, *Conservative Movement,* 289–94.
71. Godfrey Hodgson, *The World Turned Right Side Up* (Boston: Houghton Mifflin, 1996), 104.
72. Nash, *Conservative Intellectual Movement,* 184–85.

CHAPTER 8: THE MOVEMENT GAINS ALLIES, 1964–1980

1. Donald Critchlow, *Phyllis Schlafly and Grassroots Conservatism: A Woman's Crusade* (Princeton: Princeton University Press, 2005); Lisa McGirr, *Suburban Warriors: The Origins of the New American Right* (Princeton: Princeton University Press, 2001); Jonathan Schoenwald, *A Time for Choosing: The Rise of Modern American Conservatism* (New York: Oxford University Press, 2001). William F. Buckley, Jr., *The Unmaking of a Mayor* (New York: Viking, 1966).
2. Lee Edwards, *The Conservative Revolution: The Movement That Re-Made America* (New York: Free Press, 1999), 123–25. Frank Meyer, *The Conservative Mainstream* (New Rochelle: Arlington House, 1969), 160.
3. Patrick Allitt, *Catholic Intellectuals and Conservative Politics in America* (Ithaca: Cornell University Press, 1993), 115–16. Meyer, "The Violence of Nonviolence," in *Conservative Mainstream,* 207–9.

4. Meyer, *Conservative Mainstream,* 204–5. William F. Buckley, Jr., *The Jeweler's Eye* (New York: Putnam, 1968), 137.
5. Meyer, *Conservative Mainstream,* 214, 217. Nash, *Conservative Intellectual Movement,* 281–82.
6. William F. Buckley, Jr., *The Governor Listeth* (New York: Putnam, 1970), 150–51.
7. Dan T. Carter, *The Politics of Rage: George Wallace, The Origins of the New Conservatism, and the Transformation of American Politics* (New York: Simon and Schuster, 1995). George Wallace, quoted in John Micklethwait and Adrian Wooldridge, *The Right Nation: Conservative Power in America* (New York: Penguin, 2004), 66.
8. Meyer, *Conservative Mainstream,* 288. Kevin Phillips, *The Emerging Republican Majority* (New Rochelle: Arlington House, 1969). Joseph Crespino, *In Search of Another Country: Mississippi and the Conservative Counterrevolution* (Princeton: Princeton University Press, 2007).
9. Daniel Kelly, *James Burnham and the Struggle for the World* (Wilmington, Del.: ISI Books, 2002), 314–17. M. Stanton Evans, *The Politics of Surrender* (New York: Devin Adair, 1966), 357–75.
10. Meyer, *Conservative Mainstream,* 222–23 (reprinting a *National Review* column of August 1966).
11. Allitt, *Catholic Intellectuals,* 151–52.
12. Kelly, *James Burnham,* 324–33. Phyllis Schlafly and Chester Ward, *Kissinger on the Couch* (New Rochelle: Arlington House, 1975).
13. John Judis, *William F. Buckley, Jr., Patron Saint of the Conservatives* (New York: Simon and Schuster, 1988), 336–37.
14. Justin Raimondo, *An Enemy of the State: The Life of Murray Rothbard* (Amherst, N.Y.: Prometheus, 2000), 151–209.
15. Hess, quoted in George Nash, *The Conservative Intellectual Movement in America Since 1945* (1976. New York: Basic, 1979), 316.
16. Murray Rothbard, "Confessions of a Right-Wing Liberal," *Ramparts,* 1968 (on the web at http://www.mises.org/story/1842).
17. Jerome Tuccille, *It Usually Begins with Ayn Rand* (New York: Stein and Day, 1971), 13, 93.
18. Murray Rothbard, *For a New Liberty* (New York: Macmillan, 1973), 10, 132, 221. Paul Gottfried, *The Conservative Movement, rev. ed.* (Boston: Twayne, 1993), 46.
19. Robert Nozick, *Anarchy, State and Utopia* (New York: Basic, 1974), ix.
20. Buckley, *Governor Listeth,* 340–41, 343.
21. Russell Kirk, *The Sword of Imagination: Memoirs of a Half-Century of Literary Conflict* (Grand Rapids: Eerdman's, 1995), 413.
22. Tuccille, *It Usually Begins,* 54.
23. Meyer, *Conservative Mainstream,* 299.
24. Harrington used the term *neoconservatives* as a slight, but it stuck. Mark Gerson, *The Neoconservative Vision: From the Cold War to the Culture Wars* (Lanham, Md.: Madison, 1997), 6.

25. Irving Kristol, "Memoirs of a Trotskyist" (1977), in *Reflections of a Neoconservative* (New York: Basic, 1983). On the New York intellectual "family" and its journal, *Partisan Review*, see Alexander Bloom, *Prodigal Sons: The New York Intellectuals and Their World* (New York: Oxford University Press, 1986), 71–120.
26. Garry Dorrien, *The Neoconservative Mind: Politics, Culture, and the War of Ideology* (Philadelphia: Temple University Press, 1993), 88–90. Daniel Bell, *The End of Ideology: On the Exhaustion of Political Ideas in the Fifties* (Glencoe, Ill.: Free Press, 1960).
27. Norman Podhoretz, *Making It* (1967. New York: Bantam, 1969), x. Dorrien, *Neoconservative Mind*, 158–61.
28. Perter Steinfels, *The Neoconservatives: The Men Who Are Changing America's Politics* (New York: Simon and Schuster, 1979), 56–58, 285–90. Steinfels, author of the first systematic study of the neoconservatives, pointed out that although the neoconservatives were themselves members of the new class, they clearly did not share its alleged "adversary culture" principles.
29. Joseph Schumpeter, *Capitalism, Socialism, and Democracy* (1942. New York: Harper and Row, 1976).
30. Steinfels, *Neoconservatives*, 54–59.
31. John Ehrman, *The Rise of Neoconservatism: Intellectuals and Foreign Affairs* (New Haven: Yale University Press, 1995), 67. Steinfels, *Neoconservatives*, 108–12, 128–31.
32. Lee Rainwater and William Yancey, *The Moynihan Report and the Politics of Controversy* (Cambridge: MIT Press, 1967). Nash, *Conservative Intellectual Movement*, 320–26. Buckley, *Jeweler's Eye*, 158–59.
33. Edward Banfield, *The Unheavenly City Revisited* (Revised version of *The Unheavenly City*, 1970. Boston: Little Brown, 1974). Nash, *Conservative Intellectual Movement*, 328–30.
34. Gerson, *Neoconservative Vision*, 96–98.
35. Nathan Glazer, "The Limits of Social Policy," *Commentary* 52 (September 1971): 51–58.
36. Michael Novak, *The Rise of the Unmeltable Ethnics* (New York: Macmillan, 1972). Peter Berger and Richard Neuhaus, *To Empower People: The Role of Mediating Structures in Public Policy* (Washington, D.C.: American Enterprise Institute, 1977). Dorrien, *Neoconservative Mind*, 306–11.
37. Gerson, *Neoconservative Vision*, 87. 290.
38. Glazer, "Limits of Social Policy." Irving Kristol, *Two Cheers for Capitalism* (1978. New York: Mentor, 1979), ix–x. On Wills and the Convenient State, see Chap. 7, above.
39. Norman Podhoretz, "Making the World Safe for Communism," *Commentary* 61 (April 1976): 31–41. Dorrien, *Neoconservative Mind*, 167–69.
40. Arthur Hertzberg, "Israel and American Jewry," *Commentary* 44 (August 1967): 69–78. Ehrman, *Rise of Neoconservatism*, 39. Dorrien, *Neoconservative Mind*, 184–90. Gerson, *Neoconservative Vision*, 161–65.
41. Gerson, *Neoconservative Vision*, 170–73. Ehrman, *Rise of Neoconservatism*, 86.

42. Godfrey Hodgson, *The World Turned Right Side Up* (Boston: Houghton Mifflin, 1996), 233–38.
43. Ehrman, *Rise of Neoconservatism,* 111–13.
44. Peter Berger, quoted in Norman Podhoretz, *Why We Were in Vietnam* (1982. New York: Simon and Schuster, 1983), 197–98. Podhoretz, *Why We Were in Vietnam,* 217, 85–86. Podhoretz makes his admission of culpability in a personal postscript added to the paperback edition of the book, but omitted from the original, which avoided discussion of his own views. See also Podhoretz, "Making the World Safe for Communism."
45. Steinfels, *Neoconservatives,* 1.
46. Midge Deceter, "The Liberated Woman," *Commentary* 50 (October 1970): 33–44. That this point of view was already controversial can be seen from the angry rebuttals sent in by many *Commentary* readers. See "Women's Lib. and the Liberated Woman," *Commentary* 51 (February 1971): 12–36. Midge Decter, *The New Chastity and Other Arguments Against Women's Liberation* (New York: Coward, McCann and Geohagen, 1972), 56. See also Decter, *The Liberated Woman and Other Americans* (New York: Coward, McCann and Geohagen, 1971), 1–99. Arlene Croce, "Sexism in the Head," *Commentary* 51 (March, 1971): 63–68.
47. Critchlow, *Phyllis Schlafly,* 217–18.
48. Ibid., 219–23. Phyllis Schlafly, *The Power of the Positive Woman* (New Rochelle: Arlington House, 1977).
49. Allitt, *Catholic Intellectuals,* 180–83. William F. Buckley, Jr., "The Catholic Church and Abortion," *National Review,* April 5, 1966, 308.
50. Allitt, *Catholic Intellectuals,* 153–57.
51. Ibid., 189.
52. White dissent at "Roe v. Wade Supreme Court Decision," http://womenshistory.about.com/library/etext/gov/bl_roe_m.htm.
53. Allitt, *Catholic Intellectuals,* 191–94.
54. Joseph Sobran, "The Abortion Ethos," *Human Life Review* 3 (Winter 1977): 14–21. John T. Noonan, *A Private Choice: Abortion In America in the 1970s* (New York: Free Press, 1979). Charles Rice, *Beyond Abortion: The Theory and Practice of the Secular State* (Chicago: Franciscan Herald Press, 1979).
55. Walter Capps, *The New Religious Right: Piety, Patriotism and Politics* (Columbia: University of South Carolina Press, 1990), 58–88. Patrick Allitt, *Religion in America Since 1945: A History* (New York: Columbia University Press, 2003), 156–58.
56. Francis Schaeffer, *The Great Evangelical Disaster* (Westchester, Ill.: Crossway, 1984), 23.
57. Allitt, *Religion in America,* 151–54. Dinesh D'Souza, *Falwell Before the Millennium: A Critical Biography* (Chicago: Regnery Gateway, 1984). Micklethwait and Wooldridge, *Right Nation,* 83–85. Edwards, *Conservative Revolution,* 184–99.
58. Larry W. Chappell, *George F. Will* (New York: Twayne, 1997), xiii–xiv.

59. Many of his columns from the 1970s are gathered in George Will, *The Pursuit of Happiness and Other Sobering Thoughts* (New York: Harper and Row, 1978). On baseball, see George Will, *Men at Work: The Craft of Baseball* (New York: Macmillan, 1990).
60. Will, *Pursuit of Happiness*, xvi; George Will, *Statecraft as Soulcraft: What Government Does* (New York: Simon and Schuster, 1983), 19–20, 24.
61. Will, *Pursuit of Happiness*, 57, 72, 73–75.

CHAPTER 9: THE REAGAN REVOLUTION AND THE CLIMAX OF THE COLD WAR

1. Emmett Tyrrell, *The Conservative Crack-Up* (New York: Simon and Schuster, 1992), 104.
2. John Stefancic and Richard Delgado, *No Mercy: How Conservative Think Tanks and Foundations Changed America's Social Agenda* (Philadelphia: Temple University Press, 1996). John Micklethwait and Adrian Wooldridge, *The Right Nation: Conservative Power in America* (New York: Penguin, 2004), 76–80.
3. Stefancic and Delgado, *No Mercy*, 4–5.
4. See, e.g., Kevin Lynch, "Afghanistan on a Shoestring," *National Review*, January 21, 1983, 40–42, 69.
5. Editorial, "Reagan's Soviet Speech," *National Review*, February 10, 1984, 17.
6. On the politics of the Strategic Defense Initiative, see Angelo M. Codevilla, "How SDI Is Being Undone from Within," *Commentary* 81 (May 1986): 21–29. On the genesis of the project, see Ronald Reagan, *An American Life* (New York: Simon and Schuster, 1990), 547–50.
7. Patrick Allitt, *Catholic Intellectuals and Conservative Politics in America, 1950–1985* (Ithaca: Cornell University Press, 1993), 289–96.
8. Michael Novak, "Moral Clarity in the Nuclear Age," *National Review*, April 1, 1983, 354–58.
9. John Ehrman, *The Rise of Neoconservatism: Intellectuals and Foreign Policy, 1945–1994* (New Haven: Yale University Press, 1995), 139–42.
10. Jeane Kirkpatrick, "Dictatorships and Double Standards," *Commentary* 68 (November 1979): 34–45.
11. Jeane Kirkpatrick, "U. S. Security and Latin America," *Commentary* 71 (January 1981): 29–40. Constantine Menges, "Central America and Its Enemies," *Commentary* 72 (August 1981): 32–38.
12. Milton Friedman and Rose Friedman, *Free to Choose: A Personal Statement* (New York: Harcourt Brace Jovanovich, 1979), 265. Lanny Ebenstein, *Milton Friedman: A Biography* (New York: Palgrave, 2007), 199–211. William R. Allen, ed., *Bright Promises: Dismal Performance: An Economist's Protest* (collected *Newsweek* articles by Friedman) (New York: Harcourt, Brace Jovanovich, 1983).
13. Friedman, quoted in Ebenstein, *Milton Friedman*, 171.
14. Jude Wanniski, *The Way the World Works* (New York: Simon and Schuster, 1978), 97–99.
15. Wanniski, *Way the World Works*, 45–46.

16. Irving Kristol, *Two Cheers for Capitalism* (New York: New American Library, 1978), x, 3–22.
17. George Gilder, *Wealth and Poverty* (New York: Basic, 1981).
18. Ibid., 27.
19. Ibid., 49, 37.
20. Michael Novak, *Capitalism and Socialism: A Theological Enquiry* (Washington, D.C.: American Enterprise Institute, 1979), 117.
21. Michael Novak, *The Spirit of Democratic Capitalism* (New York: Simon and Schuster, 1982), 94.
22. Novak, *Spirit of Democratic Capitalism,* 249.
23. Friedman, *Free to Choose,* 38–69, 95–100.
24. Robert Bork, *The Tempting of America: The Political Seduction of the Law* (New York: Basic, 1990), 287. Michael Kinsley, "The Case Against Bork," *New Republic,* October 5, 1987; reprinted in Kinsley, *Big Babies* (New York: William Morrow, 1995), 27.
25. Bork, *Tempting of America,* 300.
26. Ibid., 6, 112.
27. David Brock, *The Real Anita Hill: The Untold Story* (New York: Free Press, 1993). Brock later regretted writing this book, as well as his services in smearing conservatives' opponents. See Brock, *Blinded by the Right: The Conscience of an Ex-Conservative* (New York: Crown, 2002).
28. Walter H. Capps, *The New Religious Right: Piety, Patriotism, and Politics* (Columbia: University of South Carolina Press, 1990), 185–217.
29. Allan Bloom, *The Closing of the American Mind: How Higher Education Has Failed Democracy and Impoverished the Souls of Today's Students* (New York: Simon and Schuster, 1987).
30. Ibid., 313–18.
31. Ibid., 73–75.
32. S. J. D. Green, "The Closing of the American Mind Revisited," *Antioch Review* 59 (Spring 2001): 371–83.
33. Wayne J. Urban, untitled review of Allan Bloom, *The Closing of the American Mind,* E. D. Hirsch, Jr., *Cultural Literacy,* and Diane Ravitch and Chester Finn, Jr., *What Do Out Seventeen-Year-Olds Know?, Journal of American History* 75 (December 1988): 869–74. Stanley Aronowitz and Henry Giroux, "Schooling, Culture and Literacy in the Age of Broken Dreams: A Review of Bloom and Hirsch," *Harvard Educational Review* 58 (May 1988): 172–94. Robert Scholes, "Three Views of Education: Nostalgia, History, and Voodoo," *College English* 50 (March 1988): 323–32.
34. E. D. Hirsch, *Cultural Literacy: What Every American Needs to Know* (Boston: Houghton Mifflin, 1987).
35. See, e.g., Leila Christenbury, "Cultural Literacy: A Terrible Idea Whose Time Has Come," *English Journal* 78 (January 1989): 14–17.
36. Charles Sykes, *Prof-Scam: Professors and the Decline of Higher Education* (New York: St. Martin's, 1989). Peter Shaw, *The War Against the Intellect: Episodes in*

the Decline of Discourse (University of Iowa Press, 1989). Martin Anderson, *Impostors in the Temple: The Decline of the American University* (New York: Simon and Schuster, 1992). David Bromwich, *Politics by Other Means* (New Haven: Yale University Press, 1994).

37. Roger Kimball, *Tenured Radicals: How Politics Has Corrupted Our Higher Education* (New York: Harper and Row, 1990), xi.
38. Ibid., 96–101.
39. Benjamin Hart, *Poisoned Ivy* (New York: Stein and Day, 1984). See also Dinesh D'Souza, *Letters to a Young Conservative* (New York: Basic, 2002), 18–34.
40. D'Souza, *Letters to a Young Conservative,* 25. Brock, *Blinded by the Right,* 17.
41. Hilton Kramer, *The Revenge of the Philistines: Art and Culture, 1972–1984* (New York: Free Press, 1985).
42. Hilton Kramer, "A Note on the New Criterion," *New Criterion,* September 1982, 1–5.
43. Hilton Kramer, "Is Everything and Anything to Be Permitted as Art?" *New York Times,* July 2, 1989, H1, H7. Editorial, "Shutterbuggery," *National Review,* September 1, 1989, 14.
44. Hilton Kramer, "Studying the Arts and the Humanities: What Can Be Done?" (1979), in Kramer and Roger Kimball, eds., *Against the Grain: The* New Criterion *on Art and Intellect at the End of the Twentieth Century* (Chicago: Ivan Dee, 1995), 74–81.
45. Eric Foner, "Lincoln, Bradford, and the Conservatives," *New York Times,* February, 13, 1982, 1:25. For conflicting accounts of the rise of the paleoconservatives, see Joseph Scotchie, ed., introduction to his *The Paleoconservatives: New Voices of the Old Right* (New Brunswick: Transaction, 1999); David Frum, "Unpatriotic Conservatives," *National Review,* April 7, 2003, 32–40; and Paul Gottfried, *The Conservative Movement, rev. ed.* (Boston: Twayne, 1993).
46. Benjamin B. Alexander, "The Man of Letters and the Faithful Heart," in Clyde Wilson, ed., *A Defender of Southern Conservatism: M. E. Bradford and His Achievements* (Columbia: University of Missouri Press, 1999),17–34. Eugene Genovese and Elizabeth Fox-Genovese, "M. E. Bradford's Historical Vision," ibid., 78–91.
47. M. E. Bradford, "Is the American Experience Conservative?" in Scotchie, *Paleoconservatives,* 147–48, 148, 151.
48. M. E. Bradford, "The Lincoln Legacy: A Long View," in *Remembering Who We Are: Observations of a Southern Conservative* (Athens: University of Georgia Press, 1985), 143–56, quotations on 148, 155.
49. Clyde Wilson, "Restoring the Republic," in Scotchie, *Paleoconservatives,* 181.
50. Ibid., 185.
51. Richard Quinn, introduction to Oran P. Smith, ed., *So Good a Cause: A Decade of the Southern Partisan* (Columbia, S.C.: Foundation for American Education, 1993), xiii. Charles Scott Hamel, foreword, ibid., xvii.

52. Sam Francis, "The Evil That Men Do: Joe McCarthy and the American Right," *Chronicles* 10 (September 1986): 16–21; Thomas Fleming, "Short Views," ibid., 10–11, 24–25. Francis sounded almost anti-Semitic here. Paul Gottfried, a regular contributor to *Chronicles* and himself a historian of the conservative movement, challenged Francis on the issue of Jewish immigrants (Letters, *Chronicles* 10 [November 1986]: 39).
53. Paul Gottfried, "Reconfiguring the Political Landscape," in Scotchie, *Paleoconservatives,* 164. Chilton Williamson, "Promises to Keep," ibid., 99–100. See also M. E. Bradford, "Sentiment or Survival: The Case Against Amnesty," in *Remembering Who We Are,* 110–23, quotation on 121.
54. Scotchie, *Paleoconservatives,* introduction, 5. Editorial, "The Divisions in the American Right," *Chronicles* 10 (July 1986): 6–7. Dan Himmelfarb, "Conservative Splits," *Commentary* 85 (May 1988): 54–58.
55. Richard Neuhaus, "Neuhaus on Rockford," *National Review,* July 14, 1989, 4–5. Richard Bernstein, "Magazine Dispute Reflects Rift on U.S. Right," *New York Times,* May 16, 1989, A1.
56. Bernstein, "Magazine Dispute"; Neuhaus, quoted in Gottfried, *Conservative Movement,* 145.
57. Dan Himmelfarb, "Conservative Splits," 55.
58. Justin Raimondo, *An Enemy of the State: The Life of Murray N. Rothbard* (Amherst, N.Y.: Prometheus Books, 2000), 266–78. Gottfried, *Conservative Movement,* 146–48.
59. Ehrman, *Rise of Neoconservatives,* 173–76, quotation on 176.
60. Dorrien, *Neoconservative Mind,* 102, quotation on 115. Ehrman, *Rise of Neoconservatives,* 177–80.
61. David Evanier and Martin Sieff, "Will the Soviet Union Survive Until 1994?" *National Review,* April 7, 1989, 24–30. Editorial, "Comrade Gorbachev's Leap in the Dark," *National Review,* April 21, 1989, 13–14. Dorrien, *Neoconservative Mind,* 200–202.

CHAPTER 10: CONSERVATIVES AFTER THE COLD WAR, 1989–2001

1. R. Emmett Tyrrell, *The Conservative Crack-Up* (New York: Simon and Schuster, 1992), 15, 200, 8. Michael Lind, *Up from Conservatism: Why the Right Is Wrong for America* (New York: Free Press, 1996).
2. Francis Fukuyama, "The End of History," *National Interest* 16 (Summer 1989): 3–18, quotations on 3, 4, 14.
3. Ibid., 15, 18.
4. Samuel Huntington, "The Clash of Civilizations," *Foreign Affairs* 72 (Summer 1993): 22–49, quotation on 22.
5. Ibid., 25, 30–32.
6. Ibid., 41.
7. Dilip Hiro, *Desert Shield to Desert Storm: The Second Gulf War* (London: Grafton, 1992).
8. Norman Podhoretz, "Enter the Peace Party," *Commentary* 91 (January, 1991):

17–21, quotation on 20. See also William F. Buckley, Jr., "Is It Worth Joey's Life?" *National Review,* February 25, 1991, 63.

9. Anon., "No Desert Quagmire," *National Review,* May 13, 1991, 14. William Rusher, "Saddam Hussein and Us," ibid., November 5, 1990, 59.
10. Angelo Codevilla, "Magnificent, But Was It War?" *Commentary* 93 (April 1992): 15–21. See also Laurie Mylroie, "How We Helped Saddam Survive," *Commentary* (July 1991): 15–18.
11. See, e.g., anon., "The New Face of War," *National Review,* February 25, 1991, 14–15. Joshua Muravchik, "The End of the Vietnam Paradigm?" *Commentary* 91 (May 1991): 17–23. Muravchik argued that nearly all the cautionary lessons of the Vietnam era were sounded during the Gulf War and that nearly all were falsified. Writing just after the war's end, he speculated about the degree to which the successful outcome of the war would dislodge these old fears.
12. Joseph Sobran, "Why *National Review* Is Wrong," *National Review,* October 15, 1990, 64–65.
13. Patrick Buchanan, *Right from the Beginning* (Boston: Little Brown, 1988). Wick Allison, "The Uses of American Power," *National Review,* November 19, 1990, 43–44.
14. Buchanan, quoted in William F. Buckley, Jr., *In Search of Anti-Semitism* (New York: Continuum, 1992), 26–28. Paul Gottfried, *The Conservative Movement,* rev. ed. (New York: Twayne, 1993), 149–51.
15. Buckley, *In Search of Anti-Semitism.* Gottfried, *Conservative Movement,* 158–64.
16. Buchanan wrote prolifically on these themes during the 1990s. See in particular Patrick Buchanan, *The Great Betrayal: How American Sovereignty and Social Justice Are Sacrificed to the Gods of the Global Economy* (Boston: Little Brown, 1998); Buchanan, *A Republic, Not an Empire: Reclaiming America's Destiny* (Washington, D.C.: Regnery, 1999); and Buchanan, *The Death of the West* (New York: Thomas Dunne, 2002).
17. William Kristol and Donald Kagan, eds., *Present Dangers: Crisis and Opportunity in American Foreign and Defense Policy* (San Francisco: Encounter Books, 2000), introduction, 4, 23–24.
18. Kristol and Kagan, *Present Danger,* introduction, 16–17. Donald Kagan, "Strength and Will," ibid., 337–62, esp. 350–54.
19. Richard Perle, "Iraq: Saddam Unbound," in Kristol and Kagan, *Present Dangers,* 99–110.
20. Patrick Allitt, *Religion in America Since 1945: A History* (New York: Columbia University Press, 2003), 198.
21. Thomas Fleming, "Trollopes in the Stacks," in Joseph Scotchie, ed., *The Paleoconservatives: New Voices of the Old Right* (New Brunswick: Transaction, 1999), 156.
22. Richard J. Neuhaus, *Catholic Matters* (New York: Basic, 2006), 31–64.
23. Richard J. Neuhaus, *The Naked Public Square: Religion and Democracy in America* (Grand Rapids: Eerdman's, 1984).

24. Richard J. Neuhaus, *The Catholic Moment: The Paradox of the Church in the Postmodern World* (New York: Harper and Row, 1987), 283.
25. Charles Colson, Richard Neuhaus et al., "Evangelicals and Catholics Together: The Christian Mission in the Third Millennium," *First Things,* May 1994.
26. Richard Neuhaus, Robert Bork, Russell Hittinger et al., "The End of Democracy? The Judicial Usurpation of Politics," *First Things,* November 1996, 18–56.
27. Ibid., 18–20.
28. Robert George, "The Tyrant State," ibid., 39–42. Charles Colson, "Kingdoms in Conflict," ibid., 34–38.
29. Gertrude Himmelfarb, letters, *First Things,* January 1997, 2–3. John Leo (p. 24), William Bennett (pp. 19–21), and Midge Decter (p. 21) in "The End of Democracy? A Discussion Continued," ibid.
30. Roger Kimball, *The Long March: How the Cultural Revolution of the 1960s Changed America* (San Francisco: Encounter Books, 2000), 4, 10.
31. Ibid., 27, 275.
32. Ibid., 59.
33. Lynne Cheney, "The End of History," *Wall Street Journal,* October 20, 1994, A22. Charles Krauthammer, "In the Politically Correct 'New History,' Victimization Is In, Facts Are Out," *Pittsburgh Post-Gazette,* November 7, 1994, B2.
34. Krauthammer, "In the Politically Correct 'New History.' "
35. Editorial, "School's Out to Lunch," *National Review,* May 6, 1996, 19–20. Lynne Cheney, "New History Standards Still Attack Our Heritage," *Wall Street Journal,* May 2, 1996, A14.
36. Gary Nash, "Lynn Cheney's Attack on the History Standards, Ten Years Later," *History News Network,* November 8, 2004. Nash, *History on Trial,* cited here from Keith Windschuttle, "The Problem of Democratic History," *New Criterion,* June 1998, 22–29. Gary Nash, Charlotte Crabtree and Ross Dunn, *History on Trial: Culture Wars and the Teaching of the Past* (New York: Vintage, 2000). Lynne Cheney, *Telling the Truth* (New York: Simon and Schuster, 1995).
37. Joseph Conti, and Brad Stetson, *Challenging the Civil Rights Establishment: Profiles of a New Black Vanguard* (Westport, Conn.: Greenwood, 1993). Martin Kilson, "Anatomy of Black Conservatism," *Transition* 59 (1993): 4–19. Shelby Steele, *The Content of Our Character: A New Vision of Race in America* (New York: St. Martin's, 1993).
38. Micklethwait and Wooldridge, *Right Nation,* 271–77, quotation on 273.
39. Charles Murray, *Losing Ground* (New York: Basic, 1984); for the "thought experiment" of abolishing all the programs, see 227–33.
40. Charles Murray and Richard Herrnstein, *The Bell Curve: Intelligence and Class Structure in American Life* (New York: Free Press, 1994).
41. Russell Jacoby, *The Bell Curve Debate: History, Documents, Opinions* (New York: Times Books, 1995).

42. Michael Barone, "Common Knowledge," *National Review,* December 5, 1994, 32–33. Ernest Van Den Haag, "Not Hopeless," ibid, 38–39. Glen Loury, "Dispirited," ibid., 56–59. Brigitte Berger "Methodological Fetishism," ibid., 54–57.
43. Chester Finn, Jr., "For Whom It Tolls," *Commentary* 99 (January 1995): 76–80.
44. Dinesh D'Souza, *Letters to a Young Conservative* (New York: Basic, 2002), 15–44. D'Souza, *Falwell, Before the Millennium: A Critical Biography* (Chicago: Regnery Gateway, 1984). D'Souza, *Illiberal Education: The Politics of Race and Sex on Campus* (New York: Free Press, 1991).
45. Dinesh D'Souza, *The End of Racism: Principles for a Multiracial Society* (New York: Free Press, 1995).
46. Ibid., 556.
47. Peter Brimelow, "He Flinched," *National Review,* November 27, 1995, 60. Clifford Orwin, "Western Man's Burden?" *The Public Interest,* Winter 1996, 108–14.
48. Thomas Sowell, "The Race Merchants," *Forbes,* October 9, 1995, 74. Herbert Wray, "Race: The End of Discussion?" *US News and World Report,* October 2, 1995, 70. Robert L. Woodson, Sr., "The End of Racism? Hardly," *New York Times,* September 23, 1995, 23.
49. Mayer Schiller and Dinesh D'Souza, "Racial Integration or Racial Separation?" *American Enterprise* 7 (January 1996): 22–23.
50. David Frum, *Dead Right* (New York: Basic, 1994). Frum, *The Right Man: The Surprise Presidency of George W. Bush* (New York: Random House, 2003).

INDEX